1

Unequal Protection

UNEQUAL PROTECTION

Environmental Justice and Communities of Color

EDITED BY
Robert D. Bullard

PREFACE BY Benjamin F. Chavis, Jr.
FOREWORD BY Congressman John Lewis

SIERRA CLUB BOOKS
SAN FRANCISCO

The Sierra Club, founded in 1892 by John Muir, has devoted itself to the study and protection of the earth's scenic and ecological resources—mountains, wetlands, woodlands, wild shores and rivers, deserts and plains. The publishing program of the Sierra Club offers books to the public as a nonprofit educational service in the hope that they may enlarge the public's understanding of the Club's basic concerns. The point of view expressed in each book, however, does not necessarily represent that of the Club. The Sierra Club has some sixty chapters coast to coast, in Canada, Hawaii, and Alaska. For information about how you may participate in its programs to preserve wilderness and the quality of life, please address inquiries to Sierra Club, 730 Polk Street, San Francisco, CA 94109.

Library of Congress Cataloging in Publication Data
Unequal protection : environmental justice and communities of color / edited by Robert D. Bullard ; foreword by Benjamin F. Chavis, Jr.
    p.   cm.
Includes bibliographical references and index.
ISBN 0-87156-450-5
    1. Green movement—United States.   2. Environmental policy—United States.   3. Race discrimination—United States.   4. United States—Race relations.   I. Bullard, Robert D. (Robert Doyle), 1946– .
363.7'03'0973—dc20   93-20942
                                            CIP

Production by Janet Vail
Cover design by Paul Bacon
Book design by Abigail Johnston
Composition by Wilsted & Taylor

Printed in the United States of America on acid-free paper containing a minimum of 50% recovered waste paper, of which at least 10% of the fiber content is post-consumer waste
10 9 8 7 6 5 4 3 2 1

Contents

Foreword

As a participant in the American civil rights movement, I witnessed the unfolding of one of the most powerful social dramas of modern time. The civil rights movement expanded and improved democracy in America. It focused the light of freedom into the darkest corners of this nation and prodded the American conscience into moral action. The movement lifted the corners of the American rug and exposed the dirt and filth of racism and oppression.

The civil rights community, under the leadership of Dr. Martin Luther King, Jr., set out to make this nation a more just and better country for all of its citizens. I, like many others, was drawn to the movement out of a sense of moral duty to defeat the institutional racism that thrived under "Jim Crow."

Segregation, an evil system, was built on a foundation of greed, hatred, and denial of basic human rights. Its symbols were everywhere in the South. I had grown up in Alabama seeing the signs that said "White" and "Colored." The signs are gone, but the residuals of Jim Crow housing and unfair industrial and land use policies are still with us. African Americans and other people of color are burdened with more than their share of toxic waste dumps, landfills, incinerators, lead smelters, dirty air and drinking water, and other forms of pollution that threaten their health in their homes and in the workplace. Even today, the area where one lives can affect one's quality of life—including environmental quality and access to health care.

The struggle for civil rights instilled in many of us the dream that through disciplined, nonviolent action we could transform this nation into a beloved community—a community of peace, justice, and brotherhood. Our tactics garnered considerable attention to the moral dimension of this struggle. Since the 1960s, the American civil rights movement has inspired many other social movements—including the environmental movement—in this country and abroad.

In the 1980s, similar moral imperatives emerged around the quest for environmental justice. This new movement is an inclusive movement. It has brought new vitality and constituent groups whose voices were seldom heard or listened to in the early environmental movement, which emphasized conservation and preservation issues. Just as African Americans and others mobilized to protest the evils of segregation and discrimination, they have now mobilized to protest unjust public policies, discriminatory facility-siting practices, unequal protection, and other forms of environmental racism.

Clearly, the goals of advocates of social and economic justice and the goals of environmentalists have begun to converge. This shared vision makes for a stronger movement when diverse groups, organizations, and communities view environmental protection as a *right* of all, not a *privilege* for a few. The quest for environmental justice has helped to renew the civil rights movement in recent years.

I first became involved with the environmental justice movement as an Atlanta city council member in the early 1980s, and I continued to follow these issues after my election to the U.S. Congress in 1986. Working with prominent activists, such as Reverend Benjamin Chavis, Jr., and former U.S. delegate Walter Fauntroy of Washington, DC, I soon became convinced that reaching the goal of environmental justice would require action on the part of the federal government. That action, I thought, could be best achieved through federal legislation.

During the 103d Congress, in early 1993, I introduced the Environmental Justice Act. This act would target the 100 most polluted locations in the United States for federal attention. These areas would be designated as environmental high-impact areas

(EHIAs). In 1992, I had introduced an earlier version of the Environmental Justice Act with then U.S. senator Al Gore of Tennessee.

The Environmental Justice Act would require assessment of health conditions in communities that have high concentrations of polluting facilities. Collection of environmental data for assessing the cumulative effects of pollution would cover air, water, and soil in a particular community. Federal and local officials would be required to remedy the adverse effects of pollution in the EHIAs.

It is my belief that all Americans have a right to know what is in the air they breathe, what is in the water they drink, and what is in the food they eat. Environmental degradation affects all of us, every hour, every day. The people who live near polluting industries pay the price with their health. The larger society pays the price in higher taxes for health care.

Unequal Protection: Environmental Justice and Communities of Color challenges the nation's leaders to develop action strategies to combat the long-term environmental and health impacts (physical and mental) of pollution on those most affected. We must find ways to leave our physical environment—the communities where we live, work, and play—a little cleaner, a little greener for unborn generations.

We have begun to realize the important connection between the environment and public health. *Unequal Protection* shows us that we cannot afford to ignore the impact of pollution and land use practices on vulnerable groups, neighborhoods, and communities. Citizens have the right to know how landfills, hazardous waste sites, incinerators, manufacturing plants, and other polluting facilities in their communities affect their health.

Indeed, *Unequal Protection* provides a wide-ranging look at environmental disputes, public health threats, and endangered communities from the perspectives of those most affected. As a policymaker, I look to the writings and wise counsel of many of the contributors to this volume in my effort to pass national legislation to combat environmental racism. The authors present compelling evidence that significant segments of our society suffer disproportionately from environmental problems. Moreover, the book places the struggle for environmental justice in a larger context—as an extension of the civil rights and human rights struggle by people of color in the United States and abroad.

Congressman John Lewis
1993

Preface

On Sunday morning, October 27, 1991, people in the United States saw the ushering in of a new environmental era. The day marked the culmination of the three-day First National People of Color Environmental Leadership Summit. With all of the bad news we had gotten from the White House, Congress, and the U.S. Environmental Protection Agency, communities of color needed some good news. The first challenge of the Summit was for us to garner out of this historic experience not only the good news but also the mechanisms that make the good news real in our communities, in the nation, and in the world.

Most of the contributors to *Unequal Protection: Environmental Justice and Communities of Color* were delegates, participants, and observers at the Summit. The issues discussed by the authors could hardly be addressed without some attention given to institutional constraints. Numerous studies—including the United Church of Christ Commission for Racial Justice's own 1987 *Toxic Wastes and Race in the United States*—show that communities of color are disparately impacted by the nation's environmental, industrial, and land use policies.

Environmental racism impacts the quality of life where people live, work, and play. Environmental racism is racial discrimination in environmental policy-making and enforcement of regulations and laws, the deliberate targeting of communities of color for toxic waste facilities, the official sanctioning of the presence of life-threatening poisons and pollutants in communities of color, and the history of excluding people of color from leadership of the environmental movement.

The discussion of environmental justice is *not* a philosophical debate, although we do need to question the philosophical ethos that allows a society to participate in its own destruction. But for us, the issue of environmental justice is an issue of life and death. In the South Side of Chicago, *our* children are dying. Some die in their mothers' wombs. In Louisiana's petrochemical corridor, "Cancer Alley," it is *our* children who are dying in record numbers. In New York City, it is *our* children who are poisoned by lead-based paint in old housing. In the Southwest and among farm workers, it is *our* children who suffer from pesticide poisoning. On Native American reservations, territories, and lands, it is *our* children who are victims of "radioactive colonialism." And for Asian American and Latino American sisters and brothers who labor in Silicon Valley, it is *our* children who are dying.

All forms of environmental injustice, at home and abroad, must be challenged and stopped. An injustice to one is an injustice to all. It is our intention to build an effective multiracial, inclusive environmental movement with the capacity to transform the political landscape of this nation. We must channel our anger into constructive organizing through which our political will is felt by those who make policy in this country. It is unlikely that this nation can solve its environmental problems without addressing the environmental justice question.

Benjamin F. Chavis, Jr.
1993

Acknowledgments

This volume represents the hard work of many dedicated leaders in the environmental justice movement. I am especially grateful for the grassroots environmental activists who took time out of their busy organizing schedules and prepared essays for this book. The work of the People of Color Environmental Justice Network was an invaluable resource to this project. Financial support was provided by grants from the Ford Foundation as part of the 1992 First National People of Color Environmental Leadership Summit, the Lawyers' Committee for Civil Rights Under Law, and the Jessie Smith Noyes Foundation for which we are especially grateful. Sierra Club Books editor David Spinner shepherded the manuscript skillfully through several permutations. Two of my colleagues at the University of California, Riverside deserve recognition: Robin Whittington, who assisted in preparing the manuscript, and Linda Bobbitt, who prepared the graphics.

Introduction

ROBERT D. BULLARD

The nation's environmental laws, regulations, and policies have not been applied fairly across all segments of the population. Some individuals, groups, and communities receive less protection than others because of their geographic location, race, and economic status. Generally, environmental problems in suburban areas pose far fewer public health threats than do those in urban or rural areas. Moreover, low-income communities and communities of color bear a disproportionate burden of the nation's pollution problems.

Whether in urban ghettos and barrios or in rural "poverty pockets" and Native American reservations, pollution presents potential threats to public health that individuals with affluence or political clout are unwilling to accept. Risk burdens are localized, yet the benefits are generalized across all segments of society. Environmental disparities between white communities and communities of color reflect larger societal inequities. Over the years, disparities have been created, tolerated, and institutionalized by local, state, and federal action.

The mood in the country has now shifted to such a degree that affected populations, or "victims," are launching frontal assaults on polluting industries and decision makers who view their communities as expendable. Affected communities are rising up against the current environmental protection apparatus—a system that is regressive in many of its applications. The current system provides greater benefits and protection for middle- and upper-income whites while shifting costs to the poor and people of color. Moreover, the dominant environmental protection paradigm reinforces, rather than challenges, the stratification of *people* (race, ethnicity, status, power, etc.), *place* (central cities, suburbs, rural areas, unincorporated areas, Native American reservations, etc.), and *work* (i.e., office workers are afforded greater protection than farm workers).

Many of our current environmental policies exist to manage, regulate, and distribute risks. As a result, the dominant environmental protection paradigm (1) institutionalizes unequal enforcement; (2) trades human health for profit; (3) places the burden of proof on the "victims," not on the polluting industry; (4) legitimates human exposure to harmful chemicals, pesticides, and hazardous substances; (5) promotes "risky" technologies, such as incinerators; (6) exploits the vulnerability of economically and politically disenfranchised communities; (7) subsidizes ecological destruction; (8) creates an industry around risk assessment; (9) delays cleanup actions; and (10) fails to develop pollution prevention as the overarching and dominant strategy.

Can our current environmental protection apparatus be reformed? Do we need a new model? There is a growing movement to turn the current environmental protection model on its head. It just does not work for many vulnerable populations, ranging from children poisoned with lead in their homes to migrant farm workers and their families poisoned in the fields. Government has been too slow in adopting a *prevention* framework for these groups.

In many instances, government *is* the problem. Residents of communities such as Northeast Houston, West Dallas, East Los Angeles, South Tucson, or Chicago's South Side are not looking to government to "save" them from industrial polluters. The impetus for changing the environmental protection apparatus has *not* come from within the regulatory agencies, the polluting industries, or the industry that has been built around risk assessment. For the most part, the environmental justice movement—a loose alliance of grass-roots and national environmental and civil rights leaders, academics, and activists—has provided the vision and leadership in challenging the shortcomings of the current environmental protection model.

Activists have targeted disparate enforcement, compliance, and policy formulation as they affect environmental and public health decision making on a wide range of issues, from toxic waste to urban transportation. They have borrowed many of their tactics from the civil rights movement. Environmental justice activists have not limited their tactics to demonstrations in the streets but have begun to mount legal challenges to unequal protection by government decision makers and industrial firms.

What do grass-roots leaders want? These leaders are demanding a shared role in the decision-making processes that affect their communities. They want participatory democracy to work for them. They are challenging the background assumptions that drive risk-based decision making, industrial policies that pit jobs against the environment, and housing policies that force families to choose between childhood lead poisoning and homelessness. All of these policies have a disparate impact, whether intended or unintended, on the quality of life in low-income areas and communities of color.

Why has it taken so long for government to act affirmatively in reducing environmental inequities? The environmental justice message is beginning to filter into the mainstream of government and nongovernmental organizations (NGOs). There is still a lot of work to be done in catching up, in educating, and in convincing some public officials that environmental disparities are real and that environmental racism exists. Nevertheless, several events in the early 1990s brought these concerns into the national public policy debate:

1. Dialogue was initiated among social scientists, social justice leaders, national environmental groups, the federal Environmental Protection Agency (EPA), and the Agency for Toxic Substances and Disease Registry (ATSDR) about disparate impact.

2. The Michigan Coalition, an ad hoc group of environmental justice activists and academics who came together at a conference

held at the University of Michigan, prompted the federal EPA to form a Work Group on Environmental Equity. The agency later created an Office of Environmental Equity and an Environmental Equity Cluster (coordinated by an assistant administrator for enforcement) and issued a final report titled *Environmental Equity: Reducing Risks for All Communities.*

3. The ATSDR established a minority health initiative (after some prodding from environmental, health, and social justice advocates), held a Minority Environmental Health Conference, and initiated a study of minority communities near Superfund National Priorities List (NPL) hazardous waste sites.

4. The First National People of Color Environmental Leadership Summit was held in Washington, DC. The Summit galvanized grass-roots and national support for strategies to combat unequal protection and to work toward environmental justice.

5. The EPA, the ATSDR, and the NIEHS (National Institute for Environmental Health Sciences) jointly sponsored a workshop titled Equity in Environmental Health: Research Issues and Needs in Research Triangle, North Carolina. The workshop initially served a data-gathering function and later expanded into a full-blown conference.

6. The Environmental Justice Act of 1992 (EJA) was introduced into Congress by Congressman John Lewis and Senator Albert Gore. With Gore moving to the vice presidency, the EJA of 1993 is undergoing major revisions with new sponsors.

Current environmental decision making operates at the juncture of science, technology, economics, politics, special interests, and ethics—and mirrors the larger social milieu, where discrimination is institutionalized. Why do some communities get dumped on while others escape? Why are environmental regulations vigorously enforced in some communities and not in others? Why are some workers protected from environmental threats while others, such as migrant farm workers, are allowed to be poisoned? How can environmental justice be incorporated into environmental protection models? What community-organizing strategies are effective against environmental racism?

These are some of the questions addressed in this book. Environmental justice advocates, however, have moved beyond the questioning stage and are seeking solutions. Their message is not about whining but about winning. Many of their struggles have ended in victories, although most of their struggles have remained invisible to the larger society. It is hoped that the relaying of the case studies in this book will further crystallize the environmental justice message for the public at large.

The major theme of this book is the cultural diversity of the environmental justice movement. We have assembled contributors who represent diverse backgrounds, including academicians, students, activists, journalists, and lawyers. The perspectives of both academicians and activists are given equal weight in this book.

Many of the authors are part of national grass-roots environmental justice networks. The vast majority of the writers are persons of color who have firsthand experience in working with poisoned communities and politically oppressed people. Many of the chapters were written by individuals who participated in the First National People of Color Environmental Leadership Summit. The contributors all offer special insights, and they bring an array of disciplines to bear on critical environmental problems that affect people of color in the United States.

Who are we trying to reach in this book? The book is written for anyone who is interested in the environment and justice. Ideally, we would like to reach the mainstream and grass-roots environmental and social justice movements, in which a common language is beginning to emerge.

The book is divided into three major parts and sixteen chapters. Part I chronicles the legacy of early environmental justice struggles in communities of color. In chapter 1, Robert D. Bullard examines the convergence of the environmental and social justice movements into a new movement for environmental justice. He also lays out an environmental justice framework for addressing regressive impacts, inequities, unequal protection, and racism.

Chapter 2 is an essay written by free-lance writer Michael Haggerty. This paper documents the environmental and health problems of Triana, Alabama, a town that was poisoned by DDT manufactured by Olin Chemical Company for the U.S. Army and by PCBs, the origins of which are yet to be determined. The essay—first published in a 1980 issue of the *Atlanta Journal and Constitution*—explores the role of the local mayor and staff scientists at the national Centers for Disease Control (CDC) in making the community aware of the health dangers of eating fish from nearby waterways. Triana was tagged as the "unhealthiest town in America" in 1980.

Chapter 3, written by environmental scientists Ken Geiser and Gerry Waneck, provides a detailed account of the controversial siting of a PCB landfill in mostly African American and poor Warren County, North Carolina, in 1982. The authors point out some glaring discrepancies in the state and federal permitting process that allowed the facility to be built on top of a shallow water table. The demonstrations, protests, and citizen arrests surrounding this decision sparked the national environmental justice movement.

In chapter 4, law professors Regina Austin and Michael Schill present a detailed historical account of environmental justice struggles in African American, Latino American, and Native American communities. Their analysis draws together the common themes of environmental justice problems experienced by these groups and the strategies they have pursued in seeking redress.

Part II examines the lives of residents who live in "sacrifice zones," or corridors where high concentrations of industrial pollution are found. In chapter 5, activist Patsy Ruth Oliver tells her story and that of her middle-income African American neighbors in Texarkana, Texas. Her Carver Terrace neighborhood, which was built on top of an abandoned wood-treating plant, is now known as the Texarkana Koppers Superfund Site. Residents in the Superfund site had to get a congressional mandate before the federal EPA would agree to buy them out and relocate them outside the contaminated community.

Chapter 6 was written by *Dallas Examiner* journalist Ronald Robinson. His essay chronicles the problem of lead contamination in West Dallas—a mostly low-income African American and Latino American community. Robinson explores the reasons for the long federal delays in cleaning up the lead-contaminated West Dallas neighborhood. He also examines litigation around Dallas's segregated public housing and its link to the lead problem.

In chapter 7, sociologists Beverly H. Wright and Robert D. Bullard and environmental activist Pat Bryant describe the plight of African Americans who live in the shadow of Louisiana's petrochemical plants in an area dubbed "Cancer Alley," the 85-mile stretch of the Mississippi River from Baton Rouge to New Orleans. They describe the plight of these communities, founded after the abolition of slavery and now threatened by industrial pollution, and the role that the Gulf Coast Tenants Organization (GCTO), a multistate grass-roots environmental network, has played in organizing, educating, and mobilizing disenfranchised communities in Louisiana, Mississippi, and Alabama.

Chapter 8, written by free-lance writer Kathy Hall, provides us with an in-depth critique of the energy industry's impact on two Native American groups, the Navajo and the Hopi. Because Native American reservations are sovereign nations, most federal and state environmental regulations do not cover these lands. Hall's essay illustrates how the Hopi and Navajo have borne the brunt of coal mining on the reservations—regressive impacts that flow from our nation's energy policies.

Chapter 9 was written by *San Francisco Examiner* journalist Jane Kay. Her essay focuses on environmental problems in California's African American, Latino American, and Native American communities. Among the topics examined are urban industrial pollution, siting of hazardous waste facilities, and the economic vulnerability of Native American lands and the practice of targeting "risky" industries for reservations.

Part III examines some of the emerging alliances, coalitions, and networks between grass-roots and mainstream environmental and social justice groups of color. There are clear signs that an environmental justice movement is alive and well in diverse communities all across the nation. Moreover, many of these groups have ties to other activist groups of color around the world, as in the case of the Third World Network and networks that emerged from the 1992 Earth Summit in Rio de Janeiro.

Chapter 10, written by longtime environmental justice activists Richard Moore and Louis Head, looks at the history of the Albuquerque-based Southwest Organizing Project (SWOP). Through the People of Color Regional Activist Dialogue for Environmental Justice (RAD), their efforts created the eight-state Southwest Network for Environmental and Economic Justice (SNEEJ). SNEEJ has become a model for organizing regional networks of color.

Chapter 11 was written by political scientist Cynthia Hamilton. Using an eco-feminist perspective, she explores the experiences of the African American women who organized Concerned Citizens of South Central Los Angeles for the purpose of blocking construction of a municipal solid waste incinerator. Concerned Citizens, along with its allies, was able to defeat the city-sponsored garbage incinerator project known as LANCER (Los Angeles City Energy Recovery). The lessons presented in this essay emphasize the strengths of multiracial and multiethnic coalitions.

In chapter 12, Gabriel Gutiérrez writes about his mother and the other Mexican American women who came together and formed Mothers of East Los Angeles (MELA). In the past, MELA mobilized to block the construction of prisons and oil pipelines. Later, the group mobilized its mostly Latino American community to block construction of a hazardous waste incinerator proposed for the nearby neighborhood of Vernon. This essay is a classic case of community empowerment centering on environmental justice.

In chapter 13, Francis Calpotura and Rinku Sen, codirectors of the Center for Third World Organizing (CTWO), write about community organizing around the problem of lead contamination in Oakland, California. They describe the organizing strategies of a local grass-roots group, People United for a Better Oakland, or PUEBLO—a group that was successful in getting a model lead abatement program instituted in Oakland.

Chapter 14, written by sociologist Celene Krauss, documents struggles of women of color and white working-class women who have provided leadership in the environmental justice movement and provides insights into their motivation for activism. Her interviews with strong female leaders of various racial, ethnic, and social backgrounds provide convincing evidence that the environmental justice movement is becoming firmly institutionalized in the family, home, school, community, and other social institutions where women have influential roles.

Chapter 15 was written by journalism professor Karl Grossman. He discusses the products of the First National People of Color Environmental Leadership Summit. In addition to examining substantive issues presented at the Summit and the resulting "Principles of Environmental Justice," Grossman discusses some of the post-Summit activities. His critique reveals that the 1991 Summit was instrumental in bringing diverse groups of color together, but the emerging networks appear to be the key vehicles that keep them in touch with one another.

The final chapter, chapter 16, was written by environmental lawyer Deeohn Ferris. This essay incorporates comments and views from a number of grass-roots leaders and environmental justice groups. The specific recommendations in the paper were submitted to the Clinton-Gore transition team working in the Natural Resources and Environment Cluster.

Finally, the question of who *pays* and who *benefits* from the current industrial and environmental policies is central to any analysis of environmental justice. We cannot separate the question of what kinds of consumer products are manufactured in this country from our mounting waste problem. We are all guilty. Thus, alteration of our life-styles and consumption behavior will play a decisive role in future solutions to local and global environmental problems. It is only just and fair that the individuals, communities, states, and countries who have the *most* will be asked to give up the most.

I

Overview and Legacy
of
Early Struggles

1

Environmental Justice for All

ROBERT D. BULLARD

People of color have always resisted actions by government and private industry that threaten the quality of life in their communities. Until recently, this resistance was largely ignored by policymakers. This activism took place before the first Earth Day in 1970; however, many of these struggles went unnoticed or were defined as merely part of the "modern" environmental movement. This chapter outlines a framework that can be used to address disparate impact, unequal protection, and environmental discrimination.

ANATOMY OF EARLY STRUGGLES

In 1967, students at predominantly African American Texas Southern University in Houston were involved in a campus riot triggered by the death of an eight-year-old African American girl, who had drowned at a garbage dump. Student protesters questioned why a garbage dump was located in the middle of the mostly African American Sunnyside neighborhood.[1] The protests got out of hand. Police were met with rocks and bottles. Gunshots were fired. A police officer, struck by a ricocheting bullet, was killed. Nearly 500 male students were cleared from the dormitories, and many of the leaders were arrested. The Kerner Commission classified the disturbance at Texas Southern University as a "serious disorder."[2]

In 1968, Reverend Martin Luther King, Jr., went to Memphis on an environmental justice mission—better working conditions and pay for striking African American garbage workers. King was killed in Memphis before he could complete this mission. Nevertheless, garbage and landfills did not disappear as an environmental justice issue.

In 1979, residents of Houston's Northwood Manor subdivision (a suburban neighborhood of African American home owners) filed the first lawsuit charging environmental discrimination. More than 83 percent of the Northwood Manor residents owned their homes. In *Bean v. Southwestern Waste Management*, Houston residents charged Browning-Ferris Industries with locating a municipal solid waste landfill in their community. An early attempt to place a similar facility in the same area in 1970—when the area was mostly white—had been defeated by the Harris County Board of Supervisors.

Houston has a long history of locating its solid waste facilities in communities of color, especially in African American neighborhoods. From the early 1920s through the late 1970s, all five of the city-owned sanitary landfills and six of its eight municipal solid waste incinerators were located in mostly African American neighborhoods. Similarly, three of the four privately owned solid waste landfills were located in mostly African American communities during this period. African Americans, however, made up only 28 percent of the city's population. Despite the overwhelming statistical evidence, the plaintiffs lost their lawsuit, and the Whispering Pines landfill was built in Northwood Manor.[3]

Some proponents of the Whispering Pines landfill suggested that the African American neighborhood would benefit from the waste facility by way of the jobs and taxes it would provide. However, Charles Streadit, president of Houston's Northeast Community Action Group, addressed the benefits and liabilities associated with the landfill in his neighborhood:

> Sure, Browning-Ferris Industries [owner of the Whispering Pines landfill] pays taxes, but so do we. We need all the money we can get to upgrade our school system. But we shouldn't

have to be poisoned to get improvements for our children. When my property values go down, that means less for the schools and my children's education. . . . A silent war is being waged against black neighborhoods. Slowly, we are being picked off by the industries that don't give a damn about polluting our neighborhood, contaminating our water, fouling our air, clogging our streets with big garbage trucks, and lowering our property values. It's hard enough for blacks to scrape and save enough money to buy a home, then you see your dream shattered by a garbage dump. That's a dirty trick. No amount of money can buy self-respect.[4]

The aforementioned examples show a clear link between civil rights and environmental justice. However, it was not until the early 1980s that a national movement for environmental justice took root in several mainstream civil rights organizations. The environmental justice movement took shape out of the 1982 protests in Warren County, North Carolina. This mostly African American and rural county had been selected as the burial site for 30,000 cubic yards of soil contaminated with highly toxic PCBs (polychlorinated biphenyls). Oil laced with PCBs had been illegally dumped along roadways in fourteen North Carolina counties in 1978; the roadways were cleaned up in 1982.[5]

More than 500 protesters were jailed over the siting of the Warren County PCB landfill. Demonstrations were led by a number of national civil rights advocacy groups, including the United Church of Christ Commission for Racial Justice, the Southern Christian Leadership Conference, and the Congressional Black Caucus. African American civil rights activists, political officials, religious leaders, and local residents marched in protest against "Hunt's Dump" (named for Texas's governor at that time, James Hunt). Why had Warren County been selected for the PCB landfill? Opponents contend that the decision made more political sense than environmental sense.[6]

Although the demonstrations were unsuccessful in halting construction of the landfill, the protests marked the first time African

Americans had mobilized a national, broad-based group to oppose what they defined as environmental racism. The demonstrations also prompted District of Columbia delegate Walter Fauntroy, who was chairman of the Congressional Black Caucus, to initiate the 1983 U.S. General Accounting Office (GAO) study of hazardous waste landfill siting in the Environmental Protection Agency's Region IV.[7] Fauntroy had been active in the protests and was one of the many who went to jail over the landfill.

The 1983 GAO study found a strong relationship between the location of off-site hazardous waste landfills and the race and socioeconomic status of the surrounding communities. The study identified four off-site hazardous waste landfills in the eight states (Alabama, Florida, Georgia, Kentucky, Mississippi, North Carolina, South Carolina, and Tennessee) that constitute the EPA's Region IV. The four sites included Chemical Waste Management (Sumter County, Alabama); SCA Services (Sumter County, South Carolina); Industrial Chemical Company (Chester County, South Carolina); and the Warren County PCB landfill (Warren County, North Carolina).

African Americans made up the majority of the population in three of the four communities where off-site hazardous waste landfills were located. In 1983, African Americans were clearly overrepresented in communities with waste sites, since they made up only about one-fifth of the region's population, yet African American communities contained three-fourths of the off-site landfills. These ecological imbalances have not been reversed a decade later. In 1992, African Americans constituted about one-fifth of the population in Region IV. However, the two operating off-site hazardous waste landfills in the region were located in zip code regions where African Americans made up the majority of the population.

A new form of environmental activism has emerged in communities of color. Activists have not limited their attacks to well-publicized toxic contamination issues but have begun to seek remedial action on neighborhood disinvestment, housing discrimination and residential segregation, urban mass transportation, pollution, and other environmental problems that threaten public safety.

Activist groups of color have begun to build a national movement for justice. In October 1991, the First National People of Color Environmental Leadership Summit was held in Washington, DC. The Summit demonstrated that it is possible to build a multi-issue, multiracial environmental movement around *justice*. Environmental activism was shown to be alive and well in African American, Latino American, Asian American, and Native American communities.

The four-day Summit was attended by more than 650 grass-roots and national leaders representing more than 300 environmental groups of color. The Summit was planned *by* people of color. Delegates came from all fifty states, including Alaska and Hawaii, as well as from Puerto Rico, Chile, Mexico, and the Marshall Islands. Delegates attended the Summit to share their action strategies, redefine the environmental movement, and develop common plans for addressing environmental problems affecting people of color in the United States and around the world.

Grass-roots groups organized themselves around a number of environmental issues, ranging from the siting of landfills and incinerators to lead pollution. At the Summit, delegates adopted the "Principles of Environmental Justice," which they are using as a guide for organizing, networking, and relating to other groups. The common thread that runs throughout the grass-roots groups of color is their demand for a *just* environment.

THE ENVIRONMENTAL JUSTICE FRAMEWORK

There is general agreement that the nation's environmental problems need immediate attention. The head of the U.S. Environmental Protection Agency, writing in the agency's *EPA Journal*, stressed that "environmental protection should be applied fairly."[8] However, the nation's environmental laws, regulations, and policies are not applied uniformly across the board, resulting in some individ-

People of Color Grassroots Environmental Groups

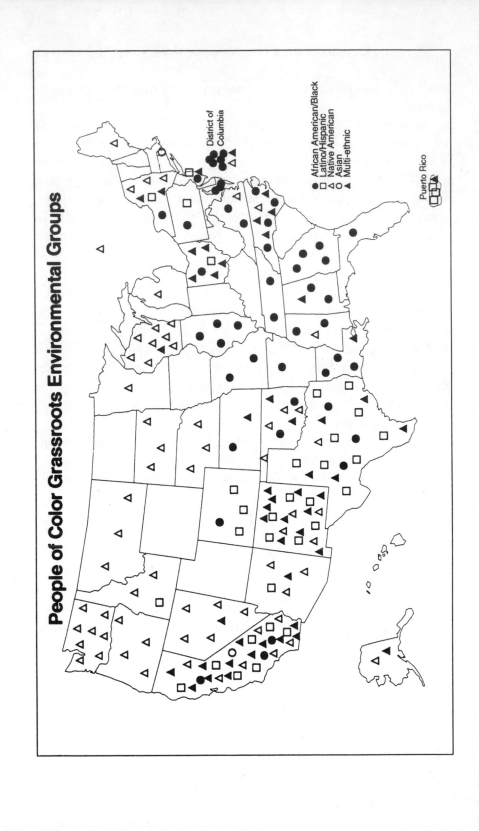

District of Columbia

African American/Black
Latino/Hispanic
Native American
Asian
Multi-ethnic

Puerto Rico

uals, neighborhoods, and communities being exposed to elevated health risks.

Environmental decision making operates at the juncture of science, technology, economics, politics, and ethics. A 1992 study by staff writers from the *National Law Journal* uncovered glaring inequities in the way the federal EPA enforces its laws. The authors write:

> There is a racial divide in the way the U.S. government cleans up toxic waste sites and punishes polluters. White communities see faster action, better results and stiffer penalties than communities where blacks, Hispanics and other minorities live. This unequal protection often occurs whether the community is wealthy or poor.[9]

After examining census data, civil court dockets, and the EPA's own record of performance at 1,177 Superfund toxic waste sites, the *National Law Journal* report revealed the following:

1. Penalties under hazardous waste laws at sites having the greatest white population were 500 percent higher than penalties with the greatest minority population, averaging $335,566 for white areas, compared to $55,318 for minority areas.

2. The disparity under the toxic waste law occurs by race alone, not income. The average penalty in areas with the lowest income is $113,491, 3 percent more than the average penalty in areas with the highest median incomes.

3. For all the federal environmental laws aimed at protecting citizens from air, water, and waste pollution, penalties in white communities were 46 percent higher than in minority communities.

4. Under the giant Superfund cleanup program, abandoned hazardous waste sites in minority areas take 20 percent

longer to be placed on the national priority list than those in white areas.

5. In more than half of the 10 autonomous regions that administer EPA programs around the country, action on cleanup at Superfund sites begins from 12 percent to 42 percent later at minority sites than at white sites.

6. At minority sites, the EPA chooses "containment," the capping or walling off of a hazardous waste dump site, 7 percent more frequently than the cleanup method preferred under the law, permanent "treatment," to eliminate the waste or rid it of its toxins. At white sites, the EPA orders treatment 22 percent more often than containment.[10]

These findings suggest that unequal environmental protection places communities of color at special risk. The environmental justice framework attempts to uncover the underlying assumptions that may influence environmental decision making. It also rests on an analysis of strategies to eliminate unfair, unjust, and inequitable conditions and decisions. The basic elements of the framework consist of five basic characteristics:

1. Incorporates the principle of the right of all individuals to be protected from environmental degradation,

2. Adopts a public health model of prevention (elimination of the threat before harm occurs) as the preferred strategy,

3. Shifts the burden of proof to polluters and dischargers who do harm or discriminate or who do not give equal protection to racial and ethnic minorities and other "protected" classes,

4. Allows disparate impact and statistical weight, as opposed to "intent," to infer discrimination,

5. Redresses disproportionate risk burdens through targeted action and resources.

The goal of an environmental justice framework is to make environmental protection more democratic. More important, it brings to the surface the *ethical* and *political* questions of "who gets what, why, and in what amount."[11] Who pays for, and who benefits from, technological expansion?

Environmental and health laws have not provided equal protection for all Americans. Most of the nation's environmental policies distribute the costs in a regressive pattern while providing disproportionate benefits for whites and individuals who fall at the upper end of the education and income scale.[12] Numerous studies, dating back to the 1970s, reveal that communities of color have borne greater health and environmental risk burdens than has society at large.[13]

Nationally based conservation and environmental groups have played an instrumental role in shaping this nation's environmental laws and regulations. It was not until recently, however, that these nongovernmental organizations (NGOs) paid attention to environmental and health threats to poor, working-class persons and to communities of color.

The environmental justice movement attempts to address environmental enforcement, compliance, policy formulation, and decision making. It defines environment in very broad terms, as the places where people live, work, and play. The question of environmental justice is not anchored in a scientific debate but rests on an ethical analysis of environmental decision making.

Current decision-making models have proven to be inadequate in protecting at-risk communities. Emphasis on defining risk as the probability of fatality addresses only part of the health threats. Should endangered communities have to wait for a "body count" for government to act? Many communities would say no to this question.

Often, environmental stressors result in adverse health effects short of death. The health effects might be developmental, reproductive, respiratory, neurotoxic, or psychological in nature. As a consequence, the assignment of "acceptable" risk, use of averages, and siting of risky technologies (i.e., incinerators, landfills, chemical plants, smelters, etc.) often result from value judgments that serve to legitimate the imposition of inequitable social policies.

ENDANGERED COMMUNITIES

Millions of Americans live in housing and physical environments that are overburdened with environmental problems including older housing with lead-based paint, congested freeways that crisscross their neighborhoods, industries that emit dangerous pollutants into the area, and abandoned toxic waste sites.

Virtually all of the studies of exposure to outdoor air pollution have found significant differences in exposure by income and race.[14] African Americans and Latino Americans are more likely than whites to live in areas with reduced air quality. For example, National Argonne Laboratory researchers D. R. Wernette and L. A. Nieves found the following:

> In 1990, 437 of the 3,109 counties and independent cities failed to meet at least one of the EPA ambient air quality standards. . . . 57 percent of whites, 65 percent of African Americans, and 80 percent of Hispanics live in 437 counties with substandard air quality. Out of the whole population, a total of 33 percent of whites, 50 percent of African Americans, and 60 percent of Hispanics live in the 136 counties in which two or more air pollutants exceed standards. The percentage living in the 29 counties designated as nonattainment areas for three or more pollutants are 12 percent of whites, 20 percent of African Americans, and 31 percent of Hispanics.[15]

The public health community has very little information to explain the magnitude of some of the health problems related to air pollution. However, we do know that persons suffering from asthma are particularly sensitive to the effects of carbon monoxide, sulfur dioxides, particulate matter, ozone, and nitrogen oxides.[16] African Americans, for example, have a significantly higher prevalence of asthma than does the general population.[17]

In the heavily populated Los Angeles air basin, more than 71 percent of African Americans and 50 percent of Latino Americans live in areas with the most polluted air, while only 34 percent of whites live in highly polluted areas.[18] For a few days in 1992, the attention of the entire world was affixed on the flames of Los Angeles. Even before the uprising, however, *San Francisco Examiner* reporter Jane Kay described the zip code region in which the now riot-torn South Central Los Angeles neighborhood is located as the "dirtiest" zip code (90058) in California.[19] This 1-square-mile area is saturated with abandoned toxic waste sites, freeways, smokestacks, and wastewater pipes from polluting industries.

Efforts to rebuild South Central Los Angeles and the other neighborhoods scarred by the uprising will need to incorporate environmental justice initiatives—rebuilding will need to encompass more than replacing the burned-out liquor stores, pawnshops, check-cashing centers, and fast food operations.

A "green" initiative will need to incorporate strategies employing incumbent residents in cleanup and rebuilding efforts that adopt environmentally sound technologies. Moreover, redlining practices must be vigorously attacked if any serious rebuilding of South Central Los Angeles is to take place. A partnership is needed between community institutions and businesses and the various government agencies (environmental protection, housing, public health, public works, human services, job training, education, business development, law enforcement, etc.) to create sustainable neighborhoods.

Threatened communities in southeastern Louisiana's petrochemical corridor (the 85-mile stretch along the Mississippi River from Baton Rouge to New Orleans) typify the industrial madness that has gone unchecked for too long. The corridor has been dubbed "Cancer Alley" by some environmentalists.[20] Health concerns raised by residents and grass-roots activists who live in Alsen, Saint Gabriel, Geismer, Morrisonville, and Lions, all of which are located in close proximity to polluting industries, have not been adequately addressed by local, state, and federal agencies, including the federal EPA and the Agency for Toxic Substances and Disease Registry (ATSDR).

A few contaminated African American communities in Cancer Alley have been bought out or are in the process of being bought out by industries under their "good neighbor" programs. Dow Chemical, the state's largest chemical plant, is buying out residents of mostly African American Morrisonville.[21] The communities of Sunrise and Reveilletown (founded by former slaves) no longer exist. The buyout settlements are often sealed. Few of the recent settlement agreements allow for health monitoring or surveillance of affected residents once they are dispersed.[22]

Some settlements have even required the "victims" to sign waivers that preclude them from bringing any further lawsuits against the polluting industry. These practices have resulted in the scattering of residents, making it difficult to carry out follow-up or long-term health monitoring.

A few health assessments have been conducted by federal agencies, but few of these reports have found their way into the hands of residents of the affected communities. An environmental justice framework could assist communities in Cancer Alley as they negotiate buyout agreements or contemplate litigation or some other risk reduction strategy.

Industrial encroachment into Chicago's South Side neighborhoods is yet another example of endangered communities. Chicago is the nation's third largest city and one of the most racially segregated cities in the country. More than 92 percent of the city's 1.1 million African American residents live in racially segregated areas. The Altgeld Gardens housing project, located on the city's Southeast Side, is one of these segregated enclaves.

Altgeld Gardens is encircled by municipal and hazardous waste landfills, toxic waste incinerators, grain elevators, sewer treatment facilities, smelters, steel mills, and a host of other polluting industries. Because of the physical location, Hazel Johnson, a community organizer in the neighborhood, has dubbed the area a "toxic doughnut." Others see their community as a "toxic soup," where residents perform the role of human guinea pigs.

The Southeast Side neighborhood is home to 150,000 residents, of whom 70 percent are African American and 11 percent are Latino American. It also has 50 active or closed commercial hazardous waste landfills, 100 factories (including seven chemical plants and five steel mills), and 103 abandoned toxic waste dumps.[23] Currently, health and risk assessment data collected by the state of Illinois and the federal EPA for facility permitting have failed to take into account the cumulative and synergistic effects of having so many "layers" of poisons in one community.

Altgeld Gardens residents wonder at what point government will declare a moratorium on permitting any new noxious facilities in their neighborhood. Can a "saturation threshold" be determined without the necessary studies (one such study would be mandated under the proposed Environmental Justice Act of 1992) that delineate the cumulative health impacts of all of the polluting industries in the area? All of the polluting industries (lead smelters, landfills, incinerators, steel mills, foundries, metal-plating and metal-coating operations, grain elevators, etc.) imperil the health of nearby residents and should be factored into any future facility permitting decision.

Environmental justice advocates have sought to persuade the various levels of government (federal, state, and local) to adopt a framework that addresses distributive impacts, concentration, enforcement, and compliance concerns. They have taken their fight to city halls, state capitals, and the U.S. Congress.

In 1990, New York City adopted a "fair share" legislative model designed to ensure that every borough and every community within each borough bear its fair share of noxious facilities. Public hearings have begun to address risk burdens in New York City's boroughs. Proceedings from a hearing on environmental disparities in the Bronx point to concerns raised by African Americans and Puerto Ricans who see their neighborhoods threatened by garbage transfer stations, salvage yards, and recycling centers. The report reveals the following:

> On the Hunts Point peninsula alone there are at least thirty private transfer stations, a large-scale Department of Environmental Protection (DEP) sewage treatment plant and a sludge

dewatering facility, two Department of Sanitation (DOS) marine transfer stations, a citywide privately regulated medical waste incinerator, a proposed DOS resource recovery facility and three proposed DEP sludge processing facilities.

That all of the facilities listed above are located immediately adjacent to the Hunts Point Food Center, the biggest wholesale food and meat distribution facility of its kind in the United States, and the largest source of employment in the South Bronx, is disconcerting. A policy whereby low-income and minority communities have become the "dumping grounds" for unwanted land uses works to create an environment of disincentives to community-based development initiatives. It also undermines existing businesses.[24]

In 1992, Chicago congresswoman Cardiss Collins offered an amendment to the bill reauthorizing the Resource Conservation and Recovery Act (RCRA), requiring "community information statements" that assess the demographic makeup of proposed waste site areas and the cumulative impact a new facility would have on the existing environmental burden.

In a similar vein, in 1992 Georgia congressman John Lewis, a longtime civil rights activist, and former senator Al Gore (now vice president) introduced their version of an Environmental Justice Act. (The 1993 version of the Environmental Justice Act was introduced in the House by John Lewis and in the Senate by Max Baucus, a Democrat from Montana.) The act (S. 2806 and H. R. 5326) was designed to "establish a program to ensure nondiscriminatory compliance with environmental, health, and safety laws and to ensure equal protection of the public health."

Some communities form a special case for environmental justice and risk reduction. Because of more stringent state and federal environmental regulations, Native American reservations, from New York to California, have become prime targets for risky technologies. Native American nations are quasi-sovereign and do not fall under state jurisdiction. Similarly, reservations are "lands the feds forgot," and their inhabitants "must contend with some of America's worst pollution."[25]

Few reservations have infrastructures to handle the risky technologies that are being proposed for their communities, and more than 100 waste disposal facilities have been proposed for Native American lands.[26] Reservation inhabitants have among the worst poverty, unemployment, education, and health problems of all Americans. Targeting Native American land for disposal of wastes is a form of "'garbage imperialism."

TOXIC WASTE TIME BOMBS

The hazardous waste problem continues to be one of the most "serious problems facing the industrial world."[27] Toxic time bombs are not randomly scattered across the urban landscape. In New Jersey (a state with one of the highest concentrations of uncontrolled toxic waste dumps), hazardous waste sites are often located in communities that have high percentages of poor, elderly, young, and minority residents.[28]

Few national studies have been conducted on the sociodemographic characteristics of populations living around toxic waste sites. Although the federal EPA has been in business for more than two decades, it has yet to conduct a national study of the problems of toxic wastes in communities of color. In fact, the United Church of Christ Commission for Racial Justice, a church-based civil rights organization, conducted the first national study on this topic.[29]

The Commission for Racial Justice's landmark study, *Toxic Wastes and Race in the United States,* found race to be the single most important factor (i.e., more important than income, home ownership rate, and property values) in the location of abandoned toxic waste sites.[30] The study also found that (1) three out of five African Americans live in communities with abandoned toxic waste sites; (2) 60 percent (15 million) African Americans live in communities with one or more abandoned toxic waste sites; (3) three of the five largest commercial hazardous waste landfills are located in predominantly African American or Latino American communities and account for 40 percent of the nation's total estimated landfill capacity; and (4) African Americans are heavily overrepresented in the populations of cities with the largest number of abandoned toxic waste sites.[31]

In metropolitan Chicago, for example, more than 81.3 percent of Latino Americans and 76 percent of African Americans live in communities with abandoned toxic waste sites, compared with 59 percent of whites. Similarly, 81.3 percent of Latino Americans and 69.8 percent of African Americans in the Houston metropolitan area live in communities with abandoned toxic waste sites, compared with 57.1 percent of whites. Latino Americans in the Los Angeles metropolitan area are nearly twice as likely as their Anglo counterparts to live in a community with an abandoned toxic waste site.[32]

The mounting waste problem is adding to the potential health threat to environmental high-impact areas. Incineration has become the leading technology for disposal of this waste. This technology is also becoming a major source of dioxin, as well as lead, mercury, and other heavy metals released into the environment. For example, millions of pounds of lead per year will be emitted from the nation's municipal solid waste incinerators in the next few years. All of this lead is being released despite what we know about its hazards to human health.

Hazardous waste incinerators are not randomly scattered across the landscape. A 1990 Greenpeace report, *Playing with Fire*, found that (1) the minority portion of the population in communities with existing incinerators is 89 percent higher than the national average; (2) communities where incinerators are proposed have minority populations 60 percent higher than the national average; (3) average income in communities with existing incinerators is 15 percent less than the national average; (4) property values in communities that are hosts to incinerators are 38 percent lower than the national average; and (5) average property values are 35 percent lower in communities where incinerators are proposed.[33]

Environmental scientists have not refined their research methodologies to assess the cumulative and synergistic effects of all of society's poisons on the human body. However, some health problems cannot wait for the tools to catch up with common sense. For example, the nation's lead contamination problem demands urgent attention. An environmental strategy is needed to address childhood lead poisoning. It is time for action.

THE POLITICS OF LEAD POISONING

Why has so little been done to prevent lead poisoning in the United States? Overwhelming scientific evidence exists on the ill effects of lead on the human body. However, very little has been done to rid the nation of lead poisoning—a preventable disease tagged the "number one environmental health threat to children" by the federal Agency for Toxic Substances and Disease Registry.[34]

Lead began to be phased out of gasoline in the 1970s. It is ironic that the "regulations were initially developed to protect the newly developed catalytic converter in automobiles, a pollution-control device that happens to be rendered inoperative by lead, rather than to safeguard human health."[35] In 1971, a child was not considered at risk for lead poisoning unless he or she had 400 micrograms of lead per liter of blood (or 40 micrograms per deciliter [µg/dl]). Since that time, the amount of lead that is considered safe has continually dropped. In 1991, the U.S. Public Health Service changed the official definition of an unsafe level to 10 µg/dl. Even at that level, a child's IQ can be slightly diminished and physical growth stunted. Lead poisoning is correlated with both income and race (see table 1.1).[36]

A coalition of environmental, social justice, and civil libertarian groups are now joining forces to address the lead problem. The Natural Resources Defense Council, the NAACP Legal Defense and Education Fund, the American Civil Liberties Union, and the Legal Aid Society of Alameda County, California, won an out-of-court settlement worth $15 million to $20 million for a blood lead–testing program. The lawsuit, *Matthews v. Coye,* involved the failure of the state of California to conduct federally mandated testing

TABLE 1.1

Estimated Percentages of Children (Living in Cities with Population over 1 Million) 0.5–5 Years Old with Blood Levels Greater than 15 µg/dl, by Race and Income (1988)

RACE	INCOME		
	<$6,000	$6,000–$15,000	>$15,000
African American	68%	54%	38%
White	36%	23%	12%

Source: Agency for Toxic Substances and Disease Registry, *The Nature and Extent of Lead Poisoning in Children in the United States: A Report to Congress* (Atlanta: U.S. Department of Health and Human Services, 1988).

for lead of some 557,000 poor children who receive Medicaid. This historic agreement will probably trigger similar actions in other states that have failed to live up to federally mandated screening requirements.[37]

CONCLUSION

Despite the recent attempts by federal environmental and health agencies to reduce risks to all Americans, environmental inequities still persist. Some children, workers, and communities are disproportionately affected by unhealthy air, unsafe drinking water, dangerous chemicals, lead, pesticides, and toxic wastes.

If this nation is to achieve environmental justice, the environment in urban ghettos, barrios, reservations, and rural poverty pockets must be given the same protection as that provided to the suburbs. All communities—African American or white, rich or poor—deserve to be protected from the ravages of pollution.

The current emphasis on waste management and pollution control regulations encourages dependence on disposal technologies, which are themselves sources of toxic pollution. Pushing incinerators and risk technologies off on people under the guise of economic development is not a solution to this nation's waste problem. It is imperative that waste reduction programs mandated by federal, state, and local government be funded that set goals for recycling, composting, and using recycled materials.

An environmental justice framework needs to be incorporated into a national policy on facility siting. In addition to the standard technical requirements, environmental justice proposals will need to require implementation of some type of "fair share" plan that takes into account sociodemographic, economic, and cultural factors of affected communities. It is clear that current environmental regulations and "protectionist" devices (zoning, deed restrictions, and other land use controls) have not had the same impact on all segments of society.

The federal EPA needs to take the lead in ensuring that all Americans are protected. It is time for this nation to clean up the health-threatening lead contamination problem and prevent future generations from being poisoned. No segment of society should be allowed to become a dumping ground or be sacrificed because of economic vulnerability or racial discrimination.

In order for risk reduction strategies to be effective in environmental high-impact areas and for vulnerable populations, there needs to be sweeping changes in key areas of the science model and environmental health research. At minimum, these changes must include a reevaluation of the attitudes, biases, and values of the scientists who conduct environmental health research and risk assessment and the officials who make policy decisions.

Acceptance of the public as an active and equal partner in research and environmental decision making is a first step toward building trust within affected communities. Government agencies and other responsible parties need to incorporate principles of environmental justice into their strategic planning of risk reduction.

We need a holistic methodology in documenting, remediating, and preventing environmental health problems. Prevention is the key. Environmental justice demands that lead poisoning—the number one environmental health problem affecting children—be given the attention and priority it deserves. It is the poorest among the nation's inhabitants who are being poisoned at an alarming rate. Many of these individuals and families have little or no access to regular health care.

The solution lies in leveling the playing field and protecting all Americans. Environmental decision makers have failed to address the "justice" questions of who gets help and who does not, who can afford help and who cannot, why some contaminated communities get studied while others are left off the research agenda, why some communities get cleaned up at a faster rate than others, why some cleanup methods are selected over others, and why industry poisons some communities and not others.

Finally, a national environmental justice action agenda is needed to begin addressing environmental inequities that result from procedural, geographic, and societal imbalances. Federal, state, and local legislation is needed to target resources for those areas where societal risk burdens are the greatest. States that are initiating fair share plans to address interstate waste conflicts need also to begin addressing intrastate environmental siting imbalances. It is time for environmental justice to become a national priority.

2

Crisis at Indian Creek

MICHAEL HAGGERTY

A CDC doctor goes to Triana, Alabama, to investigate a case of DDT contamination. Once a boon to world health, DDT poses a threat for the future.

Clyde Foster, the mayor of the tiny (pop. 600) town of Triana, Alabama, got a call one night in November of 1978 from an anonymous reporter. "Mayor Foster," the voice said, "I don't want to alarm you, but I have information leaked to me from an executive report of the Tennessee Valley Authority, and I believe you should know about it. The TVA has found fish in Indian Creek that contain forty times the DDT level considered safe by the federal government."

Foster was incredulous. Indian Creek flowed into the Tennessee River some three hundred yards from where he sat. It had once been the town's local water source. The people in Triana ate fish from that creek every day. "How long has it been contaminated?" he asked. The reporter hung up.

Foster was working late in the town's spanking new municipal building after a full day as director of equal opportunity employment at Marshall Space Flight Center at nearby Redstone Arsenal. The news left him shaken. Triana, a poor, almost totally black rural community surrounded by woods and cotton fields that hug a bend in the Tennessee River, had been doing so well. The people were excited by their new city hall and were hoping to win federal funds for a local health clinic. Foster went home to confer with his wife and ponder what to do.

The next day he called the TVA in Chattanooga, Tennessee, and asked for corroboration of what he had heard. A TVA official confirmed the news and read the report over the phone. The report ended with the suggestion that "epidemiological studies should be run on the citizens of Triana." There was also the shocking revelation that some four thousand tons of DDT lay in the sediment of Huntsville Spring Branch, another embayment that joins Indian Creek shortly before it flows into the Tennessee River at Triana. Foster is never speechless, but this news took him aback. "Sir, I must tell you that I am greatly concerned over this threat to the life of my town," he told the TVA man. "I'm sure you're aware that we swim in that creek, that we fish in it every day—for *food,* damn it, not for trophies—and it was our only local source of water until 1967." The TVA man said he was sorry.

City hall in Triana began receiving calls that day from reporters in Huntsville, fifteen miles away. Foster knew it was time to confer with the town council before the people of Triana found out about their disaster from the newspapers. At a hastily called meeting that night, they decided to take the fish from various freezers in town and send them to the TVA for analysis in the hope that there were high levels of DDT only in fish more recently caught—meaning the DDT had just been spilled—or that the DDT was not so prevalent as to be in all the fish caught in the river.

While the frozen fish were being analyzed, Foster began looking into the DDT's source, which the TVA said was a defunct chemical plant on a remote part of the Army missile base at Redstone Arsenal, some five miles from Triana by way of Indian Creek and Huntsville Spring Branch. He knew assigning responsibility for the spill would be complicated, for the creek runs through property owned by the Army Corps of Engineers, collects in a swampy basin near the Army's missile ranges, and flows through Wheeler National Wildlife Refuge where it joins with Indian Creek. The overlapping governmental jurisdictions were confusing, but at least the plant was a piece of hard evidence.

But Foster found that there was no longer a plant, only a ghostly concrete slab connected to a filled-in ditch that once dumped effluent into the Spring Branch. The Army had completely dismantled the plant in 1970, but the faint, pungent odor of DDT still hung in the air. The Army disclaimed responsibility for the plant because a private company rented the land from the government in 1943 and built the plant to manufacture poisonous chemicals like mustard gas, phosgene, and chlorine. In 1947, another private manufacturer bought the plant to make DDT. That company sold out to the Olin Chemical Corporation in 1953. Olin continued to make DDT there until the Army closed down the plant in 1970 for exceeding a mutually established set of pollution standards for DDT levels in the Spring Branch. The plant's existence was no secret to Foster. Spills intermittently killed massive numbers of fish in Indian Creek.

"Sure, we knew the plant was there," Foster told the Army, "but nobody ever told us they were dumping tons of DDT right into our water. We're afraid to fish in the creek now, and it's a prime source of food for our community."

"Mr. Foster," one general replied, "the land where the plant was built is on an Army base, but it's owned by the Corps of Engineers. We only rented it to the chemical companies, and we can take no responsibility for the pollution of Indian Creek."

Foster was beginning to lose his composure. "General," he replied, "if one of those missiles from your base lands in Indian Creek, it's sure as hell your responsibility."

He went next to the Alabama Department of Public Health in Huntsville and Montgomery. There he was reminded of the controversy surrounding DDT. Public health officers told him that DDT had never been proven harmful to human beings and that scarce resources could not be made available to run epidemiological studies on the people of Triana. One doctor stated flatly that he'd just as soon sprinkle DDT on his cereal in the morning as he would sugar: the two were equally harmful. Foster was not prepared for this. He felt he did not know enough to challenge the state public health authorities, but he didn't believe them.

Foster recalls his feelings: "I did not want a confrontation. I just wanted the scientific investigation to speak for itself. Why did the TVA suggest Triana be studied if DDT wasn't at all dangerous? How can it kill insects, fish, and birds and not be potentially harmful to people? I knew the stuff was real stable, that it stays in the body for years. Who knows what effect massive doses could have over a long period of time? The TVA has known about the presence of DDT in the fish of Indian Creek for years, and I found later that the Army checked in 1977 and found a fish with one hundred times the safe DDT level. Then we received the TVA analysis of the fish from our freezers: our fish had even higher DDT levels than those they had first tested. We needed some help."

As an employee of the federal government with more than twenty years' experience, Foster knew of a federal organization that might help his town. One afternoon in mid-December he reached for the phone and asked the long-distance operator to connect him with the Centers for Disease Control in Atlanta.

In the forty years since the discovery of its insecticidal properties, the chemical compound DDT has become the focal point of an intense scientific dispute. Clyde Foster was a boy growing up near the steel mill where his father worked in Birmingham when DDT was introduced in the rural South just after the end of World War II to combat mosquitoes and other vectors of disease. Its use against crop-destroying insects established it as a miracle of modern agriculture. In 1945 the Swiss chemist who discovered its toxicity won the Nobel Prize. It appeared he had found the "perfect" insecticide.

The future mayor of Triana had decided from boyhood that he wanted a better life than a job in a steel mill. One of thirteen children, he spent a summer after high school with a sister in Chicago, working to save money for college. By the time he graduated from a small black institution in northern Alabama cotton country in 1954 and began work as a mathematician at the Marshall Space Flight Center, countless tons of DDT had been sprayed all over the world. In its wake, some crop yields had jumped fifty percent; malaria, yellow fever, and typhus had been brought under control; the booming chemical industry in the United States was developing new insecticides at an astronomical rate. Coincidentally, a federal agency established in Atlanta during World War II—dubbed Malaria Control in War Areas—had used DDT to great advantage in its fight to control mosquitoes. The Atlanta agency proved so successful that in 1946 it was renamed the Communicable Disease Center and took on the expanded role of combating many additional infectious diseases.

DDT has been more widely used than any other pesticide, but it is still unclear exactly how it affects people. DDT attacks the nervous system of insects by penetrating directly through their outer coverings. It has also proven harmful to certain species of birds and fish. The nervous systems of higher animals are much less vulnerable, since DDT cannot penetrate our skins. When ingested directly, DDT breaks down in the body into two metabolites, DDD and DDE.

The DDD is excreted in urine, but the DDE is highly fat-soluble and collects in the fatty tissue, where it remains. There lies the heart of a controversy: scientists have discovered that the notable chemical stability of some DDT metabolites makes them nearly impervious to metabolic processes; they are not destroyed by digestion, but accumulate along the food chain as one animal devours another. And DDT has other interesting chemical properties. A nearly insoluble crystal, it can stay in the ground through a thousand rains. It also has a high vapor pressure, so it evaporates easily, and when airborne moves freely through the atmosphere. It has been sprayed with such abandon that it permeates every corner of the globe; there is hardly a human being alive who does not have DDT metabolites in his fatty tissue.

These qualities of persistence and easy dissemination, highly valued for insect control, leave nagging questions in the minds of scientists as to the long-term health effects of DDT. With the added revelation that many insects quickly developed an immunity to the compound, it fell into disfavor in the sixties and is banned in some countries today, including the United States. Still, the Alabama Department of Public Health is not alone in maintaining that DDT is innocuous in relation to human health.

Clyde Foster's phone call to the Centers for Disease Control came during a pivotal stage in the agency's development. It had changed its name (from the Communicable Disease Center) in 1970 to reflect the gradual broadening of its mission. It had gained a worldwide reputation for its skills in epidemiology, disease surveillance, and disease control, and for the high standards of its laboratory sciences. It employed more than three thousand people and had shared a crowning achievement in 1977 with other health organizations around the world: the complete eradication of smallpox from the face of the earth. But while the center had enjoyed many successes, it was facing a new, particularly twentieth-century challenge just as disturbing as the bacterial diseases that once mystified all medicine and gave birth to the science of microbiology in the nineteenth century. This challenge was the mounting number of nonbacteriological ailments, often caused by the contamination of the environment, that were known as "chronic" diseases.

The center developed its original response to chronic disease in an almost offhand way. What is now the Chronic Diseases Division within the Bureau of Epidemiology was first created in the early sixties to investigate the theory that viruses were related to cancer. A small group of scientists trained in hematology (a branch of biology that deals with the blood and blood-forming organs) assembled at CDC to look for a viral cause for leukemia and, later, to inquire about genetic causes of cancer. Eventually they abandoned this research as the theoretical pendulum swung toward the present belief that environmental factors are the chief cause of cancer. There followed a natural metamorphosis of purpose as the leukemia experts turned their attention to the new theory. Theirs was a field still largely unscouted by scientific inquiry, but by 1978 they were increasingly busy. The scope of their investigations had expanded, and their work had important implications. It was obvious that the Chronic Diseases Division was going to demand more and more of the center's resources.

Foster's call was referred to the Chronic Diseases Division and then to its newest office, called the Special Studies Branch. Special Studies was created to deal with the overflow of inquiries related to environmental hazards, especially toxic poisoning and low-level radiation exposure. Like the other two branches in the Chronic Diseases Division—the Birth Defects Branch and the Cancer Branch—Special Studies was crammed into a small set of offices in one wing of CDC's main building, which is adjacent to the campus of Emory University. Foster finally reached Dr. Kathleen Kreiss, one of several young physicians in the Special Studies Branch enrolled in the center's two-year Epidemiological Investigative Service training program. A woman of enormous energy and boundless enthusiasm for her work, Dr. Kreiss would soon become the de facto chief of Special Studies, even though she was technically a trainee.

When the phone rang after working hours, she was at her cluttered desk in a passageway between cubicles, puzzling over a case involving workers in a chemical plant who had suddenly developed severe bladder dysfunctions. She was also planning to write a report that evening about an outbreak of Rocky Mountain spotted fever that had killed the parents of a North Carolina family, and she was hoping to find time to look into a case of arsenic contamination in Alaskan well water. Though already overcommitted, she took Foster's call, writing hasty notes as she listened to his story of how the ghost of DDT had come back to haunt Triana, Alabama.

Foster explained to Dr. Kreiss about his town's plight. "Dr. Kreiss, *we are frightened,* we would like to know what this means to our health as a community. Other government agencies seem unable to help. How can I convince the Centers for Disease Control to come to our aid?"

Foster found he didn't need to convince Kathleen Kreiss of anything. He had come to the right place. She told him in her quiet, understated way that she would help. "I knew," she recalls, "that there was no information on how DDT affected pregnant women, the sick and elderly, infants, and other populations outside the venue of occupational health studies. We were so understaffed that we were pressed to the absolute limit as individuals, but I decided I had to look into this." She agreed to attend a meeting of TVA administrators with the mayor on the very next day in Chattanooga.

At the meeting, Mayor Foster was taken with the articulate self-confidence of twenty-eight-year-old Dr. Kreiss. An expansive man himself, he was impressed by the patient, studied pace with which she explained the need for an epidemiological study in Triana and requested that TVA send her samples of the fish they had already tested. He was sure of himself, too, and he liked the contrast he and Dr. Kreiss made: she with large polygonal glasses and long blond hair bound up on her head; he in black pants, socks, shoes, and shirt, with a gray herringbone coat and vest, his hairline receding to leave two tight glossy black tufts on either side of the shiny bare middle of his head. He pounded the table when he made a point and raised his voice to punctuate it. "Our people are in the food chain of that river," he told the administrators. "Many of us eat its fish every day. Already there is economic hardship among very poor people who customarily derive daily sustenance from the river. Our whole community is upset. We need help." But the TVA—overcome by the complexity and immensity of the problem—was not able to commit itself to any definite course of action.

At subsequent meetings, Foster learned that the Environmental Protection Agency's predecessor has tested fish and wildlife from the Indian Creek area, knew of high DDT levels in the water, but didn't tell anyone in Triana. He was sure that the TVA and the state of Alabama knew of Triana's reliance on fish from the river, and he was angered that no one had worried about closing the DDT plant until 1970 when the Army took action. "Of course they were aware of how much fish we ate," he told the stream of reporters now visiting Triana. "If it hadn't been a black community, the people responsible would probably have been on the plant's board of directors, and they would have prevented toxic spills from threatening their own families."

It was the mayor's job to be emotional about his town and its safety; it was Dr. Kreiss' responsibility to remain objective through an investigation that would involve a lot of frightened people. She reviewed previous DDT studies and sought expert opinion by calling a prominent university professor who is a recognized authority on pesticides. He thought her investigation would be a waste of time, and reminded her that there was no solid evidence that DDT was harmful to human health.

Dr. Kreiss remained unconvinced. She decided to take blood samples from a dozen Triana citizens. She also began devising a questionnaire to determine each donor's medical history. She asked the mayor to select twelve people from the town who had been life-time residents, were between twenty and sixty-five years old, ate fish on a regular basis, and had never been exposed to DDT as agricultural workers. "We'll do a pilot study on these twelve," she told him, "and I'll come to Triana and explain the results at a public meeting. Then we'll be able to see if there's any indication that we should test the whole community."

Clyde Foster did not qualify for the pilot testing because he was not a lifelong member of the town. He had arrived in 1957 after taking his job at the space flight center and marrying a young woman from Triana. But in many ways Foster is the father of the town. He always liked living there. He enjoyed fishing and loved to wander down the steep wooded slopes that flank Indian Creek and walk along its muddy littoral until it joined with the wide green-gray Tennessee River. Yet he was deeply bothered by the poverty of his adopted home. It was a place opportunity had abandoned. Most of its one hundred residents were elderly people, either on welfare or unemployed. Returning each day from work in the white world at the Marshall Space Flight Center, he would contemplate the contrast between the opportunities of that world and the poverty of his home a few miles away. Triana lacked even running water—there was a well in another town, and there was the river. "There is no need for this disparity in a land of plenty," Foster began telling his fellow citizens at meetings in the shack they used for a town hall. "There is no reason we should do without running water, but we aren't even officially recognized as a town, we have no charter, and we don't know where we came from."

In 1963, Foster chaired a committee of residents interested in raising Triana "from the ashes of the past." By 1964, with the help of old-timers who remembered some of the local history, the committee had unearthed the town's original charter—dated 1819—from the state archives in Montgomery: the charter had never been dissolved. The committee petitioned a local probate judge to reinstate the charter, making it possible for the town to apply to federal agencies as a local government. This is what Foster had hoped for all along. He was elected mayor, and under his persistent guidance, Triana won a federal grant/loan for a water system that was installed in 1967 (to initiate the program, Foster had his own well dug and then gave it to the town); another grant for twelve public housing units; and a contract from private industry to build a plant for electronic and mechanical assembly work that hired twenty-two local residents off the welfare roles in its first year of operation. The town grew. It won a county-supported day care center, its population topped five hundred, and it kept growing. Six months before the TVA's report on the DDT contamination, Triana had realized its fondest dream: a new municipal building, built with a federal loan.

When Dr. Kreiss arrived with her blood sample collection kit in February of 1979, Triana was a town that believed in its potential. It was both dynamic and friendly. Before setting up her collection system in the fire station, she walked with the mayor and saw the park overlooking Indian Creek that the town had built ten years ago. He pointed out for her the land set aside for a new health clinic, another of his dreams for the community. He was hoping this DDT investigation would not take the wind from the sails of Triana. It was a town that prized its future.

Dr. Kreiss took blood that day from what Foster likes to call "the twelve apostles." She collected the blood in glass tubes, allowed it to coagulate, capped the tubes, and spun them in a centrifuge she had brought along. She aspirated the clear serum into special vials, packed them in dry ice, and took them to John Liddle, a Ph.D. chemist who is chief of the Toxicology Branch of the Clinical Chemistry Division at CDC.

John Liddle's chemists—working in a set of temporary buildings in Chamblee that have since become permanent—had been examining the fish samples from the TVA and Triana's freezers, and now they took the serum from the twelve apostles and prepared it for analysis. It would be weeks before the results would be in. Work in a toxicology lab is painstakingly slow. Since chemical substances cannot be found with even the most powerful microscopes, researchers must rely on procedures of quantitative analysis sensitive to parts per billion or trillion. By contrast, bacteriological investigators are usually able to isolate a particular microbe, find a culture medium it will grow in, and study how to combat its effects by developing an antigen or a vaccine. The eradication of smallpox is paradigmatic of the success of this kind of research. Unlike toxic-related disease, smallpox is caused by a virus that produces obvious visible symptoms, it is transmitted only from human to human, and there is an excellent vaccine that conveys long-term immunity. There are no vaccines to counter chemical contamination of the body's systems, cultures cannot be grown, and symptoms are not necessarily visible for many years.

Mayor Foster called regularly to check on the lab's progress. John Liddle urged patience, explaining that the process was slow, and that it was important to be thorough.

In two weeks, the results were compiled. Test after test confirmed an emerging pattern: the level of DDT metabolites in the Triana serum was some fourteen times higher than the national average. One sample contained over three thousand parts per billion, four times as much DDT metabolite as had ever been found in previous studies.

By now, Dr. Kreiss was conferring with Renata Kimbrough, a highly respected scientist and medical doctor attached to John Liddle's toxicology lab. Dr. Kimbrough, a striking, silver-haired woman, uses her medical expertise to help guide the lab's chemists through the long, intricate maze of toxicological analysis by examining the symptoms of a reported illness and determining what compounds are the likely suspects. Like tracks in first snow, Dr. Kimbrough's clues have often melted into the body's chemistry by the time she begins looking for them. Chemicals can change form when they enter the body, damaging in the process the cells' hereditary material—DNA—and then disappear. Some complex substances are nearly impossible to analyze and are dangerous at incredibly low concentrations; others become dangerous only in the presence of another toxic substance, whereupon they combine or react to produce a dangerous chameleon that fades from view. "It is a very difficult science, and there aren't many people who are trained to do it," admitted Dr. Kimbrough with a trace of her native German accent. "I try to screen a substance thoroughly before we attempt a chemical analysis. We usually have a limited sample to work with, and it has to be saved for the lab processes. I can tell a great deal from symptoms, but sometimes I'll use animals as a screen. If one component of a substance is harmless to rats or guinea pigs, then we can turn our attention elsewhere. Unlike searching for bacteria, we often have no idea of what form the culprit will take. Even when a clue is found, carcinogenesis involves periods of latency up to twenty years that are still not understood by medical science."

While pursuing her research Dr. Kimbrough had already become a notable champion for the cause of protecting human health from toxic damage. Kimbrough is consistently nonpolitical about the opinions she ventures in relation to her work—a common attitude at the center—but she, like Kathleen Kreiss, once found herself in the middle of a well-publicized investigation of a widely used chemical. In the late sixties, she found that hexachlorophene caused brain lesions when fed to laboratory rats. It was also discovered that hexachlorophene was causing the same kind of brain lesions in premature infants who were regularly cleansed with it in hospitals to ward off staph infections. Kimbrough was eventually called to France to testify in a tragic case of hexachlorophene poisoning that killed thirty infants. The DDT contamination in Triana immediately interested her. There were many unanswered questions in the scientific literature about DDT. A study in Florida had shown premature infants have much higher DDT metabolite levels in their blood than full-term newborns, but the possible cause and effect relationship remained to be determined; DDT's metabolites had been found to have hormonal effects in some animals, but there was no research on humans. It was once believed that the body protected itself from all contaminants by transforming them into less toxic forms, but now it was known some reactions result in metabolic toxification, and the metabolites of DDT were not well-studied. No one knew if DDT metabolite levels stabilize at a certain point or continue to increase with age. Dr. Kimbrough had urged Dr. Kreiss to follow her original impulse from the beginning. Now she encouraged her to run a test on the entire Triana community.

The meeting in Triana attracted over a thousand people. It was a cold evening in mid-March, the cotton fields were freshly turned but unplanted, and the small green nodes of early spring had not yet surfaced on the bare trees towering over Indian Creek. The gymnasium at the municipal center was filled to capacity with faces that were black, white, young, old, curious, alarmed, concerned. Dr. Kreiss released the findings on the twelve residents tested and explained the situation calmly. Research with DDT was incomplete. These levels were high in relation to the national average, but there was no immediate indication that the health of the individuals tested had been harmed by DDT. "There is much research to be done," she told them, "especially among women, children, and older people. It appears that people who ingest DDT metabolites from the food chain may have higher levels than agricultural workers who are exposed directly to DDT. We are aware that, for some unknown reason, black people consistently accumulate more DDT metabolites than the white population. It may be years before we can assess the effects—if any—that DDT has on Triana's health, but this study is very important. In May, I hope to return and test every person in the community who is willing. This will involve a simple blood sample and a medical questionnaire. We'll also check your blood pressure. I hope all of you who are interested will come." Before leaving, she spent an hour answering dozens of questions.

In May, Dr. Kreiss returned to Triana with a crew of twelve friends from CDC, people she knew would be interested. They were Epidemiological Investigative Service officers, a public health adviser who flew in from Florida, and a secretary. Dr. Kimbrough flew in to help on her weekend off. Mayor Foster had seen that everything was ready. The testing would take five days; the people who chose to participate were notified by mail when to come to the municipal center's gymnasium where the crew had set up. Testing began at six in the morning on Friday through Tuesday, continuing late each night. Testees were asked to fast for eighteen hours before their blood samples were taken, and a surprising 518 people did just that. They filled out questionnaires, had their own questions answered, had their blood pressure checked. The CDC crew subsisted on doughnuts and coffee, straggling back to the hotel at the Huntsville airport each night to eat and sleep before the next day's ordeal.

Before returning to Atlanta, Dr. Kreiss and Dr. Kimbrough took the opportunity to have a look at the DDT plant site at Redstone Arsenal, only a few miles upstream from Triana. The trip by car was a lengthy drive onto the military base along roads lined with pine forests and bright green cotton fields in new growth. The plant had been built just above where Huntsville Spring Branch became a wide swamp three miles before joining Indian Creek. Besides closing the plant and dismantling it in the face of opposition by Olin Chemical Corporation, the Army had moved tons of contaminated earth away from the Spring Branch and into nonpermeable toxic waste dumps on another part of the base. There was also a new and elaborate charcoal-filtering system to assure that water running into the Spring Branch from previously contaminated ground was purified along the way. Still, nothing practical could be done to remove the thousands of tons of DDT in the sediment of the Spring Branch, property under the overlapping jurisdiction of the Army Corps of Engineers, the TVA, and the national wildlife refuge. "I think we're fortunate," the Army information officer told the two scientists, "that the Spring Branch has acted as a natural filter, preventing the bulk of the DDT from continuing on to Indian Creek and the Tennessee River. And we're lucky no one lives on the Spring Branch. I understand Mayor Foster is seeking federal help in alleviating Triana's problem, but I don't see how he's going to get this cleaned up completely. To dredge or bypass the Spring Branch would have to be done against the wishes of some government agencies because it would upset the ecology so badly. And the cost would be so astronomical it's difficult to calculate."

The lab results would be piling up for weeks. The questionnaire data had to be fed into CDC's computer, cross-referenced with the blood data, reprocessed through the computer, and painstakingly analyzed. Kathleen Kreiss knew the job had just begun. Soon after her last visit to Triana, Kreiss was made acting chief of the Special Studies Branch. She moved into a closet-size office dominated by a blackboard behind her desk listing the branch's pending and current investigations. They included a case of PCB (polychlorinated biphenyl, an outlawed chemical) poisoning of livestock feed in Michigan; a uranium mill tailings spill in Arizona; a mysterious disease connected somehow to the ventilation system in an Indiana grade school; an unexplained illness among sewage plant workers in Fulton County. Computer printouts of the Triana statistics as thick as phone books lay on the floor, her tiny desk, the windowsill. Her reading for months was also spread around her: *Dangerous Properties of Industrial Materials; Registry of Toxic Effects of Chemical Substances; Suspected Carcinogens; Poisoning.*

The Special Studies Branch was overwhelmed and understaffed, and the eight-hour day became a thing of fiction for Dr. Kreiss. New calls came in continually for advice or assistance, and on some days she found no more than a scrap of an hour here or there to think about the DDT blood serum levels in Triana. Somewhere in all those printouts could be a clue, some pattern she could not envision until it sifted out in the constant shuffling between intuition and ratiocination she had learned as an epidemiologist. But one fact emerged almost immediately: the overall blood pressure of Triana's residents was very high. The population's figures were thirty percent above the national average after they were adjusted for age, sex, and race. Could that, she wondered, be due to DDT, or simply to anxiety, or both? Or was there some other factor? There was no way of knowing.

In Triana, Mayor Foster was also feeling frustrated. Though he often conferred with Dr. Kreiss over the phone and continued to be impressed with her efforts, he watched as his town's requests for additional federal loans and grants were frozen. The DDT story was widely publicized, and he was convinced that government agencies were waiting to see if Triana's status as a flourishing community would be sustained. "Our applications for aid are in limbo," he complained to the press. "Either they're waiting to see if we fold, or they're holding back just in case we get special assistance from somewhere. Now, that's punitive and I don't like it. Before the DDT was found, we were looking for developers; now our fund-raising capabilities have been completely curtailed."

When asked about the government's action concerning the DDT incident, Foster was adamant. "Look, you list the agencies," he would tell reporters, raising both fists and bending out his fingers one by one. "The Department of the Army, the Army Corps of Engineers, the Department of the Interior, the Food and Drug Administration, the Tennessee Valley Authority, the Department of Health, Education, and Welfare, the Environmental Protection Agency, the Alabama Department of Public Health. Only Dr. Kreiss at the Centers for Disease Control has not tried to tell us someone else is responsible, even though this accident has unalterably affected our lives."

Foster is sometimes hyperbolic when defending his town, but there was truth in what he said. In many ways the changes in Triana were obvious and in some they were not. The Alabama Department of Public Health never did outlaw fishing in Indian Creek, but the TVA put up a large sign at the public boat ramp that read:

NOTICE
Fish in these waters are
heavily contaminated with
DDT

EAT THEM AT YOUR OWN RISK

The local fishing trade fell off sharply. The less obvious effects had to do with things like the Triana Volunteer Fire Department's monthly fish fry, a much cherished social event of the recent past that had been possible only because the main course had come fresh and free from the river. There was also the high blood pressure. A discussion of Triana's plight at a town council meeting uncovered the fact that all eighteen people present had high blood pressure. Joe Lewis, Triana's police chief/fire chief/city engineer, expressed the town's frustration: "We've got a wonderful community here. Fifty

percent of our people are related to one another, we're like an island, and we love it. But we can't just turn our heads and forget
about it when we hear about this DDT. What's going to happen to
our kids? They'll have to live through this all their lives."

No matter what results Dr. Kreiss' study would eventually turn
up, and despite Foster's insistence to the contrary, it was becoming
clear that not much would be done very soon to remove DDT from
the Huntsville Spring Branch swamp. The swamp is a natural filter,
but it is also a holding tank, and Triana's inhabitants may have to
live with the DDT problem into the next century. But the larger concern is not only Triana's, it is everyone's. Triana may only be a preliminary. There is mounting evidence at CDC that the next great
challenge to modern health will come from the chronic effects of
substances man himself has introduced into the environment. By
virtue of their latent carcinogenicity, many chemicals used for decades may already pose a threat to public health that will remain
unaffected by new controls.

"We need a direct response to the fact that the first era of epidemiology is over," maintains Dr. J. Donald Millar, one of many epidemiologists involved in the successful worldwide campaign to
eradicate smallpox, and the man now in charge of public health services at CDC. "Most of the diseases caused by etiologic agents are
well-studied, their effects are known, and though far from being totally eliminated, they are no longer mysteries to us. The three important factors affecting life expectancy now are unhealthy
behavior like cigarette smoking, violence, and environmental
threats—people haven't been exposed long enough to many toxic
substances for us to know their effects."

Dr. Kreiss agrees that the challenges are myriad, but she is un-
happy with the slow progress in the fight against chronic diseases.
"It's pretty obvious," she said from behind a stack of computer
printouts in her office, "that public health is more threatened by
toxic environmental factors now than by bacteriological disease. It
is also true that the private medical sector in this country is not answering the challenge. I learned in med school and afterward at the
Occupational Health Program in the Harvard School of Public

Health that occupational medicine and preventive health care are the black sheep of the private medical world. Industrial medicine evolved as a way to keep insurance premiums down, not from any direct desire on the part of the medical community to get involved with occupational threats or environmental hazards. We are obligated to study cases like Triana. Even at CDC, lip-service is paid to noninfectious problems, but the resources of the Chronic Diseases Division are terribly strained, the old structure is still here, and we all recognize the pressing need to adapt."

The pace of Dr. Kreiss' investigation is slowed by her commitments to other problems, and it will be some time before she has compiled her results. But there is a new health clinic in Triana now, and the mayor doesn't deny that the DDT controversy and the revelation that eighty percent of his town is suffering from high blood pressure ultimately helped expedite the federal grant that made the clinic possible. On the day before Thanksgiving, the clinic's new furniture and equipment arrived. It was enthusiastically unloaded into two old house trailers provided by the TVA and renovated by the town. At the nearby country store on the Triana highway, the talk drifted from the health clinic trailers to the TVA's public health efforts after the war. An elderly woman sat crocheting in a rocking chair, her ebony skin deeply creased and tanned to a luster by healthy old age. "The TVA sprayed that DDT everywhere, and thank God they did," she said forcefully. "Before that we had ticks, bed bugs, mosquitoes; people were dyin' of malaria. They put screens on all the windows and doors, and for free, too." Everyone present agreed that what she said was true.

"But I'll tell you," said a fisherman, "the good game fish know about that DDT. They haven't gone in Indian Creek for fifteen years."

"You know, it puts pressure on you mentally," added James Parcus, the store's co-proprietor and the only white man on Triana's town council. "You wonder if it's going to cause something cancerous to chop ten years off the end of your life. Way I look at it, those are the best years."

"I quit eating the fish from the river fourteen years ago because I suddenly became allergic to them," his wife said from behind the cash register. "It's my kids I'm worried about."

"And how about that liquid frost?" somebody asked.

"Now there's another thing I fear," Mrs. Parcus said. "They spray that stuff on the cotton fields, and even with the windows closed it seeps into the house. It burns and makes you choke, and I'm positive it made our allergic daughter sick twice this year. It's like that DDT; they spray it all over the place without knowin' what it'll do to people."

Up and down the highway near the store, the cotton fields lay completely dead. The white bolls stood out against brown stalks and branches so that it appeared an early snow had fallen. The plants had been sprayed with the powerful herbicide local residents call "liquid frost." Using this chemical increases the efficiency of the harvesting machines that have replaced the back-breaking process of picking cotton by hand. When the plants are dead, their bolls separate more easily and less chaff gets in the machines' hoppers. The residents of Triana have no way of knowing if liquid frost will eventually affect their health, even though they are certain it is an irritant in the immediate sense. Congress passed the Toxic Substances Control Act in 1976, forcing chemical producers to assess toxicity before they begin manufacture, but the law does not apply to substances already on the market and in use for many years.

The microbe hunters who started the first epidemiological era in the nineteenth century would probably appreciate the irony of our situation. They were always discovering that the road to better medical knowledge was full of blind curves. Nearly every infectious disease known to man is now under control, but the challenges of public health have become more complicated, its goals more elusive. There are, for example, between 30,000 and 50,000 chemicals on the market today, mixed in over two million combinations. A thousand new chemicals are developed every year. On a graph, the proliferation of these substances in our environment over the last forty years would define a line rising sharply, almost exponentially, toward an unknown limit. From some perspectives, the human population is being slowly poisoned. The dream of a world without disease is made more remote by our own shortsightedness.

Mayor Foster certainly sees the irony. The DDT spill is not Triana's fault, but it is Triana's tragedy. No amount of civic ingenuity or community pride can undo the damage. Dr. Kreiss is not alone when she describes Triana as one of the warmest, friendliest places she has ever visited. There is little crime or violence, and the jail cell in the new municipal building remains empty, the butt of many jokes about its disuse. "We've found happiness here," Foster said recently as he looked out past the town's new health clinic toward the tops of the trees lining Indian Creek. "Our opportunities exceed those of any blacks you'll find in the urban area. The DDT hasn't spoiled that for us, but it has changed our lives. Thank God Kathleen Kreiss is concerned about people. Thank God she is so technically competent. She has calmed us." He swept his hand out, taking in the whole scene before him. "I came here for the good life. I don't know what the good life means to other people, but to me it means being among friends and close to nature. It means being able to fish and hunt. It means being able to swim in the beautiful river that flows by your house. Nobody does that anymore."

EDITOR'S EPILOGUE

The story of Triana does not end here.[1] The "unhealthiest town in America" fought back and won.[2] In 1980, Mayor Clyde Foster filed a class action lawsuit against Olin Chemical Company. After years of delays and attempts to co-opt the Triana residents, the lawsuit was settled out of court in 1983 for $25 million.[3] The model settlement agreement had three main points. Olin Chemical Company agreed (1) to clean up residual chemicals, (2) to set aside $5 million to pay for long-term medical surveillance and health care of Triana residents, and (3) to pay "cash-in-pocket" settlements to each resident.[4]

3

PCBs and Warren County

KEN GEISER AND GERRY WANECK

W ater is a precious resource on the surface of this planet.[1] It is
required by all life forms—the average human consumption
is two quarts per day—and it represents most of the mass of living
organisms. It covers most of the earth's crust but it cannot escape
the earth's atmosphere—it can only move from place to place. Thus
the water cycle is a closed system.

Throughout the industrial world today, vast bodies of water are
being contaminated by synthetic toxic chemicals. Whole lakes and
rivers have been declared too dangerous for human exposure. As
these pollutants seep into creeks and groundwater, water acts as a
vehicle that carries these toxins from our physical environment into
our biological environment.

This chapter wishes to call attention to the serious consequences
of chemical contamination of the earth's water resources. It focuses
on one of the most hazardous of contaminants: PCBs, a close relative of dioxin. Some of the scientific background needed to understand the chemistry and biology of these compounds is provided. It
shows how industrial negligence and government ineffectiveness
are responsible for the crisis. As more and more communities are
faced with this threat, people often find that they themselves must
take action if they are to overcome it.

In the fall of 1982, a large protest occurred in Warren County,
North Carolina, against an effort by the state to dump over 6000
truckloads of PCBs-laden soil into what officials called "a secure

landfill." Protestors came from miles around as blacks and whites, young and old, united in a courageous attempt to block roads to the landfill with their bodies. Over 500 arrests were made as the protest drew national attention. Why are PCBs so frightening that people were willing to risk arrest while using their bodies to stop the dump trucks?

CHEMISTRY AND BIOLOGY OF PCBS

PCBs is an abbreviation for "polychlorinated biphenyls," members of the family of halogenated aromatic hydrocarbons. This family also contains DDT and TCDD (Dioxin), some of the most toxic substances known to life. . . .[2] All of these compounds are synthetic: they do not occur naturally and must be made by reacting chlorine or other halogens with certain petroleum derivatives. Commercial PCBs are inevitably contaminated with dioxin because of their common manufacturing process.

The very properties of PCBs that make them so hazardous to life are the properties that make them so attractive to industry: they are virtually indestructible. PCBs are chemically inert, heat resistant, nonflammable, and electrically nonconducting. They are most commonly used in transformers and capacitors, but have also been used in pesticides, heat exchanger fluids, paints, copying paper, adhesives, sealants, and plastics.[3]

Much of the PCBs have already escaped into the general environment, although "hot spots" have been identified. PCBs have been found in lakes, bays and rivers across the country. The list includes the Great Lakes . . . ; Escambia Bay, Florida; the Waukegan River in Illinois; the Ohio River; the Housatonic River in Connecticut; the Chesapeake Bay; San Francisco Bay; Puget Sound, Washington, and in New York's Hudson River. Most of these waters have been polluted by discharge of industrial wastes, either directly or indirectly through municipal sewer systems.[4]

The problem encountered in all attempts at disposal is how to detoxify the PCBs, contaminated soil and river sludge. Thus far, high temperature incineration is the only EPA-approved method. However, scientists debating how to dispose of PCBs from the Hudson River found that burning the contaminated sludge at temperatures as high as 1000°C merely drove PCBs out of the residues into the gas stream exiting from the furnace. Treatment in an after burner at 1800°C was necessary to completely destroy the PCBs. The main problem with incineration at such extremely high temperatures is that it consumes a tremendous amount of fuel—approximately one gallon of oil for every cubic foot of river bottom treated.[5] It is ironic that incomplete incineration is also one way in which PCBs can be converted to dioxins.[6]

Of the PCBs that have made their way into the environment, a large amount have entered the food chain, and the EPA estimates that 90% of the world's population have measurable levels of PCBs in their bodies. Although PCBs and their relatives are poorly soluble in water, they are carried by water and accumulate in the oils and fats of plants and animals where they cannot be excreted. As Joseph Highland of the Environmental Defense Fund has stated, "The levels of contamination and the number of people affected continue to increase every year. Human breast milk is so heavily contaminated that currently the average nursing infant exceeds by ten times the maximum daily intake level for PCBs set up by the Food and Drug Administration. Fish, birds and livestock in many parts of the U.S. are literally sodden with PCBs."[7] Animal studies have shown these chemicals to be carcinogenic, toxic to the liver and to interfere with reproduction. Studies of their effects on humans have been limited to accidental or occupational exposure. One such incident is described below.

In 1968, some 1200 Japanese developed severe rashes, accompanied by discharge from the eyes, dark brown pigmentation of the skin and nails, headaches and physical weakness. Scientists painstakingly traced the problem to a specific batch of rice oil that was used for cooking by all the affected families. The oil was found to be heavily contaminated with heat exchanger fluid that had leaked into the oil during processing.

PCBs, long known to produce rashes and other skin symptoms in industrial workers, was found to be the major contaminant of the fluid. When this was discovered, the doctors treating these patients focused primarily on these skin symptoms, while tending to ignore the more general complaints. As time passed, however, the skin rashes disappeared while the general symptoms persisted and grew worse. In the years since the incident, these patients have shown disturbances in the liver, blood, nerves, immune responses and reproductive function. There is also some indication that the cancer rate may be unusually high among these people, although even now it is still not long enough after the accident to be certain.[8]

The "Yusho" patients (Yusho is Japanese for "oil disease"), along with victims from a chemical plant explosion in Seveso, Italy, constitute the largest group of people known to be suffering from exposure to PCBs or dioxin. Their specific symptoms are probably a result of the close chemical resemblance of these chlorinated aromatic hydrocarbons to certain growth or sex hormones and to certain mutagens. Liver enzymes are also thought to play a role in the induction of cancer as they attempt to metabolize these chemicals.[9] The effects on the majority of the population who chronically receive much lower exposures over a lifetime can only be extrapolated from the available data on acute exposures.

THE ROLE OF GOVERNMENT AND INDUSTRY

Many of the problems caused by toxic wastes are due to a combination of negligence by industry and failure of governmental agencies to take proper action. In many cases the desire for a favorable business climate and increased profits subordinate their responsibility to society. We are just beginning to see the hidden costs of our technological society and have yet to understand how we will pay the price. According to Dr. Mary-Jane Schneider, in her book *Persistent Poisons:*

> Even if no further pollution were to occur, enough PCBs are already dispersed throughout the environment to cause concern for the indefinite future. The cumulative production of PCBs in North America through 1970 (after which production fell off)

has been estimated at 500,000 tons, and worldwide production was about twice that. In North America, an estimated 300,000 tons have been disposed of into dumps and landfills and may or may not be leaking into air and waters. About 30,000 tons have been released into the atmosphere and were probably carried back to earth by rain and snow. And about 60,000 tons were released into fresh and coastal waters.[10]

With clean and inexpensive detoxification technologies still years off, what actions can be taken to reduce the PCBs threat to our environment? One step has already been taken—that of "source reduction."

The effort to reduce the source actually began some time ago. Although little concern was raised over the chemical between 1929 (when Monsanto first began production) and 1968, the news of the "Yusho" poisoning incident in Japan brought the issue squarely to public attention. The reaction here in the U.S. was so significant that in 1972 Monsanto voluntarily restricted sales of PCBs to closed electrical and hydraulic systems. In 1976 the U.S. Congress took an even bolder step with the passage of the Toxic Substances Control Act by specifically banning the manufacture or continued use of PCBs except in sealed systems. Monsanto ceased production of all PCBs in 1977, which left only the problem of regulating continued use and disposal.

In regulating use and disposal of PCBs manufactured prior to 1977, the government has been less than aggressive. In 1979 the EPA published regulations limiting the use of PCBs to intact, non-leaking capacitors, electromagnets and transformers. The Environmental Defense Fund petitioned the U.S. Court of Appeals to review these regulations as less than adequate and in 1981 the court ruled the regulations invalid and granted an 18 month interim period to promulgate new regulations. The new regulations proposed by the EPA in 1982 are limited to providing for indefinite use of current transformers containing PCBs and a ten year phase out of PCB containing capacitors.

The U.S. Food and Drug Administration first established standards for PCBs in food in 1973. Those regulations permitting 2.5 parts per million in milk and dairy products were later reduced to even lower levels in 1979. Similarly, the National Institute of Occupational Safety and Health has recently reviewed Occupational Safety and Health Administration standards for worker exposure and recommended tighter standards, but OSHA under the [Reagan] administration has failed to act.

Regulations outlawing PCBs have now left us with large amounts of PCBs-laden substances facing disposal. The government has been procrastinating here as well. Almost two years elapsed between the time EPA promulgated disposal regulations and the first incineration facilities were licensed. Presently there are only two licensed incinerators on land and the incinerator ship *Vulcanus* is occasionally provided temporary permits to burn PCBs at sea. There are nine landfills permitted to accept solid PCBs wastes (less than 500 ppm) and several Mobil chemical treatment plants are permitted to detoxify PCBs-contaminated oil. With such limited facilities the problem of backlog and storage of PCBs, particularly in discarded transformers, remains serious.

Thus, although PCBs production has actually stopped, the struggle to regulate the use and disposal has moved more slowly. One of the primary impediments to more aggressive government action has been the pressure of current industrial users for whom tighter regulations on use would increase costs. The . . . federal administration's reluctance to advance regulations will mean that any increased efforts to reduce the source of PCBs contamination must come from interests outside the government. Neither government nor industry is likely to move forward on further source reduction or clean-up of existing water and soil contamination without public pressure. That message has clearly been read in neighborhoods and communities across the country and the result has been a groundswell of local citizen action.

COMMUNITY ACTION: THE SOURCE OF REAL SOLUTIONS

In many communities across the country, citizens have come together into local voluntary organizations to struggle against the threat of PCBs. These grassroots organizations have become the wellspring for generating the political muscle necessary to confront government officials and irresponsible industries.

Citizens have organized to press for state enforcement of existing laws and regulations. Citizen groups have also pushed ahead in researching, advocating and demanding many new and innovative approaches to toxic chemical contamination. In clean-up efforts, citizen groups have pressured state agencies for studies of contaminants, removal of above-ground containers and remedial action to contain chemicals discharged into the ground. In the area of health, citizens groups have conducted their own door-to-door health surveys, pressed for professional epidemiological studies of potentially affected populations and advocated long term health screening programs for monitoring exposure victims. Recently citizen groups have initiated campaigns aimed at the industrial sources of the chemicals themselves.

Broad-based coalitions have formed in several states advocating source reduction, "right to know" and "right to inspect." *Source reduction* as discussed in the case of PCBs above, generally involves a whole series of technological changes in industrial production ranging from simple chemical substitution to complex treatment and detoxification processes whereby the amount of hazardous material produced as waste is reduced. *Right to know* provides workers in plants and community residents living near plants the right to gain the name of and information about toxic chemicals used in the plant. *Right to inspect* provides workers and community residents the right to tour industrial facilities and review current health and safety features.

While much of this citizen action is recent, it is off to a strong start, offering hope of a comprehensive approach to the massive and widespread problem of chemical contamination in water and soil. The character of the citizen action is yet emerging, but so far it appears to be based in working-class communities where the hazards are most prevalent and to draw upon the direct action tactics developed over years of community organizing experience. The protest in Warren County, North Carolina is a good example.

PCBs contamination in the state of North Carolina was caused by the deliberate criminal dumping of PCBs fluid from the Ward Transfer Company of Raleigh by the Robert J. Burns trucking operation of Jamestown, New York. Court records show that, faced with an economic loss brought about by the EPA's ban on resale in 1979, Burns and Ward chose to illegally dump the PCBs. Burns and Ward are now serving sentences for their crimes,[11] but there are only a handful who have been brought to justice for similar actions.

Meanwhile, thirty-thousand gallons of the PCBs fluid remained on 270 miles of roadway in fourteen North Carolina counties for four years before the EPA and the state began the clean-up. Because of the technical difficulty and prohibitive expense of permanent detoxification, the state decided to build a landfill in which to store the contaminated soil indefinitely.

As soon as the state announced that Warren County was being chosen as a potential site for the landfill, Warren County Citizens Concerned About PCBs was formed under the leadership of Ken Ferruccio, one of the residents of the town of Afton (in Warren County).

Warren County is the poorest county in the state with per capita income of around $5,000 in 1980. Its population is 65% black. According to Ken Ferruccio, "The trend is very clear. They would rather experiment with poor black people, poor white people, than to experiment with the middle and upper classes . . . The regulations are such that allow landfills to be placed in environmentally unsafe, but politically powerless areas."

Landfills were discussed at a citizens meeting in Moore County in February 1982, attended by Ken and his wife Deborah. Moore County is one of several that are being considered by the Chemical Wastes Management Co. for siting of landfills. Speaking at this meeting were William Sanjour, branch chief of the EPA's Hazardous Wastes Management Division, and Ms. Lois Gibbs, organizer of the Love Canal residents. According to Deborah Ferruccio, "Mr. Sanjour supervised studies on the damages caused by hazardous wastes, on industries which generate hazardous wastes, and on the technology to handle these wastes. Nearly $20 million [was] spent in these studies. The results, which were quite conclusive, were that *landfills inevitably leak;* and that safe landfill technology is only a concept, not a reality."[12] In New Jersey, construction of landfills with the same basic design has been outlawed because of leaching problems.

There are economic factors involved in the political decision of where to site landfills. Landfills have federal common law liability regulations that absolve landfill operators from all liability after five years. The producer passes the responsibility for damages from hazardous wastes onto the landfill operator. Landfill operators usually operate at the edge of bankruptcy, so when a landfill leaks, the company goes bankrupt and the taxpayers are left with the burden.

In the case of Warren County, it became clear that the state of North Carolina had other economic and industrial considerations in mind when Afton was sited. According to Ken Ferruccio, "The Afton site is only three miles from a new regional industrial waste water treatment plant connected by pipeline to Soul City, potentially one of the industrial parks in North Carolina. The Afton site would begin the completion of an industrial package consisting of Soul City (production), the treatment plant (waste processing), and landfills (waste storage).

"As the plot unfolded, the scenario became even more depressing. Documents revealed that the overriding consideration for the state's desire to acquire the Afton site was the need for a legal chemical waste dump in North Carolina. This would mean that Afton would have to eventually store not only the PCBs, and not only waste eventually generated during production at Soul City, but also waste imported from various parts of the region as well."[13]

The site at Afton was not even scientifically the most suitable. The water table of Afton, N.C. (site of the landfill) is only 5–10 feet below the surface, and the residents of the community derive all of their drinking water from local wells. Only the most optimistic could believe that the heavy concentration of PCBs in the Afton landfill will not eventually leach into the groundwater. Unless a more permanent solution is found, it will only be a matter of time before the PCBs end up in these people's wells.

The October 1982 protest by the Warren County Citizens Group represented the first time people have gone to jail trying to stop a toxic wastes landfill. Actions like these have been characteristic of the civil rights and anti-nuclear movements. Both analogies have merit. The issue at Warren County *is* a question of civil rights; and the danger of the toxic wastes threat *is* related to the nuclear threat. In the case of the toxic wastes, however, "meltdowns" have already occurred all over the country.

The PCBs protest failed to prevent the landfill from being completed, but it succeeded in a number of ways. The governor, James Hunt, had initially refused to meet with the group but was then forced to make concessions to their community. These were that no more landfills would be built in Warren County and that well water and body levels would be monitored. The Concerned Citizens Group is still actively pressuring the state to remove or detoxify the landfill as soon as possible.

The Warren County protest illustrates some of the real opportunities of citizen action. The common threat of the waste dump in Afton united the community in a concerted action of defense. Black and white residents met together, worked together and were arrested together. In fact, the presence of national civil rights figures and members of the national Black Congressional Caucus served to link the protest to larger civil rights and "poor people's" movements. Participants in the community organization educated themselves about the technical issues, learned about PCBs and health hazards and developed an in-depth analysis of the policy and financial questions which led to the selection of Afton as the dump site. United and educated, the citizens of Warren County have developed a true sense of community and a heightened sense of community efficacy.

4

Black, Brown, Red, and Poisoned

REGINA AUSTIN AND MICHAEL SCHILL

People of color throughout the United States are receiving more than their fair share of the poisonous fruits of industrial production. They live cheek by jowl with waste dumps, incinerators, landfills, smelters, factories, chemical plants, and oil refineries whose operations make them sick and kill them young. They are poisoned by the air they breathe, the water they drink, the fish they catch, the vegetables they grow, and, in the case of children, the very ground they play on. Even the residents of some of the most remote rural hamlets of the South and Southwest suffer from the ill effects of toxins.[1]

This chapter examines some of the reasons why communities of color bear a disparate burden of pollution. It also brings into focus the commonality of their struggles and some strategies that are useful in overcoming environmental injustice.

THE PATH OF LEAST RESISTANCE

The disproportionate location of sources of toxic pollution in communities of color is the result of various development patterns. In some cases, the residential communities where people of color now live were originally the homes of whites who worked in the facilities that generate toxic emissions. The housing and the industry sprang

53

up roughly simultaneously.[2] Whites vacated the housing (but not necessarily the jobs) for better shelter as their socioeconomic status improved, and poorer black and brown folks who enjoy much less residential mobility took their place. In other cases, housing for African Americans and Latino Americans was built in the vicinity of existing industrial operations because the land was cheap and the people were poor. For example, Richmond, California, was developed downwind from a Chevron oil refinery when African Americans migrated to the area to work in shipyards during World War II.[3]

In yet a third pattern, sources of toxic pollution were placed in existing minority communities. The explanations for such sitings are numerous; some reflect the impact of racial and ethnic discrimination. The impact, of course, may be attenuated and less than obvious. The most neutral basis for a siting choice is probably the natural characteristics of the land, such as mineral content of the soil.[4] Low population density would appear to be a similar criterion. It has been argued, however, that in the South, a sparse concentration of inhabitants is correlated with poverty, which is in turn correlated with race. "It follows that criteria for siting hazardous waste facilities which include density of population will have the effect of targeting rural black communities that have high rates of poverty."[5]

Likewise, the compatibility of pollution with preexisting uses might conceivably make some sites more suitable than others for polluting operations. Pollution tends to attract other sources of pollutants, particularly those associated with toxic disposal. For example, Chemical Waste Management, Inc. (Chem Waste) has proposed the construction of a toxic waste incinerator outside of Kettleman City, California, a community composed largely of Latino farm workers.[6] Chem Waste also has proposed to build a hazardous waste incinerator in Emelle, a predominantly African American community located in the heart of Alabama's "black belt." The company already has hazardous waste landfills in Emelle and Kettleman City.

According to the company's spokeswoman, Chem Waste placed

the landfill in Kettleman City "because of the area's geological features. Because the landfill handles toxic waste, . . . it is an ideal spot for the incinerator"; the tons of toxic ash that the incinerator will generate can be "contained and disposed of at the installation's landfill."[7] Residents of Kettleman City face a "triple whammy" of threats from pesticides in the fields, the nearby hazardous waste landfill, and a proposed hazardous waste incinerator. This case is not unique.

After reviewing the literature on hazardous waste incineration, one commentator has concluded that "[m]inority communities represent a 'least cost' option for waste incineration . . . because much of the waste to be incinerated is already in these communities."[8] Despite its apparent neutrality, then, siting based on compatibility may be related to racial and ethnic discrimination, particularly if such discrimination influenced the siting of preexisting sources of pollution.

Polluters know that communities of low-income and working-class people with no more than a high school education are not as effective at marshaling opposition as communities of middle- or upper-income people. People of color in the United States have traditionally had less clout with which to check legislative and executive abuse or to challenge regulatory laxity. Private corporations, moreover, can have a powerful effect on the behavior of public officials. Poor minority people wind up the losers to them both.[9]

People of color are more likely than whites to be economically impoverished, and economic vulnerability makes impoverished communities of color prime targets for "risky" technologies. Historically, these communities are more likely than others to tolerate pollution-generating commercial development in the hope that economic benefits will inure to the community in the form of jobs, increased taxes, and civic improvements.[10] Once the benefits start to flow, the community may be reluctant to forgo them even when they are accompanied by poisonous spills or emissions. This was said to be the case in Emelle, in Sumter County, Alabama, site of the nation's largest hazardous waste landfill.[11]

Sumter County's population is roughly 70 percent African American, and 30 percent of its inhabitants fall below the poverty line. Although the landfill was apparently leaking, it was difficult to rally support against the plant among African American politicians because its operations contributed an estimated $15.9 million to the local economy in the form of wages, local purchases of goods and services, and per-ton landfill user fees.[12]

Of course, benefits do not always materialize after the polluter begins operations. For example, West Harlem was supposed to receive, as a trade-off for accepting New York City's largest sewage treatment plant, an elaborate state park to be built on the roof of the facility.[13] The plant is functioning, fouling the air with emissions of hydrogen sulfide and promoting an infestation of rats and mosquitoes. The park, however, has yet to be completed, the tennis courts have been removed from the plan completely, and the "first-rate" restaurant has been scaled down to a pizza parlor.[14]

In other cases, there is no net profit to distribute among the people. New jobs created by the poisonous enterprises are "filled by highly skilled labor from outside the community," while the increased tax revenues go not to "social services or other community development projects, but . . . toward expanding the infrastructure to better serve the industry."[15]

Once a polluter has begun operations, the victims' options are limited. Mobilizing a community against an existing polluter is more difficult than organizing opposition to a proposed toxic waste–producing activity. Resignation sets in, and the resources for attacking ongoing pollution are not as numerous, and the tactics not as potent, as those available during the proposal stage. Furthermore, though some individuals are able to escape toxic poisoning by moving out of the area, the flight of others will be blocked by limited incomes, housing discrimination, and restrictive land use regulations.[16]

THREAT TO BARRIOS, GHETTOS, AND RESERVATIONS

Pollution is no longer accepted as an unalterable consequence of living in the "bottom" (the least pleasant, poorest area minorities can occupy) by those on the bottom of the status hierarchy. Like anybody else, people of color are distressed by accidental toxic spills, explosions, and inexplicable patterns of miscarriages and cancers, and they are beginning to fight back, from Maine to Alaska.[17]

To be sure, people of color face some fairly high barriers to effective mobilization against toxic threats, such as limited time and money; lack of access to technical, medical, and legal expertise; relatively weak influence in political and media circles; and ideological conflicts that pit jobs against the environment.[18] Limited fluency in English and fear of immigration authorities will keep some of those affected, especially Latinos, quiescent. Yet despite the odds, poor minority people are responding to their poisoning with a grass-roots movement of their own.

Activist groups of color are waging grass-roots environmental campaigns all over the country. Although they are only informally connected, these campaigns reflect certain shared characteristics and goals. The activity of activists of color is indicative of a grass-roots movement that occupies a distinctive position relative to both the mainstream movement and the white grass-roots environmental movement. The environmental justice movement is antielitist and antiracist. It capitalizes on the social and cultural differences of people of color as it cautiously builds alliances with whites and persons of the middle class. It is both fiercely environmental *and* conscious of the need for economic development in economically disenfranchised communities. Most distinctive of all, this movement has been extremely outspoken in challenging the integrity and bona fides of mainstream establishment environmental organizations.

People of color have not been mobilized to join grass-roots environmental campaigns because of their general concern for the environment. Characterizing a problem as being "environmental" may carry weight in some circles, but it has much less impact among poor minority people. It is not that people of color are uninterested in the environment—a suggestion the grass-roots activists find insulting. In fact, they are more likely to be concerned about pollution than are people who are wealthier and white.[19] Rather, in the view of many people of color, environmentalism is associated with the preservation of wildlife and wilderness, which simply is not more important than the survival of people and the communities in which they live; thus, the mainstream movement has its priorities skewed.

The mainstream movement, so the critique goes, embodies white, bourgeois values, values that are foreign to African Americans, Latino Americans, Asian Americans, and Native Americans. Environmental sociologist Dorceta Taylor has characterized the motivations of those who make donations to mainstream organizations as follows:

> [In part, the] motivation to contribute is derived from traditional Romantic and Transcendental ideals—the idea of helping to conserve or preserve land and nature for one's own present and future use, or for future generations. Such use involves the ability to get away from it all; to transcend earthly worries, to escape, to commune with nature. The possibility of having a transcendental experience is strongly linked to the desire to save the places where such experiences are likely to occur.[20]

Even the more engaged environmentalists, those whose involvement includes participation in demonstrations and boycotts, are thought to be imbued with romantic and transcendental notions that favor nature over society and the individual's experience of the natural realm over the collective experience.

There are a number of reasons why people of color might not share such feelings. Their prospects for transcendental communion with nature are restricted. Parks and recreational areas have been closed to them because of discrimination, inaccessibility, cost, their lack of specialized skills or equipment, and residence requirements for admission.[21] They must find their recreation close to home. Harm to the environment caused by industrial development is not really their responsibility because they have relatively little economic power or control over the exploitation of natural resources. Since rich white people messed it up, rich white people ought to clean it up. In any event, emphasis on the environment in the abstract diverts attention and resources from the pressing, concrete problems that people of color, especially those with little or no income, confront every day.

Nonetheless, communities of color have addressed environmental problems that directly threaten them on their own terms. The narrowness of the mainstream movement, which appears to be more interested in endangered nonhuman species and pristine, undeveloped land than at-risk humans, makes poor minority people *think* that their concerns are not "environmental." Cognizant of this misconception and eschewing terminology that artificially compartmentalizes people's troubles, minority grass-roots environmental activists take a multidimensional approach to pollution problems. Thus, the sickening, poisonous odors emitted by landfills and sewage plants are considered matters of public health or government accountability, while workplace contamination is a labor issue, and lead-based paint in public housing projects is a landlord-tenant problem.[22]

The very names of some of the organizations and the goals they espouse belie the primacy of environmental concerns. The Southwest Organizing Project of Albuquerque (SWOP) has been very successful in mobilizing people around issues of water pollution and workplace contamination. For example, SWOP fought for the rollback of charges levied against a group of home owners who were forced to hook up with a municipal water system because nitroglycerine had contaminated private wells. SWOP then campaigned to make the federal government assume responsibility for the pollution, which was attributed to operations at a nearby military installation. Yet in a briefing paper titled "Major National Environmental Organizations and the Problem of the 'Environmental Movement,'" SWOP describes itself as follows:

> SWOP does not consider itself an "environmental" organization but rather a community-based organization which ad-

dresses toxics issues as part of a broader agenda of action to realize social, racial and economic justice. We do not single out the environment as necessarily having a special place above all other issues; rather, we recognize that issues of toxic contamination fit within an agenda which can (and in our practical day-to-day work, does) include employment, education, housing, health care, and other issues of social, racial and economic justice.[23]

In some ways, minority grass-roots environmentalism reflects the interrelationship among various forms of subordination, about which Daniel Zwerdling wrote in an early attack on the parochialism of the mainstream environmental movement:

Pollution, poverty and worker insecurity reflect three different ways that American corporations express themselves as they exploit people and resources for maximum profits. When corporations need raw materials, they strip them from public lands as cheaply as possible and leave behind great scars on the earth. When they need labor, they hire workers as cheaply as possible and leave behind women and men broken by industrial injuries, diseases, and debt. When corporations produce their goods they use the cheapest and fastest methods available and leave behind vast quantities of waste. The corporations dump the wastes in the poorest and most powerless parts of town. And when they earn their profits, the corporations divide them up among company executives and investors, leaving behind poor people who cannot afford medical care or food or decent homes.[24]

Ordinary, plain-speaking people who are the casualties of toxic poisoning articulate the critique somewhat more pointedly. As Cancer Alley resident Amos Favorite put it:

We are the victims. . . . Not just blacks. Whites are in this thing, too. We're all victimized by a system that puts the dollar before everything else. That's the way it was in the old days when the dogs and whips were masters, and that's the way it is today when we got stuff in the water and air we can't even see that can kill us deader than we ever thought we could die.[25]

In the estimation of the grass-roots folks, however, race and ethnicity surpass class as explanations for the undue toxic burden heaped on people of color. Activists see these environmental inequities as unfair and unjust—practices that many feel should be illegal. Of course, it is hard to prove that racial discrimination is responsible for siting choices and government inaction in the environmental area, particularly in a court of law. One need only point to the examples of *Bean v. Southwestern Waste Management* (Houston, Texas), *Bordeaux Action Committee v. Metropolitan Nashville* (Nashville, Tennessee), and *R.I.S.E. v. Kay* (King and Queen County, Virginia) to see the limited utility of current anti-discrimination doctrine in redressing the plight of poisoned communities of color.

Environmental activists of color draw a good deal of their inspiration from the modern civil rights movement of the 1960s. That movement was advanced by hard-won Supreme Court decisions. These organizers hope that a civil rights victory in the environmental area will validate their charges of environmental racism, help to flesh out the concept of environmental equity, serve as a catalyst for further activism, and, just possibly, force polluters to reconsider siting in poor minority communities.

CAPITALIZING ON THE RESOURCES OF COMMON CULTURE

For people of color, social and cultural differences such as language are not handicaps but the communal resources that facilitate mobilization around issues like toxic poisoning. As members of the same race, ethnicity, gender, and even age cadre, would-be participants share cultural traditions, modes, and mores that encourage cooperation and unity. People of color may be more responsive to organizing efforts than whites because they already have experience with collective action through community groups and institutions such as churches, parent-teacher associations, and town watches or informal social networks.[26] Shared criticisms of racism, a distrust of corporate power, and little expectation that government will be responsive to their complaints are common sentiments in communities of color and support the call to action around environmental concerns.

Grass-roots environmentalism is also fostered by notions that might be considered feminist or womanist. Acting on a realization that toxic poisoning is a threat to home and family, poor minority women have moved into the public realm to confront corporate and government officials whose modes of analysis reflect patriarchy, white supremacy, and class and scientific elitism. There are numerous examples of women of color whose strengths and talents have made them leaders of grass-roots environmental efforts.[27]

The organization Mothers of East Los Angeles (MELA) illustrates the link between group culture and mobilization in the people of color grass-roots environmental movement.[28] Persistent efforts by MELA defeated proposals for constructing a state prison and a toxic waste incinerator in the group's mostly Latino American neighborhood in East Los Angeles.

Similarly, the Lumbee Indians of Robeson County, North Carolina, who attach spiritual significance to a river that would have been polluted by a hazardous waste facility proposed by the GSX Corporation, waged a campaign against the facility on the ground of cultural genocide. Throughout the campaign, "Native American dance, music, and regalia were used at every major public hearing. Local Lumbee churches provided convenient meeting locations for GSX planning sessions. Leaflet distribution at these churches reached significant minority populations in every pocket of the county's nearly 1,000 square miles."[29]

Concerned Citizens of Choctaw defeated a plan to locate a hazardous waste facility on their lands in Philadelphia, Mississippi. The Good Road Coalition, a grass-roots Native American group based on the Rosebud Reservation in South Dakota, defeated plans by a Connecticut-based company to build a 6,000-acre garbage landfill on the Rosebud. Local residents initiated a recall election, defeating several tribal council leaders and the landfill proposal. The project, dubbed "dances with garbage," typifies the lengths that the Lakota people and other Native Americans will go to preserve their land—which is an essential part of their religion and culture.

Consider, finally, the Toxic Avengers of El Puente, a group of environmental organizers based in the Williamsburg section of Brooklyn, New York.[30] The name is taken from the title of a horror movie. The group attacks not only environmental racism but also adultism and adult superiority and privilege. The members, whose ages range from nine to twenty-eight, combine their activism with programs to educate themselves and others about the science of toxic hazards.

The importance of culture in the environmental justice movement seems not to have produced the kind of distrust and misgivings that might impede interaction with white working-class and middle-class groups engaged in grass-roots environmental activism. There are numerous examples of ethnic-based associations working in coalitions with one another, with majority group associations, and with organizations from the mainstream.[31] There are also localities in which the antagonism and suspicion that are the legacy of white racism have kept whites and African Americans from uniting against a common toxic enemy. The link between the minority groups and the majority groups seems grounded in material exchange, not ideological fellowship. The white groups attacking toxins at the grass-roots level have been useful sources of financial assistance and information about tactics and goals.

THE PRIMACY OF HANDS-ON TACTICS

Participation through direct action is crucial to the grass-roots environmental movement, just as it is for its white counterpart. Direct action includes a panoply of legal and extralegal activities such as circulating petitions; holding demonstrations, marches, and sit-ins; conducting candidate and agency accountability sessions, during which panels of prepared community members conduct the quizzes; and picketing shareholders' meetings. The commitment to maximum participation may, of course, represent a matter of necessity for persons without disposable income, but it also seems to be a matter of belief. Again, as stated by Amos Favorite: "The ordinary person who works the fields and walks the streets, who has to live everyday with this mess, he's the warrior of the future. He's got the power to save the world. He's the real environmentalist."[32]

Legal expertise is decidedly deemphasized. The grass-roots folks spend a good deal of their time battling experts—bureaucrats, engineers, epidemiologists, lawyers—in an effort to make questions of risk distribution not simply a matter of science and technology but also a matter of politics and social responsibility. They have reason to be wary of undue reliance on their own experts. The stress placed on direct action means that the law and access to legal forums are more important to grass-roots environmentalists than are lawyers themselves.

Regulation of toxic producers is quite varied and extensive. The permits, licenses, zoning variances, and reporting requirements demanded of polluting concerns all represent openings for activism; lawyers are not invariably required for aggrieved people to take advantage of these requirements.[33] Lawyers still have a role to play, however. They facilitate the release of demonstrators from police custody; secure protection of protestors' First Amendment rights; represent complainants before regulatory agencies; and accompany activists to meetings and conferences at which the other side is sure to be represented by legal counsel. Lawyers clarify the power of government agencies to do what the activists are demanding and assist in the assessment of available strategies to determine which will have the most impact on the polluter.

Both community organizers and lawyers have a certain skepticism about the efficacy of litigation in advancing the goals of minority grass-roots environmentalism, but citizen suits and tort actions are not wholly missing from the list of tactics employed by those involved in the minority grass-roots environmental movement. Plaintiffs do sometimes prevail, and even when they do not, their suits at least perform an educational function. They serve notice to the larger community that there is a problem and that people are upset about it. At the same time, however, litigation requires resources and takes a long time to complete. Losses in court can be demoralizing if too much hope is pinned on achieving legal victories. As activist Richard Moore contends, the judicial system is, after all, not "ours." According to Moore, keeping an organization going for the extended campaigns needed to produce results requires a creative mixing of means and methods.[34]

Direct action tactics can work. How poor minority people come to be powerful is not entirely clear. According to activist Ellie Goodwin, minority grass-roots groups win concessions when they have a clear agenda, dogged determination, and a stubborn resistance to buy-offs and side deals that spell co-optation.[35] The extension of voting rights has increased the number of local and state public officials who are from minority groups or who are responsive to complaints coming from poor minority citizens. The grass-roots movement is also riding on the coattails of the mainstream movement's triumph. The general interest in environmental problems makes industry susceptible to embarrassment and makes government authorities shy about ignoring environmental complaints. Although the media are generally accused of paying too little attention to protests in low-income minority communities, environmentalism there, as elsewhere, is attracting an audience.

ROADBLOCKS TO RELIEF

The success of grass-roots approaches to environmental problems should be judged by whether they produce the desired remedial results. The aspirations of the participants in the minority grass-roots environmental movement parallel those of whites—compensation; restoration of the land, water, or air; inspection of the polluter's facilities; and pollution reduction and prevention. People of color, however, must grapple with circumstances that make the achievement of their goals either more difficult or more imperative.

Limited power can turn victories into disappointments. For example, grass-roots environmentalists in general seem to agree that one of the most desirable concessions they can extract from a polluter is the right to inspect its facility and to monitor its operations.[36] Inspections require direct participation and may result in a reduction of pollution or of the risk of harm. It interjects the community into the company's business. At least two of the attempts poor minority communities have made to undertake inspections have been frustrated. After agreeing to an inspection in the wake of a chemical spill at its inner-city Philadelphia plant, the Welsh Chemical Company reneged because no accommodation could be reached regarding distribution of the information that would have been acquired.[37] Similarly, Chevron attempted to turn an inspection of one of its Richmond, California, facilities into a one-day "tour."[38] Nonetheless, with the assistance of an industrial hygienist, the inspection team produced a list of concerns and released the information to the media. The company objected and broke off dialogue with the community. In these cases, citizens apparently lacked sufficient clout with which to demand greater access. The right to inspect is clearly an area in which policy reform is needed.

People of color have also been handicapped in redressing their pollution-related injuries through tort actions. People whose land and water have been contaminated and whose health has been impaired by toxic poisoning want to be compensated for the harm that has been done to them. Compensation is one goal as to which race, ethnicity, and class clearly do matter. Toxic tort litigation can be quite costly, and poor minority people may encounter difficulties with finding and negotiating a deal with attorneys who are both experienced in handling toxic tort cases and capable of advancing the necessary expenses.

Establishing a claim or entitlement depends on documenting the harm the claimants have experienced or proving a link between the polluter's toxic emissions and the symptoms about which complaint is made. People of color may be at a disadvantage in this regard because their access to medical care is often limited. Building a record may be difficult even when victims are organized, health complaints are ongoing, and medical intervention is timely. For example, within days of a sooty, foul-smelling spill at a chemical plant in the Kensington-Richmond section of Philadelphia, some of the residents and an environmental organizer who worked with them suffered extensive skin rashes.[39] Residents held a sit-in at the health commissioner's office and demanded clinical monitoring to determine the source of the problem. Certain hours were set aside at a public clinic outside the community for investigation of the problem, and arrangements were made to get people there. But the logistics proved to be too onerous, and some residents thought that they had accomplished as much as they could, so the scheme broke down.

The life-styles of people of color may affect their ability to link their health problems to toxin exposure and may also provide a defense to their claims. Many consume diets consisting mainly of junk food, soul food, or processed food, all of which are cheap but high in fat, salt, and sugar.[40] Minorities' consumption of cigarettes, alcoholic beverages, and illicit drugs tends either to be greater than that of the white population or to have more serious health consequences. To compound the causation puzzle, available statistics indicate that poor minority workers are disproportionately exposed to toxins on the job.[41] All of these activities are correlated with the same sorts of disorders (cancer and heart and lung disease) that environmental pollutants promote.[42]

In a few cases, monetary settlements in the millions of dollars have been awarded to poor minority victims of toxic poisoning. The aftermath of such settlements has not really been explored. There is a tendency to underestimate the competence of poor minority people to make financial decisions or to handle substantial sums of money like those involved in court settlements. At the same time, it is likely that poor minority people have fewer local financial institutions or private service organizations (banks, rehabilitation facilities, training programs) interested in meeting their needs. The postsettlement experience needs systematic study and is an area with which lawyers should be concerned.

Compensation may be paid in lieu of restoration of the land and prevention of future harm. For those hard pressed by immediate perils, restoration and prevention, which require a longer time frame, may be impossible goals. Some poor people may have such strong social or cultural reasons for wanting to preserve the integrity of their communities that they are prepared to hold on and hold out, but it seems likely that resolve is related to resources.

To create a buffer zone around a petrochemical plant, Dow Chemical bought the town of Morrisonville, Louisiana, by offering landowners $20,000 per acre, home owners between $50,000 and $200,000, and tenants $10,000 for resettlement.[43] Dow "built a subdivision four miles down river where some of Morrisonville's families could move into new brick homes and establish another community."[44] Georgia Gulf has done the same thing in Reveille-town, Louisiana. These buyout programs have been attacked by environmentalists because buffer zones do not decrease accidents or pollution, though the buffer zones may reduce the direct harm toxins will cause. This criticism seems more justified when directed at the companies responsible for the pollution than at the residents who accept the companies' buyout offers. It is difficult to criticize the compromises people make when they have spent their lives in toxic danger and have few financial resources.

Compensation can have a more disruptive effect on communal life than other forms of relief. Individual monetary settlements can threaten communal solidarity, and there is no precedent for pursuing claims of harm to an entire group or for treating compensation payments as a group asset to be invested for the benefit of the group. These are matters that will likely be of concern to environmental justice activists of color.

The breakdown in the communitarian ethos with regard to compensation is very likely attributable to dichotomies in the law. In the environmental area, there is a real separation between common law and statutory law, between equitable relief and legal remedies, between suits brought by organized groups and class actions initiated by representative individuals, and even between toxic tort litigators and environmental regulatory attorneys. For example, a common-law nuisance is easy for ordinary people to detect and prove, and plaintiffs are not obligated to notify the polluter prior to bringing suit.[45] Unfortunately, there is no provision in the common law for attorneys' fees; restoration and rehabilitation of the environment may be unavailable options unless they are cheaper than compensation; and the deterrent effect of damages is attenuated.

Actions based on public law tend not to have such limitations, but there is generally no provision in the statutes for recovery of damages. Legal policy analysts should consider whether it is possible to combine in one cause of action the strengths of both common law and statutory claims. Furthermore, there should be further inquiry into the viability of communal rights of action.

BRIDGING THE JUSTICE-ENVIRONMENT GAP

At the same time that environmental justice activists are battling polluters, some are engaged on another front in a struggle against elitism and racism that exist within the mainstream environmental movement. There are several substantive points of disagreement between grass-roots groups of color and mainstream environmental organizations. First, communities of color are tired of shouldering the fallout from environmental regulation. A letter sent to ten of the establishment environmental organizations by the Southwest Organizing Project and numerous activists of color engaged in the grass-roots environmental struggle illustrates the level of exasperation:

> Your organizations continue to support and promote policies which emphasize the clean-up and preservation of the environment on the backs of working people in general and people of color in particular. In the name of eliminating environmental hazards at any cost, across the country industrial and other economic activities which employ us are being shut down, curtailed or prevented while our survival needs and cultures are ig-

nored. We suffer the end results of these actions, but are never full participants in the decision-making which leads to them.[46]

Although the indictment standing alone seems fairly broad, it is backed up with specific illustrations of the adverse impact mainstream environmentalism has had on poor minority people. In response to pressure from environmentalists concerned about saving wildlife and protecting the health of the general population, pesticides of great persistence but low acute toxicity, such as DDT and chlordane, have been restricted or banned. They have been replaced by pesticides that degrade rapidly but are more acutely toxic, such as parathion. The substitutes, of course, pose a greater risk to farm workers and their children, who are for the most part people of color.[47] Baldemar Velasquez of the Farm Labor Organizing Committee characterizes the mainstream's failings in regard to pesticides as follows:

> [T]he environmental groups are not responding to try to right the wrongs and change the motivation of industry, which is greed and profit at the expense of everyone. When you start dealing with that issue, you're dealing with structural change in terms of how decisions are made and who benefits from them. The agenda of the environmental movement seems to be focused on getting rid of a particular chemical. This is not enough, because they'll replace it with something else that's worse. . . .[48]

Another threat to communities of color is the growing popularity of NIMBY (not in my backyard) groups. People of color have much to fear from these groups because their communities are the ones most likely to lose the contests to keep the toxins out. The grassroots environmentalists argue that rather than trying to bar polluters, who will simply locate elsewhere, energies should be directed at bringing the amount of pollution down to zero. In lieu of NIMBY, mainstream environmentalists should be preaching NIABY (not in anyone's backyard).[49]

Finally, conservation organizations are making "debt-for-nature" swaps throughout the so-called Third World. Through swaps, conservation organizations procure ownership of foreign indebtedness (either by gift or by purchase at a reduced rate) and negotiate with foreign governments for reduction of the debt in exchange for land.[50] Grass-roots environmental activists of color complain that these deals, which turn conservation organizations into creditors of so-called Third World peoples, legitimate the debt and the exploitation on which it is based.[51]

The positions staked out by environmental justice activists regarding fallout from environmental regulation are consistent with the values that are ingrained in the rest of the movement's activities. The fallout critique is not opposed to environmentalism or environmental regulation. In attacking the political conservatism of the mainstream, the grass-roots environmentalists are not themselves lapsing into environmental conservatism. In fact, the fallout from which communities of color suffer can be cured with *more*, not less, environmentalism, provided it is antielitist, antiracist, sensitive to the cultural norms and mores of people of color, mindful of the impact of domestic regulation on brothers and sisters abroad, and cognizant of the substantial need for economic development in disenfranchised communities.

Unlike those in the mainstream organizations, people involved in the environmental justice movement cannot afford to lose sight of the material circumstances of the black, brown, red, and yellow folks who are their compatriots and constituents. Nor do the grass-roots activists intend to abandon their environmental agenda. The "eco" in eco-justice stands as much for "economic" as for "ecological." For many communities of color, it is too late for NIMBY. They already have a dump, an incinerator, a smelter, a petrochemical plant, or a military base in their neighborhood. They do not necessarily want the polluters " 'to pack up and move away. That's not what we're asking for. We just want them to clean up the mess they've made. They can do it. It's only fair.' "[52] What they want is accountability from existing polluters.[53]

The dual environmental-economic agenda of the minority grass-roots movement is reflected in two items of the Bill of Rights drafted by the Southwest Organizing Project's Community Environmental Program:

> *Right to Clean Industry:* We have the right to clean industry; industry that will contribute to the economic development of our communities and that will enhance the environment and beauty of our landscape. *We have the right to say "NO" to industries that we feel will be polluters and disrupt our lifestyles and traditions.* We have the right to choose which industries we feel will benefit our communities most, and we have the right to public notice and public hearings to allow us to make these decisions.
>
> *Right to Prevention:* We have the right to participate in the formulation of public policy that prevents toxic pollution from entering our communities. We support technologies that will provide jobs, business opportunities and conservation of valuable resources. As residents and workers, we have the right to safe equipment and safety measures to prevent our exposure in the community and the workplace.[54]

Prevention of toxic accidents and communal participation in risk allocation decisions should be the key components of future negotiations regarding industrial sites in poor minority communities. It is hard to envision a world without trade-offs, and it is too soon to tell what sort of compromises enlightened minority communities might be willing to make (or, more likely, might feel compelled to make) when presented with proposals from industries that are mostly clean but a little bit dirty. They might be willing to accept some exposure in exchange not for cash or credit but for control. To the extent that communities do not create and carry out their own plans for economic development, their right to reject poisonous enterprises will be limited. Therein lies the next hurdle for environmental activists of color.[55]

The struggle to contain the poisoning of poor minority communities requires resources, which the grass-roots environmentalists do not have and the mainstream environmentalists do. Environmental justice advocates reject the romantic view of the mainstream and stress that its power is material, not transcendental. As one grass-roots activist put it: "'They're going to have to get off the stick of preserving birds and trees and seals and things like that and talk about what's affecting real people. . . . Organizations of color are forcing the issue.'"[56]

In addition to challenging some of the goals of the mainstream movement, environmental justice activists are going after the mainstream for failing to integrate their staffs and boards, for failing to enlarge their agendas to include the concerns of poor minority communities, and for failing to share their bountiful resources with poorer grass-roots groups. These challenges strike a nerve in organizations that view themselves as being faithful to the liberalism of the 1960s. Whether their guilt, concern, or embarrassment will translate into greater cooperation between minority environmental groups and the mainstream or integration of the organizations' bureaucracies remains to be seen. The grass-roots folks seem to think that if they achieve the second goal, they will be closer to achieving the first. They may be fooling themselves. Some consideration should be given to devices for ensuring the accountability of people of color who find positions in mainstream organizations as a result of complaints from the grass roots.

People of color have provided the crucial leadership for the growing environmental justice movement in the United States. This movement, in all aspects of its operations, is antielitist, antiracist, class conscious, populist, and participatory. It attacks environmental problems as being intertwined with other pressing economic, social, and political ills. It capitalizes on the social and cultural strengths of people of color and demands in turn that their lifestyles, traditions, and values be respected by polluters and mainstream environmental organizations alike.

The environmental justice movement is still in its embryonic stages. Its ideology has yet to be fully developed, let alone tested. Moreover, it is too easy for outsiders to criticize the trade-offs and compromises poor people and people of color bearing toxic burdens have made. It is important to understand the movement on its own terms if one hopes to make policy proposals that will be of use to those struggling to save themselves. Grass-roots people have proven that they are capable of *leading, speaking,* and *doing* for themselves.

II

Surviving Environmental "Sacrifice" Zones

5

Living on a Superfund Site in Texarkana

PATSY RUTH OLIVER

A neighborhood in Texarkana provides a real-life example of a community killed by toxic contamination. Texarkana is a twin city that straddles the Texas-Arkansas state line. In 1990, the Texas side had a population of 31,656 persons, of whom about one-third were African Americans. The Carver Terrace neighborhood was our American dream that turned into a nightmare.[1] This is my story and the story of the destruction of my family, my home, and my community. The Carver Terrace community is lost forever.

The Carver Terrace subdivision in Texarkana began in 1964. It was a nice neighborhood where African Americans could buy nice homes and enjoy the fruits of their hard work. As a matter of fact, it was one of the few places in Texarkana where upwardly mobile and middle-income African Americans could own homes. Life in Texarkana was ruled by Jim Crow. Segregation was the common practice in housing, education, employment, and other arenas.

Residents pursued their dreams of happiness and freedom by buying a home in Carver Terrace. I moved into the neighborhood in 1968. However, that is not the whole story. Little did I know that I was living on a time bomb. It was ticking, but we could not hear it. It was like a rattlesnake that had lost its rattles: it is still a rattlesnake, but it is even deadlier because you do not know it is there—

and it may kill you before you ever see it. That is the way Carver Terrace was—a nightmare camouflaged as a dream.

THE MAKING OF AN AFRICAN AMERICAN "LOVE CANAL"

Carver Terrace was built in a 100-year floodplain, on top of an old wood-treating site. The Koppers Company operated its wood-treating facility on the site until 1961.[2] Over the years, we residents suffered from repeated flooding of our homes. Deadly poisons lay in the soil beneath our homes, and when the temperature and weather were right, those poisons rose into the air for us to breathe, and rainfall moved the poisons around.

The neighborhood contained poisonous chemicals I had never heard of—none of us had—and it was a long time before I even knew how to pronounce them. I still have trouble pronouncing the names of some of the deadly poisons that lay beneath my home. The poisons had been there, piling up, for more than fifty years before we moved there. In 1910, the National Lumber and Creosote Company had set up a creosote wood treatment plant on the ground where we later lived.

In 1938, the Wood Preserving Corporation bought the land. Later, that company, with the land, became a part of the Koppers Company, which operated the creosoting business there until 1961, when the operations ended and some of the buildings were relocated. So for fifty years, creosote and other poisonous chemicals went into the land. In 1962, speculators bought 34 acres of the old creosoting site, and in 1964, after a series of land deals, the development of Carver Terrace as a residential subdivision began. The all-white Texarkana zoning officials permitted Carver Terrace, Inc. to build houses on the site. By 1967, a total of twenty-eight homes had been completed.

We did not know all this history. We were just thrilled to be able to buy such nice homes in Texarkana, a city long noted for its dismal race relations and a city where an African American man had been publicly lynched—murdered by a mob of white men without any opposition from law enforcement officers—as late as 1941.

Carver Terrace ended up with seventy-nine upscale homes and approximately 250 residents—all African Americans. The subdivision covered half of the original land used for the creosoting operations. The other half, where there were no homes, was sold to the Kennedy Sand and Gravel Company in 1975; that company began mining the sand and gravel on its site and selling it for use elsewhere. That meant that Carver Terrace soon existed next to gravel pits, not an environment of aesthetic excellence but at least a safe one—as far as we knew.

How little we knew!

Our education came slowly. What set it in action was a new law passed by Congress in 1979 that required the fifty largest chemical companies to report their hazardous waste sites. This was when Carver Terrace—the old Koppers site—came to the attention of the Environmental Protection Agency. In 1980, the Texas Department of Water Resources, working with the EPA to explore old, abandoned industrial sites like this one, inspected the site and followed up the next year with a field investigation team that inspected, photographed, and sampled the site.

The 1980 study showed that the soil and groundwater were contaminated with chemicals commonly used in wood preserving: pentachlorophenol (PCP), arsenic, and creosote. The first inkling residents had that they were living on a time bomb came then—but not in any official communication. During the field investigation, some of the investigators gave informal warnings to some residents, telling them that they should be careful about their children playing outdoors in the community. One mother was told that after her children rode their bicycles outside they should take care to wash the bicycle tires before taking them inside the house, because of contamination. But officially, the residents were told nothing of the hazards of living in Carver Terrace.

Over the next few years, a number of steps were taken to compile more data on the site. Koppers, the previous owner of the land and its creosoting operation, inspected the site and a year later did a hydrogeologic investigation. In 1984, the Texas Department of Water Resources recommended that the site be placed on the National

Priority List (NPL) of Superfund sites. Later that year, the EPA ordered the Kennedy Sand and Gravel Company to cease its sand and gravel operations. A month later, the Emergency Response Branch of the EPA confirmed the high levels of contaminants in the neighborhood, and that same month—October 1984—the old Koppers site was placed on the Superfund National Priority List.

The Agency for Toxic Substances and Disease Registry (ATSDR) conducted a health assessment and concluded that the Koppers Superfund Site posed a "potential risk to human health resulting from possible exposure to hazardous substances at concentrations that may result in adverse health effects."[3] Nevertheless, the ATSDR's inconclusive health assessment failed to provide the residents with the information they needed to support a neighborhood buyout.[4]

The next year—1985—the EPA investigated the site for dioxins, which, as we know, are among the most toxic molecules known to humankind, and a month later Koppers signed a consent order to pay for the remedial investigation. A lot of things happened that year. Following a technical investigation, the EPA ordered immediate soil and sod barriers on certain lots in Carver Terrace. Tap water and soil samples were tested. Air samples were taken—and on two of the three test days, the air quality results exceeded the EPA's own guidelines.

Government officials were testing everything, but they never did a health survey or gave any attention to what was going on in the lives of the people of Carver Terrace. *They were studying the site to death, but they seemed to forget about the people living there.* After much delay, in 1988 the EPA came up with its record of decision (ROD) for cleanup of the site. EPA officials concluded that a cleanup could be accomplished that would allow Carver Terrace residents to remain in the neighborhood. Residents, however, were concerned about the safety of the cleanup efforts and wanted out of the area.

In late summer of 1988, while the EPA was foot-dragging, Jim Presley and Don Preston, members of a new environmental organization headquartered in Texarkana, Friends United for a Safe Environment (FUSE), came to Carver Terrace and offered their assistance to the residents. A number of Carver Terrace residents attended the subsequent FUSE meetings and joined the organization.

An informal FUSE poll demonstrated that the Carver Terrace people wanted a buyout of their homes so they could relocate elsewhere and lead normal, unpoisoned lives. The FUSE board made Carver Terrace one of its priority projects. Don Preston, who later became president of FUSE, became one of our regular workers and played a central role in the struggle to get us out.

Then, in November 1988, a very interesting thing happened. The Department of the Interior's U.S. Fish and Wildlife Service released to the EPA its study of a small stream next to Carver Terrace. The report emphasized that the waters there were unhealthy for fish and stated that the remedial investigation had been flawed. The Department of the Interior's report concluded that there were "severe health risks" to the people living near the stream.

This was the "smoking gun" we needed. When FUSE obtained a copy of the report, it went to the news media, to television and to the *Texarkana Gazette*. One of the Carver Terrace residents, interviewed by KSLA-TV reporter Jan Morgan on camera, put it exactly the way we all felt: "It looks like the government's more concerned with the fish in the creeks than with the people who live here!"

Other people who lived in the Texarkana metropolitan area were beginning to learn about the plight of Carver Terrace. From that point on, different residents of Carver Terrace began to appear regularly on television, on the radio, and in the newspapers. And these first small steps began to pay off. We had to inform the general public about our plight if we were ever going to win; we knew we could not leave it up to the EPA or the state of Texas.

ENVIRONMENTAL JUSTICE COMES TO TOWN

We had a big break in February 1989. FUSE—a biracial, bistate group—hosted a national meeting of environmentalists that month, due mostly to the efforts of Jimmie Hays, a FUSE member, and Patty Frase of Jacksonville, Arkansas, both of whom had attended a national antitoxics rally in Kansas and urged that the next rally be held in Texarkana. We called it the Texarkana Conference on Environmental Justice. We held the first day's meeting at the Mount Zion Missionary Baptist Church, which is on the Superfund site in Carver Terrace. It was a lively day and night.

Environmentalists from all over the country swarmed into Carver Terrace and saw what we were up against. They saw the "KEEP OUT" signs the EPA had posted in the gravel pits next door, warning of the toxins there. The gravel pits were fenced off with chain link fences; nobody was supposed to go there because it was so dangerous. About 250 of us lived on *our* side of the fence, without a warning, as if the fence had sanitized the poisons and kept them on the other side. Our visitors were amazed, to put it kindly, that the government had demonstrated such insensitive and twisted thinking.

The weekend was a great success, for it enabled activists from the outside to see Carver Terrace, interact with its people, and carry the word forth to the rest of the nation. This was a landmark event for Carver Terrace and probably did more to help us eventually get out of our nightmare than the years of administrative foot-dragging of the EPA.

We had some memorable moments. Richard Grossman of Washington, DC, publisher of the *Wrenching Gazette,* conducted a "wrenching debate" at Mount Zion Church the first afternoon, and for the first time people of Carver Terrace took part in a spirited discussion over some of the larger issues that we face everywhere. Environmentalists from fourteen states, from California to Massachusetts, took part.

At first, many of the Carver Terrace residents felt a little uneasy about these people—mostly white, but not entirely—from other parts of the country who came in and said they were concerned about us. But as the day wore on, residents came to feel, "We are not alone. They have come here to work *with* us."

That night in the church was a deeply moving experience. We had leading environmentalists from all over the country, from leading national and regional organizations, speaking. John O'Connor, director of the National Toxics Campaign, came from Boston, Massachusetts. Lois Marie Gibbs, head of Citizens' Clearinghouse for Hazardous Wastes (CCHW), came from Arlington, Virginia, and told how she and others had won the fight for relocation in Love Canal, New York—another poisoned paradise. We began to see that what she and her neighbors had done in Love Canal could be done in Carver Terrace. Carver Terrace was Texas's Love Canal.

Darryl Malek-Wiley, a white man from New Orleans who was active with the Sierra Club, gave us a rousing plea for forgetting racial barriers and working together. Pat Bryant, an eloquent African American man from New Orleans who led the Gulf Coast Tenants Organization, reminded us of what had been done to people years ago who poisoned the land and the water—and that we needed to start thinking about what should be done to those who were poisoning us today in this country.

That night, after the last speech, all of us—African American and white, male and female, young and old, visitor and resident—linked hands all around the church and sang environmental verses to "We Shall Overcome." It was a high point emotionally for all of us that night, and a powerful feeling that those who came from afar would never forget. I know. I have talked with many of them since. They remember—and they have told others.

The next day, at another location on the Arkansas side of town, featured testimony from victims and activists. We heard Dick Russell and Lauri Maddy from Kansas, Dr. Peter Montague from Princeton University, Cathy Garula from Pennsylvania, Patty Frase and Mardell Smith from Arkansas, Kay Kiker from Alabama, Pat Moss of Native Americans for a Clean Environment (NACE) in Oklahoma, George Baggett from Missouri, Walter Hammerschick from Texas, Les Ann Kirkland from Louisiana, Larry Wilson from Kentucky, and Mike Roselle from California. Chris Bedford from Washington, DC, recorded the weekend on film for the Organizing Media Project.

Sunday afternoon, the third and concluding day of the Conference for Environmental Justice, became the emotional climax to the weekend. This did not seem likely, considering the exciting two days that had preceded it. On top of all else, it started raining that afternoon. But that did not stop us. It all built up, for Sunday afternoon the conference ended with participants marching through Carver Terrace, chanting and singing together and carrying placards and a huge banner that proclaimed "Team Up Texarkana, Clean Up TOXICANA!" Three television stations in the Texarkana–Shreveport, Louisiana, area covered the demonstration. As people joined the march of local and visiting environmentalists in the rain, the line of demonstrators stretched for several blocks. From Carver Terrace, we marched to another nearby Superfund site—the Texarkana Wood Preserving Company's abandoned creosote plant. We made speeches there and then returned to the Mount Zion Church at Carver Terrace, where we vowed to keep in touch and to keep the fight going. And we have.

Writer Jim Presley wrote a long article for the *Texas Observer* about the conference, which was distributed widely. Dick Russell wrote about it in *In These Times*. George Baggett, from Kansas City, Missouri, wrote in the next issue of his publication *Toxic News:* "Environmental activists that missed this meeting missed an important turning point in the environmental movement. . . . We shall overcome!"

From that point until the present, it seems that events followed without much breathing space in between. One of the most important events was the organization that same year of the Carver Terrace Community Action Group, as an affiliate of FUSE, with its members holding membership in both organizations. Some of the non–Carver Terrace members of FUSE also joined CTCAG.

We elected J. E. ("Sonny") Fields as president of the Carver Terrace Community Action Group and Talmadge Cheatham as vice president. A number of us served on the board. This gave us an available spokesman anytime an emergency or a newsworthy event came up. And there were a lot of newsworthy events. When Carver Terrace flooded—and this happened every time there was a heavy rain—bringing creosote-laced water down our streets and sometimes into our homes, the television cameras were not far behind. The images began to pile up, so that people outside Carver Terrace could not miss the point.

THE IMPACT OF A BUS RIDE TO AUSTIN

Residents from Carver Terrace and other FUSE members joined with another environmental group, Citizens Opposing Pollution (COP), about 60 miles south of us in northeastern Texas, to fill a bus for a rally in Austin, the state capital. This came in March, the month after the conference, and linked us with other groups in Texans United and Texas POWER, statewide environmental organizations. Our network was growing.

At this time, we marched from our buses, which came from different parts of the state, to the offices of the Texas Water Commission. A COP leader had made an appointment to see an official at the Texas Water Commission—and all of us, 100 or more strong, appeared with him. Surprise! It took the people at the Texas Water Commission some time to restore their equilibrium, but they finally found a room large enough to accommodate us and did hear us out. We wanted them to know we meant business, and Carver Terrace made its voice heard along with the others from all over the state.

One of the most important things that happened that day in Austin was that we also went to see our elected officials. A delegation went to see the state senator, who lived several counties away from us; as far as I know, he never did anything about our problems. But four of us went to see our state representative, Barry Telford, from our county, and he immediately became interested and involved. He took copious notes on what we told him about Carver Terrace. And he did something about it—pronto. Representative Telford began writing letters on our behalf—to the EPA, to Congressman Jim Chapman, to our U.S. senators.

I count this as the first official step, on elected politicians' part, to get the ball rolling for a buyout because after that, Congressman Chapman began applying pressure on the EPA. He became our most powerful and effective ally in the federal government. It is hard to measure all the good that trip to Austin and our visit with Barry Telford did.

After that, we began to get support from public bodies in our area. The Texarkana, Texas, city council made a resolution urging the EPA to buy us out. The resolution was offered by Councilman Grady Wallace on the first night he served on the council. The Bowie County Commissioners Court gave similar official support.

The Carver Terrace Community Action Group organized a march from our community to the city hall in downtown Texarkana, Texas. Even though the march was held on a Saturday, when city offices were closed, we had front-page coverage in the *Texarkana Gazette* the next day. Pam Stone of CCHW came over to be with us, along with FUSE friends. A big plus was the presence of Grady Wallace, the city council member who represented the ward containing Carver Terrace. Also an African American, Wallace was one of our staunchest supporters from the first day he was elected to the council, working both publicly and behind the scenes on our behalf.

Carver Terrace representatives began attending the STP (Stop The Poisoning!) workshops run by the Highlander Center in New Market, Tennessee. Jimmie Hays from FUSE had gone earlier, and because Jimmie recommended me, I became the first one from Carver Terrace to go. It was an exhilarating weekend. I was beginning to realize that people can empower themselves, but the STP school gave me some special tools. Larry and Shelia Wilson and others drew upon years of experience, and on the experiences of many before them, to show how a few people can make a difference in a community.

After that, I attended another STP session at Highlander Center, this time taking Linda James and Betty Jean Davis from Carver Terrace with me. Our third STP school was held in Texarkana in November 1990. Larry and Shelia Wilson of the Highlander Center came to Carver Terrace and enabled more of the residents to attend—and to learn how to deal with the EPA, other government agencies, and industry.

Carver Terrace attracted the attention of Greenpeace when it was having a series of advertising "spots" made for television to be shown nationally on VH-1. The camera crew came to Texarkana to film our story. Soon, people who had never heard of Carver Terrace knew of it.

After the Conference on Environmental Justice that was held in

Texarkana in early 1989, I was selected to be a representative to a Greenpeace action on the "penta" issue in Washington, DC. I joined other activists from all over the country in a visit to EPA administrator William Reilly's office, where we made him aware—directly—of our concerns over the EPA's lack of action on the issue.

Later, FUSE and Carver Terrace Community Action Group members traveled by bus to join other environmentalists, organized by Texans United and Greenpeace, in a protest at the EPA's Region VI headquarters in Dallas. Out of fear of us, the EPA officials shut down their offices. They sent their personnel home for the rest of the day and locked us out.

On April 10, 1989—just a few months after our Conference on Environmental Justice in Texarkana—the Agency for Toxic Substances and Disease Registry of the U.S. Public Health Service in Atlanta, Georgia, completed its health assessment for the Koppers Superfund Site in Carver Terrace. The report went to the EPA and some other agencies.

By law, the report was supposed to go to the local public library, among other points of distribution. We never got it. So we never knew anything about it until we learned about it through the grapevine. FUSE had a copy of it faxed from the ATSDR and held a joint news conference with the Carver Terrace Community Action Group in the parking lot of the Mount Zion Missionary Baptist Church, right where the television and newspaper cameras could see the "KEEP OUT" warning sign across the chain link fence in the gravel pit area.

Linda James for the Carver Terrace group and Don Preston for FUSE presented the facts, highlighting the fact that the report had been available for nearly a full year, yet the EPA had not disclosed its contents to those it affected most—us.

This report confirmed everything we had been saying about our nightmare. Some of the sizzling facts in it included: "Long-term exposures to contaminated soils in the residential area pose a potential health risk for ingestion and dermal absorption of soil contaminants. Ground water beneath the site is contaminated and would pose a potential health risk if used for potable purposes."

At least thirty-five on-site contaminants were identified, including cancer-causing dioxins and furans. They found fifteen off-site contaminants of concern, some of them in more than one medium, such as subsurface soil, groundwater, and sediment. On top of this, a lot of data had not been looked for and therefore were left out. This told us that conditions might be even worse than the report let on. No plants or animals were tested. They found only two fish big enough to eat in Wagner Creek nearby.

But the report backed up what we had already known in our hearts—that we were being poisoned. They found "substantially higher than background" levels of bad actors like PAHs (polynuclear aromatic hydrocarbons) and PCP (pentachlorophenol), as well as other phenols and toxic metals.

Later, when some of us charged that the EPA had hidden this report from us—the people it affected—for almost a year, the EPA representatives said that it had not been concealed; it just had not been sent due to an unintentional error. Well, who was responsible for us not getting the report on time?

Later, in 1990, the EPA's Region VI office sent over a group of "experts" to tell us how well they were doing their job. Larry and Shelia Wilson came over from the Highlander Center a short time before the scheduled EPA visit and briefed us on what the EPA probably would try to do in order to soothe us down. One tactic might be to split us up into little groups, where the "expert" could confound us with technical talk and keep us from asking questions as a group—embarrassing questions for them.

The EPA's dog and pony show did not work. When the time came and the EPA representatives said they would divide us up into small groups so they could show us what they were doing, Sonny Fields, president of the Carver Terrace Community Action Group, rose and informed them that the residents of Carver Terrace had already discussed it and would not be breaking up into groups. Anything the EPA had to tell them, it should tell them as a group.

The Carver Terrace residents, our allies from FUSE, other interested persons from city government, Congressman Chapman's representative, and others just stayed together as we had planned. And we showered the EPA team with hard questions. That night, I am sure they understood that if we had anything, we had unity!

About a week later, we received a statement from Jesse Jackson in support of a buyout and relocation. We held another news conference—well attended by media as well as public officials—and read his statement.

All of these events just started snowballing and building up pressure on the EPA. But the EPA kept saying: "Well, we're not in the real estate business. We don't go around buying people out and relocating them." We held letter-writing sessions at meetings of FUSE and the Carver Terrace Community Action Group, sending letters to our senators and congressmen. Congressman Jim Chapman began to lead the fight in Congress for a buyout.

In November 1990, our "impossible" dream came true. Our long shot came home. Congress approved a buyout and relocation for the victims of Carver Terrace, *mandating* the EPA to amend its 1988 record of decision—and appropriated $5 million for the purpose. It was understood that the EPA would go to the "responsible party"—by then, the Beezer Corporation, which had taken over Koppers—for reimbursement of the expenses.

Along the way, we had a lot of help from "outsiders," and, thank God, they kept coming and helping us. Cathy Garula from the Relocation Assistance and Information Network (RAIN) in Pennsylvania, Linda King from the Environmental Health Network in Louisiana, and Cathy Hines of the National Toxics Campaign in Boston (Cathy is headquartered in Maine), as well as others, came in. Cathy Garula came to Texarkana repeatedly, giving us the benefit of her wisdom and vast experience. Cathy had led a successful buyout fight in her hometown of Centralia, Pennsylvania, years before.

This, of course, is not the end of the story. Government action is always slow. We are not out of Carver Terrace yet. It was January 1991 before the EPA record of decision noted the buyout action ordered by Congress. The U.S. Army Corps of Engineers was designated as the federal agency to appraise our homes on the way to the buyout. The corps held a public hearing in Texarkana on July 30, 1991. Not much later, the first appraisals began. Then the EPA raised another barrier. It needed more action from Congress. Congressman Chapman put the additional requested legislation through Congress in late September. He said that the original legislation should have been enough, but he went ahead and added to the law.

The sad part of all this is that we have won our fight, as I write this in August 1992—but we have also lost, because most of the residents are still *in* Carver Terrace, still breathing the same old poisoned air, still living on top of toxic soil, still seeing each new flood mix up a devil's brew of creosote-spiked water to run through our neighborhood and then to run off our land and contaminate other neighborhoods and even, finally, those downstream from us. So far, it is only a paper victory, but we are hopeful, and we are still fighting for the EPA to expedite our relocation from this poisoned paradise before it is too late.

It is already too late for about thirty Carver Terrace residents who have died in the meantime. I lost my own mother, Mrs. Mattie Warren, to cancer on July 27, 1990. She had been as vocal an activist as anyone. She had gone with us on the bus to Austin—a 350-mile trip and back. She had marched in the rain on that day in February 1989 when we concluded the Conference on Environmental Justice. So she had ended up giving her life. But as a memorial to her, I have dedicated the rest of my life to environmental work.

I am an environmentalist. I always will be, so long as God gives me breath. I have been fortunate to meet environmental activists in the movement who are dedicated to the cause of justice. Serving on the national board of directors of the National Toxics Campaign was one of the highlights of my life. To be a member of the Southwest Organizing Project and to be on the coordinating committee of the Southwest Network for Economic and Environmental Justice—not only would something like that have seemed impossible a few years ago, but I would not even have known what these groups were.

LEARNING FROM A BAD SITUATION

What are the lessons of Carver Terrace that other poisoned communities can learn from? I think they are many. First, you cannot fight a fight like this by yourself. You need help. But even if you start out by yourself—just one person—you will find friends. We were lucky in Carver Terrace. Friends—FUSE friends—came in from outside the community, found out what we wanted, and helped us get it. They helped us organize and plugged us into a larger environmental and political network out there in this big world, and once we were started, there was no stopping us.

So the first lesson is to start out the best way you can—and look for friends. Through allies, plug into other networks. Lobby your government—local, state, and federal. Tell everybody you can about your problem, what is causing it, what it is doing to you and your community, and what needs to be done. Most of all, use every opportunity to show the media—newspapers, television, and radio—how the people are suffering. This is a vital part of education.

Join hands with other environmentalists, social justice activists, and concerned citizens far and wide. Make contact with the national environmental groups that have expertise you feel will be useful to your struggle. I probably have not named even half of the people from afar who helped us in one way or another. They are out there, and they *want* to help you. At the same time, *always* help other grass-roots environmental organizations.

You will need to keep building the network. Somebody else's cause that you help will be your own—because we all live downstream from someone. You may make mistakes; we did. But you will learn from them. Keep growing and learning. Never say die, and keep on, even when winning your fight looks like an impossible dream. We learned in Carver Terrace that even an impossible dream, like getting out of our prison of poison, can become a reality.

Remember what the great poet Langston Hughes said—that without dreams, "life is a broken-winged bird that cannot fly." Hold fast to your dream. Making your dream come true is what makes life worth living and what makes us human.

6

West Dallas versus the Lead Smelter

RONALD ROBINSON

The federal government estimates that 3 to 4 million American children are potentially exposed to lead in sufficient amounts to raise their blood levels to those of health concern.[1] African American children are especially at risk because of where they live and play. African American children represent about 60 percent of children at risk for lead toxicity in families whose annual income is less than $6,000 and 46 percent of those with annual family incomes of more than $15,000.

In general, people of color and the poor are disparately affected by industrial toxins, dirty air and drinking water, and the proximity of noxious facilities such as municipal landfills, incinerators, toxic waste dumps, and lead smelters.[2] Despite the attempts made by government to level the playing field, environmental inequities still persist. Even in today's society, racial discrimination influences where people live, work, and play. Moreover, institutional discrimination influences the likelihood of exposure to lead.[3] This chapter examines the government response to a lead contamination problem in a major southwestern city.

THE CASE OF DALLAS, TEXAS

Dallas is the seventh largest city in the United States, with a population of just less than 1 million. The 265,594 African Americans
who live in Dallas represent about 30 percent of the city's population. Dallas is still a racially segregated city, with about eight of
every ten African Americans living in primarily African American
areas. In 1980, the population of West Dallas consisted of 13,161
residents, of whom more than 85 percent were African American.[4]
The 1980–1990 period saw a rapid increase in the Latino American
population, which now constitutes more than one-third of West
Dallas neighborhoods. The low-income neighborhood lies west of
the Trinity River and only a short distance from the sparkling Dallas
skyline. This 13.5-square-mile area has 10,262 housing units, one-
third of which are public housing projects.

West Dallas has always been a largely African American community. Before the area was annexed by the city, few basic services
were provided to local residents. However, the city did allow the
area to be used as a garbage dump and a dumping ground for all
kinds of throwaways—including old battery casings.[5] Over the
years, Dallas's African Americans have been forced to cope with
lead smelters operating in their communities. All three of the lead
smelters that operated in the city were located in mostly African
American and Latino American neighborhoods. One of the city's
oldest lead smelters, which dates back to the 1930s, is located in
West Dallas.

The 63-acre Murph Metals (later named RSR Corporation) lead
smelter is located next door to an elementary school and across the
street from the West Dallas Boys Club and the 3,500-unit George
Loving public housing project. The West Dallas housing project is
located just 50 feet from the sprawling lead smelter's property line
and directly in the path of the prevailing southerly winds.

In the mid-1960s, during its peak period of operation, the plant
employed more than 400 persons, few of whom lived in the West
Dallas neighborhood. The smelter pumped more than 269 tons of

lead particles each year into the West Dallas air. Lead particles were blown by prevailing winds through the doors and windows of nearby homes and onto West Dallas streets, ballparks, and play-grounds.

PAYING THE PRICE WITH THEIR LIVES

Life in West Dallas is hard, and this fact shows on the faces of its people. Reva Agent is sixty-four years old and lives on Toronto Street. She has five children (one was stillborn) and a few medical problems. She has cataracts in her right eye. She has bone and breast cancer. Doctors have amputated both legs, and she suffers from kid-ney failure. She has had surgery on her back and right arm. She has problems breathing; her arthritis constantly hurts, and there is a numbness in her joints following the pain. She just came home from Parkland Hospital after her fifth heart attack.

Reva's next-door neighbor recently died. Doctors told the family it was "bad blood." Johnny Tyler lives just down the street from Reva. He has suffered from high blood pressure and heart trouble ever since both his legs were amputated. Elmo Carlyte's legs were also amputated, and he, too, suffers from heart trouble. He lives just around the corner from Reva.

Jean Tansley is blind, with one leg amputated, and also suffers from heart trouble. She needs a machine to help her breathe, and her body is always swollen. Booker T. Washington, who recently died, had had both of his legs amputated. And then there is Mr. Hutchi-son, who also had to have both legs amputated; he died not long ago, at the age of sixty-one.

All of these people have a few more things in common. They all have children and grandchildren who are constantly sick. Many of these children have been diagnosed with learning disabilities. As you move through West Dallas, you notice a curious thing on streets named Palacious, Griffin, and Toronto, to name a few. Many of the small wood frame homes built in the past thirty years have disabil-ity ramps leading up to the front doors.

Something quiet and horrendous is happening to the families in

West Dallas. For more than fifty years, companies have dumped toxic waste products in their neighborhood without regard for the people living there. At last count, there were eleven dump sites under or around these residents.

In 1950, the city of Dallas built one of the nation's largest public housing projects in West Dallas. The West Dallas project was constructed on land contaminated by a nearby lead smelter, whose 300-foot smokestack had belched lead emissions into the area for three decades. West Dallas is also home to seventy other industries, which add to the area's pollution problem.

Dallas passed a stringent lead ordinance in 1968. However, lax enforcement rendered the ordinance worthless. City officials were informed as early as 1972 that lead was finding its way into the bloodstreams of children who lived in two mostly African American and Latino American neighborhoods: West Dallas and East Oak Cliff.[6] The Dixie Metals smelter operated in the East Oak Cliff neighborhood.

Living near the smelters was associated with a 36 percent increase in blood lead levels. The city was urged to restrict the emissions of lead into the atmosphere and to undertake a large screening program to determine the extent of the public health problem, but it failed to take immediate action to protect the mostly African American and poor residents who lived near the smelters.

In 1980, the federal EPA, informed about possible health risks associated with the Dallas lead smelter, commissioned another lead-screening study. This study confirmed what had been known a decade earlier: children living near the smelters were likely to have greater blood lead concentrations than children who did not live near them.

Lead concentrations in the soil near the RSR Corporation's smelter in West Dallas, for example, averaged nine times that in the control area, while the average near the Dixie Metals smelter in East Oak Cliff was thirteen times the norm. Lead levels in the soil were so high that the director of the nearby West Dallas Boys Club was forced to suspend outdoor activities.

In 1981, after nearly decades of complaining to city officials, local residents organized themselves into the West Dallas Neighborhood Committee on Lead Contamination. The group was assisted by staff from the Common Ground Community Economic Development Corporation, a grass-roots self-help group. Common Ground assisted the West Dallas residents in getting their case into the public domain, testifying at hearings, producing reports, and providing general technical assistance.

The city took action only after a series of lead-related news articles made the headlines in Dallas newspapers.[7] The *Dallas Morning News* broke the headline-grabbing story of the "potentially dangerous" lead levels discovered by EPA researchers in 1981. The articles triggered widespread concern, public outrage, several class action lawsuits, and legal action by Texas's attorney general.

Although the federal EPA was armed with a wealth of scientific data on the West Dallas lead problem, the agency chose to play politics with the people by scrapping a voluntary plan offered by RSR to clean up the "hot spots" in the neighborhood. John Hernandez, a deputy administrator of the EPA, blocked the cleanup and called for yet another round of tests, to be designed by the Centers for Disease Control in conjunction with the EPA and the Dallas Health Department.

The results of the new study were released in February 1983. This study once again established the smelter as the source of the elevated blood lead levels in West Dallas children.[8] Residents saw the response by government as insensitive, unjust, and racist; Hernandez's delay of cleanup actions in West Dallas was said to be tantamount to "waiting for a body count."[9]

Public pressure forced the Dallas City Council to appoint a task force (the Dallas Alliance Environmental Task Force) to study the lead problem in 1983. The task force concluded that "the city has missed many opportunities to serve and protect the community-at-large and two neighborhoods in particular in relation to the lead problem we now address."[10]

After years of court delays, the West Dallas plaintiffs negotiated an out-of-court settlement worth more than $45 million. The lawsuit was settled in June 1983, with RSR agreeing to a soil cleanup in West Dallas, a blood-testing program for children and pregnant women, and installation of new antipollution equipment. The settlement, however, did not require the smelter to close.

The settlement was made on behalf of 370 children—almost all of whom were poor, African American residents of the West Dallas public housing project—and forty property owners. The agreement was one of the largest community lead contamination settlements ever awarded in the United States.

The antipollution equipment for the smelter was never installed. In May 1984, the Dallas Board of Adjustments, a city agency responsible for monitoring land use violations, requested the city attorney to order the smelter permanently closed for violating the city's zoning code. Four months later, the Dallas Board of Adjustments ordered the West Dallas smelter permanently closed.

As it turns out, the lead smelter had operated in the mostly African American West Dallas neighborhood for fifty years without having the necessary use permits. After repeated health citations, fines, and citizen complaints against the smelter, one has to question the city's lax enforcement of health and land use regulations in African American and Latino American neighborhoods.

For more than sixty years, the RSR Corporation's smelter disposed of crushed automobile battery chips by dumping them as landfill in West Dallas. The plastic batteries were boiled at high temperatures, with the leftovers resembling molten lava. These leftovers, or lead "slag," can be found throughout the community, just about anywhere one looks in West Dallas. Slag can be found in parks, on playgrounds, in household gardens, and in residents' driveways.

In 1982, Alicia Hracheta, who lived on Clymer Street, ordered gravel for her driveway and garage. The gravel was to cover an area 50 feet by 10 feet. When, over the years, her family began to suffer various ailments, such as hair loss, liver damage, and slow learning for the children, Mrs. Hracheta decided to have her residence tested for lead. As it turned out, the gravel company had delivered crushed battery casings instead of the soil she had ordered.[11]

The battery casings had been compacted into the soil of her

driveway. Soil sampled in her driveway tested at 99,000 parts per million (ppm) of lead. According to the EPA, 500 ppm of lead is considered dangerous for industry, and 250 ppm is considered a health risk for residents. This level of toxic material makes Mrs. Hracheta's residence the most contaminated home in Dallas.

The Texas Water Commission tested another West Dallas residence and found contaminated dust. A windowsill in a house on Gallagher Street contained 1.1 milligrams of lead per cubic centimeter of surface area. The U.S. Department of Housing and Urban Development rates .54 milligram as a potential danger. No standards for lead in dust have been set by state and federal environmental agencies.[12]

Because of the contamination, Mrs. Hracheta had her garage removed, and the Texas Water Commission collected soil samples. With the garage gone, more rainfall than normal collects in her yard, then flows under the house, causing corrosion and contamination. As a result of these worsening conditions, Dorca Zaragoza of the Texas Water Commission (TWC) promised Mrs. Hracheta that she would be moved to a local hotel with a food allowance of $50 per day. The cleanup, however, was met with snags and delays.[13] More important, the decision to store the lead-tainted soil temporarily at the closed smelter, until a permanent hazardous dump could be located, heightened fears of West Dallas residents.[14]

More than 260 tons of toxic waste have been dumped into West Dallas—enough toxic waste to fill both Arlington Stadium, with 43,500 seats, and the Cotton Bowl, with 50,000 seats, six times over. Yet for years, the people of West Dallas have been told that their health problems had nothing to do with their environment. One woman, whose entire family suffers from lead poisoning (she is afraid to give her name, for fear of reprisal), was told by the TWC inspectors, "The reason your family suffers health problems is because you don't clean your home properly."[15] This same woman has been cleaning the stately homes in the affluent and mostly white North Dallas for more than twenty years. Slag found in the soil around this West Dallas family's home tested at more than 7,000 ppm of lead.[16]

It is clear that West Dallas was a community of residents long before the arrival of the lead smelter. The segregated neighborhood was made up of home owners and renters. As part of the city's urban renewal and slum clearance efforts, scores of single-family homes were razed to make way for the massive West Dallas public housing project, a project built for African American families under Dallas's Jim Crow housing policies. The 3,500-unit public housing project was constructed just across the street from the lead smelter.

SEGREGATED HOUSING AND TOXIC POLITICS

African Americans were purposely moved to West Dallas and segregated into an area with a severe housing shortage, where absentee landlords built the infamous "shotgun shacks" for newly arrived East Texas migrant workers in the late 1940s to 1950s. For decades, West Dallas was a neighborhood with squalid health conditions, where houses were without running water or indoor plumbing.

The early 1950s witnessed a population surge, with more than 24,000 poor laborers working in the growing heavy industry in West Dallas. With a potentially excellent tax base just across the Trinity River coming from the lead smelters, cement plants, gravel pits, and brick factories, the Dallas city fathers decided to incorporate the area. Along with the newfound cash came a newfound problem: the "Negro" problem. A deal had to be worked out that would annex the area yet keep the people "down on the dump." The formula would have to include the federal government.

The West Dallas neighborhood was annexed into the city in 1954. Dallas whites viewed annexation as an unavoidable burden to stop the spread of disease to other areas. Still, it was not until federal funds were promised for public housing that the tide turned in favor of annexation. By the time of annexation, the health of the community was already threatened by nearby polluting industries. The legacy of these industries is lead, nickel, chromium, arsenic, zinc, cadmium, and asbestos that permeate the soil, homes, and bodies of West Dallas residents.

In January 1985, Debra Walker filed a lawsuit against the U.S.

Department of Housing and Urban Development over its discriminatory housing policies. The lawsuit, *Walker v. U.S. Department of Housing and Urban Development,* charged the government with purposely moving African American residents into segregated, unsafe, and polluted West Dallas public housing.

For some government officials, the "steering" policy was seen as a solution to the "Negro housing problem." For example, Dallas city council member Roland Pelt, one of the authors of this plan, called for "an entire Negro City" to be built next to the Trinity River. The lawsuit contends that whites in South Dallas were demanding that the city of Dallas take action to prevent "black" families from spilling over into "white" districts. Several homes owned by African Americans in the South Dallas area were bombed.

Another component of this plan that did not become part of the lawsuit was the federal government's formula. In order for Dallas to receive money to build the West Dallas public housing project, it had to reserve 500 of the 3,500 units for poor whites. Within two years after the project opened, most of the white tenants were moved from the development. Several longtime West Dallas residents say that "the city moved those poor white folk out overnight" while allowing poor African Americans to remain in unsafe housing.

The city of Dallas was the substantial cause of segregation in public housing built in this contaminated area. The Walker lawsuit contends that Dallas supported the active participation of its city attorney in illegal tenant assignment and selection plans by the Dallas Housing Authority (DHA). The DHA was ordered to forfeit more than $31 million in federal funds from 1969 to 1974, and this loss resulted in the rapid and irreversible deterioration of every DHA housing project, including West Dallas.

The Sullivan family was typical of families living in West Dallas's George Loving housing project, located directly across from the RSR Corporation's lead smelter. Mae Sullivan moved to the project and raised two children there. One afternoon in 1987, she received a notice from the DHA telling her that she would have to move until the DHA rehabilitated the projects.

Dallas city authorities never formally notified these residents as to *why* they had to move. The DHA never informed Mae Sullivan and thousands of her neighbors that they were being moved because of the consent decree in *Walker v. U.S. Department of Housing and Urban Development.* The purpose of the consent decree, granted on January 20, 1987, was simply to remedy violations by the DHA and to remove all vestiges of racial segregation in public housing within the city of Dallas. The decree was signed by United States District Judge Jerry Buchmeyer in September 1990.

In January 1992, the federal judge threw out the 1987 settlement because the Dallas Housing Authority and the Department of Housing and Urban Development (HUD) had not met their obligation of providing better housing for the plaintiffs in neighborhoods across the city.[17] The agencies were supposed to demolish 2,600 dilapidated public housing units in the West Dallas project and replace them with housing elsewhere. However, only 1,400 alternative units were provided.

Opposition to the consent decree from city hall based on the desire to find alternatives to West Dallas public housing caused demolition time to pass with no viable alternative presented to the court. Until 1991, there had been no offer from Dallas for the $88 million from HUD that would rehabilitate West Dallas public housing. The Dallas City Council took no action, partly because it was involved in litigation of its own calling for increased "minority" representation on the city council. African Americans and Latino Americans constitute a majority of the Dallas population; however, these groups are severely underrepresented at city hall.

THE LEGACY OF GOVERNMENT INACTION

The Texas Water Commission and the EPA were quietly testing the West Dallas public housing projects for contamination. They discovered more than 500 "hot spots" considered dangerously saturated with contamination from lead, nickel, chromium, arsenic, zinc, and cadmium, as well as asbestos found in and around the schools. The city of Dallas, the state of Texas, and the national Centers for Disease Control (CDC) also knew as far back as 1982 that West Dallas was a toxic time bomb.[18]

In 1982, for example, the Texas Water Commission tested 440 West Dallas children. A total of 237, or 54 percent, fell into the higher-risk groups, with lead contamination ranging from "extreme to severe." On Westmoreland Street in the late 1960s and early 1970s, the risk level of lead exposure was "extreme," at 5,000–6,000 ppm. Seventeen children, aged nine to fourteen, were tested and found to have extreme levels of lead in their blood.

On Delhi, Porter, Morris, Nomas, and Toronto streets, sixty-six children aged eight to seventeen were tested and found to have extreme levels of lead contamination. Levels of lead on those streets contained no less than 5,000 ppm. On Pueblo, Hendricks, Applegrove, and Toronto streets from 1968 to 1975, lead levels were found to be "very severe" among sixty-five children aged seven to fourteen. Levels of lead on streets were measured at 3,500–5,000 ppm.

On Rupert, Pringle, Gallagher, and Magdeline streets, eighty-nine children, ranging from infants to fifteen-year-olds, had a lead risk level described as "severe," with 2,000–3,500 ppm found on street levels. On all of these streets, the numbers then and the numbers now far, far exceed current city, state, and federal health standards, sometimes by twenty or thirty times or more.

In 1992, the West Dallas children who had been found to have extraordinary lead levels in the 1982 study were adults, ranging in age from eighteen to twenty-seven. Many of these individuals are now fighting to have their children tested and treated. The legacy of West Dallas's lead contamination is still with the people who remain in the area.

By February 1992, the city's dirty little secret was out, and the people of West Dallas were organizing and demanding a cleanup. Mayor Steve Bartlett had just been elected to an at-large seat on the city council, with five of the fourteen district seats going to African American and Latino American council members. (Dallas has a fourteen-member council elected from districts and a mayor elected at large. The system is commonly referred to as "14 + 1.") Two West

Dallas districts were represented by African American community activist Mattie Nash and Mexican American attorney Domingo Garcia.

At the same time, changes were going on quietly at the federal and state levels. Buck J. Wynne, former chairman of the Texas Water Commission, was appointed to head the EPA's Region VI, which includes West Dallas. On February 3, 1992, Mayor Steve Bartlett held a press conference. Curiously enough, the mayor's office never bothered to notify the African American or Mexican American press of his news conference, which was so critical to the West Dallas community. The mayor announced that the EPA had obtained a site on which to dispose of lead-tainted soil from West Dallas. He then introduced Wynne, the new regional administrator of the EPA, to his first West Dallas news conference.

Wynne announced the "good news" that the EPA had concluded a contract with Waste Management Inc. (WMI)—a company that leases a nontoxic industrial waste facility in Monroe, Louisiana— for shipment of contaminated soil accumulating at the RSR site. The lead-tainted soil scraped from "hot spots" was to be piled on the old RSR smelter site until a permanent disposal site could be found.

The entire West Dallas cleanup project (excavation, testing, and transportation) is estimated to cost $3 million to $4 million. The federal Superfund is picking up the cost of the project, even though West Dallas was not on the official Superfund cleanup list. An estimated 11,000 truckloads (30,000 to 40,000 cubic yards) of lead-contaminated soil will be removed from several West Dallas sites, including school property and about 140 private homes.[19]

West Dallas residents are glad that cleanup actions have finally begun after more than two decades of foot-dragging. However, some community leaders are not totally satisfied with the way the cleanup action has been handled. Luis Sepulveda, president of the West Dallas Coalition for Environmental Justice and a lifelong resident of West Dallas, is an ardent critic of the EPA. His childhood home has been declared contaminated by lead, and most of his nine brothers and sisters—as well as his mother and father—suffer from health problems. Sepulveda challenged the federal action at a press conference: "They have yet to clean up the rest of Amelia Earhart [elementary school grounds]. There are over 111 homes. We're finding churches, grounds, underwater contamination. We need to focus on this. Where is the contaminated soil going? Is it leaving one minority community and going into another minority community?"[20]

According to sources at the EPA, trucks were ready to roll with the contaminated West Dallas soil as early as Thursday, February 6, 1992. Under the cover of darkness, the trucks started moving out to Monroe. On Friday afternoon, Louisiana's governor, Edwin Edwards, received a call from Ouachita Parish officials, who had never been contacted by the EPA or anyone about plans to dump 1,818 truckloads of contaminated soil into a class I sanitary landfill there.[21]

Ouachita Parish police juror (equivalent to a Texas county commissioner) Arlan Rawls said, "People have a habit of moving whatever they want into the parish without permission, and I resent that." Governor Edwards then ordered Louisiana state officials to monitor the site and make sure that no hazardous materials were accepted. When contacted, Buck Wynne told Ouachita Parish officials that the lead-contaminated soil from West Dallas was "nontoxic."

When confronted by members of the West Dallas Coalition for Environmental Justice, Wynne told them that the "nontoxic" lead-contaminated West Dallas soil would be dumped at the Magnolia landfill, which was not located near any residential area. In fact, however, the Ouachita High School campus is just half a mile from the dump site.

At 5:30 on the same afternoon, Ben Marshall from District C of the Ouachita Parish Police found out about the 1,818 truckloads of contaminated West Dallas soil headed his way. "It was the first time we had heard about it, and it made us angry. It scared us. We decided right then and there that we had to do something about this." That night, the parish police jurors voted to take immediate action by calling their congressional representatives, their state legislators, the governor, and the state secretary of environmental quality— they all got involved.

The EPA agreed to shut down shipments voluntarily for the time being while tests were performed to determine the extent of the toxic hazard. During this brief shutdown, the EPA began to tinker with the definitions of "hazardous" waste. The Dallas regional headquarters of the EPA maintained that the West Dallas soil headed for Monroe contained only 5 ppm of lead. As mentioned earlier, the formula for contaminated toxic soil is that 250 ppm is considered toxic for residential areas and 500 ppm is considered toxic for industry—and some of the West Dallas soil had been shown to be contaminated with more than 99,000 ppm of lead.

Why would the EPA remove soil with only 5 ppm, as it was maintaining it had done to officials of Monroe, Louisiana? The people of Monroe were committed to independent testing of the soil and were fighting any attempt to dump the toxic West Dallas soil in their parish. Monroe, the government seat of Ouachita Parish, has a population of 57,000, and African Americans constitute more than 60 percent of the community.

On Tuesday, February 11, 1992, the people and their Louisiana federal and state representatives held a town hall meeting at the Louisiana State University campus and invited the West Dallas Coalition for Environmental Justice to attend. State representative Frances Thompson addressed the meeting early on, explaining that she was upset at the way the whole thing was being handled. "I felt that it was poorly handled by the EPA. I felt they should have notified us. They didn't even know the representative in the area," she added.

Charles Guiser, an EPA official, addressed the packed auditorium of Monroe residents, federal and state authorities, and local and national media: "I don't want people to think that we're trying to run over people, that we're trying to force something down people's throats. We launched this action under the Superfund to remove the danger and threat of lead-exposed soil from West Dallas

by using the Superfund to remove that soil that had been exposed."
The exchange between the EPA and parish residents became intense:

Woman in audience: "Is the soil from West Dallas hazardous?"

EPA: "We have to be very careful about how we use that word.
The classification can be . . ."

Woman: "I don't want to know about the classification—is it
hazardous? If it's not hazardous, why can't you leave it there [West
Dallas]?"

EPA: "It is a hazard to the people of West Dallas in its present
state."

Woman: "And it won't be hazardous to the people of Monroe?!"

The truckloads of lead-contaminated West Dallas soil were
scheduled to be dumped at the Magnolia landfill beginning on
Thursday, February 13.[22] Residents of Monroe and members of the
West Dallas Coalition for Environmental Justice vowed to demonstrate in front of the RSR smelter to prevent trucks from returning
the lead-tainted soil. State district judge Michael Ingram granted an
injunction against the dumping.

EPA officials decided to reroute the trucks to a class I sanitary
landfill (operated by Republic Waste Industries, owned by Waste
Management Inc.) in Avalon, located in Ellis County, 45 miles
south of Dallas. Ellis County has lush green pastures as far as the
eye can see and cotton fields that occasionally give way to small,
neat white wood frame homes. Reverend O. C. Johnson, Jr., is pastor of the predominantly African American Saint John's Baptist
Church, located not more than two blocks from the Republic Waste
landfill.

Reverend Johnson could see the site from his office at the rear of
the church. One day, he noticed that the men working at the landfill
were wearing "white moon suits" and had what appeared to be gas
masks covering their faces. Reverend Johnson adds:

We were told by EPA officials that they were preparing some
kind of "water treatment" plant; then it came to our knowl-

edge that they were planning on dumping some contaminated soil from the West Dallas area over in back of us. We don't want that lead dumped back here because our land is too precious. This is agricultural land. We provide food here for many families in the state of Texas, and we don't want to destroy what we have going for us at this particular stage with some freak accident of nature.

The Ellis County towns of Ennis, Italy, and Avalon vowed to stop any shipments of the lead-laced soil, despite the EPA's threats of lawsuits and heavy fines of $25,000 per day for Ellis County. EPA Region VI administrator Buck Wynne was determined to override the Ellis County towns' efforts. He released a statement to the media saying, "Continued human exposure to waste materials at the West Dallas Lead Site constitutes an imminent and substantial endangerment, particularly to children and pregnant women; the agency has authorized an emergency removal action at the site under Section 104(a) of CERCLA."

What did all of this mean? In lay terms, it meant that no one, no town, no county can block shipments of contaminated soil slated for disposal under these Superfund regulations. Still, Ellis County officials stood fast in their opposition to the shipments. However, the weight of the EPA eventually won out, and tainted West Dallas soil is now a part of Ellis County.

According to EPA officials, there are some 1,300 Superfund sites throughout America. Superfund sites are used when the EPA has tested a particular site and declared it hazardous, then put it on a list for the hazardous waste to be cleaned up. The West Dallas area was not on the list of Superfund sites. However, because of the lead levels at the site, the EPA said that it had to consider West Dallas an emergency. Because of this new designation, all of a sudden West Dallas was added to the Superfund site list in a position ahead of hundreds of other sites already designated.

Why were cleanup actions taken in 1992? Some residents speculate that the city's bid to win a horse racing track had something to do with the cleanup. The newly elected mayor headed Dallas's effort to win the right to build a racetrack in West Oak Cliff (Pinnacle Park), near West Dallas.

The city endorsed Pinnacle Park unequivocally and passed a resolution authorizing issuance of municipal bonds to cover the construction cost. Dallas did not want to lose out to its southwestern neighbor, the city of Grand Prairie. A month earlier, Grand Prairie had voted to approve a half-cent increase in sales tax to allow for $65 million in bonds as partial payment of $95 million to build the $100 million racetrack.

A group of investors unveiled plans to build a $109 million class I horse racing track in West Oak Cliff—next door to the city's largest known lead slag heap. William Moriarity, an engineering and environmental consultant for Pinnacle Park developers, did not see any threat to the track's grandstand, a mile from the lead slag. He did, however, see a threat to the horses, whose barns would be built on top of a West Dallas landfill.

West Dallas activist Luis Sepulveda is convinced that the proposal to build a racetrack was the real motivation for "emergency removal" of lead slag from West Dallas. Sepulveda adds: "I asked Steve Bartlett, 'You mean you're going to build a racetrack on top of an area where, regardless, you think it's okay for residents of West Dallas to die; aren't you concerned that these million-dollar horses are going to come in and be contaminated? We can't stand for that; those horses are worth millions of dollars.'" Dallas lost out, and Grand Prairie eventually got the racetrack.

The story of West Dallas and its lead problem does not end with the shipment of contaminated soil to Ellis County. The West Dallas Coalition for Environmental Justice filed a lawsuit against the EPA, the state of Texas, and the city of Dallas alleging civil rights violations in West Dallas spanning decades. The suit states that residents were discriminated against and were not given equal protection under the law from polluting industries, including the RSR Corporation's smelter. It asks for a thorough cleanup, follow-up medical care, job training, educational programs, and new zoning, among other remedies. Federal district judge Jerry Buchmeyer has given permission for the suit to proceed.

CONCLUSION

The smelter is now closed. Still, West Dallas residents wonder why they had to wait twenty years for the government to act. Why were the people in this community deserted by the city and the federal government? It certainly was not because the officials did not have sufficient evidence or documentation of the lead problem. Residents of the mostly African American and Latino American neighborhoods have had to wait longer than their white counterparts for environmental protection. Environmental racism proved to be a major obstacle in West Dallas. Nevertheless, local residents persisted over the years in making government more responsive to their needs and in getting the lead removed from their community.

7

Coping with Poisons in Cancer Alley

BEVERLY H. WRIGHT, PAT BRYANT, AND ROBERT D. BULLARD

The South has always been an important battleground for African Americans' struggle for social justice. In recent years, southern activists have added environmental justice to their agenda. Until the turn of the century, more than 90 percent of African Americans lived in the southern states. With the advent of World Wars I and II, African Americans began to migrate from the small rural towns of the region to the Northeast, Midwest, and West.

All across the southern "black belt," in counties with predominantly African American populations, a steady stream of men, women, and children pulled up stakes and embarked on a new life away from the cotton fields, sugarcane plantations, and sharecropping farms. This migration was stimulated by both the "push" of Jim Crow and the "pull" of economic and political freedom expected outside the region.[1] It was not until the mid-1970s that this exodus was reversed. Today, more than 53 percent of all African Americans live in the South, the same percentage as in 1980.

The South has always been thought of as a backward land, based on its social, economic, political, and environmental policies. By default, the region became a "sacrifice zone," a sump for the rest of the nation's toxic waste.[2] A colonial mentality exists in the South, where local government and big business take advantage of people who are politically and economically powerless. Many of these attitudes emerged from the region's marriage to slavery and the plantation system—a brutal system that exploited humans and the land.[3]

The South is stuck with this unique legacy—the legacy of slavery, Jim Crow, and white resistance to equal justice for all. This legacy has also affected race relations and the region's ecology. Southerners, both African American and white, have less education, lower incomes, higher infant mortality, and shorter life expectancy than Americans elsewhere. It should be no surprise that the environmental quality Southerners enjoy is markedly different from that in other regions of the country.

The South is characterized by "look-the-other-way environmental policies and giveaway tax breaks."[4] It is our nation's Third World, where "political bosses encourage outsiders to buy the region's human and natural resources at bargain prices."[5] Lax enforcement of environmental regulations has left the region's air, water, and land the most industry befouled in the United States.

LOUISIANA AS "PARADISE" LOST

African Americans have always constituted a sizable share of the population in southern states where the plantation economy was dominant—as in Louisiana. Louisiana has tagged itself a "sportsman's paradise." However, in the early 1900s the state's economy slowly began to change from an agricultural and fishing economy, based on its cypress swamps, waterways, and fertile soil, as oil exploration led to the construction of a refinery in Baton Rouge. The Mississippi River served as a magnet for petrochemical companies because of its access to barges and its capacity for disposal of chemical waste.

With the collapse of the sugar plantation system after World War II, Louisiana became a prime location for the petrochemical industry, which became the new plantation system. In the 1940s, the state's population could be seen shifting as jobs were created by this

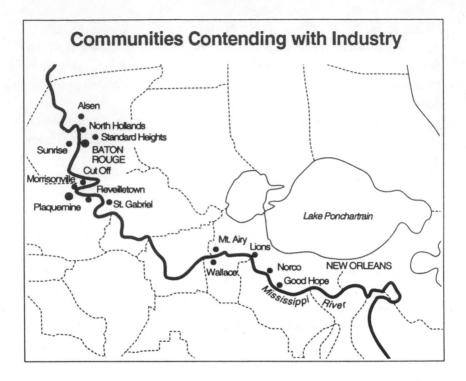

Communities Contending with Industry

new oil-based economy. By 1956, some 87,200 Louisianians were directly employed by the petrochemical industry. In the 1960s, much of the growth was related to the generous tax exemption and other inducements offered by Governor John McKeithen. By the 1970s, Louisiana's industrial corridor, an 85-mile stretch along the Mississippi River from Baton Rouge to New Orleans, was producing 60 percent of the nation's vinyl chloride and nitrogen fertilizer and 26 percent of the nation's chlorine.

In 1990, African Americans made up nearly 31 percent of Louisiana's population. How have African Americans fared under this new system, in which the petrochemical industry is king? Amos Favorite, a World War II and civil rights veteran and resident of Geismer, Louisiana, agrees that the petrochemical industries are the new "masters." "We are the victims. . . . We are all victimized by a system that puts dollars before everything else. That's the way it was in the old days when the dogs and whips were masters, and that's the way it is today when we got stuff in the water and air we can't even see that can kill us deader than we ever thought we could die."[6]

Many of these industries are located next to African American communities that were settled by former slaves—areas that were unincorporated and where the land was cheap. Local residents had few political rights (most African Americans were denied the right to vote or to hold public office). While the promise of jobs was the selling point for industries coming to towns along the Mississippi River, only a few jobs were actually offered to African American residents—and these were usually the dirtiest jobs, at the lowest wages.

The petrochemical industry has played an important role in the state's economy, especially in southern Louisiana. More than 165,000 workers were employed in the state's petrochemical industry at its peak in 1982. This single industry accounted for one out of three tax dollars collected by the state.[7] Even though Louisiana is a poor state, many of the giant corporations get special tax breaks. For example, thirty large corporations, many of which are major polluters, received $2.5 billion in Louisiana property tax exemptions in the 1980s. Only a few permanent new jobs resulted from these exemptions.[8]

Louisiana is not a large state; it ranks thirty-first in land area for all of the states. Yet despite its compact size, Louisiana has become a hazardous waste "importer" state. It disposed of 819 million pounds of hazardous waste shipped from other states in 1988, the latest year for which Louisiana Department of Environmental Quality figures are available.[9] On the other hand, Louisiana sent 307 million pounds of hazardous waste to other states for disposal, giving the state a net import of 512 million pounds of hazardous waste.

In 1992, the Institute for Southern Studies' "Green Index" ranked Louisiana forty-ninth of fifty states in overall environmental quality. The Green Index is based on seventy-seven federal and state policy indicators.[10] Louisiana ranked fiftieth in toxic release to surface water, high-risk cancer facilities, per capita toxic underground injection, and oil spills in state waters. On community and work force health, it also ranked toward the bottom: infant mortality, forty-ninth; households with only septic tanks, forty-fourth; households without plumbing, forty-third; doctors delivering patient care, forty-first; and workers in high-risk jobs, fortieth. Toxic waste discharge and industrial pollution are correlated with poorer economic conditions. The state could actually improve its general welfare by enacting and enforcing regulations to protect the environment.[11]

Nearly three-fourths of Louisiana's population—more than 3 million people—get their drinking water from underground aquifers. Dozens of the aquifers are threatened by contamination from polluting industries. The three biggest industrial threats to the state's groundwater are Dow Chemical, Vulcan, and PPG.[12] Some of the state's residents fear that someday they will be forced to become dependent on bottled drinking water, which would be cost prohibitive for many low- and moderate-income households.

Louisiana's industrial corridor accounts for nearly one-fourth of the nation's petrochemical production. Some 125 companies in this corridor manufacture a range of products including fertilizers, gasoline, paints, and plastics. More than 2 billion pounds of toxic chemicals were emitted from these plants between 1987 and 1989.

This corridor has been dubbed "Cancer Alley" because the air, ground, and water are full of carcinogens, mutagens, and embryotoxins. The area was described in a *Washington Post* article as a "massive human experiment" and a "national sacrifice zone."[13] Residents of Cancer Alley have also described their environment as a "toxic gumbo." Linda King of the Environmental Health Network, a grass-roots group based in Louisiana, expressed a similar view: "We don't live in areas that spew out only copper, only benzene. . . . We live in chemical stews."[14]

Alsen, situated at the beginning of Cancer Alley, is one of these endangered communities. The unincorporated community sits several miles north of Baton Rouge on the Mississippi River. In 1980, Alsen's population stood at 1,104, of whom 98.9 percent were African Americans. Beginning as a rural community of African American landowners, Alsen developed into a stable working-class suburban enclave. More than 77 percent of the residents own their homes.

Tiny Alsen sits in the shadow of the towering petrochemical plants that line the Mississippi River. Rollins Environmental Services operates hazardous waste facilities near the community—the only hazardous waste disposal facilities in the Baton Rouge area. In 1986, the Rollins landfill was the fourth largest in the nation in terms of remaining capacity.[15]

The Rollins hazardous waste landfill and incinerator have been a constant point of contention for nearby Alsen residents. Rollins's facilities have been the source of numerous odor and health complaints from home owners and workers at the plants. Rollins was cited for more than 100 state and federal violations between 1980 and 1985, but it did not pay any penalties.

Fed up with the poisoning of her community, seventy-five-year-old grandmother Mary McCastle organized her neighbors into the Coalition for Community Action (CCA). The group, determined to protect the health of the community and bring Rollins into compliance with state and federal environmental regulations, filed a lawsuit against Rollins. After years of delays, the lawsuit was settled out of court for several hundred thousand dollars. The CCA has also pursued cleanup of a Superfund site near an area called Devil's Swamp. In 1992, the group was successful in obtaining a technical assistance grant (TAG) from the federal Environmental Protection Agency.

Ascension Parish typifies what many people call a toxic "sacrifice zone." The rural and mostly African American parish lies just 10 miles south of Baton Rouge. In the two parish towns of Geismer and Saint Gabriel, some eighteen petrochemical plants are crammed into a 9.5-square-mile area. Companies such as BASF, Vulcan, Triad, CF Industries, Liquid Airbonic, Bordon Chemical, Shell, Uniroyal, Rubicon, Ciba-Geigy, and others discharge 196 million pounds of pollutants annually into the water and air.[16] Discharges include the carcinogens vinyl chloride and benzene; mercury, which is harmful to the nervous system; chloroform; toluene; and carbon tetrachloride, which can cause birth defects.

Free-lance writer Conger Beasley, writing in *Buzzworm,* described some of the health threats posed by the petrochemical industry in Cancer Alley:

> People living within a mile of the plants have a 4.5 percent greater chance of contracting lung cancer than those who live one to three miles away. They are least knowledgeable about hazardous waste effects. A quarter-century after enactment of major civil rights laws, they remain distrustful of politicians, black and white, who historically have manipulated the system for their own benefit.[17]

It takes Amos Favorite to describe the hellish nightmare in his hometown of Geismer, a small, mostly African American river town: "You ought to see this place at night. . . . When these companies burn off their waste the air lights up like a battlefield. I'm telling you it's scary. Nighttime around here is like an evil dream."[18] Favorite is convinced that government officials have written off entire communities along the river. Policymakers appear to rate the lives of African Americans and poor people as expendable.

Government has often cooperated with industry in disenfranchising communities of color. A prime example of this practice is the case of Wallace, a small community located on the eastern bank of the Mississippi River in Saint John the Baptist Parish. Wallace is 95 percent African American. As an unincorporated area, the community does not have a governing body of its own. It relies on the Saint John the Baptist Parish Council to protect the health, welfare, and environment of the community. But the white parish officials have not provided equal protection for all of the parish citizens. It seems that some communities are more equal than others.

Wallace is a close-knit community of home owners whose landholdings have been in their families for several generations. The community has always been zoned as residential—until the parish council voted to make way for a proposed industrial plant. In 1990, the Formosa Plastics Corporation asked the parish council to re-zone 1,800 acres of land, which included Wallace, from residential to industrial.[19] Wallace residents were surprised and angered by the parish council decision. Kelly Colquette and Elizabeth Robertson, writing in the *Tulane Environmental Law Journal,* voiced some suspicion of the parish officials' decision:

> First, residential property usually receives the utmost protection from parish zoning commissions. . . . Second, because other industrially zoned properties already existed on the west bank [of the Mississippi River], the Parish Council could have allowed Formosa to use the industrial land already available. . . . Third, and most offensive, it is widely known that Formosa has a well-earned reputation as a world class environmental outlaw.[20]

In 1992, after intense grass-roots organizing by Gulf Coast Tenants Organization (GCTO), an alliance of grass-roots environmental and social justice groups in Alabama, Mississippi, and Louisiana, and a lawsuit filed by the Sierra Club Legal Defense Fund, Formosa was forced to withdraw its proposal, and the plant was not built. This represented a victory for the local organizers, yet it was only a partial victory for Wallace residents, who still needed jobs. The residents, however, had drawn a line in the sand, refusing to trade their health and the life of their community for a few dirty, low-paying jobs.

BUYOUTS, PUSH-OUTS, AND SELLOUTS

Important organizing work is under way in southern Louisiana and along the Gulf Coast of Mississippi. Some communities are now under siege from nearby industries. Many of these threatened communities were there long before the petrochemical industry came to the region. A number of chemical companies have begun to take aggressive steps to limit their liability by buying out nearby communities. Several buyouts along the river have occurred in recent years. For example, Reveilletown was bought out by Georgia Gulf; Good Hope, by a refinery in Saint Charles; Morrisonville, by Dow Chemical; and Sunrise, by Placid Refining Company.

Actions taken by some of the polluting industries have sparked citizen activism all across the Gulf Coast. Many of the leaders are women. A leader in this movement is Janice Dickerson, an African American who grew up in Reveilletown, a community founded by former slaves after the Civil War. The community is located across the Mississippi River from Baton Rouge. Janice does not live in Reveilletown anymore. The entire community was poisoned by vinyl chloride emissions released from Georgia Gulf's manufacture of plastics.

After traces of vinyl chloride were found in the blood of local children in 1987, thirteen Reveilletown property owners filed a lawsuit against Georgia Gulf. The case was later settled out of court. Twenty other families subsequently agreed to sell to Georgia Gulf for a reported $1.2 million, and the company completed a program in 1990 to move a total of fifty families away from its vinyl chloride plant.[21]

At a candlelight vigil held in 1990 in which African American and white environmentalists mourned the death of Reveilletown, Dickerson said that racism and corporate greed were at the heart of the poisoning of Reveilletown. "I really think white politicians thought years ago that the ill effects of Georgia Gulf would be contained in Reveilletown," she said. Dickerson's concerns are not that different from those expressed in other communities of color that have fallen victim to environmental racism. Nevertheless, she continues her fight for environmental justice along the river.

Morrisonville, founded in the 1870s by former slaves, is another community that was bought out. The town's founder, Robert Morrison, was a minister who struggled to create this community around the church he led, the Nazarene Baptist Church. The community survived flooding from the Mississippi and it survived Jim Crow, but it could not survive Dow Chemical.

Some Morrisonville residents can still recall when the land that Dow stands on was part of a huge sugarcane empire owned by the Mayflower and Union Plantation. The plantation house is still standing and can be seen inside the fence owned by Dow. In 1959, the community sold some land to Dow. Many of the residents now see this transaction as the mistake that marked the beginning of their demise as a community. The land sold to Dow created a greenbelt, but Dow expanded and built on the land—up to the property lines of some Morrisonville residents.[22]

The Morrisonville chemical plant is Dow's largest facility in Louisiana. "Dow built right out to the fence until they were on top of us," says Jack Martin, a longtime Morrisonville resident. The buyout has brought sadness to the community. Doretha Thompson sums up the demise of her community: "It's like a big death taking place. . . . I always thought I'd spend the rest of my life in Morrisonville with my relatives. But it seems like what Dow wants, Dow gets."[23]

The chemical conglomerate spent more than $10 million in a voluntary buyout of the town's 250 home owners—the first of its kind in the absence of a lawsuit. Dow compensated people for the cost of their homes, but the "community" is lost forever. Presently, the town's residents have moved upriver, downriver, and to Baton Rouge. Many of them return every Sunday to worship in the Nazarene Baptist Church, the only surviving symbol of the community.

The community of Sunrise was purchased in 1874 from a white landowner by Alexander Banes, a former slave. The property changed hands in 1904, when Banes sold the property to Benjamin Mayer, a white businessman from Baton Rouge. Mayer subsequently subdivided the land and sold parcels to individuals.

In the 1930s, Sunrise was inhabited by mostly white residents, but by 1970, the community was 17 percent white and 83 percent African American. Sunrise is the home of Placid Refining Company, an independent oil-refining and oil-marketing company. Placid converts crude oil and material resources produced in Louisiana into gasoline and diesel and jet fuel. In 1980, on the streets closest to the Placid refinery, 48 percent of the residents were white and 52 percent were African American.[24]

In 1979, Placid initiated a program to purchase the property of employees of the refining company who lived in Sunrise. The program resulted in Placid's acquiring more than 100 parcels of land—about one-third of the lots in Sunrise. By 1985, the company had purchased $947,000 worth of property in the community. However, African American Sunrise residents were not offered the same opportunities to be bought out as their white counterparts. White residents who lived closest to the plant at the time of the buyout and other white residents were bought out first. In 1985, some African American property owners in Sunrise were told that the company would get back to them. This, however, did not occur.

The remaining residents of Sunrise who lived in the shadow of Placid filed a lawsuit against the company in 1990. The suit listed as plaintiffs 241 individuals who owned thirty-six houses and 89 residents who were renters. In March 1991, in response to the lawsuit, Placid initiated its "Sunrise program," which offered to buy the homes of any nonplaintiff owners in Sunrise. An offer was made to property owners to purchase homes at prices that would allow owners to buy or build new homes that are similar in size and materials to the ones they owned in Sunrise. In addition to the purchase price, owners were provided $5,000 per household.

This program resulted in Placid's acquiring more than 90 percent of the homes of the nonplaintiff owners. Plaintiffs in the lawsuit were not eligible; nor did they desire to participate in Placid's Sunrise program. Placid and the plaintiffs finally reached an out-of-court settlement under which Placid would purchase all property of the plaintiffs.

BREAKING DOWN BARRIERS

The Achilles heel of the environmental movement in the United States is its whiteness.[25] Especially in the Deep South, the environmental movement is locked up in traditions of liberal do-gooding and racial inequities that make it very difficult to build a mass-based movement with the power to change the conditions of our poisoning. The key to building a multiracial drive against toxic pollution is—first—to have people of color talking and organizing among themselves.

Les Ann Kirkland, a progressive white environmentalist in the area, agrees that "racism is rampant" and discusses it if somebody "brings it up." But she worries that if color is made a central issue, environmentalists will not be able to take on a broader organizing agenda. And she does not agree that race is the most important variable in the siting of toxic facilities.

It is very easy to postpone dealing with questions of racism until later. That seems to be the strategy of leaders of major environmental organizations. These groups cannot reach out to African Americans and people of color as long as they are nearly all white.

The understanding of GCTO activist Janice Dickerson and other African Americans that the environmental movement is a critical arena in which to fight racism is a bright light for the future. Dickerson is involved in a two-state (Louisiana and Mississippi) organizing effort through the Gulf Coast Tenant Leadership Development Project, a predominantly African American organization. The primary focus of the project is to encourage African Americans in schools, churches, and communities to organize around environmental concerns and to provide African Americans with the organizational support to nurture their development as environmentalists.

Weekly meetings are held in Baton Rouge in which African American activists openly discuss interrelationships of issues such as community poisoning, racism, environmentalism, and housing. Staff members from New Orleans, Baton Rouge, and Gulfport, Mississippi, counsel members and visit leaders in their towns.

One of the tenant leaders' first efforts is to confront major industrial powers over the poisoning of Monte Santo Bayou. The bayou meanders from the completely African American Scotlandville section of Baton Rouge through many communities and past Exxon's refinery and chemical plants to empty like a sewer into the already poisoned Mississippi River. When the river is high in the spring, a backwash reverses the flow, sending the poisons upstream past a public housing complex called Monte Santo Village.

Harvesting of crawfish is a favorite springtime activity here. African American children from the housing projects wade and swim in the bayou, too. But Sharon Lewis, mother of three children and vice president of the Monte Santo Tenants Organization, wants these activities curtailed until she is convinced that the bayou is safe. Since Lewis began attending GCTO meetings, she has received strength and support from Janice Dickerson and others. And at least for now, she and her community have Exxon's tiger by the tail.

Both Lewis and Dickerson know that their effort to clean up the bayou will take years of struggle and a strong movement that has the power to build multiracial coalitions—under the leadership of African American communities that suffer most. They know that building that movement will take time. They believe that their work has realized significant accomplishments that can serve as models for multiracial organizing around environmental issues elsewhere.

ENVIRONMENTAL SUMMIT— MILESTONE OF HOPE AND SOLIDARITY

The most threatening occurrence in recent times for the multinational corporations and their institutional allies, and the most empowering recent event for oppressed ethnic and racial groups in the United States, was the First National People of Color Environmental Leadership Summit, held in Washington, DC, in October 1991. Key ethnic community leaders previously separated by geography, culture, and history united to make a clear statement of intent to build a national and international social justice movement that pivots on stopping the rape of the earth and the poisoning of all of its people.

Leaders from all sectors of the United States (corporate; religious; government, both state and federal; and environmental) watched in amazement. The rules of the progressively funded social justice game are set so that this kind of uniting of people of color, if not forbidden, seldom occurs. And the one thing that made it possible—people of color having the good sense to meet for two days by themselves—is the very thing that, before and after the Summit, many white and African American progressives have sought to prevent from happening again.

The Summit's product, the "Principles of Environmental Justice," is so commonsense that any progressive group, whether labor, religious, youth, or human rights, should leap to endorse the Principles and be guided by the spirit of united purpose among people of color that authored them. The Principles are truly the summation of diverse struggles for survival and propagation of the total human family and all species. They certainly map out a set of beliefs on which to base a strong movement to continue pursuit of that kind of beloved society professed in so many indigenous cultures—societies based on serving human needs rather than capitalistic greed.

The planners of the Summit expected the obvious: that religious, government, and national environmental leaders would find fault in any process in which people of color put their heads together to break up the genocidal games all the major institutions play on them. Delegates to the Summit demonstrated to themselves that African Americans, Native Americans, Latino Americans, and Asian Americans must plot a course together and ask other progressives to join their vision and struggle for a just world.

For leaders in the GCTO, the Summit did not come quickly enough. For more than six years, the GCTO had been educating African American leaders in Louisiana's Cancer Alley to stop the practice of industries poisoning African American communities. The GCTO's involvement in environmental issues was not planned; it was undertaken in response to demands of tenant leaders in many communities that the group had assisted to beat bad landlords and the federal government's desire to destroy public housing. Many of them, especially those in Saint Charles Parish, Louisiana, found that having better homes helped little when the poisons spewed from industries sickened and killed them.

In Hahnville, an unincorporated community in Saint Charles Parish, the GCTO found that the incidence of cancer was eighteen times the national average. While university and corporate scientists could not document causation between the petrochemical industry and cancer deaths, our common sense, or what folks used to call "mother wit," taught local leaders differently. The most poisonous industries known, petrochemical industries, locate here as close to African American and poor communities as they possibly can, and cancer incidence is highest in those communities. Funerals exceed births and marriages as the most frequent social occasion.

The GCTO held out its poor, black hands to join with environmental groups and labor to do something about this, but at almost every juncture white environmental, religious, and labor activists told us, "Okay, African Americans are being poisoned disproportionately, but it is not because they are African American; it is because they live in poor neighborhoods."

And community activists have responded so many times with the question: "Why are people of color disproportionately poor, sick, illiterate, in jail, unemployed, starving, homeless, and dying? Is it any surprise that institutions and corporations in the United States have heaped the greatest risk of industrial and government poisoning on people of color?"

The GCTO seized on the opportunity to demonstrate that African American and white unity could occur around this issue if the concerns of environmentalists were expanded to include labor's concerns and those of the African American communities and poor communities in general. The GCTO took a busload of tenants and a few environmentalists to the Southern Environmental Assembly in Atlanta. It would have been a very white affair if these activists had not gone.

Shortly thereafter, the GCTO encouraged an ad hoc coalition of labor, religious, environmental, tenant, and civil rights organizations to join an eleven-day march and participate in related activities to highlight the extremely dangerous conditions in Cancer Alley. That African Americans and whites would join together in Louisiana shook up folks in industry and environmental circles. State and local governments passed resolutions supporting the GCTO's demands to clean up the state's air, land, and water. And the groups in the coalition adopted principles that are remarkably similar to those recently passed by the Summit delegates.

That march was a great success. The Louisiana Chemical Association, a group that represents the new plantation owners in Louisiana, the chemical companies, polled registered voters across the state. The voters responded, saying that they had learned more about environmental destruction during the days preceding, during, and after the march than at any other time. It is not surprising that the state's conservative legislature passed a law in its next session requiring a 50 percent reduction of airborne chemicals by 1994.

During Earth Day 1990, the GCTO got a piece of the national media with its week-long Second March Against Poisons. It was obvious that the group had to join hands with the Latino American–led Southwest Organizing Project (SWOP), the African American–led United Church of Christ Commission for Racial Justice, academics and scientists of color, and other community organizations of color to defend our right to live. By joining hands with sisters and brothers all across this nation, activists of color defined their oppression and mapped out strategies to make their communities whole again.

What is so encouraging is that these leaders are not apologizing for who they are. The Summit clearly affirmed the sanctity of diverse cultures and the commitment to social, economic, and racial justice as a basis for a clean environment. These environmental justice leaders continue to ask: How can any community, white or African American, be safe as long as our nation's policy allows communities of color to accept the risk of poisoning? And how long will Americans believe that poisons deposited in communities of color will stay in those communities and not migrate across the tracks to suburban America?

The roughly 2 billion pounds of poisons put into the air, land, and water in Cancer Alley find their way sooner or later into the homes of all Americans. In about three days, ethylene and thousands of other lethal gases make their way from Cancer Alley refineries to the Great Lakes and the Northeast. A few more days, and those same gases, although somewhat diluted, poison the air of Europe, Asia, Africa, and the other continents. Many of the pesticides and fertilizers produced here poison us first and farm workers second, then finally wind up on America's and the world's dinner tables.

Likewise, fish and seafood from Louisiana's waters find their way to most dinner tables. Louisiana is the second largest seafood-exporting state in the United States. Fish in Louisiana's largest river system, the Calcasieu Estuary, have been studied and found to be poisoned with cancer-causing chemicals. The state and federal governments have said and done very little to protect the public except to post advisories warning people against fishing and consuming fish caught in this estuary.

Largely African American communities are up against the wall of chemical facilities along the Mississippi River. "Keep quiet," the industries say. "Here's a few dollars to keep the African American churches from preaching. A couple more dollars to keep universities from teaching and researching. Here are a lot of dollars for national and local media to repeat the lie that petrochemical companies are fine, clean businesses that propagate blue herons in restored marshlands next to petro refineries." Implied in their message is that sickness and death from the chemical companies and defense contractors are perfectly acceptable.

THE ROAD AHEAD

Which leaders in which communities and organizations will lead the way toward restructuring our society and liberating our people? People of color have to develop unbought, dedicated, and skilled leadership that can make every sector of American society accept a vision of a just United States and world order. This vision, articulated in the Principles of Environmental Justice, calls for industrialized and nonindustrialized, rich and poor communities and nations to share equally in the productive resources—jobs, income, leisure, education, health care, and clean environment.

"Accountability" has to become a key word in the environmental justice movement. When one looks at overlays of areas where poisonous wastes are stored in the United States and compares them to the communities that have elected large numbers of African American and Latino American officials to public office, they become one and the same. How could this happen? How could elected officials of color in the southern and southwestern states, home of the majority of African Americans, Latino Americans, and Native Americans, join forces with these poisoning companies?

Since the first passage of the Voting Rights Act in 1965, communities of color more often than not have elected officials who were acceptable to whites or who were able to acquire the money to buy radio advertisements and other media attention. Too many of these leaders are accountable to interests outside their communities; in the South, those interests are often the big hazardous waste–producing companies and polluting industries. The interests of people of color must be taken more seriously by the politicians. Many elected leaders of color earnestly thought that bringing in high-risk poisoning industries was better than unemployment. Today, they are beginning to rethink the long-term environmental and health effects associated with hosting risky industries.

For many conscientious leaders, the choice—starve now or maybe be sick later—has not been so clear. It is, in fact, no choice, but it is the reality in which people of color have continued to find themselves in the United States and across the globe.

Unfortunately, this will not change until the fundamental assumptions on which our society is built are challenged and restructured. Where are the resources needed for production, where will they be obtained, and at what costs to host communities and the environment? What is produced for whom, and what is the social utility of the product? And how are the net gains from the industrial process distributed among all points in the production cycle?

New and old leadership must organize communities around the reality of toxic poisoning. Bold and innovative approaches must be devised to stop the poisoning and to clean up the mess that we live in. The single most labor-intensive job market developing today is hazardous waste cleanup. It will certainly be a measure of shortsightedness if the cleanup jobs that become available from our sharpened political demands contribute to lower unemployment for the rest of America. But unless people of color get the training now and develop our own cleanup corporations now, we will be left out.

Many of us have watched Superfund cleanups: outsiders coming into communities and doing the work with few local hires. In some cases, the companies who poisoned the communities in the first place get Superfund monies to hire other folks to come into these communities, stir up the chemicals and make residents and workers sicker, and leave the mess unabated. That is the story of the Devil's Swamp cleanup near the community of Alsen.

The nation's churches, religious organizations, civil rights and human rights organizations, universities, youth organizations, and labor organizations must be involved. Removing the poisons in urban and rural communities across this nation is a great moral issue that is connected to everything that faces our people.

An example is the tremendous amounts of lead that our children ingest in inner-city areas. Another is the poisons spewed from municipal incinerators and industries, often in densely populated areas. These problems can be tackled, but people of color must be allowed to lead the efforts to ensure that real cleanup takes place. If America is to be cleaned up from the past fifty years of chemical poisoning, there will be jobs for everyone.

In the South and other regions, economic development must be revitalized through cooperative models that do not rob workers and the environment. We must support minority and small farmers to produce unpoisoned, healthy food.

There is a multiplicity of economic development models from which to choose. The bottom line all over the world is the question of how to capitalize on these models. Environmental groups of color must learn the ways in which some national environmental organizations knock on doors, use direct mail, and use workplace solicitations to fund community building. Health programs, counseling, cleanups, and university research must be funded by cutting the obscene military budget, especially since there is no longer a Soviet threat.

None of this will happen without great organizing skill exhibited by community leaders of color across the country—people whose lives depend on it. The same kind of leadership development training by and for people of color that occurred in the South in the 1950s and 1960s must continue at heightened levels in the 1990s.

8

Impacts of the Energy Industry on the Navajo and Hopi

KATHY HALL

The indigenous cultures of the southwestern region of the United States have developed adaptations that work within the fluctuations of the semiarid ecosystem of the Colorado Plateau. This chapter examines two of these tribes, the Hopi and the Navajo, who live on Black Mesa. The Hopi reservation is located within the boundaries of the Navajo reservation. The reservation borders have been imposed on the Hopi and Navajo peoples by the United States government. The Hopi people differ greatly from the Navajo.

The traditional Hopi are an agricultural people who live in settled villages located on three mesas. The traditional Navajo are seminomadic, living in hogans on the open country, herding sheep, and planting gardens. Until recently, trade between members of both tribes in the Black Mesa region occurred regularly. At least in this region, the two tribes lived alongside each other in a symbiotic relationship. The common portrayal of both tribes is that the Hopi were the first people, invaded by the marauding Navajo, and that there always has been and always will be conflict between the tribes. While this portrayal may be accurate in some cases, at a gathering in April 1993 on Big Mountain, located on Black Mesa, a Hopi spokesperson for the Hopi spiritual leaders and an initiated Hopi priest reconfirmed an oral agreement made between the traditional people of both tribes: the traditional Navajo have every right to live on Black Mesa and are considered good neighbors.

Many of the traditional Hopi and Navajo people who currently live in the Black Mesa region firmly believe that the earth cannot be owned. They view themselves as the caretakers of the earth, believing that they must live in harmony with the laws of the Creator in order to maintain balance for the entire planet. To both the traditional Hopi and the traditional Navajo, this means living a simple life without electricity or running water, completing cycles of ceremonies and offering prayers every day. Traditional members of both tribes manifest these beliefs through very different practices, yet a similar theme appears: humans are linked between earth and the Creator and, because of this link, must act with respect and honor toward all of creation. Theoretically, then, action is based on maintaining harmony through daily practices that acknowledge the beauty, mystery, and intricacy of earth cycles.

Changing Woman is one of the most highly revered and dependable of the Navajo Holy People. She is the source of life and the giver of sustenance and destiny to all beings. She is the symbol of the Female Rains and the psyche of lakes, rivers, and mountains. She is in control of vegetation everywhere for the benefit of Earth People.[1]

Tukunavi is the area, including Black Mesa, that the Hopi say is part of the heart of Mother Earth. Within this heart, the Hopi have left a seal by leaving religious items, clan markings, plantings, and ancient burial grounds as landmarks and shrines.[2]

The appearance of the Anglo-American in the Southwest introduced a very different ethic and value system toward the land and its inhabitants. Many Anglo-Americans, especially those in positions of decision-making power, view the land and its resources as a commodity that can be quantified and manipulated for mass production. One assumption of modern Western society is that natural limitations can be overcome by applying technological innovations in order to transform ecosystems. This transformation is considered an improvement and is correlated with progress. The modern Western idea of progress assumes an expanding economy, and expansion demands the creation of new commodities and markets. Electricity has become crucial for this process; electrical power is now an integral part of daily life in modern societies. In the United States, Japan, and western Europe, public concern about the negative impact on the environment from current sources of fuel used to generate electricity has led to implementation of national standards that regulate industrial consumption of these fuels. In the United States, one of these standards calls for a reduction in the amount of ventilated sulfur from coal-fired generation plants. Currently, the coal industry utilizes at least one of the following strategies to resolve this dilemma: first, the installation of equipment designed to "scrub out" sulfur; second, the use of low-sulfur coal.

Coal is one of the most abundant fuel resources found in the United States. There are two basic types of coal. Large deposits of high-sulfur metallurgic coal exist in the Midwest and on the East Coast; these are mined via subsurface shafts and used in the manufacture of steel. Steam coal is found in the western states, fairly close to the surface, and is accessible through strip-mining techniques. The sulfur content of steam coal varies, but compared with metallurgic coal, it is low.[3] Approximately one-third of U.S. steam coal resources lie under reservation lands, territory held "in trust" by the United States government.[4]

In 1990, the Office of Surface Mining Reclamation and Enforcement (OSMRE), a federal agency in the U.S. Department of the Interior, endorsed the continuation of strip mining of coal by Peabody Coal Company (PCC) on Black Mesa in the Four Corners region of the American Southwest. Although Peabody Coal Company has been exploiting the area since the 1960s, an environmental impact statement (EIS) was not produced until June 1990, when the OSMRE finally issued an EIS for the proposed Black Mesa–Kayenta Mine. The permit requests that an additional 13,800 acres be mined, stating that "the unique desert landscape will be changed from abrupt landforms to gently rolling hills and swales."[5] Water has been and will continue to be used to transport coal to one of the power stations through a slurry pipeline. The water is extracted from the confined portion of the N-aquifer under Black Mesa via five deep wells.[6] This aquifer is one of the major sources of water for the traditional Hopi village of Moenkopi, 70 miles from the mining area. It is also one of the major sources of water for many springs and shallow wells on Black Mesa used by the Navajo for domestic purposes and subsistence farming and for watering livestock.

After the mining is over, Peabody is required by federal law to reclaim the land. According to the proposed permit, this acreage, which is now covered by pinyon, juniper, sagebrush, and saltbush, will become grassland complete with fifty-eight ponds; artificial perches for owls, eagles, hawks, and other raptors (one per every 400 acres); reconstructed rock and brush piles (one per every 10 acres); and carefully constructed wildlife corridors, including special plantings of pinyon and juniper trees.[7] Humans, however, will be unable to utilize these resources, as "harvesting of the trees or pinyon nuts could be detrimental to the wildlife for which the habitat was designed."[8] Grazing of livestock, an important survival activity for many Black Mesa residents, will not be permitted for at least thirty-eight years—the estimated time frame for the reestablishment of vegetation. Individuals who are "able to establish a customary use area claim" will receive $50 per acre.[9]

Peabody and the OSMRE state that range conditions will improve; 99 acres, which now support only one sheep, will, it is claimed, be able to support ten. However, this depends on the survival of at least one-third of all vegetation planted and strict enforcement of a grazing plan that Peabody has developed.[10] Peabody has the option of extending the reclamation period beyond ten years. Once the land is released, it is to be "turned back to the lessor, in this case the BIA, who has final say as to when and whether the land can be returned to the original premining land use of grazing and wildlife habitat."[11]

The authors of the background document used for the EIS concluded that the project as outlined by Peabody would not damage the hydrologic balance associated with the proposed mining operation. They also concluded that cultural impacts would be potentially significant but could be mitigated through careful consultation with tribal members and payment for spiritual ceremonies on sites that will be destroyed.[12] Federal agencies mandated to oversee mining operations have heartily endorsed Peabody's mining permit.

THE NAVAJO AND HOPI AND THE
TRANSFORMATION OF BLACK MESA

The Black Mesa region is not empty. Many of the traditional Navajo people from this area rely on sheep as their economic base. "Sheep are our bank," explained one Navajo resident at a 1993 spring gathering on Big Mountain. "We don't take away your credit cards; why do you take away our sheep?" The sheep provide food for direct consumption and wool, which is woven into products and sold for cash. The cash, in turn, is used for purchasing needed items. Some of these people perceive the mine and mining operations as an invasion; somebody is making money, but none of that income is redistributed to households in the area. Furthermore, some residents feel as if their physical health has been directly affected. One woman at this same gathering complained of health problems related to the coal dust. Others complain about the emotional stress of seeing the pipeline and mining operations and of direct adverse effects from the operations, such as sound and physical vibrations from dynamite blasts. Other Navajo residents of the Black Mesa region rely on the mine for wages yet supplement their income with the sheep flocks and by gathering wild food and wood for domestic purposes.[13]

A portion of the economy of the Black Mesa region, then, is mixed: some residents produce for direct consumption, while others produce for exchange. Both the Navajo and the Hopi mix the two types of production. While some Navajo residents on Black Mesa have been able to maintain a more traditional life-style, the economy of the Navajo Nation as a whole has undergone dramatic transformations. However, these changes have occurred over many decades.

In the 1860s, under the auspices of a U.S. government military campaign, Kit Carson forcibly removed most Navajo from their land, destroying hogans, gardens, and orchards and incarcerating thousands at Bosque Rondondo. During the next few years of internment, many Navajo became dependent on military-supplied manufactured items for basic necessities and were forced to "begin producing for exchange rather than production [consumption]."[14] By the time Navajos were released from Bosque Rondondo and returned to reservation land, outside merchants dominated "all forms of Navajo domestic production."[15] This pattern continued for half a century or more, and production for subsistence purposes declined further. However, many Navajo did continue to raise sheep, thus ensuring customary land use rights.

In the 1930s, federal agencies attributed soil degradation in the arid Southwest to overgrazing by the Navajo sheep herds. A 10 percent reduction in the size of livestock herds was decreed. As herds were reduced below sustainable levels, smaller herders were forced to sell or eat their remaining sheep. As herd sizes fell and some families were no longer able to keep their animals, access to customary rights of land use was lost. In this way, land was taken from many of the Navajo, who were forced into wage labor in order to survive. This wage labor was controlled by nontribal, often multinational, industrial capital. Many Navajo no longer produced items for exchange with merchants but rather produced labor in exchange for wages. Land tenure patterns, however, allowed for a continuation of production for direct consumption (i.e., sheep for food). Both of these processes helped to create a shift from merchant to industrial capital in the Navajo Nation.

Ultimately, the "Navajo Nation was prevented from developing internally a significant strata [sic] of industrial capitalists or a significant amount of industrial capital."[16] Instead, an elite composed of tribal council officials dominates the accumulation and distribution processes on the reservation.

A large portion of capital, in the form of mineral royalty payments to the Navajo and Hopi tribal councils, continues to be generated by nontribal, multinational corporations that extract and export mineral resources from reservation land. Royalties from these projects are supposed to help establish "a more independent and self-sustaining reservation economy."[17] However, the cruel reality of poverty has not been eliminated, despite resource development on reservation land since the 1960s.[18] In 1977, the Navajo Nation received approximately $2.5 million from mineral-related leases and millions of dollars in federal aid. Yet half of the people on the reservation lived below the poverty level.

Energy-related projects and the prosperity they are supposed to generate appear to benefit some but not all. Many have grown poorer as the projects consume land and destroy resources that were once available for subsistence living. Others have grown richer, accumulating more capital, assets, and access to land rights. And sadly, there are some who experience a temporary rise in living standards through wages earned by working in the uranium and coal mines but who are now living in even greater poverty due to injuries and deaths directly related to occupational hazards that continue to go unrecognized and uncompensated by the mining corporations.[19] Navajo miners, previously nonunion, have formed unions in order to improve work standards and receive better wages and benefits. Needless to say, all of these struggles continue.[20]

Extraction of coal, gas, and uranium, as well as construction of dams and water diversion projects, has occurred on reservations in the Southwest at a vigorous pace since World War II, but without any mechanisms by which the tribes could guarantee equitable income distribution, control multinational corporate activities, or even gain direct benefits from these projects.

The development of the Native American reservations has been examined from many perspectives, including theories of internal colonization and domestic dependency.[21] The fact that the economy of the Navajo Nation relies heavily on exportation of minerals suggests important consequences associated with mineral enclave economies in developing countries. For example, the positive effects of a mineral economy include foreign exchange earnings, the generation of additional government revenue, increased employment, and the creation of a skilled labor force. Negative aspects include the creation of an enclave industry that relies on imported technology, absorbs only a limited amount of indigenous labor, and often repatriates profits out of the country. At the same time, the mining industry "tends to create environmental damage and is often operated under poor working and living conditions."[22]

Furthermore, once the resources are mined out, there is nothing left to generate revenues or employment in the local economy. The mining industry "is often characterized by a highly monopolistic industrial structure" that "competes with agriculture for the utilization of fertile soil and scarce water resources." Finally, it "creates a group of labor elites whose interests do not coincide with those of the nation and whose pattern of consumption tends to be higher and different from that of most of the rest of the population."[23]

Many of these negative effects correlate with the situation on Black Mesa. However, in the case of the Navajo Nation, the elite, whose pattern of consumption and interests appears to be different from that of many of the residents of Black Mesa and the traditional Hopi villages, also include tribal council members. The difference in interest goes beyond inner tribal issues to intertribal conflicts between Hopi and Navajo tribal council members and has culminated in the proposed relocation program on Black Mesa.

The establishment of reservations and boundaries that gave each tribe exclusive land rights has set the tone for disputes over land—disputes that continue to this day. Prior to the setting of reservation boundaries, the Navajo and Hopi had lived together with minimal conflict, the Hopi living in permanent villages and the Navajo living dispersed on the land.[24] According to Thomas Banyaca, spokesperson for some traditional Hopi spiritual leaders, an agreement was made between traditional members of the Hopi and Navajo peoples. This agreement basically confirmed that the traditional Navajo were welcome to remain on Black Mesa indefinitely.[25] Most of Black Mesa is under the jurisdiction of both the Navajo and Hopi tribes, in what has been commonly known as the Joint Use Area (JUA). The first dispute over land appears to have occurred in 1943, with the creation of Grazing District 6, an area set aside for exclusive Hopi use. One hundred Navajo families who had lived in that area for generations were forced to relocate. In 1974, the remainder of the area was partitioned, with each half of the land being placed under the exclusive jurisdiction of each tribe. All Navajo living on the Hopi side of the partition are scheduled for relocation, and Hopi on the Navajo side will also have to relocate. The entire JUA had been occupied mainly by Navajo families. The justification for the partition was that the two "warring groups" needed to be physically separated before fatalities occurred.

In 1973–1974, Hopi tribal rangers arrested and beat up Navajo sheepherders who trespassed on District 6 in order to retrieve their wandering sheep. Navajo herders had put up fences in an attempt to keep their sheep out of the district, but the fences were subsequently torn down by Hopi tribal police. The media portrayed these incidents of violence as range wars; however, investigations by the *Washington Post* found that the "war" had been staged by Evans and Associates, a Salt Lake City public relations firm. Evans and Associates also wrote speeches for the Hopi chairman and had as one of its clients WEST, a consortium of utilities whose grand electric plan included strip mining of coal in the JUA.[26]

The partition of land and relocation were regarded by some as the only way to settle a long-standing dispute over land between two conflicting tribes. Many residents of Black Mesa perceive the land dispute as an issue manufactured by the Peabody Coal Company and implemented by Hopi tribal council officials. While lawmakers and tribal council officials state that there is no connection among the partition line, forced relocation, and coal mining, documents have been submitted by the Hopi tribe that indicate an interest in developing coal in the partition area.[27]

A handful of Navajo people and their Hopi supporters are attempting to stop relocation and what they perceive to be the destruction of Black Mesa, an area considered sacred by both peoples. As early as 1971, Hopi people began to oppose mining operations there. A lawsuit was filed, and a coalition of Hopi, Navajo, environmentalists, and other concerned citizens formed to reach out to the local, national, and international communities.[28] Unfortunately, the lawsuit failed. Despite the beginning of forced relocation, a building freeze, and selective stock reductions for residents of the JUA, the struggle continues.

Elderly Navajo women and their families have stood in front of bulldozers, torn down fences, turned away government officials, and been thrown in jail. Traditional Hopi religious leaders have revealed portions of their sacred teachings in support of their Navajo neighbors and in an attempt to stop the strip mining.[29] Indigenous groups worldwide, community groups throughout the United States, and international solidarity and environmental groups continue to provide material support, to send financial and legal aid, and to lobby their governments to pressure the U.S. government to reconsider relocation as livestock reductions and loss of land bring about starvation conditions for those who choose to stay. The Navajo and Hopi peoples who oppose strip mining have not "won the battle." They have, however, repeatedly extended deadlines for relocation. As a result, the debate over the rights of indigenous people to democratic sovereignty regarding development, assimilation, and religious freedom has been brought to the attention of the national and international public.

Recently, the debate has expanded to include discussions of diminishing water supplies on the reservation and transformation of the Black Mesa ecosystem. The movement, storage, and outflow of surface and subsurface water will be changed as thousands of acres of earth are strip-mined to a depth of 250 feet. Not only will native vegetation be removed from the direct mining site, but off-site vegetation, which has adapted to fluctuations of the water cycle in the arid and semiarid desert region, may also be affected.

The possible disruption of the hydrologic cycle limits the survival options for the Navajo and Hopi peoples, as well as development plans of both tribes. In addition, emissions from coal-fired generation plants in the Four Corners region degrade the visual quality of the Grand Canyon and spew ash and pollution into the upper reaches of the atmosphere.[30] Present plans for reclaiming the land have major social and cultural implications, as rights and access to land will become regulated by the state rather than by customary use.

Neither tribal protest nor international public outcry, however, has significantly changed the plans of the multinational corporations, government agencies, or tribal councils. For example, in July 1990, at the request of Hopi and Navajo tribal council leaders, Secretary of the Interior Manuel Lujan opposed OSMRE recommendations and decided not to approve Peabody's extended mining permit. However, also at the urging of tribal council leaders, Lujan granted Peabody a temporary permit to continue operation of the present strip mine and slurry line.[31] It appears as if the council leaders do not want the government to issue a blanket approval of the operation, nor do they want a complete moratorium on strip mining or use of water for coal slurry transportation. This is because royalties from mineral resource extraction continue to be a major source of income for the Navajo and Hopi nations.[32] The contradiction between long-term survival and maintenance of resources for future generations and the need to generate income for tribal council budgets becomes a painful battleground, where tribal members are in conflict with each other and with their neighboring tribe.

THE TRIPLE ALLIANCE

In his book *Dependent Development,* Peter Evans examines the interrelationship of foreign capital, local capital, and the state in building an industrialized economy. He describes the process whereby international capital became "an integral part of the domestic Brazilian economy and the representatives of international capital . . . an integral part of the Brazilian political and social order."[33] Evans describes a split between the masses, who do not benefit from industrialization, and the elite, who do. The elite are actively involved in the decision-making process of accumulation and distribution, whereas the masses are not involved and for the most part do not have a "legitimate political voice."[34] While much of the analysis is specific only to Brazil, Evans's description of the "triple alliance" may help to elucidate the socioeconomic and political mechanisms that have allowed the strip mining of Black Mesa to continue despite vigorous protests by reservation residents. Of particular interest is Evans's argument that "it is unlikely that foreign capital would have sponsored industrialization on its own without continual stimulation and pressure from the local elite."[35]

On Black Mesa, Peabody, the state, and the Navajo and Hopi tribal councils form a triple alliance. Singly and together, each of these social actors has a stake in mineral development. Peabody will be allowed to mine coal and continue making profits; the state will be guaranteed a supply of fuel for the generation of electricity as well as for export commodities; and tribal council officials will be assured high incomes and sources of revenue for council-approved and council-funded projects. What is equally clear as well is that "the gap separating the local capitalists [in this case, the tribal council] who are able to play a role in shaping the process of accumulation from those who are not in a position to do so grows."[36]

THE PEABODY COAL COMPANY

In 1883, Francis Peabody bought a horse and began a coal delivery service in Chicago. Within two years, wholesale coal operations were begun; by 1901, the company was operating four mines; and by 1928, Peabody had purchased six large mines in Illinois and held long-term contracts to supply utilities with coal. Production peaked shortly after World War II, only to crash in 1953. A 1955 merger with Sinclair Coal Company of Missouri provided new capital and access to the largest strip mine in the country. All that remained of the old Peabody operation was the name.

By 1963, Peabody Coal Company was the number one U.S. producer of coal. Kennecott Copper Company bought Peabody in 1968, only to have the Federal Trade Commission (FTC) order its sale. In 1977, a consortium of six companies bought Peabody: Newmont Mining, The Williams Companies, Bechtel Investments, Boeing, the Equitable Life Assurance Society, and Fluor. At this time, Peabody was described as a "high-cost producer with far too many low-profit, long-term contracts." A onetime Exxon executive, Robert Quenon, was hired, and a program that "ruthlessly pursued lower costs" was implemented.[37] In 1983, Fluor sold its share to the other companies. In 1989, high profits from coal leases led executives of Newmont to look to Peabody (of which it owned a 49 percent interest) as a way to pay for costs incurred while Newmont fought a hostile takeover by a corporate raider, Texas oil magnate T. Boone Pickens.[38] Continued financial woes left Newmont one choice: to sell its stake in Peabody to a British mining conglomerate, Hanson PLC.[39]

The coal industry has been undergoing a major restructuring process that has resulted in the concentration of ownership. While at one time a coal-supplying company could depend on long-term contracts with utility companies, recently many utilities have turned to the "spot market" in order to fill fuel needs. In 1987, an article in the industry journal, *Coal Age,* said:

> While the loss of companies is regrettable, a restructured coal industry will be better able to deal with the nation's energy needs over the long term. . . . Larger companies can better deal with the environmental issues already at hand and can also better raise the capital necessary to prepare for a rising long-term trend in usage and production. By the same token, larger and better capitalized industry members will have a greater financial strength for weathering over short-term swings in demand and prices . . . [and] will be able to take advantage of stock and bond markets for underwriting capital projects.[40]

Peabody's history confirms that concentration within the coal industry is occurring. It was the fear of such concentration that inspired the FTC to order Kennecott to sell Peabody. Twelve years later, Peabody is again a one-owner corporation—only this time as one of the many assets of a British-based international conglomerate.

THE STATE

The federal government has been actively promoting the development of domestic sources of coal reserves in the West since the

1950s. In 1964, WEST proposed what was called the "Grand Plan." The "entire Southwest was to be arranged into a power grid," with the "infrastructural development costs largely underwritten by tax dollars." This grid was to include coal-fired generation plants, dams, nuclear reactors, and transmission lines.[41] Government support for this project was enthusiastic. In 1968, the secretary of the interior had become "a direct financial participant" in the Navajo plant, one of the "WEST six."

The Persian Gulf crisis was a rallying point for a renewed call for energy independence. Energy proposals by the Bush administration promoted coal and clean coal technologies as the best source of fuel for production of electricity. The Bush administration and the coal industry assumed that the Clean Air Act Amendments of 1990, which require that sulfur dioxide emissions be decreased by 1995, can be met by increasing mining and use of steam coal for generation of electricity. It is estimated that one-eighth of U.S. coal-fired generation plants will shift to supplies of coal that is low in sulfur content. Thus, the use of low-sulfur coal becomes more profitable as environmental standards rise. The geography of the coal industry in the United States also will shift to areas where low-sulfur deposits are located.[42]

Switching sources of coal may help to alleviate some types of pollution; however, other costs to the environment undoubtedly will increase, such as the current conflict over water and land rights in the Black Mesa region. Present strategies for the use of low-sulfur coal legitimate centralized corporate, federal, and tribal council planning, production, and regulation of coal and electricity. In short, neither Peabody's nor Bush's plans, nor those of the Hopi or Navajo councils, include democratic decision making in order to sustain the people or the ecology of the region.

TRIBAL COUNCILS

Energy corporations have been involved in Navajo politics since 1921, when a vast oil field was discovered by Standard Oil on reservation land. In order to gain access to that resource, the corporation persuaded the Bureau of Indian Affairs (BIA) "to come up with some 'chiefs' to sign the leases. The five Navajo who cooperated were given a semblance of dignity by being appointed as a 'tribal council.' "[43] The "Navajo tribal council" had virtually no political power. "It met only at the call of the BIA Commissioner and its members could be removed by the Secretary of Interior. The only power it appeared to have, the power to approve leases, was ceded to the Commissioner in its first session."[44]

A complete restructuring of all Native American reservations was initiated under the auspices of the Tribal Reorganization Act of 1934. Reservations nationwide were offered "some control of their own affairs and the right to own land communally" if a tribal council and tribal structure were set up. After the 1934 reorganization act, traditional Native American political systems and decision making went unacknowledged by the United States government.

Tribal council systems became the only federally recognized legitimate representatives of Native American policy and transactions. This "reorganization brought about a situation through which U.S. developmental policies could/can be implemented through a formalized agency composed of the Indians themselves."[45] In many respects, tribal governments operate as do corporate boards, with the tribal councils acting as "representatives of the Indian 'landowners,' and tribal attorneys acting as their agents." Decisions are made by these representatives over the entire resource base of the reservation, without their necessarily sharing the benefits that result from the decisions.

While many tribal council officials may sincerely be working toward the betterment of the entire reservation, the behavior of others is very suspect. For example, former chairman of the Navajo Council Peter MacDonald and his son, Rocky, were recently charged with and convicted of extortion and accepting kickbacks from private businesses.[46]

Actions undertaken by Navajo tribal council officials and family members may contradict the needs and desires of reservation residents themselves. One of the facts that came out of the MacDonald trial was that the younger MacDonald had been hired for $6,000 per month by Paul Wood "to try to obtain a site on the reservation to build a $40 million hazardous waste incinerator." While Rocky MacDonald was looking for a toxic waste incineration site, residents in the Navajo reservation community of Dilkon discovered that Waste Tech, a Colorado-based company and subsidiary of AMOCO Oil, wanted to build a toxic waste incinerator on the reservation. A community group was formed; group members educated themselves and the rest of the community about the dangers of the incinerator and toxic waste dumping. This self-education effort was successful in that the Navajo kicked Waste Tech and other toxic waste companies off the reservation.[47]

A tribal council was also set up for the Hopi people in 1934. Hopi council officials face similar types of decisions and enjoy similar privileges as do Navajo tribal officials. For example, the only beneficiaries of Grazing District 6, an area created for exclusive Hopi use and occupancy in 1943, were the Sepaquaptewa family and their followers.[48]

While the U.S. government and international corporations recognize tribal councils as the legitimate and only representatives of Native American people, many reservation residents do not and have not from the beginning. In fact, a traditional Hopi political structure continues to operate alongside the "legitimate" council. Marilyn Harris, an elder who represents the traditional Hopi of the Second Mesa, recently stated: "We're glad to see the elected [tribal] government trying to protect our water. But these governments don't represent the Hopi people, and if they hadn't allowed mining in the first place, our water wouldn't be in danger now."[49]

Many Navajo feel that the government and the tribal council officials have betrayed traditional Navajo spiritual and cultural beliefs. Roberta Blackgoat, in the Declaration of Independence of the Independent Dine Nation at Big Mountain, stated that the "U.S. government and the Navajo Tribal Council have violated the sacred laws of the Dine Nation. . . . They have divided the Indigenous people by boundaries of politics, Euro-American education, modernization and Christianity. The U.S. denies our rights to exist as Indigenous people on Mother Earth."[50]

The Navajo have resisted being removed from the lands that Peabody, the state, and the Hopi tribal council wished to strip-mine. A moratorium on forced relocation was implemented in 1986, and the Relocation Commission was dissolved. Two years later, during an October 1988 meeting between Peabody officials and Hopi tribal council members, a plan that would involve the strip mining of an additional 54,000 acres on reservation land was confirmed. However, without the relocation of as many as 9,500 Navajo, the plans of Peabody and the Hopi tribal council would have gone unrealized.[51] Then, in 1989, Arizona senator John McCain pushed a bill through Congress that quickly became public law. The Relocation Commission was reactivated, with the mandate that relocation be completed by the end of 1993.[52] With relocation completed, the Black Mesa coal deposits could then become an integral part of the steam coal export market to Japan.

Nevertheless, the Navajo continue to resist leaving Black Mesa. Roberta Blackgoat, a seventy-five-year-old elder, says:

> If they come and drag us all away from the land, it will destroy our way of life. That is genocide. If they leave me here, but take away my community, it is still genocide. If they wait until I die and then mine the land, the land will still be destroyed. If there is no land and no community, I have nothing to leave my grandchildren. If I accept this, there will be no Dine, there will be no land. . . . I will die fighting this law.[53]

For many of the Navajo who have chosen the option of moving from their customary use lands, relocation benefits have not been forthcoming. As of 1990, there were 700 Navajo refugee families. These families have applied for relocation benefits; many have been declared eligible to receive housing, yet some have been waiting as long as eleven years for promised benefits.[54] Furthermore, the new lands sit on a radioactive spill site, where the water contains radioactive materials. Reduction of livestock continues once the relocatees move to the new lands. Lack of acreage for their flocks, and bills, which were never a part of life on Black Mesa, cause many Navajo relocatees to go broke and become homeless.

Throughout the 1980s, the Reagan and Bush administrations' national energy strategies were very explicit about increasing exports of coal and coal technologies. Predictions were made of dramatic increases in the capacity of coal-fired electric generation facilities of the Pacific Rim nations by the year 2000. The Bush administration wanted to ensure that the United States had a share of this emerging multibillion-dollar market. The Department of Energy (DOE) was instructed to set up initiatives specifically for the coal export market. The DOE researched the ways in which U.S. industry could work with export trading companies to expand the market share in coal and clean coal technologies. Of course, what these plans rarely discuss, much less emphasize, are the ecological and cultural losses that will result from such policies, as well as the undemocratic political-economic processes that will be encouraged by the strip mining of Black Mesa.

COAL MINING AND CONFLICTS OVER
WATER ON BLACK MESA

Some indigenous peoples of the American Southwest say that the Kachinas come dancing down from the mountains, bringing with them precious rainfall. The Kachinas are also known to emerge from the depths of the earth bearing gifts of water. Hydrologists from the Office of Surface Mining Reclamation and Enforcement (OSMRE) and the U.S. Geological Survey (USGS) confirm what the Navajo and Hopi have known for centuries. The headwaters of Moenkopi Wash flow with water on a seasonal basis, depending on precipitation and/or snowmelt. The lower portion of Moenkopi Wash flows with water on a continuous basis because its base flow is fed by two main sources: discharge from an underground aquifer, which geologists have named the N-aquifer, and discharge from the alluvial aquifers. Base flow does not include direct surface runoff resulting from snowmelt or precipitation, but surface runoff is an important source of recharge to the alluvial aquifer.

The N-aquifer is one of the main sources of water in the Black Mesa area. It consists of three formations and exists under confined conditions in the central part of the region. In 1965, the aquifer was in equilibrium: the amount of water flowing into it was equal to the amount flowing out. However, from 1976 to 1979, Peabody withdrew approximately 3,700 acre-feet per year. In addition, community withdrawals of water amounted to approximately 2,000 acre-feet per year. As a result of a combination of these withdrawals, water levels in the aquifer have declined.[55]

The major use of N-aquifer water in the Peabody coal-mining operation on Black Mesa is for transportation of coal via slurry lines. The federal government, along with coal associations and pipeline companies, has been promoting coal slurry pipelines as the most efficient way to transport coal since 1979. However, conflicts over the use of federal eminent domain and questions about water rights have left only one coal slurry pipeline in operation today: the Black Mesa Pipeline.

Water for the slurry line was negotiated by Peabody with the Navajo tribe in a separate lease when the coal leases were signed in the 1960s. Peabody officials and agency representatives from the USGS and the OSMRE state that depletion of the aquifer will occur, with, however, only minimal impact to water users on Black Mesa.[56] It is claimed that water levels will return to prepumping levels fifteen years after mining and pumping have ceased.

One area of major controversy is the impact that Peabody mining operations may have on Hopi water supplies. For example, the Hopi town of Moenkopi is located 70 miles from the mining site. For the first time in many Hopis' memories, Moenkopi Wash has dried up. To many Hopi, traditional and progressive alike, this is perceived as a direct result of Peabody's operations. The controversy surrounding this issue is very heated.

The Office of Surface Mining Reclamation and Enforcement was required by federal law to conduct an assessment of the cumulative impact that strip mining and water withdrawals for coal transport would have on water availability and quality. The original cumulative hydrologic impact assessment (CHIA) predicted that the threshold value for base flow material damage in Moenkopi Wash at Moenkopi would be 2.40 cubic feet per second (cfs). Threshold values are flows that maintain the system. If base water flows drop below this value, the water system can be adversely affected. Theoretically, damage to the water flow would not occur as long as the baseline water flow did not drop below 2.40 cfs. However, after the report was published, it was discovered that a typing error had been made: the revised threshold value is 0.94 cfs. While the figures indicate that material damage will most likely occur if flow goes below these threshold levels, the OSMRE asserts that mining and water withdrawals for slurry lines can occur with minimal damage. The OSMRE stated that if water flow or quality does decrease, it will be the result of drought and of water uses other than those related to mining. The Hopi tribal council was not convinced. A consulting firm, HydroGeoChem, was hired to conduct a private analysis of the system. HydroGeoChem calculated a value of 0.0 cfs, which could mean that any withdrawals from the N-aquifer system may degrade flow at Moenkopi.[57]

Most of the attention is directed toward impacts associated with withdrawals from the N-aquifer; however, other impacts to surface water flows, and to other aquifers, may also occur from the mining operations. The bulk of the strip-mining operation has occurred and will continue to occur in the headwaters of Moenkopi Wash, as well as in one portion of the upper watershed of Dinnebito Wash. Other ways in which strip mining of coal can affect surface and underground water are through pollution, diversion, and depletion. The acids that are a by-product of coal mining and processing may leach into any one of a number of the underground aquifers in the region and also may contaminate surface water. In addition, chemicals used as explosives may also pose problems to surface water; chemicals caused the death of eighty-six sheep in the Black Mesa area in June 1989.[58] The capacity of the water to drain into, or discharge from, various aquifers may be disrupted when places of recharge and discharge are dug up or blown up during strip-mining operations.

Water not only is stored deep underground in various aquifers but also can be found in the alluvium of washes and intermittent streams. The alluvium is recharged through direct precipitation and by discharges from the underground aquifers. Alluvial aquifers in the mining area will be dug up and eliminated. Recharge of the alluvial aquifer from surface runoff events may also be affected.

The Wepo formation contains the coal that will be mined; hence, it will be destroyed. Wells, seeps, springs, and discharges to the alluvium and washes associated with the Wepo aquifer in the mine area may dry up. Some of the washes that are tributaries to Moenkopi Wash carry small, intermittent flows that may derive from Wepo discharge. In addition, open or reclaimed mining pits might cause the dewatering of nearby wells in the Wepo formation. Also expected are depletion of some spring flows and accumulation of water with high mineral content in certain areas.[59] Another indirect impact from the mining operations regards the interaction between surface and subsurface water flows and wild vegetation. The maintenance of historically consistent water table fluctuations is necessary for the survival of vegetation that grows along the banks of the washes and arroyos. The importance of this vegetation in maintaining erosion control is often overlooked: a drop in the water table or a decrease in surface flow for even a relatively short time could cause the wild vegetation to suffer further stress from desiccation, eventually leading to death. Without the vegetation, the soil along the banks would be washed out during rainstorms. This would not only add to the sediment load downstream but also contribute to flash floods. Thus, the quality and quantity of surface water can be potentially affected by the loss of vegetation along the washes.

Currently, Navajo and Hopi people are upset because wells and springs in the area are drying up. They feel that this is due to withdrawals by Peabody for the slurry line.[60] Peabody and the USGS join the OSMRE in claiming that changes to water at Moenkopi and in many other areas will be due to drought conditions and community usage of water. There is no denying the fact that climatic conditions are a very important variable in this region. In 1992, the governor of Arizona declared Black Mesa a national disaster area because of drought conditions and the drying up of domestic water sources.

But many residents of Black Mesa firmly believe that the drying up of springs and wells is a direct result of Peabody pumping water from the N-aquifer. It is true that cycles of drought are a part of the area. Navajo elders remember droughts—and springs that continued to flow despite years of low precipitation, springs that have recently dried up. To many of these people, the cessation in water flow correlates with the time when Peabody began mining operations.

Water attracts water; this is the belief of some traditional Hopi. Western scientists still cannot explain many of the intricate details that make up the water cycle of the Black Mesa region. Perhaps scientists may never be able to explain fully the dynamic interactions of climate, geomorphology, and vegetation that create the ebb and flow of water in that area. The debate among experts in different agencies continues, yet the consequences of depleting water resources or transforming the mechanisms that maintain the hydrologic cycle in this desert ecosystem can be problematic. Peabody Coal Company admits that wells and springs in the direct path of the strip-mining operation will be destroyed. It promises replacement of water through the drilling of new wells that tap the N-aquifer. Should the levels of other springs, seeps, and washes drop, water will have to come from deep wells, thus confining livestock and their caretakers to one specified area, as opposed to an open territory with cultural significance.

"To plant corn in semi desert country, one must use the same earth only every other year, and sometimes the holes in which kernels are sown must be very deep, in order to reach moisture."[61] The Navajo and Hopi have developed forms of farming that best utilize the small amounts of water that the desert region offers. These traditional dryland farming techniques could become obsolete if water tables drop or if mechanisms of alluvial recharge are interrupted.

To the traditional Hopi and Navajo, water, as it appears on the earth in the form of springs, is a source of sustenance not only for the body but also for the spirit. Water from wells pumped by electric motors cannot hold the spiritual significance associated with natural water outflows. The transformation and/or depletion of water supplies in the Black Mesa area constitute an assault on traditional ways of living. In addition, survival strategies for those reservation residents who are underemployed and who must supplement their income by gathering wild food, by growing traditional foods, and by raising livestock will be limited. Indigenous people who choose to practice an inherited way of life will be further denied their heritage. This cultural tradition embodies an ecological ethic, one that seeks not to control or dominate sources of water but rather to understand the natural rhythms and live by accepting them.

If the Black Mesa–Kayenta Mine permit is approved and the Hopi and Navajo councils agree, mining will continue until 2034. Peabody and the Black Mesa Pipeline Company will have primary rights to the surface and underground water on Black Mesa for the next four decades. Navajo and Hopi who rely on the various wells, seeps, springs, and base flows associated with the N-aquifer, as well as other aquifer and surface water flows on Black Mesa, will have secondary rights to that water.

CONCLUSION

Just as the sun supplies energy to plants, which are then able to manufacture chlorophyll and provide food for themselves and grazers and predators, coal supplies electricity, which is used to manufacture a myriad of items that constitute the "food" of industrial society. Concentration of ownership, expansion of markets, and accumulation of capital have led to the internationalization of capital; a corporation can extract a resource in one place, process the resource in another, manufacture goods in still another, assemble the product in yet a different region, and market the product all over the globe. Increasing the production of electricity is perceived as "progress" and necessary for the expansion of a "healthy economy." Global concern about pollution demands a supply of fuel that is least harmful to the environment. Coal that is low in sulfur content has been targeted as the way to deliver society from the ill effects of air pollution and global warming yet allow the economies of industrial society to continue expanding.

Along with sunlight, water is necessary for survival on this planet. Water supplies cycle through various mechanisms. If these mechanisms are transformed or destroyed, the ability of water to recharge and discharge in a specific area will be interrupted, resulting in changes in water supply. Various societies throughout time have developed systems to cope with fluctuations in water. Some, like the current population of Los Angeles, pipe water for hundreds of miles in order to ensure an abundant supply. Other societies, such as the traditional Hopi and Navajo, have learned to live within a local cycle of water.

Reserves of low-sulfur coal lie just barely under the surface in the Navajo and Hopi reservation lands. Internationally focused American capital, in the form of Peabody Coal Company and its corporate owner, Hanson PLC, wants access to those reserves in order to make profits selling the coal to utilities in the United States and Japan. A triple alliance between an international corporation (Peabody), the state (the BIA, the OSMRE, the USGS, and the Reagan and Bush administrations), and an indigenous elite (the Hopi and Navajo tribal councils) created a situation in which mineral reserves on reservation land were exploited despite the opposition of residents of the reservations.

The triple alliance benefits its partners at the expense of members of the Hopi and Navajo nations who are not involved or who consciously choose not to participate in the process of deciding how capital is accumulated and distributed. The extraction of coal and its transport via the slurry pipeline on Black Mesa accelerates the expansion of capital outside the region while disrupting the cycle of water within the region. As surface and underground water supplies are polluted, depleted, diverted, transformed, or destroyed, seeps and springs may dry up. The source of water then becomes a well, which requires electricity for pumping and pipes for distribution.

People who have chosen to live within the delicate cycle of water in the desert region of the Southwest will be unable to continue doing so. A way of life in which the individual, clan, or village has some degree of autonomy and control outside the capitalist sector will disappear—and with it, say the Hopi, the balance that maintains life as we know it on this planet.

The struggle on Black Mesa over land use and water rights continues. The latest episode involves the Hopi tribal council issuing lease agreements to Navajo residents on Black Mesa. These agreements have come about through mediations due to a lawsuit filed in 1992 by a Navajo family. Many residents feel that the lawyer misrepresented their case and signed the wording for the lease agreement without consulting them. Resistors to relocation see four flaws of this settlement agreement: (1) secrecy of the negotiating process; (2) divisions between traditional and tribal councils; (3) inadequacy in terms of the number of home sites that will be leased (150), their size (13 acres each), terms of occupancy (payments), and minimum age (sixty-five); and (4) lopsidedness in favor of the Hopi tribal council. Conditions of the lease agreements make it almost impossible for traditional Navajo people to continue living in the area even if they sign these agreements. They will be unable to cut green wood, have overnight visitors, or hunt.

Some traditional Hopi people, in addition to protesting the forced relocation of the traditional Navajo on Black Mesa, are also attempting to halt water development projects and electrification of the traditional village of Hotevilla. Research into the effects of community- and mine-related withdrawals of water from the N-aquifer continues, as does research into the interaction between surface and subsurface waters.

While the lawyers and tribal council officials haggle over the terms of the lease agreements and relocation procedures, traditional Navajo women from Black Mesa continue weaving rugs from the wool of the sheep they have raised, many of these sheep being descendants of sheep that their great-grandmothers raised. The rugs are displayed and sold nationwide, generating direct income for these women. A permaculture project has been initiated on Big Mountain in an attempt to recharge depleted aquifers in the area, halt erosion, and create more available arable land for farming.

For more information and to send donations, contact the Big Mountain Dineh Nation, P. O. Box 1042, Hotevilla, AZ 86030.

9

California's Endangered Communities of Color

JANE KAY

California has often been portrayed as a haven for progressive environmentalism. Environmental groups thrive all across the "Golden State." Each year, new rounds of environmentally oriented propositions are placed on the ballot for Californians to vote up or down.

Although the state is a leader in controlling pesticides, toxic lead, offshore oil drilling, energy inefficiency, and dirty cars, California has failed to address environmental disparities that exist between its Anglo communities and communities of color. This chapter examines some of these differences and the strategies that local grassroots organizers are using to level the playing field.

Nobody wants to live or work in a toxic environment. Even small amounts of chemicals released into the environment and the workplace—scientists still debate how much—can cause cancer or reproductive, nerve, and respiratory damage. But as the nation's need to put the waste somewhere grows, more U.S. corporations are moving into impoverished communities where people's need for jobs surpasses concern for a clean environment. Evidence is plentiful of disproportionate, and unhealthy, pockets of pollution in communities of color.

CALIFORNIA'S "DIRTIEST" COMMUNITIES

Dozens of communities of color in California, and hundreds across the country, are now actively involved in environmental issues and are saying no to the toxic waste incinerators, the dumps, and the poisonous air and water. They call the trend to put America's waste in communities of color "eco-racism" and say that mainstream environmental groups, in part, are to blame because many have been slow to take on these fights, concentrating instead on resource and preservation issues.

Ironically, one of the first communities in California to rebel was South Central Los Angeles. When the city tried to build a state-of-the-art municipal solid waste incinerator in the neighborhood in 1985, residents fought back.[1] After hearings, marches, and political pressure, the proposal was defeated by Robin Cannon and her neighbors, who had formed Concerned Citizens of South Central Los Angeles, a grass-roots environmental group made up of African American women.

After the city failed to win a garbage burner in South Central, a private company sought approval for a hazardous waste incinerator a few miles away, in Vernon. In an unusual alliance of African American and Latino American communities, Concerned Citizens joined with Mothers of East Los Angeles, an activist group born in a Catholic church in East Los Angeles, and sued the government. In March 1991, they won and brought to a halt plans to build the incinerator.

"It was the first time the African American and Latino communities had come together on a common interest," said Juanita Tate, a South Central organizer. "We think they dump on minority communities because they feel no one's out there."

Amazingly enough, the state's most toxic zip code region lies within Vernon, wedged between South Central and East Los Angeles.[2] This 1-square-mile section of Los Angeles County—zip code 90058—is dotted with waste dumps, smokestacks, and wastewater pipes from polluting industries. Here, eighteen big manufacturers in 1989 discharged 33 million pounds of waste chemicals into the environment, as much as that generated the year before in the San Francisco Bay Area and five times the amount in the next-worst zip code region, which lies in Orange County.

Environmental justice activists say that it is no accident that zip code 90058, where the population is 59 percent African American and 38 percent Latino American, is the state's "dirtiest." It is just one example, they say, of a newly recognized form of discrimination, a toxic racism.

A full year before Los Angeles erupted in violence triggered by the Rodney King verdict, longtime South Central resident and organizer Juanita Tate warned: "We've got no drug rehabilitation centers, no treatment center, no jobs, no programs to upgrade the falling population between 35 and 40 years old. But we've got toxic industries and 75 percent of the prisons here in South Central."

California's dirtiest zip code was discovered in April 1991 during research conducted by the *San Francisco Examiner* according to zip code and ethnicity under the federal Community Right to Know Act, which requires the largest manufacturers to report a portion of toxic discharges.[3] The *Examiner*'s researchers found that the industrial zone and surrounding communities of color of South Central and East Los Angeles, Watts, Compton, Huntington Park, and Bell Gardens have more than their share of the state's industrial chemical emitters.

Spewing from zip code 90058 were, among other chemicals, 380 tons of 1,1,1-trichloroethane, a chlorinated solvent that can depress the nervous system; 28.7 tons of lead, a potent toxicant impairing intelligence, behavior, and growth, especially in the developing young; and 1.5 tons of methylene chloride, a solvent that can cause memory loss and respiratory damage and is a suspected carcinogen.

Juana Gutiérrez, a mother of five and a founder of Mothers of East Los Angeles, said: "They wanted to put everything here: a prison, a pipeline, and an incinerator. I guess they didn't realize the community has awakened. We no longer sit back and let ourselves be manipulated."

Because of these cases, when Congresswoman Lucille Roybal-Allard, a Democrat from Los Angeles, was in the California assembly,

Los Angeles: California's "Dirtiest" County
County with greatest concentration of major polluting industries,
broken down by ZIP Code.

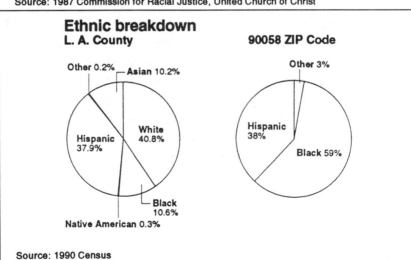

South Central
Los Angeles

Watts

East
Los
Angeles

Los Angeles
International
Airport

ZIP Code
90058
See Profile
on facing
page

Area of detail

CALIFORNIA

Los Angeles

Long Beach

Pacific Ocean

⬤ Uncontrolled toxic waste sites
(number of sites included)

▤ 50% or greater
Hispanic population

▥ 20–49%
Hispanic population

Source: 1987 Commission for Racial Justice, United Church of Christ

Ethnic breakdown
L. A. County

Other 0.2% — Asian 10.2%

White
40.8%

Hispanic
37.9%

Black
10.6%

Native American 0.3%

90058 ZIP Code

Other 3%

Hispanic
38%

Black 59%

Source: 1990 Census

TABLE 9.1
PROFILE OF 90058, CALIFORNIA'S DIRTIEST ZIP CODE*
(Zone 6 on map on p. 158)

• LOCATION: Wedged between South Central and East Los Angeles, the state's largest Hispanic and Black neighborhoods

• SIZE: Less than 1 square mile

• TOTAL POPULATION: 4,500

• TOTAL DISCHARGES, 1989*: 33 million pounds

• TOTAL DISCHARGES NINE-COUNTY BAY AREA, 1988*: 35 million pounds (for comparative purposes)

Biggest discharges among 18 companies reporting emissions to air, land, water, sewage plants or off-site disposal:

1. Aluminum Co. of America
2. Atlas Galvanizing Co.
3. Chase Packaging Co.
4. Fitrol Corp.
5. GNB Inc.
6. Ivy Hill Acquisition Inc.
7. Jensen Industries
8. NI Industries
9. Oscar Mayer Foods
10. Owens-Brockway Inc.

MAJOR DISCHARGES TO AIR IN 90058

• 1,1,1-TRICHLOROETHANE: 380 tons. Used as a cleaning solvent; can cause mutations in living cells and may damage livers, kidneys and skin.

• LEAD: 28.7 tons. Used in manufacturing and as a gas additive; can cause damage to fetuses, may increase blood pressure, can cause damage to the brain and kidney.

• METHYLENE CHLORIDE: 1.5 tons. Used as industrial solvent and paint stripper; chronic exposure can result in memory loss, high levels cause respiratory irritation, sluggishness, limb tingling and unconsciousness.

• AMMONIA: (A corrosive) 167.1 tons.

• HYDROGEN CHLORIDE: (A corrosive) 18.4 tons.

* Based on discharges to environment of chemicals by largest manufacturing companies; self-reported by manufacturers under Community Right to Know Act, 1986.

Sources: Community Right to Know reports, Western Economic Research Co.

she introduced successful bills in 1991 and 1992 requiring appli-
cants for toxic facilities to present demographics on ethnicity, language, age, and income. Governor Pete Wilson vetoed both bills,
saying that they would place an unnecessary burden on the appli-
cants. The communities lobbied again in 1993.

The fight in ethnic Los Angeles inspired other communities.
Some struggled alone. Many had assistance from such environmen-
tal groups as Greenpeace, California Rural Legal Assistance, the
National Toxics Campaign, Citizens for a Better Environment, the
United Farm Workers, the Catholic church, and the Center for
Third World Organizing.

From the Los Angeles and San Diego ghettos and barrios and San
Joaquin Valley fields, from the Contra Costa County industrial
town of Richmond to Native American lands across the nation, the
pattern is clear: minorities bear the brunt of toxic pollution. The
nation's largest toxic waste dumps and incinerators operate near
their homes in cities and in rural areas. They have the dirtiest jobs.
Their children are exposed every day to pesticides, lead, asbestos,
PCBs, chemical emissions, and hazardous waste.

SAN DIEGO'S BARRIO LOGAN

San Diego's Barrio Logan is starting to clean up the neighborhood,
linking a clean environment with a sound life for the young people.[4]
Social worker Rachel Ortiz directs the Barrio Youth Station, a service center in the 99 percent Latino American community located
beneath hydrocarbon-belching Highway 5, which runs through San
Diego.

"Enough is enough," Ortiz cried in 1990 to a large chemical recycling plant across the alley from the center. After a tough public
hearing, Pacific Treatment agreed to move its 12 million pounds a
year of recycled chemicals. Ortiz works with the Environmental
Health Coalition, which is campaigning for an environmentally
aware city council and new ordinances that provide buffers between residents and dangerous chemicals.

Jose Pacheco, sixty-nine, a member of the San Diego Organizing

San Diego County's "Dirtiest" Communities

Oceanside

Area of detail

San Diego

CALIF.

Escondido

Tierra Santa
Sierra Mesa

La Jolla

Mira Mesa

Linda Vista

El Cajon

Barrio Logan

Spring Valley

National City

Chula Vista

▲ Storage of toxic liquid and solid chemicals

○ Hazardous waste generation

■ Storage of gases on site

● Hazardous waste treatment, storage, and disposal facilities

Top 10 areas for:

Hazardous waste generation
(in millions of pounds)
1. Barrio Logan: **63**
2. Chula Vista: **35**
3. National City: **26**
4. Downtown: **13**
5. Tierra santa/Sierra Mesa: **10**
6. Mira Mesa/Sorrento Valley: **9**
7. Linda Vista: **7**
8. Oceanside: **6**
9. Spring Valley: **6**
10. La Jolla/Pacific Beach: **5**

Toxic liquid and solid chemical storage (in millions of pounds)
1. Downtown: **152**
2. Chula Vista: **89**
3. Barrio Logan: **58**
4. La Jolla: **49**
5. Linda Vista: **33**
6. National City: **13**
7. Escondido: **12**
8. Tierra Santa/Sierra Mesa: **11**
9. Mira Mesa/Sorrento Valley: **11**
10. El Cajon: **10**

Ethnic breakdown

San Diego County

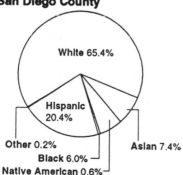

White 65.4%

Hispanic 20.4%

Other 0.2%

Asian 7.4%

Black 6.0%

Native American 0.6%

Barrio Logan

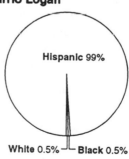

Hispanic 99%

White 0.5%

Black 0.5%

Sources: Environmental Health Coalition, U.S. Bureau of Census, 1990

Project, said: "Children are breathing all this stuff. They should take the houses out, or they should take the factories out. They shouldn't be together."

The barrio, the fast-beating *corazón,* or heart, of San Diego's Mexican American community, is a haven for the biggest toxic waste generators in the county. The old barrio, home to generations of Latino Americans, is part of Southeast San Diego, a larger, mixed-minority sprawl crisscrossed with freeways and historic sites. The streets teem with parents pushing baby strollers. The neighborhood is home to numerous landmark restaurants, such as Chuey's.

In Chicano Park, murals are emblazoned with slogans: "*Varrio, Si—Yonkes, No*" (Barrio, Yes—Junkyards, No) and "*Más Casas— Menos Yonkes*" (More Homes—Fewer Junkyards). San Diego tried to make up for the freeway that halved the old barrio and shut off access to the bay. In 1989, it build a little park at the water's edge. But the park is hardly a nature experience; it is next to fuel storage tanks, and a chain link fence keeps people from the bay because the water is so polluted there.

At its worst, there were "twenty-three major junkyards in Barrio Logan, almost one on every block," Ortiz said. "All of our properties were drenched with oils and battery acids. They leaked out after rains, and dogs would die. Sidewalks turned black and corroded."

A lot of the junk is gone now. But every year, 127 companies in Barrio Logan produce 63 million pounds of chemical waste—one-third of all chemical waste generated in the county, according to a community group's research of federal, state, and local records. Nearly 100 companies in the area's 5 square miles keep hazardous materials on site. And wedged between houses in the neighborhood are a chemical supply house; a plater, with tanks of cyanide; a toxic gas company; and a San Diego Gas and Electric Company power station.

The neighborhood in Barrio Logan changed with the construction of the freeway system in the 1950s. The community was cut in two, recalls Maria Riveroll, whose parents settled there after moving from Mexico. "You couldn't even walk to church." Industry began buying up cheap land. The city and county looked the other way as companies put up concertina wire, stacks of flattened cars, and chemical-rich operations.

The community, glad to have low rent, did not complain. "We didn't have enough education," Pacheco said. And Ortiz added: "They know we don't respond to public hearing notices. We weren't used to dealing with white-man policy."

San Diego's Environmental Health Coalition provided the documentation of Barrio Logan's suspicions: the county's minority neighborhoods had the largest concentrations of toxic materials and hazardous waste.

"The roots of this organization were in communities of color," said Diane Takvorian, who helped found the coalition a dozen years ago. "The first project we ever had was in Southeast San Diego." After years of fighting one hazardous project after another, the people who lived across the street from the toxic facilities wanted an institutional fix, Takvorian said.

In the works is a proposed pioneer zoning ordinance, part of a "Toxics Free Neighborhood" campaign. It would amend current zoning laws to create a buffer between industry and sensitive populations—parks, houses, and schools. Within five years, companies would have to cut the amount of chemicals they use and store on-site and decrease pollution and noise or move out. New ones could not move in.

Meanwhile, before a vote, the city manager has been charged by the San Diego City Council with identifying the key hazardous areas in Barrio Logan and Southeast San Diego. A group of agencies dealing with the environment, workers, and community health is to investigate the worst sites and recommend enforcement action and methods to stop pollution and worker exposure.

Barrio Logan's Ortiz says that urban blight affects children's behavior. "If you want to take away violence, you take away this ugly deterioration around them," she said. Now that action is being taken, "the kids' behavior is 500 times better. You've got to take care of living conditions or the social problems are never going to go away."

Toxics in the City of Richmond

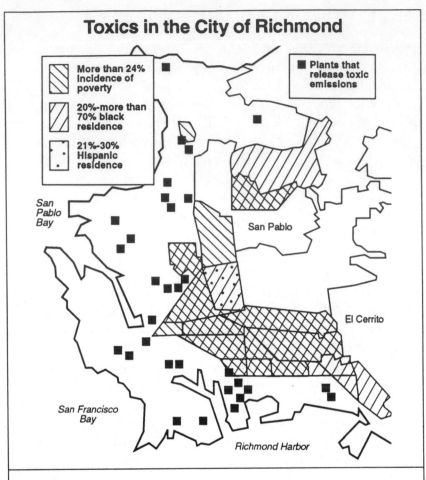

Legend:
- More than 24% incidence of poverty
- 20%-more than 70% black residence
- 21%-30% Hispanic residence
- ■ Plants that release toxic emissions

San Pablo Bay

San Pablo

El Cerrito

San Francisco Bay

Richmond Harbor

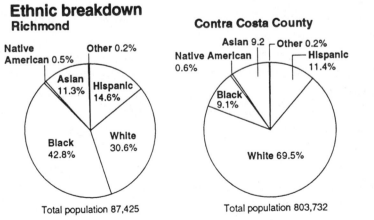

Ethnic breakdown

Richmond

- Native American 0.5%
- Other 0.2%
- Asian 11.3%
- Hispanic 14.6%
- Black 42.8%
- White 30.6%

Total population 87,425

Contra Costa County

- Asian 9.2
- Other 0.2%
- Native American 0.6%
- Hispanic 11.4%
- Black 9.1%
- White 69.5%

Total population 803,732

Sources: 1990 Census, Citizens for a Better Environment

CHEMICAL RISKS IN RICHMOND

In Richmond, the San Francisco Bay Area's most heavily industrialized city, dozens of pesticide, fertilizer, and other chemical companies lie next to lower-income African American and Latino American neighborhoods. In the past five years, the West County Toxics Coalition, an activist group, has changed "business as usual" for the Chevron Corporation and some of the largest corporations in the state.

"It makes no difference whether the industry or the communities came first," said Henry Clark, director of the group. "No planning agency should allow the community to come up so close [to toxic industries]." It ultimately comes down to power. Are the corporations going to exploit the community and use it as a dumping ground? Or will the people who live there be able to exercise their self-determination and hold the industries accountable?

Like Barrio Logan, Richmond is rebelling, organizing against the disproportionate share of pollution it is burdened with. In this city of 87,425 on northern San Francisco Bay, one out of five families lives in poverty. In the fourteen neighborhoods closest to heavy industry, African American residents make up 72 to 94 percent of the population.[5]

In 1986, minority neighborhood activists, angered by the chemicals over North Richmond, formed the West County Toxics Coalition. "We had a toxic cloud coming to us and the jobs going somewhere else. People wanted to be protected," said Henry Clark, director of the coalition.

The coalition uses as ammunition a 1989 report by Citizens for a Better Environment titled *Richmond at Risk*. The report—based on wastewater, air, hazardous waste, and federal Community Right to Know reporting—shows that 350 companies produce hazardous waste in the greater Richmond area and shows a link between racial composition of neighborhoods and location of hazardous waste facilities.[6]

Industry has dominated the area since 1902, when the Standard Oil Company built the first oil refinery. There are now hundreds of manufacturing companies in the area, employing thousands, many of whom live nearby. But, said Clark, "It doesn't make any difference who was here first, us or industry. It just shows us it was the county's fault for not having a buffer zone."

In 1989, nearly 100 large manufacturing companies in Richmond reported 1.7 million pounds of chemical discharges. One of them, Bio-Rad, which manufactures medical equipment, was accused by the state attorney general of releasing into the air as much as 60,000 pounds per year of cancer-causing chloroform near Highway 580 in Richmond.

In March 1991, the company, while not admitting wrongdoing, paid $550,000 for failing to warn under California's Proposition 65, the Safe Water and Toxic Enforcement Act of 1986. The company also paid $150,000 to the Bay Area Air Quality Management District (BAAQMD) for permit violations and agreed to stop using chloroform.

Debate continues over the risk from toxic discharges, and studies by the Environmental Protection Agency show that industrial exposures to neighborhoods are relatively low compared with exposures residents get inside houses and cars. Other studies indicate higher chemical concentrations outside plants. Dr. Wendel Brunner, director of the Contra Costa Health Department, has cautioned that environmental causes are difficult to prove. "There would have to be an eco-disaster to find an environmental problem," he said. "We know these things aren't good for you. You don't have to be a rocket scientist to know they have to be cleaned up."

Residents conducted their own unscientific study by knocking on doors in Parchester Village and other neighborhoods closest to factories and incinerators. They found people who reported cancer, respiratory problems, and skin rashes. Lucille Allen, a teacher who joined the West County Toxics Coalition three years ago, then ran for city council armed with her newfound knowledge, said that people at every other house reported breathing difficulties.

The BAAQMD samples the air in central Richmond twice each month for about a dozen toxic contaminants. "We don't see higher concentrations than we see anyplace else," said toxicologist Pat

Holmes. However, there are no permanent air monitors in North Richmond near two dozen chemical plants or hundreds of others. Nor do the BAAQMD or the state or federal government have standards of toxicity for the poisonous airborne organic discharges that are measured in tons at the stacks by the companies and measured in tumors in laboratory animals by scientists.

In 1990, the West County Toxics Coalition tried to establish "good neighbor agreements," or deadlines for improvements, with the companies, including the largest California company, Chevron, which has five plants and two chemical research facilities in Richmond.[7] Chevron, which grew from the original Standard Oil in the early 1900s, says that it wants to be a good neighbor in Richmond.

"I think these discussions are beneficial," said Jeff Krag, a spokesman for the refinery. "It gives us a perspective that we don't have." Reductions in chemicals are coming from long-term company policy and "simple good business," Krag said, not necessarily as a direct result of neighborhood requests.

Chevron replaced liquefied, pressurized chlorine for cooling water treatment, as a precaution against Bhopal-type accidents. Then the company reduced the size of its ammonia tanks. The citizens' group is now asking for a Chevron-funded community inspector who would serve as a scientific adviser. An example of such an inspector is an independent industrial hygienist who came to the neighborhood a few years ago and recommended some measures that have since been adopted by the Bay Area Air Quality Management District. But Chevron does not think a community inspector is necessary. "We don't believe there is any health risk to our neighbors as a result of our operations," Krag said. Under Proposition 65 reporting requirements, the refinery has found no discharges to the community so far that require a warning.

Richmond is trying to solve its pollution problem by encouraging companies to modernize, voluntarily reduce chemical use, and cut the load to Chevron's toxic waste incinerator. Because Chevron has rejected the community inspector concept, the citizens' group has asked the BAAQMD to make it mandatory, arguing that the people need unbiased technical help because they bear the brunt of the toxic burden. If they get a community inspector, he or she will be the first in the nation.

"We're not going to allow them to get away with disrespecting people and blowing toxic smoke in their faces," Clark said. "We can't just move away. We've got roots here."

On July 26, 1993, a railroad car servicing Richmond's General Chemical Corp., a company which has had repeated violations, ruptured and exploded, spewing an estimated 9,500 gallons of concentrated sulphuric acid into the air. More than 24,000 people were sent to the hospital.

TRIPLE JEOPARDY IN KETTLEMAN CITY

Up close, California reveals every abuse faced by U.S. racial and ethnic minorities in their struggle to keep the country's waste from contaminating their lives. In the rural town of Kettleman City in Kings County, Joe and Esperanza Maya do not want a commercial toxic waste incinerator in their backyard.[8] They already have Chemical Waste Management's huge toxic dump—the largest facility of its kind west of the Mississippi River. Residents are already threatened with the triple jeopardy of poverty, poisoning on their jobs, and risks associated with the nearby hazardous waste landfill. Esperanza Maya, who owns a comfortable house in the 95 percent Latino American farm worker town, sums up her community's feelings: "Our little town is mainly Hispanic. It's a migrant town. We don't always have 1,000 people. It goes up and down. Chem Waste is banking on people migrating in and out for seasonal work. But Chem Waste is finding out differently. When there are new people, we go door to door. We tell them what's going on here, and they tell us stories about their children's chronic colds and fatigue. Chem Waste's started to see that we mean business."

But Chem Waste, the nation's biggest hazardous waste disposal and treatment company, is moving ahead with permits to build a burner here. Joe Maya, a self-made farmer and the first Latino American mayor of the Imperial Valley city of Brawley, says that Chem Waste looks for vulnerable communities when selecting

Polluted Well Water

Results are from sampling reported between July 1989 and June 1990

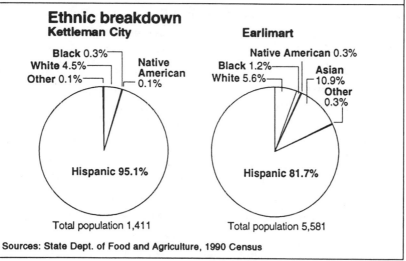

STANISLAUS

■ Townships (36-square mile area) with one or more pesticides detected in well water

MADERA   FRESNO

SANTA CRUZ

Kettleman City

KINGS

Pacific

Ocean

Earlimart

Area of detail

KERN

Ethnic breakdown
Kettleman City

Black 0.3%
White 4.5%
Other 0.1%

Native American 0.1%

Hispanic 95.1%

Total population 1,411

Earlimart

Native American 0.3%
Black 1.2%
White 5.6%
Asian 10.9%
Other 0.3%

Hispanic 81.7%

Total population 5,581

Sources: State Dept. of Food and Agriculture, 1990 Census

burner sites, choosing areas where people are too poor or powerless to fight back.[9]

Sylvia Vickers, a Chem Waste spokeswoman in Kettleman City, says that the sites are chosen because they are environmentally sound, not because of social conditions. Yet the company's three other incinerators are located in poor African American neighborhoods—Chicago's South Side; Sauget, Illinois; and Port Arthur, Texas. Chem Waste also owns the nation's largest hazardous waste disposal and treatment facility, in Emelle, in Alabama's Sumter County, which is nearly 70 percent African American and in which more than one-third of the residents live in poverty. The company has an incinerator plan under development at its Sumter County site. The fifth burner would be built in Kettleman City, where in 1980 the average family income was $13,714.

Chem Waste already has won permission from Kings County and is now seeking state and federal permits. The town is united against the burner. Residents feel that they have taken their share of toxic waste. The landfill, which the Mayas say was sneaked into town in 1979, is the nation's fifth largest and accepts hazardous waste from all over the country. Every day, as many as two hundred 20-ton trucks filled with chemical wastes—including PCBs, benzene, and asbestos—pass 4 miles from the heart of town.

It is the same pattern all over the country, say environmental justice activists. People too busy working for a living do not see the legal notices, usually printed only in English, do not know what facilities are coming their way. "The first we knew that Chem Waste was here was when a company official came to the Rotary Club meeting in Avenal after they got all the permits," Joe Maya said. "They kept it quiet. Some people didn't know it was there until they smelled it."

But Steve Drew, formerly with Chem Waste and now a Bechtel community relations representative, said that back then, "toxics weren't an issue. Now people ask why they weren't told." Drew said he was surprised at how few people in Kettleman City knew that Chem Waste had a hazardous waste facility there. His job was to publicize the hearings for additional permits.

"We took out display ads in the papers and were disappointed at the low turnout. There wasn't interest at the time," Drew said. Yet Drew himself represents another pattern faced by small communities: he is among those regulators who leave agencies to work for better-paying industry jobs. The community protectors become community foes.

Drew came to Chem Waste from the EPA Superfund program's community relations office in 1985, at a time when the company was seeking additional EPA landfill permits. In 1990, Charles White, then chief of the San Joaquin permit branch of the state Toxic Substances Control Department, retired to accept the job of Chem Waste lobbyist in Sacramento.

The next year, James Breitlow, head of permits within the EPA's hazardous wastes division, was hired by Chem Waste when it was attempting to expand significantly the Kettleman landfill. California Rural Legal Assistance, which provides legal assistance for farm workers, filed conflict of interest charges against Breitlow with the EPA and the inspector general. In 1992, a hearing panel ruled that Breitlow had properly separated himself from direct decisions on the Chem Waste permit, and Breitlow was cleared of charges of any wrongdoing.

"It's a whole pattern in itself," said Esperanza Maya. "We're supposed to trust our government. They're supposed to listen to us. They say they are. Then they turn around and give the permit. Then they go work for the person they give the permit to. That's not right. That's terrible. We're small; by the time we find out, it's already happened."

Chem Waste's record is mixed. Chemicals have leaked into the groundwater. Spokeswoman Vickers said that the company believes the pollution occurred before the landfills were lined under current regulations. "So there won't be any long-term harm done, we're removing the water," Vickers said.

In 1985, the company was fined $3.5 million by the Environmental Protection Agency and the state for faulty record keeping and other violations. The company claims to have a good worker safety record. "We're affected daily where we live," Esperanza

Maya said. "We have the largest landfill in our backyard, with 200 trucks or more coming in a day. Do you think that's not being affected?"

When she and others go door to door and talk to seasonal workers, she said, "they tell us that when they leave and go back to Mexico for two or three months, they feel much better. Here, their children have chronic colds, nosebleeds, coughs, and rashes. We don't have a doctor who can diagnose us if we're being affected. It just scares me that Chem Waste can get away with it."

In February 1991, El Pueblo para el Aire y Agua Limpio, or People for Clean Air and Water, worked with California Rural Legal Assistance to file a lawsuit against Chem Waste charging environmental racism. Representatives of the organization said they had been left out of the process that led to county approval because the documents had not been translated into Spanish. In December 1991, the judge agreed with them. Chem Waste appealed in July 1992. "Suppose the government wanted to site a dump off Market Street and all the documents for public review were in Cambodian?" asked lawyer Ralph Abascal when the suit was filed in Sacramento County Superior Court.

In September, 1993, Chem Waste surprised everyone when it withdrew its plan to build the controversial incinerator in Kettleman City.

PESTICIDES AND FARM WORKERS

Seven miles north of Delano, in Earlimart, California, the deaths from leukemia of Mirian Robles, age ten, and Monica Tovar, thirteen, revive worries over whether poison in the fields is endangering farm workers' children.

In the nation's market basket, the San Joaquin Valley, residents worry that these daughters of farm workers may be only two of dozens of children who will die of leukemia while scientists debate whether the disease is related to pesticides in surrounding farmland.

In Earlimart, a little town of 6,000 people on State Route 99, from 1984 to 1989 six Latino American children were diagnosed with cancer, three times the number expected over a period of ten years. Of every afflicted child, one or both parents works in the fields. Similar childhood cancer rates have been observed in two nearby farm towns, Fowler and McFarland.

"They're the wrong color. They don't speak the right language. And they're poor. They're not part of the dominant culture. People in a position to do something are not doing it, and I say, Why?" asked Dr. Marion Moses, a physician who founded the Pesticide Education Center in San Francisco in 1990 to bring science into the fields.

Every day in U.S. fields, farm workers are exposed to pesticides routinely applied to the crops.[10] They work largely unprotected and carry home chemical residue on their clothes, their hands, and their tools. They eat sprayed food directly from the fields and drink water containing pesticide runoff. And they are not protected by the federal Occupational Safety and Health Administration (OSHA).

Ninety-two percent of California's 750,000 farm workers are foreign-born, and 89 percent are born in Mexico, according to the National Agricultural Workers Survey conducted by the U.S. Department of Labor. Of the 8 percent born in the United States, the overwhelming number are persons of Mexican descent, according to the California Institute for Rural Studies.

Thousands of lethal pesticides are formulated from 175 chemicals, or active ingredients. Yet only 41 of them, less than one-fourth, have passed California's full battery of tests to determine whether they cause cancer, birth defects, nerve damage, or other chronic diseases.[11] Nationwide, the EPA lists 65 pesticides used on food crops as possible, probable, or known carcinogens.

California identifies about 900 agricultural pesticide–related illnesses a year, yet officials admit that the figure is unrealistically low. Minorities lack the clout to complain about poor working conditions and government inaction, said Michele Gonzalez Arroyo of the Labor Occupational Health Program at the University of California, Berkeley.

If the workers have come from Mexico, where there is 50 percent unemployment, "they're concerned," she said. "But the bigger concern is, 'How can I eat from one day to the next?'"

Health experts caution that pockets of cancer incidence can occur as statistical anomalies and not as the result of environmental or other causes. But residents suspect that exposure to chemicals in the fields and tainted drinking water are to blame.[12] And there is growing anger among those who say that the lack of safety precautions for farm workers—88 percent of whom are Latino—exposed to toxic chemicals is environmental racism.

The workers breathe air heavy with chemical drift. Chemicals splash on their hands and clothes. They work without protective gear, some working in the fields while the chemicals are still toxic to humans. They drink water from wells contaminated by a dozen farm pesticides, half of them now banned because they are known to cause cancer or reproductive damage. The notorious DBCP, once widely used on grapes and soybeans, is found in more than 2,000 wells, including more than 230 public drinking water wells, in the state's agricultural areas. In 1989, a well that provided water for the Earlimart elementary school was found to be tainted with DBCP.

Workers bring their young children to the fields because there is no one to watch them. Parents bring home chemicals on their clothes, exposing unborn children to a vast array of poisons. Gloria Hernandez, a community worker for California Rural Legal Assistance in Fresno, said, "I've seen mothers coated with pesticides nursing their babies, with no place to wash, no place to get clean drinking water. Anytime a child is in the fields, it's racism. That child is being discriminated against by the fact that the government isn't providing any kind of day care." Despite inroads in federal and state programs, many families still live without adequate food, clothing, and medical attention.

A survey by the California Department of Health Services found that the per capita income in the farm town of McFarland was $4,300 and that 44 percent of the population had no health insurance.[13] In one case, Hernandez said, grower Mike Gerawn of Sanger was sued by farm workers for failing to provide proper housing, toilet and washing facilities, and drinking water for migrant workers. "Overcrowding caused the whole problem. He was sticking 35 to 40 people in each apartment."

Gerawn responded by tearing down the barracks, Hernandez said. He was sued again by California Rural Legal Assistance (CRLA) for unlawfully evicting the people. "Now they live in chicken coops and on the backs of trucks, if they can find that. People buy camper shells and rent them to farm workers."

Gerawn has declined to talk with the *San Francisco Examiner* about the reasons for his actions. Three CRLA lawsuits against him are proceeding in the courts.

"The attitude is, 'You quit and we'll get some other Mexicans to take your place,'" said Martha Salinas, a leading organizer in the San Joaquin Valley against abuses in the fields.

Most growers do not purposely mistreat their workers, Salinas added. Farmer Walter Shubin, who grows grapes west of Fresno, said that pesticides are more strictly controlled in California than anywhere in the world. Yet, he said, "farming is so tough nowadays that some say, 'Use the chemicals and let the workers be damned.' I know there's a lot of abuse of workers, putting them in the fields before the time is up. There's just less compassion for people nowadays."

Some in the San Joaquin Valley criticized the late Cesar Chavez, founder of the United Farm Workers Union, for his relentless push for worker rights, poor record keeping and other failings. Yet almost everyone agrees that since the virtual collapse of the union, advocacy groups that work on behalf of farm workers are dwindling.

In the 1980s, CRLA lost 40 percent of its attorneys and paralegals because of federal funding cuts. Latinos are especially vulnerable to exploitation because of the threat of deportation, their desperation for a job, and their disadvantage in not knowing the language or how the system works.

"The people from Mexico are so glad to be here that they'll work for anything," said Tomas Hill, director of the Tri Valley Migrant Headstart Center in Fresno. More than fifty years after the struggle of farm workers was movingly portrayed by John Steinbeck in *The*

Grapes of Wrath, the work continues to be backbreaking and fraught with toxic exposure.

Federal and state governments regulate pesticides as "economic poisons," but farm workers are the first human line of defense against the 230 million pounds used every year in California. Studies in several nations suggest a relationship between pesticide exposure and certain types of cancers, birth defects, neurobehavioral damage, psychological changes, and reproduction and fertility problems.[14]

The cancers include non-Hodgkin's lymphoma, soft tissue sarcoma, and leukemia. The first two were named in the government's settlement with veterans who were exposed to the herbicide Agent Orange. And there is increasing evidence that brain cancer may be associated with pesticide exposure.

A preliminary state study of the thirteen cases of childhood cancer in McFarland—four would be expected in a town of that size—showed a weak link to the father's occupation in farm work.[15] But the state has never followed up with an occupational study on farm workers regarding pesticide exposure, saying that such a study would cost $1 million. Instead, it conducted a $340,000 study that merely compared numbers of childhood cancer cases in agricultural and urban counties; the rates were similar.

Dr. Adolph Nava, formerly the only physician in Earlimart and now in private practice in Visalia, is angered by what he says is the state's lack of financial commitment to the children of farm workers.

In Earlimart, most of the parents do not know what, if anything, to blame for their children's illness. Maria and Guillermo Robles, who worked side by side in the grape vineyards until their daughter, Mirian, was diagnosed with leukemia, try to think back.

Maria Robles pruned and tipped sprayed grapes until she was seven months pregnant with Mirian. "I remember the only thing I did differently with Mirian," she said. "I'd eat the little grapes right off the vines. They'd feel good in my stomach. I didn't know that was bad for her."

"Is there a relationship between pesticides and cancer, especially in farm workers? If we do a proper study, we could lay the fear to rest." Dr. Lyn Goldman, director of the epidemiology investigation branch for the state health department, is trying to find a new way to link pesticides and cancer. She is applying for grant money to conduct a study examining the cancerous tissue, thereby either ruling out a genetic cause or leaving open the possibility of an environmental cause.

Meanwhile, in Earlimart the battle for the children's lives has been tragic. One baby died in 1989, then Monica, then Mirian. Mirian's parents, sisters, and brothers gathered a year after her death for the premiere of a videotape called *Harvest of Sorrows,* produced by the Pesticide Education Center to train field workers and educate the public.

Her family remembered that until the day Mirian died, they tried to keep up their spirits. Mirian's mother now recalls: "In front of her, we tried not to look sad. We tried to act like a normal family."

TOXIC WASTES AND NATIVE LANDS

Isolated Native American reservations across the country are starting to band together in loose networks to address the environmental issues deep at the core of past and future development. Day to day, Native Americans are thrashing out the conflict of poverty and environmental degradation in painful confrontations, some ending in death threats and drive-by shootings among tribal members.[16]

On the Mexican border, the tribal governments of the Campo and La Posta Native American reservations have agreed to the siting of a multimillion-dollar garbage dump and a hazardous waste incinerator on their lands. If the dump is approved by the Bureau of Indian Affairs and the federal EPA, it will take in hundreds of railroad cars of garbage from across the nation. Campo tribal chairman Ralph Goff, who grew up on the high-desert reservation, said: "We're doing it to better ourselves. It's more than economic; it's our self-esteem.

"In southern California, we're being surrounded. We can't be traditional. We have to adapt; we have to create our own economics.

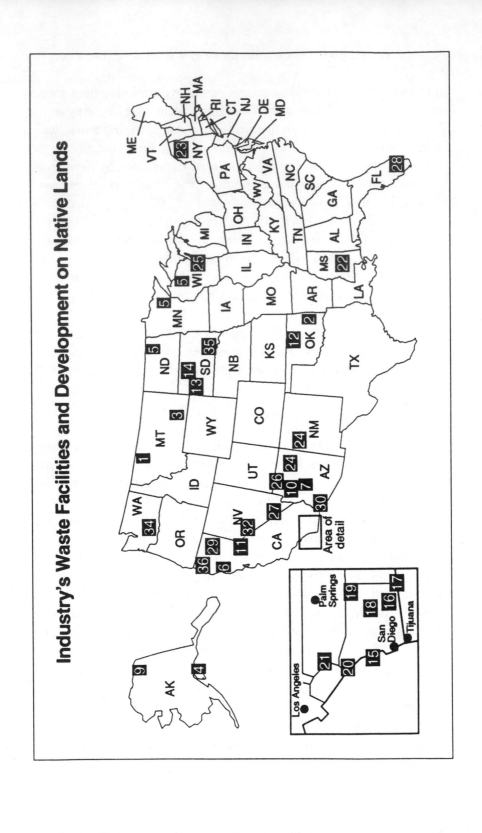

Industry's Waste Facilities and Development on Native Lands

TABLE 9.2
INDUSTRY'S WASTE FACILITIES AND DEVELOPMENT
ON NATIVE LANDS (See map on p. 158)

1. BLACK FEET
• OPPOSED: Natural gas exploration and mining in Badger–Two Medicine, an area used for age-old fasting and vision quest.

2. CHEROKEE
• OPPOSED: A U.S. Department of energy-licensed General Atomics facility, which manufactures nuclear reactor fuel and weapons. Tons of uranium have been dumped near reservation land on the Illinois and Arkansas rivers.

3. CHEYENNE
• OPPOSED: U.S. government coal sale, which includes a 100-mile tract of land in Wyoming, Montana and South Dakota, and a U.S. Forest Service plan to turn Cheyenne and Arapajo sacred prayer ground into a tourist attraction.

4. CHICLALOON
• HALTED TEMPORARILY: A coal mine and a commercial toxic waste furnace on the Kenai Peninsula, proposed by the Waste-Tech Service Inc.

5. CHIPPEWA
• OPPOSED: Kennecott Copper Co. open pit copper mine, which threatens fishing habitat and the Lac Courte Oreilles' environment.

6. CORTINA RANCHERIA
• HALTED: Dumping of asbestos bags stopped by the Bureau of Indian Affairs after protests from farmers and Colusa County officials.

7. GILA RIVER
• REJECTED: $10 million offer from Waste Management to build a 640-acre landfill and a plan by Product Development Industries Inc. for a "recycling and materials recovery" facility. Product Development now approaching the Yaquis outside Tucson.

8. GOSHUTE
• REJECTED: Hazardous waste incinerator proposed by Golden Eagle Recycling.

9. GWICHIN
• OPPOSED: Oil development in the Arctic National Wildlife Refuge, which threatens the porcupine caribou herd. About 20 other traditional Alaska native villages also opposing.

10. HUALAPAI AND HAVASUPAI
• OPPOSED: Energy Nuclear Fuels mining uranium in Canyonlands, which could contaminate water and sacred Red Butte on land near reservations.

11. JACKSON RANCHERIA
• REJECTED: An IT Corp. medical waste incinerator.

12. KAW
• REJECTED: Hazardous waste furnace and 100-acre toxic ash dump offered by Waste Tech Service Inc. after tribe accepted $100,000 and the company had spent $4 million for studies and design.

LAKOTA INDIANS (13, 14)
13. PINE RIDGE
• REJECTED: 5,000-acre garbage dump and incinerator by Amcor, a subsidiary of O&G Industries Inc. First accepted by a few tribal leaders, reversed by the tribe.
• OPPOSED: Zeolite mining and a controversial water project proposed by Bechtel.

14. ROSEBUD SIOUX
• OPPOSITION GROWING: Same 5,000-acre dump and incinerator rejected by Pine Ridge Indians, offered by RSW Inc., another subsidiary of O&G Industries.

MISSION INDIANS (15–21)
15. BARONA
• REJECTED: Waste Management landfill and furnace, first accepted by tribal officials, turned down by General Council.

16. CAMPO
• UNDER WAY: Mid-American garbage dump for U.S. waste, accepted by the tribal council and awaiting BIA and EPA approval based on environmental-impact statement.

17. LA POSTA
• UNDER WAY: Commercial toxic waste incinerator built by W. R. Grace, American Waste Recovery and Canonie, approved by the nine voting members of the tribe.

(continued on next page)

TABLE 9.2 (*continued*)

18. LOS COYOTES
• OPPOSED: Chambers Development's garbage dump, operating under a conditional lease and an armed security company brought to the reservation by Chambers to protect testing activities.

19. MORONGO OR TORRES MARTINEZ
• HALTED: Food wastes and solvents dump near the Salton Sea after three years of dumping after federal government said it threatened wetlands.

20. PALA
• OPPOSED: County landfill operated by Waste Management, abutting Sacred Mountain near Pala.

21. SOBOBA
• UNDER INVESTIGATION: 1,000 truckloads of lead-contaminated soils dumped near homes and dairy farms by a company, RANPAC.

22. MISSISSIPPI CHOCTAW
• UNDER WAY: Toxic waste dump and possibly an incinerator by National Disposal Systems. Company incorporated in 1990, bought 400 acres next to the reservation and sold to tribe for $10. Land placed in trust and leased to company. Members protesting.

23. MOHAWK
• REJECTED: Recycling plant for construction-demolition

debris by Browning Ferris Industries, Waste Management and others.

24. NAVAJO
• REJECTED: A toxic waste incinerator, first approved by chapters in Dilkon, then turned down by members along with another proposal for a hazardous waste dump by Waste Tech Services Inc. and another company.

25. OJIBWAY
• OPPOSED: Construction of a copper and zinc mining facility.

PIUTE INDIANS
26. KAIBAB
• REJECTED: Toxic waste incinerator for 70,000 tons a year and a toxic ash dump in Arizona and Utah 60 miles from the Grand Canyon by Waste Tech Service Inc.

27. MOAPA
• OPPOSED: Hazardous waste incinerator by Waste Tech Service Inc.

28. SEMINOLE
• OPPOSED: Mercury contamination in air emissions from an operating garbage incinerator off Florida tribal land. Proposed: Medical waste incinerator in Oklahoma.

29. SHASTA AND PITT RIVER
• OPPOSED: Mt. Shasta ski resort.

30. TOHONO O'ODHAM
• REJECTED: Two garbage in-

cinerators by a new company, Loralaur.

31. UTE
• REJECTED: Toxic waste incinerator by Global Telesis Corp. of Walnut Creek.

32. WASHOE
• REJECTED: Garbage incinerator. Under consideration: Multi-county garbage dump.

33. WESTERN SHOSHONE
• OPPOSED: U.S. underground nuclear testing and aircraft test flights and cyanide-leaching in gold mining. Yucca Mountain is on disputed territory so alternative transport for high-level wastes goes through Ely, Wells, Battle Mountain, South Fork, Yomba, Duckwater and Timbisha.

34. YAKIMA
• OPPOSED: Waste dump on the Columbia River.

35. YANKTON
• OPPOSED: Medical waste facility, a top candidate among several.

36. YUROK AND KARUK
• REJECTED: Logging and road building in sacred sites in the Siskiyou Wilderness Area.
• OPPOSED: Herbicide spraying that destroys weaving grasses and medicines and contaminates environment.

People can leave if they want, but we have to provide jobs here and do something for ourselves. We can't be dependent on government grants."

A few miles away, La Posta is negotiating with W. R. Grace & Company, a chemical conglomerate, to build a toxic waste incinerator on its tiny reservation. Nine of the band's sixteen members are of voting age, and according to Frank La Chappa, tribal manager, at one time were all for it. But in 1991, some were raising questions about health and safety.

Yet the neighboring Mission band, Los Coyotes, is deeply suspicious of Chambers Development's proposal for a garbage dump. Los Coyotes backed off from a conditional lease with the Pittsburgh, Pennsylvania, company in 1991, which would have placed a garbage dump in South Palm Canyon. The river there flows into the wild Anza-Borrego Desert State Park.

"I'm a poor old Indian, but I wouldn't take $10 billion for this land," said Catherine Saubel, seventy-one, a Los Coyotes elder in Banning. "It's sacred for me. It's where our medicine is growing, our food is growing, and our animals are taken care of."

Now, a growing Native American network says that the small, isolated tribes are vulnerable to the corporations because the United States lacks a national policy to address the onslaught.

"We know what jobs we're hoping to get," said Lance Hughes, a Cherokee who directs Native Americans for a Clean Environment (NACE) in Tahlequah, Oklahoma. "If anyone suffers, it'll be the Indian people because it's the low-level jobs that are the first contact—unloading trucks, digging ditches, handling wastewater. We're not going to be in the control rooms pushing buttons."

Oglala Lakota Joanne Tall, who for fifteen years has been wary of a string of projects proposed for the Pine Ridge Reservation in South Dakota, said, "All these proposals have to be put on hold until we can educate ourselves."

Environmentalists and Native Americans themselves say that the reservations are being cultivated as possible sites for waste disposal. It is yet another example, they say, of toxic racism, in which the largest minority communities get the dregs of U.S. industrial life.

The dumps and incinerators could bring in millions of dollars for impoverished Native Americans. But along with the paychecks, say many opponents, comes a loss of sovereignty over revered ancient land.

In California, twelve tribes were under economic pressure to pick a development project in 1991; most of the projects were associated with toxic waste. In 1990, the *San Francisco Examiner* found that nationwide, corporations and the government were negotiating with at least thirty-five Native American tribes regarding hazardous waste landfills, toxic incinerators, mines, or other development.[17]

State environmental laws do not apply to Native American lands, and the U.S. Environmental Protection Agency admits that its laws are weaker than many state laws and that it cannot oversee all projects. On Native American lands, the government has already allowed the disposal of more than 2 million tons of radioactive uranium mill waste. Many closed mines and nuclear sites are on or near reservations. Native American scholar Ward Churchill has tagged this practice "radioactive colonialism."[18]

Generally, industry says that such projects enhance a community's economic and social circumstances. Bechtel Enterprises, for instance, offered a full range of projects—garbage, cogeneration, trash furnaces, and hydropower facilities—in 1990 to the Oglala Sioux on the Pine Ridge Reservation.

A lawyer representing Bechtel of San Francisco said that the enterprises would be "commercially legitimate and environmentally sound." Chemical Waste Management, Inc., the nation's largest hazardous waste disposal company, says that it does not pick sites for social reasons. Waste Tech Services, which has sought projects on Native American land in Alaska, Oklahoma, and New Mexico, says the same thing. "We'll attempt to site wherever there is community support for a project, whether it be on tribal land or private land," said Doug Johnson, spokesman for Waste Tech in Golden, Colorado. "From a regulation standpoint, there is really no advantage to being on an Indian reservation because we've agreed to meet all the state environmental regulations if they're more stringent than the federal."

Waste Tech, bought by Amoco from Bechtel Enterprises in 1988, is one of the most active companies seeking deals with Native Americans. Even though Waste Tech has approached at least four tribes in Arizona, Oklahoma, Utah, and Alaska, the company says that it is not targeting tribes. "We'll do business with anyone who's interested," said Johnson. There is no advantage, he said, to operating on land exempt from state environmental law because the company has volunteered to meet state standards.

With no working projects by 1991, Waste Tech came away poorer after the failed deals. When the Oklahoma Kaw rescinded a contract for a toxic waste incinerator and 100-acre ash landfill on their land, they did not return the $100,000 payment from Waste Tech. The company has said that it would be "a nice gesture" for the Oklahoma Kaw to give it back. The company spent $4 million in studies, Johnson said.

Some Native Americans blame the U.S. government and the Bureau of Indian Affairs for putting tribes in a position of having to accept waste contracts. "I'd like to see how much money the government has put into economic development on Indian lands over the past two decades," said Lance Hughes, NACE's director in Oklahoma. "Now people are waiting for a waste management company to slap a couple hundred thousand on the table and call it economic development. It's a clear example of the BIA being unable to do it with economic development on native land. There's hardly been s—— done for these tribes."

In 1991, a single BIA official in Riverside, Gilbert Stuart, was responsible for natural resources on thirty southern California reservations, which include mining and minerals, forestry, range management, wildlife and parks, and agriculture—and now waste. The new waste deals started emerging two years ago, Stuart said. "If it's approached cautiously, I think it can be a good deal for the Indian people. I suppose there could be other economic development, but I haven't seen any."

Although former secretary of the interior Manuel Lujan had assured opponents of some of the projects that he was not in favor of them, the environmental reports keep churning out toward the BIA office in Sacramento. To bring in state oversight, Assemblyman Steve Peace, a Democrat from San Diego, authored controversial legislation to regulate hazardous waste haulers and generators and to require state permits to operate any waste facility on tribal lands.

Native Americans are divided over the legislation, which passed. Most say that it is a threat to sovereignty; others, such as Los Coyotes elder Catherine Saubel, say: "We need all the help we can get. When these big companies come in, we've already lost our sovereignty."

Lance Hughes of Oklahoma said: "It would be wonderful if the BIA would get off their butts and say that unless the tribe has the infrastructure to deal with these problems, forget it. Some big corporations that form waste management companies have no track record. They have a lot of capital, and with BIA, that seems to be okay."

On the Campo Reservation, the tribe has taken into its own hands regulation of the proposed $20 million to $30 million, 300-acre garbage dump. Tribal chairman Ralph Goff said: "We formed our own EPA so we can protect the environment. We never feel comfortable with the state or federal government because they don't have enough manpower to address the problems. We have the most self-interest. We'll do the best job to protect ourselves."

But opposition to the Campo garbage dump is growing, both on and off the reservation. The county nixed the site for a dump because the groundwater there is shallow, it is a "recharge" area for rain, and it is the only source of drinking water in the region. But the county has no authority there. Nor does the San Diego Regional Water Quality Control Board, which has warned of "a serious threat to the waters of the state." The EPA, too, has warned of possible contamination of the aquifer.

Historically, nearly every dump built over an underlying water supply has leaked into it. Off the reservation, Ed and Donna Tisdale, whose ranch abuts the Campo hill where the tribe wants to place the dump, spent $8,000 on an independent review of the suitability of placing the dump over the water supply.

They do not want a garbage dump next door and fear that their property's value will plummet. Ed Tisdale bought 60 acres of land in 1963, when "there was nothing here except brush." He dug nine wells and built a house, and he now raises organic alfalfa and Hereford cattle. Two years ago, the Tisdales turned down an offer of $750,000 for the property.

"This is the only high desert left in southern California where you can see, where you can drink water out of the ground, where you can breathe. Now these Indian tribes are taking it and trashing it," Arol Wolf, a former neighbor, said. The tribal council—the reservation's governing body—has already approved the project, Goff said. A consultant is scheduled to complete the environmental impact statement; then the project will face federal approval.

Yet Native Americans, from the Kaw and the Tohono O'odham southwest of Tucson to the Oglala Lakota in the Pine Ridge and Rosebud reservations in South Dakota, are backing away from deals with waste companies. The attraction of jobs and money begins to fade, members say, as they learn more about the amounts of water necessary to maintain projects, loss of access to land, private security forces, dangerous jobs, and odor and air pollution.

"Our land is our most valuable asset, next to our children and our elders," said Catherine Holsbo, a Barona member. "Once you poison it, there's no getting it back again. We have to stop these insane projects that are coming into the reservations. It'll be a domino effect."

For three years, representatives of dozens of native groups have held an annual conference on toxins on tribal lands called Protecting Mother Earth. Hosts of the gatherings have been the Navajo in Arizona and the Oglala Lakota on the Rosebud, on the eastern edge of the Black Hills of South Dakota, and in Celilo Village, on the banks of the Columbia River, 90 miles east of Portland.

Out of the 1992 meeting came a strong independent statement from the Indigenous Environmental Network calling for an end to uranium mining, milling, testing, reprocessing, and storage and disposal of radioactive materials on indigenous land. The push for new development is frightening some of the native peoples, who have lived undisturbed on their lands for thousands of years, including Sarah James, a member of the Gwichin Tribe of Alaska, which depends on the porcupine caribou herd on the Arctic coast.

James's protest has brought her to California and even to the Earth Summit in Rio de Janeiro in 1992, working with environmental groups to stop the drive by some in Congress to drill for oil in the Arctic National Wildlife Refuge.

"We are the caribou people," she said. "We depend on the caribou for food, clothes, and tools. If the calving ground is disturbed or polluted in some way, or the caribou decrease in number or change the migratory route, it will change our way of life. We will be a people no more."

GOVERNMENT RESPONSE TO INEQUITIES

Little has changed in California nearly a decade after civil rights leaders pointed out that while all Americans produce household garbage and toxic waste, all do not share equally in the cost of waste disposal. Charles Lee, who directed the United Church of Christ Commission for Racial Justice's landmark study, *Toxic Wastes and Race in the United States,* said in an interview, "As long as there are communities to put these things in, there's no incentive to change chemical dumping practices and no power to influence decision making."

The state is just beginning to recognize the barriers of language and education in protecting the health and safety of workers in hazardous jobs. Because of a new state law, Cal-OSHA is setting up training classes for hazardous jobs in languages other than English. The University of California, Davis, has published a booklet in Spanish educating farm workers about pesticides.

The Labor Occupational Health Program at the School of Public Health at the University of California, Berkeley, is starting multicultural training for hazardous waste workers. But the federal government has been slow to respond to growing evidence that minorities bear a disproportionate burden of toxic dangers.

After the issuance in 1987 of *Toxic Wastes and Race in the United States*,[19] things started changing, said Cynthi Harris, chief of the Community Health Branch in the U.S. Public Health Service's Agency for Toxic Substances and Disease Registry (ATSDR). Also, the U.S. Department of Health and Human Services published an eight-volume document, *Black and Minority Health,* which raised questions about the environmental effects of such heavy metals as toxic lead on minority populations, she said.

The ATSDR has set up a special program for minorities who suffer health effects from Superfund sites, the worst dumps in America. Congress ordered the agency to conduct nearly 1,000 health assessments in communities harboring Superfund sites. Although the agency has said that it would pinpoint the threatened minority communities on the list, it has yet to do so.

"I couldn't give you a percentage right now of which communities are minority, but we are working on it. I definitely feel there's an agencywide commitment to minority health issues," said Harris. Yet the EPA does not even attempt to classify a contaminated community by its ethnic makeup, which could be a first step in identifying the extent of toxic racism.

The EPA established an Office of Environmental Equity in 1992. But its first report, *Environmental Equity,* stopped short of saying that there is environmental racism in the United States.[20] In fact, the findings of the report kicked off internal wars in the EPA as well as criticism from environmentalists outside the agency.

Nevertheless, further investigation showed that the U.S. government, although saying that it was color-blind, had its own double standards. Indeed, a 1992 study by the *National Law Journal* discovered that government actions contribute to unequal protection of minority and white communities.[21] White communities get on the Superfund cleanup list faster and get better results and stiffer penalties than do communities of color.

For example, in the Midwest, the pace of cleanup was 13.8 years in minority census tracts, compared with 9.7 years in white areas. In the West, the time was 12.3 years, compared with 9.3 years in white areas. In the Great Plains, it was 12.3 years in minority areas, compared with 9.6 years in white areas.

Once a site is placed on the Superfund list, in more than half of the ten EPA regions that administer the laws, action on cleanup begins 12 to 42 percent later at minority sites than at white sites. As for penalties, under hazardous waste laws, sites having the largest white population had penalties five times as high as did sites with the largest minority populations. The disparity under the law occurs by race alone, not by income level. Penalties imposed on polluters in white areas averaged $335,566, compared with $55,318 in minority areas, the journal found.

For all federal environmental laws, including laws to regulate air and water quality and waste management, penalties in white communities were 46 percent higher than in minority communities, the *National Law Journal* found. These findings did not come as a surprise to families who live in California's environmental "sacrifice zones." Similarly, environmental racism scholars, who have been tracking pollution trends for more than a decade, were not shocked by these disparities. These and other data, however, point to the urgent need for equal enforcement of the current laws and the need for new antidiscrimination legislation to fill in the gaps where current environmental protection measures have proven inadequate.

III

Networking
and
Coalition Building

10

Building a Net
That Works: SWOP

RICHARD MOORE AND LOUIS HEAD

On April 6 and 7, 1990, the Southwest Organizing Project (SWOP) held the People of Color Regional Activist Dialogue for Environmental Justice (RAD) in Albuquerque, New Mexico. SWOP is a multiracial, multiissue, community-based organization located in Albuquerque. One hundred activists from eight states—Arizona, California, Colorado, Nevada, New Mexico, Oklahoma, Texas, and Utah—attended the gathering.

Our mission is to empower the disenfranchised in the Southwest to realize social, racial, and economic justice. A substantial part of our effort over the past five years has been devoted to work on toxic contamination issues, with special emphasis on how these problems affect communities of color.

We are not an "environmental" organization but rather address toxic contamination issues as part of a broad set of racial and social justice concerns. We do not single out the environment as necessarily having a special place above all other issues; rather, we recognize that issue of toxic contamination fit within an agenda that can—and, indeed, in practical, day-to-day work does—include employment, education, housing, health care, and other issues of social, racial, and economic justice.

We were primarily community activists working on both environmental and economic issues, coming from such organizations as

Neighbors for a Toxic-Free Community in Denver, Native Americans for a Clean Environment in Oklahoma, and the West County Toxics Coalition in Richmond, California. The meeting included many people from the indigenous nations, including the chairperson of the Havasupai people of the Grand Canyon and representatives of the Navajo of Utah and Big Mountain and the Western Shoshone of Nevada. The meeting was facilitated by SWOP.

The gathering built on years of grass-roots work in the region. For decades, activists had been immersed in fights over police repression, immigration, food and nutrition, health care, campus issues, land rights, and water rights. We had been networking with one another because we had found common interests. We were all being affected by the deadly combination of environmental racism and economic blackmail, so we saw the need to exchange experiences, and to go beyond community and statewide strategies to develop a regional network.

Two very significant things came out of that April 1990 gathering. First, SWOP initiated a process of dialogue among Latino Americans, Asian Americans, African Americans, and Native Americans that resulted in formation of the Southwest Network for Environmental and Economic Justice (SNEEJ). The Network has brought together hundreds of activists and organizations from eight states—those directly affected by these issues. Second, we set up the Southwest Training and Action Institute, established by the Network as a mechanism through which we may strengthen one another's work throughout the region.

The Network and the Institute were formed in response to the following:

1. The need for Southwestern activists and organizations to work together to broaden regional strategies and perspectives on environmental degradation and other social, racial, and economic justice issues.

2. The recognition that a strong and viable regional effort will strengthen the local work of our organizations and further em-

power us to pursue campaigns of regional and national significance.

3. The need to maximize and share the existing internal resources
of organizations in the Southwest.

4. The need for people of color to assist one another in, and take the
leadership of, efforts addressing the poisoning of communities of
color.

5. The need for training and leadership development efforts relevant to the history and cultures of the Southwest.

6. The recognition of the inherent relationship between economic
and environmental issues and the need to strengthen work that
draws the links in practice between the two.

7. The need to build, along with others, a multiracial movement
that addresses toxic contamination issues as part of a broad
agenda for social and economic justice, one that is fully inclusive
of people of color. The Institute is designed to provide training in
specific skills—community organizing workshops, coalition
building, leadership development, and membership development.

The Network has grown steadily since its founding. We now have
more than thirty member groups, both grass-roots organizations
and Native American nations. Our people come from the bottom
of the Grand Canyon and from urban areas, from San Francisco,
Denver, and Dallas to rural villages in northern New Mexico and
Arizona. We take especially seriously the need to bring rural communities into the decision-making process. Many rural communities find themselves isolated. Other people advocate *for* them
instead of advocating *with* them.

The Network's Coordinating Council is made up of twenty-three
people. These are not officially "representatives" of their organizations but represent their states. They are elected at our annual gath-

ering, during which states caucus and nominate people for the body; the general body then votes in the individual members. The current group is 50 percent women and consists entirely of people of color; council members come from twenty grass-roots organizations.

The Institute is a vehicle for studying economic issues, for examining what is happening worldwide, and for bringing information to grass-roots groups. It provides technical knowledge: What are aquifers? What are plumes? What is benzene, what is formaldehyde, and what can these chemicals do to you? Another key function is leadership development—defined broadly to include training on the history and culture of the Southwest and on the relationship of economic and environmental issues. We cannot separate economics from environmental issues, nor from issues of racism and culture.

For centuries, people of color in the Southwest have been subjected to racist and genocidal practices, including the theft of lands and water, the murder of innocent people, and the degradation of our environment. Mining companies extract minerals, leaving economically depressed communities and poisoned soil and water. The U.S. military takes lands for weapons production, testing, and storage, contaminating surrounding communities and placing minority workers in the most highly radioactive and toxic work sites. Industrial and municipal dumps are intentionally placed in communities of color, disrupting our cultural life-styles and threatening the future of our communities. Workers in the fields are dying, and babies are born disfigured as a result of pesticide spraying. Even more devastating are the effects on women, who suffer the consequences in bearing our future generations.

In order to strengthen our local work on toxic contamination, we have reached out to other groups across the country that are fighting toxic waste problems in both predominantly Anglo communities and communities of color. In so doing, we have become more fully aware of the lack of government attention given to environmental and health problems in communities of color.

SHATTERING A MYTH

Few people of color have been attracted to the mainstream environmental groups.[1] However, this does not mean that there is a lack of concern among Chicanos, Mexicanos, or other people of color. Environmental justice issues are bringing disenfranchised communities into the environmental arena. Many of these issues have historically been perceived as a poverty issue, an issue of social and racial justice inseparable from others, such as housing, unemployment, lack of health services, or poor educational opportunities.

Our communities are threatened by the environmental problems caused by racism inherent in land use decisions that result in the location of dirty industries, toxic dumps, incinerators, and military bases close to low-income communities of color. In the Southwest, as in many other regions, social and economic impacts include loss of resources such as clean water, land, and air. The human costs are staggering.

New Mexico, best described as a colony of the United States, is a case in point. Since its incorporation into the United States in the 1840s, New Mexico has been economically dependent on mineral and forest extractive industries and, since the 1940s, the United States military. It is one of the poorest states in the country, with permanent official unemployment rates of 20 percent or more common in many rural and urban communities. Indigenous New Mexicans, both Chicanos and Native Americans, now constitute more than half of the state's population; along with Mexican immigrants and a small African American population, they have long made up the majority of New Mexico's working class and poor.

Indigenous land loss, the privatization or rangelands, and the coming of the railroad in the 1880s dramatically changed the Southwest and left people of color in New Mexico economically disenfranchised. State and local governments have largely functioned at the behest of the federal government and for the benefit of outside industries. Barriers have prevented poor communities from exercising effective electoral power or economic influence even in this limited political arena.

Water is an extremely precious material and cultural resource in New Mexico. Groundwater is used for domestic, agricultural, commercial, and industrial purposes nearly everywhere. In many parts of the state, including the entire inner Rio Grande valley, accessible groundwater that is affordable to working-class people lies only a few feet below the surface. These aquifers are extremely vulnerable to contamination from industrial, military, agricultural, and waste disposal activities. Tremendous amounts of groundwater and surface water have been reserved for military and military-related use, for industry and agribusiness. While poor communities have continually had their rights to groundwater and surface water stolen over the years, that which is still accessible is now being poisoned.

New Mexico's path of development has led to environmental degradation that has most acutely affected people of color in the state. The following are a few examples:

- Military and military-related operations such as Kirtland Air Force Base and Sandia and Los Alamos national weapons laboratories, located in and around communities of color, are known polluters, with hundreds of contamination sites located within their boundaries.[2]

- In Mountainview, a primarily Chicano neighborhood in Albuquerque's South Valley, an infant almost died after drinking formula mixed with contaminated water from the family's well. Mountainview is downstream from Kirtland Air Force Base, a suspected source of groundwater contamination in the area.

- The Department of Energy has admitted that Chicanos and Mexicano workers at Los Alamos National Weapons Laboratory were more likely to be assigned to work in the "hot" areas of the facility.[3]

- New Mexico has been targeted as a disposal site for the nation's nuclear waste. The Waste Isolation Pilot Project (WIPP), one of the largest U.S. underground disposal facilities for military nuclear waste, is sited 15 miles east of Loving, New Mexico. This poor rural community is more than 80 percent Chicano.

Industries come to New Mexico to avoid stringent regulations and to take advantage of an unorganized labor force. Mining and wood-processing industries have historically endangered workers and communities. Working-class Chicano communities have grown around railroad facilities, which have in turn attracted slaughterhouses, rendering plants, and other polluting industries that utilize this form of transport. Modern high-tech manufacturers likewise threaten our groundwater and air and expose workers to the most dangerous chemicals.

In Las Vegas, New Mexico, fifty-two Chicano fiberboard workers were fired when they went on strike for a livable income, a healthy and safe workplace, and a clean environment in their community downstream from the plant. The company is blackmailing the community, threatening to move elsewhere if the workers and residents demand higher wages and environmental regulations.

Large numbers of Chicanas who have entered the microelectronic industry over the past fifteen years have suffered job-related illness and death. Birth defects are increasingly common among children of women working for high-tech manufacturers. In Albuquerque, New Mexico, more than forty children of women who unknowingly used dangerous chemicals at General Telephone Electronics' (GTE's) Lenkurt plant were born with birth defects. Many weighed only 20 to 22 pounds at five years of age. Sixteen women who were poisoned at the Albuquerque GTE plant have died; many more are extremely sick from cancer and other illnesses.[4]

Pesticides are a constant danger to Chicano and Mexicano farm workers in southern New Mexico. With the blessings of the state agriculture department, agribusinesses routinely use organophosphates and other insecticides, which poison farm workers and their families and groundwater supplies of local communities, causing cancer and other diseases among many people.

Local governments and private waste disposal corporations routinely poison poor Chicano and Mexicano communities through the siting of landfills, incinerators, and sewage treatment plants. In Sunland Park, located on the Mexico–United States border, residents have been subjected to poisonous air emissions from a medical waste incinerator located only 200 yards from local elementary schools. The company took advantage of an unorganized community of Mexican immigrants to place both the incinerator and a regional landfill that accepts wastes from several states and *maquiladora* industries along the Mexican border. Nearly 2,000 *maquiladoras*, or "twin plants," operate along the Mexico–United States border. Industries operating on the Mexican side of the border are mostly American and Japanese assembly plants that employ low-wage Mexican workers.

The community of Mountainview, south of Albuquerque, has repeatedly fought off attempts by public and private interests to place solid waste landfills and transfer facilities there. Industrial land use zoning in the area, meant to attract job-generating industry, has instead opened the doors to polluting industries. Local government has followed the lead of these interests by placing the Albuquerque municipal sewage facilities in Mountainview.

These are truly endangered communities. Poor communities are usually the least informed of existent toxic threats, and many lack the power and organization to make polluters correct them. Too often, our communities become the sites where toxic wastes not wanted by more privileged neighborhoods end up being dumped.

These cases are not confined to New Mexico but also can be seen and heard throughout the Southwest and in communities where there are large numbers of Latinos. For example, more than 8 million of the nation's 15 million Latinos live in communities with one or more uncontrolled toxic waste sites.[5] Los Angeles has more Latinos living in communities with uncontrolled toxic waste sites than any other metropolitan area in the United States.[6] And the greatest concentration of hazardous waste sites in the United States is located in predominantly Latino American and African American sections of Chicago's South Side.[7]

An estimated 300,000 U.S. farm workers, most of them Latino Americans and African Americans of Caribbean descent, are poisoned each year by pesticides, according to the World Resources Institute.[8] Free trade zones along the Mexico–United States border have promoted the development of thousands of twin plant *maquiladora* industries. The resulting urbanization along the border, coupled with little or no evironmental regulatory enforcement by either the United States or Mexico, has created extremely dangerous public health conditions for communities there. Neural birth defects, including babies being born without brains, occur at a rate six times the U.S. average in the Brownsville, Texas, area.[9]

Government regulatory agencies such as the U.S. Environmental Protection Agency (EPA) have often ignored problems affecting Latino American communities and other communities of color. Since the inception of the EPA, we have requested its assistance in alleviating the disproportionate impacts from which we suffer. Our requests—our pleas for help—have fallen on deaf ears. Instead, we have seen the EPA pursue policies that have been detrimental to us and to poor communities.

Kettleman City, California, more than 95 percent Latino American, is home to the fifth largest commercial landfill in the United States, a facility owned by Chemical Waste Management, Inc. Yet the EPA attempted to approve an expansion of the landfill without allowing any input on the matter from the local farm workers' community. The agency further encouraged Chem Waste to pursue a hazardous waste incinerator application in Kettleman City, over the strenuous objections of the community, which was systematically excluded from real participation in the permitting process.

In response to severe lead contamination near schools and housing projects in heavily Latino American and African American West Dallas, the EPA refused to meet with affected residents until forced to do so by a regional grass-roots effort. The EPA is now proposing cleanup levels for West Dallas that fall short of those it has used as standards in white communities, and it has further proposed to dump the lead-contaminated soil near an African American community in northern Louisiana.

The McFarland, California, "childhood cancer cluster" is an area where farm workers and their families live in a federally funded housing tract, built right on top of a highly contaminated site previously used as a pesticide dump. Despite this, the EPA has taken no steps to relocate residents from the area. In fact, the agency has failed to release results of tests made in 1989 to residents of the affected area.

We are calling on the Environmental Protection Agency to carry out its obligation to treat us equally as provided by law, to be accountable to those communities most directly affected by toxic poisoning. In the face of environmental racism and the inaction of regulators who are supposed to protect us, Latino Americans and other people of color have won many victories and, when organized, have incredible power and resources.

But the Network and SWOP are not alone in this work. Much grass-roots activity in the Southwest and throughout the country is addressing the poisoning of our communities. These activities generally receive little or no recognition, in part because they have not been carried out by "environmental" organizations. Rather, these efforts are part of a broader agenda to bring about social, racial, and economic justice.

We see our efforts to educate, organize, and mobilize as an expression of our self-determination. We are putting industries, the military, and the EPA—as well as state, county, and municipal governments—on notice. No longer will we allow our communities, whether they be urban or rural, to be the dumping ground for everything other people do not want in their communities.

INFLUENCING NATIONAL POLICY

Besides assisting local grass-roots work, the Network has been an important force in projecting the questions of environmental racism and economic blackmail into the national debate among environmental organizations and onto the agenda of government agencies. This has been possible because we have taken seriously the need to affect national policy. We could spend the rest of our lives—and in many cases, we may have to—fighting off one garbage transfer station or incinerator after another in our communities. We have to "put out those fires" because our communities are being poisoned every day. But strategically, we need to think in terms of a preventive situation, a way to affect city, county, state, and national policy.

This is the kind of thinking that led nine activists of color from around the country to write our January 1990 letter to the "Group of Ten" national environmental organizations, calling on them to engage in dialogue about the environmental crisis affecting communities of color and to include people of color on their staffs and boards of directors.

The January letter and a subsequent letter written by SWOP in March 1990, and the work we did around them, received a tremendous response among grass-roots activists of color. We began to receive responses, some from the Big Ten, indicating a willingness to open a dialogue. Also, a number of national environmental groups became willing to sit down and discuss with the Network their staffing and advocacy work.

In the three years since the letters stirred things up, progress has been very slow. A few people of color have been hired and appointed to boards of mainstream environmental organizations. Some of the organizations have begun to share resources—which was one of the key points in our letter.

The mainstream groups have scientists, technicians, and attorneys whose skills could be shared with grass-roots organizations. We were talking about a bottom-line question of *sharing power.* We did not expect power to be shared overnight—that is one reason why we have emphasized self-sufficiency, having our staff paid by and accountable only to the members of the Network.

We have also focused in particular on the federal Environmental Protection Agency, which has to be forced to live up to its own mandate, and that means to protect working-class communities and communities of color. We want regulations on the books that will protect our communities from being targeted for waste facilities and incinerators. We also demand *equal* enforcement of laws and regulations. Right now, many of our communities are not protected.

We sent a letter in July 1991 to EPA administrator William Reilly laying out specific examples of how the agency is responsible for a large part of the environmental racism that exists in our communities. In some cases, staff people from the EPA who were involved in granting permits to companies are now working for those same companies. We demonstrated that the EPA has aligned itself historically with industry, against the interests of communities of color and working people.

We asked that Reilly come to the Southwest and meet with leaders of our choice. We have had press conferences outside EPA offices in San Francisco, Denver, and Dallas—the three regional offices that cover the eight states participating in the Network. There is one single demand: that the regional administrators themselves go on a tour led by community representatives. After much prodding, Reilly made a visit to the Southwest in 1992. We gave him a close-up and personal tour of our poisoned communities.

We have built a base over the years; we can bring it out, and we expect to sit at the table. We have operated from the point of view that in order to sit at the table, the first thing we need to do is bring ourselves together as people of color. We know that if we cannot strengthen our relationships with one another, building a multicultural and multiracial movement to go up against the multinational corporations will be quite difficult.

Nothing we have been doing has been easy. But what we have been attempting to build, and the dialogue and networking we have attempted to create, can move us toward the kind of solidarity that can actually wield some power. Latino Americans are beginning to empower themselves in the barrios of Albuquerque, Denver, Houston, East Los Angeles, South Tucson, East Austin, the South Bronx, and West Dallas.

A PEOPLE'S STRATEGY

A people's strategy for environmental justice is needed that will fully involve those who have historically been powerless in this so-

ciety and throughout the world. As Ruben Solis, a dialogue participant and member of the Southwest Public Workers Union, stated
in a recent letter to SWOP:

> No longer will the "Green" movement be the exclusive "coun-
> try club" for whites; now it will have to include the victims of
> poisons, be they animals of the human species or the endan-
> gered species they already include in their [the top ten environ-
> mental groups'] agenda.

The perspective of SWOP that led us to take the leading role in
making the dialogue possible is illuminated by several points that
we try to address in our work, on which our thoughts were further
nourished by the dialogue itself:

1. Ample evidence confirms that toxic contamination problems in-
   ordinately affect communities of color and that there is a direct
   relation between the powerlessness of Third World communities
   (both within and outside the United States) and their vulnerability to toxic contamination hazards. Environmental issues are
   thus issues of social and racial justice. Actions that lead to toxic
   contamination of communities of color thus are acts of institutional racism, if not of systematic racial violence.

2. The colonial heritage of Southwest has resulted in its high vulnerability to toxic contamination. Weak local and state environmental regulations and government structures have resulted in
   capitulation by local and state governments to corporate polluters. Chronically depressed job markets, small shops, weak regulations, and a lack of organization of industrial workers all
   contribute to increased exposure to toxins in the workplace. Extractive industries and the federal government have moved virtually at will to control and remove vast mineral resources on
   Native American reservations. Government and industry have
   been the biggest polluters of the land and water—the two most
   important resources to indigenous peoples of the region.

3. In the Southwest, as in other parts of the United States and the world, militarism—itself a primary historical vehicle for colonization—has begotten toxic waste hazards affecting people of color and the poor. In New Mexico, mining of uranium used for nuclear research and weapons production has resulted in the poisoning of Native American communities. Workers are routinely exposed to toxic and radioactive substances during weapons development and production. The operations of military installations have resulted in contamination in nearby communities. The U.S. Department of Energy, frantically searching for sites at which to store radioactive waste accumulating around the country, has chosen New Mexico as the place to begin doing so.

4. Toxic contamination has no respect for political boundaries. Runaway shops and *maquiladoras* (twin plants) along the Mexico–United States border frequently, if not consistently, expose low-paid workers to some of the worst toxic chemicals. Highly toxic and radioactive wastes from the United States are dumped in Mexico and other Third World countries.

5. In the Southwest, where agribusiness is a major industry, pesticides are utilized with intentional disregard for their physical effects on farm laborers and surrounding communities. Migration, insufficient skills, job shortages, and demand for crop production augment the increased exposure to toxins in the fields as a result of pesticide spraying. Despite the increase of unionized farm labor and its efforts to lobby state and federal government concerning regulatory uses of pesticides, agribusiness continues its negligence, which can be attributed only to the continuation of genocidal practices on people of color.

CONCLUSIONS

The dialogue represented the first time that African Americans, Chicanos, and Native Americans had come together in the United States to discuss environmental issues from the perspective of people of color. The dialogue consistently reaffirmed the need for technical assistance and leadership development training with consideration for the cultural traditions of people of color and rural and urban distinctions; it also confirmed the necessity for a training and action institute to provide such resources.

In addition, the dialogue confirmed the need for communication among people of color and the urgency to develop further the Southwest Network for Environmental and Economic Justice (SNEEJ), which will contribute to our collective support. It brought longtime activists, leaders, and organizers from the African American, Chicano, and Native American movements together with others representing grass-roots organizations from communities of color throughout the Southwest who work directly or indirectly on environmental issues.

The diverse representation contributed to a clearer perspective of the commonalities of the problems and to a broader vision of similar concerns affecting Third World communities. It served as a vehicle to strengthen communication between unions and community organizations to begin laying the framework for pursuing our own agenda. It also was critical for us in empowering ourselves as individuals and as organizations, on a local as well as a regional level.

This was the first time people of color in the Southwest had been offered the opportunity to have their struggles against environmental injustices acknowledged as economic, cultural, racial, and social injustices as well. Some organizations not involved directly with environmental issues were able to relate their work in economic, cultural, and social justice to the effects of environmental injustices.

The dialogue served as a means by which collectively, as people of color, to support a ban on the export of hazardous waste, which is devastating Third World communities, and to oppose the taking of land from Third World people in order to repay the so-called Third World debt.

In addition, the dialogue was televised nationally on NBC's "Today Show" and was the first time that the links between environmental and economic issues from the perspective of people of color were raised on national television. Furthermore, the dialogue was instrumental in breaking the stereotype that people of color are not concerned about or active in environmental issues.

Finally, the dialogue represented a significant step for SWOP organizationally. It made headway in the course of our work on environmental and economic injustice issues in New Mexico and throughout the Southwest. No other grass-roots network exists in the United States that is multicultural and multinational in scope and that focuses on the fact that communities of color, as well as economically oppressed communities, suffer disproportionately from toxic contamination. Ultimately, the dialogue consolidated the relations that we had been slowly cultivating with many organizations throughout the Southwest and established our power as a group that will give direction in building a movement and will put forth an agenda for people of color.

11

Concerned Citizens of South Central Los Angeles

CYNTHIA HAMILTON

The mainstream environmental groups do not have a long history of working with African American and Latino American groups.[1] For the most part, national environmental groups have failed to adequately address environmental problems that disproportionately affect people of color. Although there are some exceptions, most of the large national environmental groups were late in making the connection between environmental and social justice issues.[2]

This chapter addresses the specific problems and developments associated with community organizing in South Central Los Angeles—the area that was at the center of the spring 1992 uprising.[3]

THE CITY AND THE INCINERATOR

Los Angeles is the nation's second largest city, with a population of 3.5 million. The city is one of the most culturally and ethnically diverse big cities in the country. People of color (Latino Americans, Asian Americans, Pacific Islanders, African Americans, and Native Americans) now constitute a majority (63 percent) of the city's population.

South Central Los Angeles has long been neglected socially, politically, and physically. Long before the fires in the spring uprising,

business disinvestment, redlining, and industrial pollution acceler-
ated the economic decline of the area. South Central Los Angeles, a
neighborhood that is more than 52 percent African American and
44 percent Latino American, was slated for the city's first state-of-
the-art municipal solid waste incinerator. Local residents organized
themselves into a group called Concerned Citizens of South Central
Los Angeles to fight a solid waste incinerator known as the LAN-
CER (Los Angeles City Energy Recovery) project.

The majority of the activists engaged in this community organizing were African American women. This analysis focuses on the
evolution of political organization and political consciousness
among the working-class women involved in this effort, using their
own voices.

In 1956, women in South Africa began an organized protest
against the "pass laws." As they stood in front of the office of the
prime minister, they began a new freedom song with the refrain
"Now you have touched the women, you have struck a rock." This
refrain describes the personal commitment and intensity women
bring to social change, qualities that society has summarily dismissed.

In reviewing the two-year battle in South Central Los Angeles
against a solid waste incinerator, we see these same tenacious characteristics. When the city council decided that a 13-acre incinerator, burning 2,000 tons per day of municipal waste, should be built
in a poor, residential African American and Mexican American
community, the women there said no. Officials had indeed encountered a boulder of opposition.[4]

> I noticed when we first started fighting the issue how the men
> would laugh at the women . . . they would say, "Don't pay no
> attention to them, that's only one or two women . . . they won't
> make a difference." . . . But now, since we've been fighting for
> about a year, the smiles have gone.   (Charlotte Bullock)

Communities of color shoulder a disproportionately high share
of the burden of housing the by-products of industrial development:
waste, abandoned factories and warehouses, leftover chemicals,

and debris. These communities are also asked to house the waste and pollution no longer acceptable in white communities in the form of hazardous landfills or dump sites.

In 1987, the United Church of Christ Commission for Racial Justice published a report titled *Toxic Wastes and Race in the United States*. The report concluded that race is a major factor in the presence of hazardous wastes in residential communities throughout the United States. Three out of every five African Americans and Mexican Americans live in communities with uncontrolled toxic sites.[5]

These problems are not limited to hazardous waste sites. For example, 75 percent of the residents in rural areas of the Southwest are drinking pesticide-contaminated water; the majority are Latino American. More than 2 million tons of uranium tailings have been mined and dumped on Native American reservations. The result is that Navajo teenagers are said to have reproductive organ cancer at seventeen times the national average.[6] Native American reservations are truly forgotten lands because they are not covered by state or federal environmental laws.

Urban environmental problems abound. Several million inner-city children suffer from lead poisoning, which results in learning disorders—the majority of these children are African American, Latino American, and Asian American. Working-class women of color are therefore motivated to organize around very pragmatic environmental issues rather than those normally associated with middle-class organizations.

> I did not come to the fight against environmental problems as an intellectual but rather as a concerned mother. . . . People say, "But you're not a scientist. How do you know it's not safe? . . ." I have common sense . . . I know if dioxin and mercury are going to come out of an incinerator stack, somebody's going to be affected. (Charlotte Bullock)

When Concerned Citizens of South Central Los Angeles came together to oppose the solid waste incinerator planned for the community, no one thought much about environmentalism or even feminism. These were just words in a community with a 78 percent unemployment rate, an average yearly income ($8,158) less than half that of the general Los Angeles population, and a residential density more than twice that of the whole city.

In the first stages of organization, what motivated and directed individual actions was the need to protect home and children; for the group, this individual orientation emerged as a community-centered battle. What was left in this deteriorating district on the periphery of the central business and commercial district had to be defended; a "garbage dump" was the final insult after years of neglect. Downtown flourished while residents in this area were prevented from borrowing enough to put up even a new roof.

The organization was never gender restricted, but it became apparent after a while that women were the majority. The organization of the group, the actions it engaged in, even the content of what was said all were not only a product of the issue itself—the waste incinerator—but also a function of women's oppression and what happens as the process of consciousness-raising begins.

Women often play a primary part in community action because it is about things they know best. They also tend to use organizing strategies and methods that are the antithesis of those of the traditional environmentalist movement.[7] Minority women in several urban areas have found themselves part of a new radical core of environmental activists, motivated by the irrationalities of capital-intensive growth. These individuals are responding not to "nature" in the abstract but to their homes and the health of their children.

> I have asthma, my children have asthma, my brothers and sisters have asthma, there are a lot of health problems that people living around an incinerator might be subjected to, and I said, "They can't do this to me and my family." (Robin Cannon)

Women are more likely than men to take on these issues precisely because the home has been defined as a woman's domain. According to Cynthia Cockburn, "In a housing situation that is a health hazard, the woman is more likely to act than the man because she lives there all day and because she is impelled by fear for her children. Community action of this kind is a significant phase of class struggle, but it is also an element of women's liberation."[8]

This phenomenon was most apparent in the battle over LANCER. Women with no political experience, who had no history of organizing, responded first as protectors of their children. Many were single parents; others were older women who had raised families. While the experts were convinced that their smug dismissal of the validity of health concerns raised by these women would send the women away, it only reinforced their determination.

> People's jobs were threatened, ministers were threatened . . . but I said, "I'm not going to be intimidated. . . ." My child's health comes first . . . that's more important than my job.   (Charlotte Bullock)

None of the officials was prepared for the intensity of concerns or the consistency of agitation. In fact, the women leading the opposition in South Central Los Angeles did not fit the prototype opposition as detailed by Cerrell Associates, a Los Angeles consulting firm. The firm was hired by the California Waste Management Board to find out the best places to site waste-to-energy facilities. Rather, Cerrell Associates concluded:

> Certain types of people are likely to participate in politics, either by virtue of their issue awareness or their financial resources, or both. Members of middle or high socioeconomic strata (a composite index of level of education, occupational prestige, and income) are more likely to organize into effective groups to express their political interests and views. All socioeconomic groupings tend to resent the nearby siting of major facilities, but the middle and upper socioeconomic strata possess better resources to effectuate their opposition. Middle and higher socioeconomic strata neighborhoods should not fall at least within the one mile and five mile radii of the proposed site.
> . . . [A]lthough environmental concerns cut across all

subgroups, people with a college education, young or middle-aged, and liberal in philosophy are most likely to organize opposition to the siting of a major facility. Older people, with a high school education or less, and those who adhere to a free-market orientation are least likely to oppose a facility.

The organizers in South Central Los Angeles are the antithesis of the prototype: high school educated or less; middle-aged, elderly, and young; nonprofessionals and the unemployed; low-income persons with no previous political experience—these were the characteristics of the protest group. The consultants and politicians persisted in their disbelief, however, that opposition from this group could be serious.

> In the 1950s, the city banned small incinerators in the yard, and yet they want to build a big incinerator. . . . The council is going to build something in my community which might kill my child. . . . I don't need a scientist to tell me that's wrong.   (Charlotte Bullock)

The intransigence of the city council intensified the agitation, and the women became less willing to compromise as time passed. Each passing month gave them greater strength, knowledge, and perseverance. In the end, the men of the corporation and the city had a more formidable enemy than they ever expected, and in the end they had to compromise—politicians backing away from their previous embrace of incineration as a solution to the trash crisis and the corporation backing away from a site in a poor African American residential area. While the issues are far from resolved, it is significant that willingness to compromise has become the official position of the city and the corporation, as a result of the determination of "a few women."

How successful was this grass-roots group in attracting supporters from outside its community? The African American leaders of Concerned Citizens were able to form allies and strong working relationships with a diverse set of international, national, and grass-roots environmental groups. Greenpeace was the first national environmental group to join Concerned Citizens in the fight to kill LANCER. Other environmental groups would later join the fight, including Citizens for a Better Environment (CBE), the National Health Law Program, and the Center for Law in the Public Interest.

Concerned Citizens of South Central Los Angeles was able to forge alliances with two white Westside "slow-growth" groups: Not Yet New York (a coalition of environmental and home owner groups) and the anti-incineration group called California Alliance in Defense of Residential Environments, or CADRE. The group and their allies used a wide range of tactics to fend off what was seen as a threat to their quality of life.

The grass-roots leaders borrowed many of their tactics from the earlier civil rights movement. They used some form of public protest, demonstrations, petitions, lobbying, reports and fact finding, and hearings to educate the community and intensify public debate on the dispute. Similarly, community workshops and neighborhood forums are used to keep local residents informed about the disputes and any new developments.

Similarly, Concerned Citizens targeted the various levels of government (local, state, and federal) for their role (direct or indirect) in siting and enforcement decisions. For example, they sought to have government intervene in their disputes. The LANCER dispute was infused into local city politics and was a contributing factor in the defeat of pro-LANCER city council president Pat Russell and the election of environmental advocate Ruth Galanter.

The women in South Central Los Angeles were not alone in their battle. They were joined by women from across the city, white, middle-class, and professional.

> I didn't know we all had so many things in common . . . millions of people in the city had something in common with us . . . the environment. (Robin Cannon)

Together, these two groups of women have created something previously unknown to the city of Los Angeles—unity of purpose across neighborhood and racial lines.

> We are making a difference. . . . When we come together as a whole and stick with it, we can win because we are right. (Charlotte Bullock)

This unity has been accomplished by informality, respect, tolerance of spontaneity, and decentralization. Activities that we are told destroy organizations have in reality worked to sustain this movement. For a year and a half, the group functioned without a formal leadership structure. The unconscious acceptance of equality and democratic process resulted in a rotation of the chair's position at meetings; theoretically, it was an expression of what analysts have come to refer to as the feminist critique of bureaucracy, which we have also seen in other women's actions, such as Greenham Commons.[9] Representatives of the news media were disoriented when they asked for the spokesperson and the group responded that everyone could speak for the neighborhood.

"It may be the case that women, unlike men, are less conditioned to see the value of small advances," says Cynthia Cockburn.[10] These women were all guided by their vision of the possible: that it was possible to stop completely the construction of the incinerator, that it is possible in a city like Los Angeles to have reasonable growth, that is possible to humanize community structures and services.

> My neighbors said, "You can't fight City Hall . . . and besides, you work there." I told them I would fight anyway. (Robin Cannon)

None of these women was convinced by the consultants and their traditional justifications for capital-intensive growth: that it increases property values by intensifying land use; that it draws new business to the area; that it removes blight and deterioration; and the key argument used to persuade the working class, that growth creates jobs.

> They're not bringing real development to our community. . . . They're going to bring this incinerator to us and then say,

"We're going to give you fifty jobs when you get this plant. . . ." Meanwhile, they're going to shut down another factory (in Riverside) and eliminate 200 jobs to buy more pollution rights . . . they may close more shops.   (Robin Cannon)

Ironically, the consultants' advice to industry backfired. They had suggested that emphasizing employment and a "gift" to the community (of $2 million for a community development fund for park improvement) would persuade opponents. But promises of heated swimming pools, air-conditioned basketball courts, and fifty jobs at the facility were more insulting than encouraging. Similarly, expert assurance that health risks associated with dioxin exposure were less than those associated with "eating peanut butter" unleashed a flurry of dissent. All of the women, young and old, working-class and professional, had made peanut butter sandwiches for years.

The experts' insistence on referring to congenital deformities and cancers as "acceptable risks" angered the women, who rose to speak of a child's asthma, a parent's influenza, or the high rate of cancer, heart disease, and pneumonia in this poverty-stricken community. The callous disregard of these human concerns by the experts brought the women closer together. They came to rely more on one another as they were subjected to the sarcastic rebuffs of men who referred to their concerns as "irrational, uninformed, and disruptive." These men used gender as the basis for discrediting women's concerns. Their laughter and contempt were directed at professionals and the unemployed alike; both whites and African Americans were castigated as irrational and uncompromising. As a result, new levels of consciousness were sparked in these women.

The reactions of the men of the corporation and the city provided a very serious learning experience for women, both professionals and nonprofessionals, who came to the movement without a critique of patriarchy. That critique was developed in practice. And in confronting the need for equality, these women forced men to a new level of recognition—that working-class women's concerns cannot be dismissed, even if it means more years of organizing.

Individual transformations accompanied the group process. As the struggle against the incinerator proceeded to take on some elements of class struggle, individual consciousness matured and developed. Women began to recognize something of their oppression as women. This led to new forms of action directed not only toward changing the offending institutions but also toward transforming social relations in the home.

> My husband didn't take me seriously at first either. . . . He just saw a whole lot of women meeting and assumed we wouldn't get anything done. . . . I had to split my time. . . . I'm the one who usually comes home from work, cooks, helps the kids with their homework, then I watch a little TV and go to bed to get ready for the next morning. Now I would rush home, cook, read my materials on LANCER. . . . Now the kids were on their own. . . . I had my own homework . . . my husband still wasn't taking me seriously. My husband had to learn to allocate more time for baby-sitting. Now on Saturdays if they weren't at the show or the park, I couldn't attend. . . . In the evenings there were hearings. . . . I was using my vacation time to go to hearings during the work day.   (Robin Cannon)

For single mothers, time in the home was strained. Children and husbands complained that meetings and public hearings had taken priority over the family and relations in the home.

Ironically, it was concern for family, love of family, that had catapulted these women into action to begin with; but in a pragmatic sense, the home did have to come second in order for health and safety to be preserved. These were hard learning experiences. But meetings in individual homes ultimately involved children and spouses alike. The transformation of relations continued as women spoke up at hearings and demonstrations and husbands transported children, made signs, and looked on with pride and support at public forums.

The critical perspective of women in the battle against LANCER went far beyond what the women themselves had intended. For these women, the political issues were personal, and in that sense they became feminist issues. In the end, these women were fighting for what they felt was right rather than what men argued was reasonable. The coincidence of the principles of feminism and ecology found expression and development in the consciousness of participants; the concern for earth as a home; a recognition that all parts of a system have equal value; the acknowledgment of process; and, finally, the awareness that capitalist growth has social costs.

> This fight has really turned me around; things are intertwined in ways I hadn't realized. . . . All these social issues as well as political and economic issues are really intertwined. Before, I was concerned only about health, and then I began to get into politics, decision making, and so many things.
> (Robin Cannon)

In two years, what started as the outrage of a small group of mothers transformed the political climate of a major metropolitan area. These women have strived for a greater level of democracy, a greater level of involvement, not only in their organization but also in the development of the city. They have demanded accountability regarding land use and landownership—very subversive concerns in a capitalist society. The group process, collectivism, was of primary importance. It allowed women to see their own power and potential and therefore allowed them to consolidate effective opposition.

The movement has also underscored the role of principles. In fact, we all have lived so long with an unquestioning acceptance of profit and expediency that sometimes we forget that our objective is to do "what's right." Women are beginning to raise this point in a very forthright manner, emphasizing that "the experts" have left us no choice but to follow our own moral convictions rather than accept neutrality and capitulate in the face of crisis.

The environmental crisis will escalate in the 1990s, and women of color are sure to play pivotal roles, for the reasons discussed in this chapter. If women are able to sustain for longer periods some

of the qualities and behavioral forms that they display in crisis sit-
uations (direct participatory democracy and the critique of bureaucracy, for example), they may be able to reintroduce equality and
democracy into progressive action. They may also reintroduce the
value of being moved by principle and morality.

Pragmatism has come to dominate all forms of political behavior, and the result has been disastrous as individuals and groups negotiate issues that must be understood in their totality. If women
maintain leadership positions and resist the "normal" organizational thrust to barter, bargain, and fragment ideas and issues, they
may help to set new standards for action in the environmental
movement.

Concerned Citizens proved that local citizens can fight city hall
and win. Opponents of the city-initiated incinerator project applied
pressure on key elected officials, including Mayor Tom Bradley.
Mayor Bradley later reversed his position on the incinerator project
and asked the Los Angeles City Council to kill the project—a project that had been in the planning stage since 1969 and included a
commitment of $12 million.[11]

CONCLUSION

It is unlikely that the United States will experience a mass infusion
of people of color as members of the national environmental groups
anytime soon. However, there are clear signs that we will see continuing growth in grass-roots environmental groups led by women
of color. As long as American society is separate and unequal, grass-
roots environmental groups of color will serve a positive function.

A growing number of African American groups, like Concerned
Citizens of South Central Los Angeles, are taking up the struggle for
environmental justice. Generally, these grass-roots environmental
groups emphasize social and economic justice. Their special brand
of environmentalism is broad and includes issues such as housing,
parks and playgrounds, and discriminatory redlining and attacks
policies that accelerate economic and physical decline of inner-city
neighborhoods.

It is not surprising that the women of Concerned Citizens are leading the resistance in Los Angeles's disenfranchised communities. Environmental struggles mirror the social justice struggle in other arenas. The targeting of communities of color for noxious facilities is a question of social justice.

Environmental racism and the social problems confronting communities of color force grass-roots leaders to incorporate many of the tactics learned from the earlier civil rights movement. Environmental justice groups can make a difference in the quality of life enjoyed in disenfranchised communities, and national environmental groups can learn a few lessons from these groups.

Although somewhat fragile in nature, the alliances formed between grass-roots and national groups can produce positive results. Moreover, working together provides a forum for breaking down stereotypes and mistrust on both sides. These new alliances have the potential of reshaping environmental policy debates around the issue of justice.

12

Mothers of East Los Angeles Strike Back

GABRIEL GUTIÉRREZ

Since the annexation of the Southwest, people of Mexican descent in the United States have suffered grave social and political injustices. Los Angeles, home to the second largest concentration of Mexicans in the world, is no exception. Its residents, both citizens and noncitizens, taxpayers nonetheless, have historically and systematically been excluded from both governance and economic opportunity. During the Reagan-Bush years, the income gap between the elite and the working class grew, worsening the plight of Latinos. In his acclaimed study, "A Community Under Siege: A Chronicle of Chicanos East of the Los Angeles River, 1945–1975," Rodolfo Acuña documents the corporate encroachment and political manipulation by the downtown elite on the unsuspecting Eastside.[1]

The truth be told, although Mexican Americans are concentrated throughout the region, the plight of Chicanos in East Los Angeles best reflects the history of Anglo-Mexican relations. In the late 1950s, Mexican American families were uprooted and displaced in order to make way for the infamous "East L.A. Interchange," which today connects Interstate Highways 5 and 10, California Route 60, and U.S. Highway 101. This was one to create better access to downtown Los Angeles for mostly Anglo suburban commuters.

While a predominantly Mexican American community was demographically anatomized, such a project would eventually result in environmental and health concerns in the years that followed.[2] For example, my parents, Juana Beatríz Gutiérrez and Ricardo Gutiérrez, were forced out of their homes on two separate occasions while the freeways were being built. Again, in the late 1950s and early 1960s, more Mexican American families were forced out of their homes in the Chavez Ravine area near Elysian Park to make way for the construction of Dodger Stadium.

Acuña writes that this resulted in resistance from members of the Arechiga family, who were joined by friends and relatives as they attempted to save their homes of thirty-six years from the bulldozers in May 1959. Despite efforts to evict the Arechigas, this family stood its ground for almost two years. Among the most vocal proponents of this project was Los Angeles Mayor Norris Poulson. As Mrs. Arechiga, age sixty-six, was being bodily removed, she shouted in Spanish, "Why don't they play ball in [Mayor] Poulson's backyard—not ours!"[3]

THE AWAKENING

Some scholars and politicians have argued that the Latino community and the Mexican American community in particular, has suffered injustices as a result of being apolitical. This theory was debunked, however, by a group of mothers from East Los Angeles in the mid-1980s. This group, known as Mothers of East Los Angeles (MELA), first stormed into the political arena by strongly opposing a proposed state prison in East Los Angeles.[4]

Immediately successful, MELA pursued other quality of life issues—including environmental issues. Besides leading the fight against the state prison, they participated in the Coalition Against the Pipeline and spearheaded the defeat of a proposal by California Thermal Treatment Services (CTTS) to locate an incinerator in the neighboring community of Vernon.[5] Without doubt, MELA's origins and tactics have had an irrevocable impact on policymakers and on the surrounding community. In short, the participants have become more demanding of government, not accepting the traditional concealment of information by bureaucrats.

In early May of 1985, Juana Beatríz Gutiérrez, a homemaker, Neighborhood Watch Program organizer, and mother of nine, was approached by California state assemblywoman Gloria Molina, who was informing community leaders and organizations about plans by the Department of Corrections to construct a state prison in East Los Angeles. Shortly thereafter, Gutiérrez held a meeting of fellow Neighborhood Watch block captains at her residence to discuss the state's plans to locate the prison at 12th Street and Santa Fe Avenue. This meeting, held on May 24, 1985, was attended by Juana Gutiérrez; her husband, Ricardo; Juanita Senteno; Teresa Soto; and Lucy Mendoza, in addition to Father Luis Carbo, pastor of Santa Isabel Church, and Martha Molina, an aide to Assemblywoman Molina. It was this meeting that ignited a standoff between a very stubborn corporate and political elite and an even more relentless group of Latina mothers, giving birth to the Mothers of East Los Angeles.

After the founding meeting, several of the participants began to spread the news by word of mouth. Meanwhile, Molina's staff approached other organizations and business leaders. Most notable were Steve Kasten of Lincoln Heights, José Luis Garcia of Boyle Heights, and Frank Villalobos of Montebello.

The community was especially upset by the lack of information and public awareness caused by the state's clandestine handling of the prison proposal. The Department of Corrections had first begun to consider the East Los Angeles site, known as the "Crown Coach site," on April 10, 1984, more than a year before the initial opposition was raised in May 1985.[6] In doing so, the department violated its own policy, which calls for "community input and feedback" in the process of *selecting* a prison site. This sparked a sense of moral outrage in the founders of MELA, who began to mobilize, informing other members of the community about yet another injustice.

Members soon came up with reasons why a prison should not be built on the Crown Coach site. These included "its proximity to the heavily populated community of Boyle Heights and to 26 schools within a two mile radius of the proposed site."[7] Also, there was concern about the half dozen or so prisons and jails already in and around East Los Angeles. In spite of this opposition, proponents of the prison called for bypassing an environmental impact report until *after* the purchase of the proposed site, a move that indicated that they felt they could impose their will on the surrounding community by investing millions of taxpayers' dollars in the project.

As a rule, affluent communities handily oppose locally unwanted land uses (LULUs) that threaten their property values. In contrast, MELA rested its case on the defense of the community's youth. Gutiérrez, quoted in the *Los Angeles Times,* said: "I don't consider myself political. I'm just someone looking out for the community, for the youth . . . on the side of justice." Aurora Castillo, a vocal participant who traces her family origins to a time "before the first Anglo set foot on California soil," agrees: "We were compelled to unite, because the future quality of life for our children is being threatened. And we've been fighting every which way."[8] Castillo continues, "You know, if one of [her] children's safety is jeopardized, the mother turns into a lioness."[9]

Efforts to inform other members of the community and to seek the community's support proved very fruitful. Gutiérrez recalls: "On one Sunday alone, my husband Ricardo and I gathered 900 signatures [of persons who opposed construction of the prison in East Los Angeles] among the parishioners of Santa Isabel and Saint Mary's churches."[10] This action moved beyond Neighborhood Watch; its objective, to mobilize opposition to the prison within the church network.

One of those who was most touched by this issue was the pastor of Resurrection Parish, Father John Morreta. Father Morreta opposed the prison construction by approaching parishioners after Sunday mass. It is he who is credited with coining the name "Mothers of East Los Angeles." Taking his cue from *The Official Story,* an Argentine film featuring mothers who demonstrated for the return of their children, who had been kidnapped and, at times, sold to wealthy families, Father Morreta "transformed the name 'Las Madres de la Plaza de Mayo' into 'Mothers of East Los Angeles.'"[11] After consultation with various members, the name was adopted.

As word spread through the street corners and church halls of East Los Angeles, more people and organizations became outraged that their community once again was being targeted for an unwanted facility. Among these were the Boyle Heights, Lincoln Heights, and El Sereno chambers of commerce, the Central City Business Association, the Boyle Heights Kiwanis Club, and the Rotary Club of Boyle Heights. Along with MELA, they formed the Coalition Against the Prison.[12]

One prominent Eastside group that was notably absent from this coalition was the United Neighborhood Organization (UNO). Juana Gutiérrez recalls: "I personally called Sister Modesta [a spokesperson for UNO]. She responded by saying that we shouldn't continue to fight this cause because it was a lost one. UNO never came in with us until they saw that we were winning . . . they came in *con sus cuellos parados* [expecting to save the day]."

Meanwhile, events moved rapidly. MELA helped to organize weekly Monday-night candlelight vigils in an effort to attract media attention and thus garner more support for its cause. These weekly marches on the Olympic Boulevard bridge helped to increase awareness and galvanize community support. Accordingly, the demonstrations attracted more than 3,000 participants in only a few weeks' time.

Other tactics included lobbying by MELA in Sacramento, the state capital. Because of the lack of funds to hire professional lobbyists, MELA did its own lobbying. Together with the coalition, MELA created its own access to information by launching a research and informational campaign.

On several occasions, members of MELA traveled by bus to Sacramento (more than 350 miles one way) to lobby state assemblypersons. One of the most energetic members of MELA, Erlinda Robles, recalls, "We broke up into groups and went to lobby the different legislators." Castillo adds, "In one week, we went to Sacramento twice." The impact that MELA had on state senators was damaging to Governor George Deukmejian's insistence on locating the prison in East Los Angeles. It was largely because of the media coverage and lobbying that the state senate reversed its previous stand and defeated the bill authorizing construction of the East Los Angeles prison that had recently been passed by the state assembly.

The impact was astounding. Ricardo Gutiérrez describes MELA's effect on the state legislators: "They were very surprised that a group of mothers from East Los Angeles knew so much of what was happening, of the laws. They were expecting that once these persons would be asked a question, they would not know how to answer. Every question they were asked, the Mothers of East Los Angeles had answers for."[13] As Gutiérrez points out, "MELA was not expected to be prepared for the legislators." In retrospect, the legislators were not prepared for MELA.

Inclusion in the decision-making process and the accumulation of information proved to be empowering mechanisms. Moreover, trust grew among members of MELA as the group began to increase in number. This trust made possible the effective lobbying campaign.

For the most part, poverty-stricken, misrepresented Latino American communities have been restricted to confrontation on a local level. That is, workers have dealt primarily with bosses, and tenants have dealt with landlords and other authority figures. Consequently, Latino American residents have traditionally been ignored until after the fact when unwanted state projects were being considered. Usually, seemingly irrevocable projects have gone uncontested. However, in the case of MELA's fight against the prison, access to pertinent information separated the group's struggle from past battles.

With fund-raising efforts by local chambers of commerce as well as buses donated by a local bus company, MELA went on to confront the California Department of Corrections, the state assembly, and the governor in state and local arenas. In more than a few instances, after discovering that Governor Deukmejian would be making appearances in southern California, members of MELA would hop on a bus and hold impromptu press conferences in an effort to keep their message in front of the governor. Gutiérrez recalls hearing from a reporter that Deukmejian's aides were irritated and his affluent Anglo audiences were bewildered by MELA's presence. The research and information campaigns also helped to bring a better understanding of the "invisible" forces responsible for dumping undesirable projects on East Los Angeles. In the fall of 1986, the *Daily News* ran a story questioning the history of the lot involved in the proposed prison site.[14] Interestingly, the Crown Coach lot had been purchased in February 1982 by Llewelyn Werner and Richard J. Nathan—of whom the latter was described as "a close friend" of Los Angeles County supervisor Michael D. Antonovich. The supervisor, who was state chair of the Republican party in 1984, was instrumental in opposing a similar prison proposal in Lancaster, an area that he represents.

According to a report in the *Daily News,* Antonovich's aides also played a "key role in bringing the Crown Coach site to the attention of state Department of Correction officials" as an alternative to the Lancaster site. In the meantime, the property value of the 8.2-acre site had more than doubled, rising from $2.5 million to more than $5 million in just a year and a half. Quipped state senator Bill Greene, a Democrat from Los Angeles, "The site selection [represents an effort of] Republican hustlers to buy the property, shove the prison down the minority community's throat, and make a bundle of money."[15]

In December 1986, the auditor general of California issued a report finding that "the Department of Corrections did not follow its established procedures in selecting the 'Crown Coach site' in Los Angeles County."[16] The report also revealed that there was "hazardous waste contamination adjacent to the Crown Coach site and that the site itself [had not been] tested for hazardous waste."[17] Despite these setbacks, proponents of the East Los Angeles prison, led by Governor George Deukmejian, vowed to construct the prison on the Crown Coach site in spite of strong community opposition. Consequently, the opposition became more emotional and personal. Resentment toward those favoring the prison became more vehement. Soon MELA began to take note of various legislators' positions on the prison issue.

It was during this time that MELA learned one of its most painful lessons. As a group working on its first major issue, MELA was soon exposed to the cruel world of politics. Many politicians who had promised to oppose the prison soon found themselves in politically compromising positions and betrayed the community. Politics proved to be a "dirty" business.

PRISONS, PIPELINES, AND POLLUTION

Gloria Molina's successor to the assembly, Lucille Roybal-Allard, arrived at about the same time that other quality of life issues began to surface. Among these were a plan to build a pipeline from Santa Barbara County to Long Beach, avoiding affluent coastal communities in favor of East Los Angeles. Incredibly, this pipeline was to detour about 20 miles inland before returning to the coast. Mary Pardo, a graduate student at the University of California, Los Angeles, who worked with MELA, described a community meeting at which representatives of several oil companies tried to gain support from community members for the pipeline's passage through East Los Angeles:

> "Is it going through Cielito Lindo [Ronald Reagan's ranch]?" The oil representative answered, "No." Another woman stood up and asked, "Why not place it along the coastline?" Without thinking of the implications, the representative responded, "Oh, no! If it burst, it would endanger the marine life." The woman retorted, "You value the marine life more than human beings?" His face reddened with anger and the hearing disintegrated into angry chanting.[18]

This proposal was eventually defeated, much to the credit of the Coalition Against the Pipeline, of which MELA was an active participant. However, a new, similar proposal is currently being considered. MELA soon learned that even when unwanted projects are defeated, new proposals are generated. Little time can be set aside for East Los Angeles residents to celebrate victories before new battles must be waged.

The next, and potentially most dangerous, issue to surface was the 1987 proposal of a hazardous waste incinerator, which was to be the first of its kind in a major metropolitan area. Just three years earlier, Cerrell Associates, a Los Angeles–based consulting firm, had prepared a report for the California Waste Management Board.[19] This report advised government and industry to target "lower socioeconomic neighborhoods" for waste-to-energy facilities. Professor Acuña criticized the Cerrell report, which sanctioned the practice of targeting certain neighborhoods for noxious facilities.[20] Mary Pardo asserts that this same report provided "personality profiles" that outlined the dos and don'ts of locating sites:

> Middle and higher socioeconomic strata neighborhoods should not fall within the one-mile and five-mile radii of the proposed site. Conversely, older people, people with a high school education or less are least likely to oppose a facility.[21]

Given the socioeconomic realities, this description points to low-income minority communities. Indeed, a 1987 study by the United Church of Christ's Commission on Racial Justice titled *Toxic Wastes and Race in the United States* conveyed a similar facility-siting pattern. The study found that of 15 million Latinos, 8 million live in communities with one or more licensed toxic waste sites.[22] Specifically, more than 60 percent of Los Angeles's Latino population lives in zip code regions where there are abandoned toxic waste sites, compared with 30 percent of the city's Anglo population.

The fight against the hazardous waste incinerator attracted a diverse group of allies. Among the leaders in this bout to derail the toxic waste incinerator proposal was Miguel Mendivil, a recent graduate of the University of Notre Dame who at the time was a field representative of Assemblywoman Lucille Roybal-Allard. Because of Mendivil's persistence, the assemblywoman's office had become involved. Also, Martha Molina, who now worked for Roybal-Allard and who had been present at the founding meeting of MELA, was credited with providing much-needed support. Both typified the increasing number of young people from the barrios who were taking leadership roles.

The South Coast Air Quality Management District (SCAQMD) and the state Department of Health Services insisted that the incinerator would have no significant impact on the surrounding community. Consequently, California Thermal Treatment Services (CTTS) was not required to file an environmental impact report (EIR). Ironically, CTTS had been cited dozens of times before for health and safety violations at its infectious waste incinerators in other southern California communities, including twenty-nine citations over a ten-year period for air emission violations in Garden Grove and twenty over a six-year period in Long Beach.

As the saying goes, *Una mano no se lava sola* ("One hand does not cleanse itself"). In a cyclical manner, first, government agencies responsible for enforcing health and safety regulations look the other way when minority communities are involved, paving the path for large private firms like CTTS to practice environmental laissez-faire. Then, on making their obligatory runs, these same agencies discover that there have been infractions—all, of course, after millions of dollars have been made and thousands of tons of toxins have been deposited into the air. Some environmental activists have labeled this practice as environmental racism.

MELA, which was still fighting the prison, responded in December 1987 by assembling more than 500 people at a Department of Health Services hearing and demanding an environmental impact report. In the early months of 1988, two toxic chemical accidents resulted in the forced evacuation of thousands of Eastside residents, igniting further hostility toward the incinerator.[23]

In pursuing this environmental issue, MELA, recalling the effectiveness of coalitions during its fight against the prison, joined with national organizations such as Greenpeace and the Natural Resources Defense Council. Also through this issue, it began to see that other communities were involved in similar struggles throughout the state. Juana Gutiérrez and Erlinda Robles, for instance, are among those who have participated in other demonstrations against similar undesirable projects in various parts of the state.

MELA's network was now expanding beyond the borders of East Los Angeles. This was best exemplified in a statewide demonstration against the Vernon incinerator held in November 1988. Environmental activists from Casmalia, Kettleman City, Richmond, Martinez, El Centro, and other locales where similar problems exist converged in East Los Angeles. Together, they marched from Resurrection Church to Bandini Boulevard, the site of the proposed incinerator, to take part in a demonstration that involved more than 1,000 persons.

Because of mounting pressure, the SCAQMD refused to extend CTTS's incinerator permits, but the Environmental Protection Agency and Superior Court Judge Kurt Lewin in effect undermined this action by allowing CTTS to receive permits without a full EIR. By this time, MELA had involved itself in fights against other proposed toxic burners in the area; among these was a Chem-Clear facility across the street from Huntington Park High School. There, the students organized an impressive demonstration involving more than 500 persons. Martin Smith, who would become general manager of the plant, conceded that he was "surprised by the student demonstration and . . . impressed by the turnout."[24]

In spite of the never-ending battles, persistence finally paid off. On its sixth anniversary, May 24, 1991, MELA received word that California Thermal Treatment Services, amidst costly court battles (organizations and individuals had joined to file a lawsuit against the different agencies) and public pressure, had abandoned its plans to build a hazardous waste incinerator in Vernon.[25] This prompted Juana Gutiérrez to write a public thank-you letter in which she acknowledged Senator Art Torres, who was instrumental in opposing this project, as well as Assemblywoman Lucille Roybal-Allard and her father, Congressman Edward Roybal. In expressing her gratitude, Gutiérrez noted:

> It is no secret that chemical- and toxic-producing corporations looking to make a fast dollar target communities of color be-

cause of their stereotypical powerlessness. Through this victory, let it be known that communities of color throughout the
state of California will unite whenever our children are threatened.

The tremendous effect on policy that MELA has had with respect
to the prison, the pipeline, and the incinerator has attracted offers
of contributions from sympathetic organizations and individuals.
This moved some members of MELA from the Resurrection Parish
to incorporate the group. The mothers at the founding parish of
Santa Isabel, though at first considering incorporation, decided
against it, citing their need to remain autonomous, self-sufficient,
and uncensored. Erlinda Robles explains, "We should not take
money from anybody so that we won't be dictated to by anybody."
No membership dues or staff exists.

The running of MELA at the founding parish of Santa Isabel has
continued as always. Occasional menudo breakfasts are served, and
rummage sales are held, with the proceeds going to such activities
as Christmas toy drives for neighborhood children. An attempt was
made to establish a scholarship fund for students at Santa Isabel Elementary School. Also, the founders of the group maintain that any
governance of MELA should be done on a parish-by-parish basis.

BUILDING FAMILY, HOME, AND COMMUNITY

Contrary to what some may suspect, the Mothers of East Los Angeles did not abandon their families to pursue political issues. Actually, they have gained tremendous support from their husbands
and children. Valentín Robles, husband of Erlinda, when asked
what his role in MELA was, responded:

> I have no role; I'm part of a coalition. My wife is involved with
> MELA. They have put up a successful fight. All I can do is back
> my wife up. I can't be a Mother of East L.A., since I'm a man.
> They should be in control. They have started this fight. Person-
> ally, I believe that no one priest or one man should be in charge.

To the same question, Ricardo Gutiérrez, who was present at the founders' meeting of MELA, responds: "We [husbands] are not involved in running MELA, but we're behind them 100 percent. We choose to stay in the background and do not feel that we are being bypassed."

At the time they began, it seemed highly impossible that a group of six women would be capable of mobilizing a movement that would exceed 3,000 persons. Yet after more than six years, MELA received national and international recognition for its valiant effort to preserve its community. MELA soon began to tackle other issues of major concern, including the struggle to preserve Olvera Street from developers and an unfriendly councilman; water conservation; and the demand for a Chicano/Chicana Studies Department at the University of California, Los Angeles, and more Chicano professors in the University of California system.

These lifetime community advocates-turned-activists have brought about an exciting sense of hope among younger activists within the community, many of whom have returned from distinguished universities to make it "back *into* the barrio," despite having been encouraged by society to "make it *out*." In an effort to put into context the community's response to MELA, one can cite a letter by a concerned individual that appeared in the *Los Angeles Times:* "Jimmy Stewart, in an old movie, quoted his father as saying, 'The only causes worth fighting for are the lost causes.' Well, I hope that the East L.A. prison fight is not a lost cause. It is something certainly worth fighting for, and if the Eastside residents have room for one more, I am certainly willing."

Gloria Molina could not have imagined what she was igniting when she first informed the community of plans to build a state prison. A community, one often taken for granted, was suddenly transformed. As mothers came out in defense of their children and community, they became familiar with the forces that for many years had held a tight grip on their East Los Angeles. This time, the community said, No! And it continued to say no to every other undesirable project. Such a sentiment is reflected in a statement by Juana Gutiérrez:

As a mother and resident of East L.A., I will continue fighting with perseverance, so we will be respected. And I will do this with much affection for my community. I say "my community" because I am part of it; I love my *raza* [people] as my family, and if God allows, I will continue fighting against all the governors who try to take advantage of us.

Indeed, Governor Pete Wilson, despite promising the opposite during his campaign, included the East Los Angeles prison in his 1992 budget. This action did not come as much of a surprise and has been met with continued resistance. After approximately seven years, the prison issue has become a symbol of resistance for many. On September 14, 1992, Governor Wilson signed a bill that killed the East Los Angeles prison proposal. This action came just two days before observance of Mexican Independence Day. After hearing the news, about 200 Eastside residents gathered at Resurrection Catholic Church, shouting "We won the war!" The struggle was summed up by Lucy Ramos, president of MELA:

The politicians thought we wouldn't fight but we united and said, *Ya basta,* enough, this [is] a dumping ground no more. . . . The kids around here were babies when we started. Now they too will fight for what they believe in because we showed them their voices count.[26]

Something irrevocable has happened. The one sure thing is that East Los Angeles will never be the same. Because of this newfound determination and activism, the community can no longer be taken for granted. The members of MELA demonstrated that they are well adapted to long-term struggles. These women are long-distance runners for environmental justice. In the end, their work sends a clear signal that hard work does pay off.

13

PUEBLO Fights
Lead Poisoning

FRANCIS CALPOTURA AND RINKU SEN

This chapter is less an attempt to explore the issues surrounding lead poisoning, about which much has been written by people more qualified than we are, than it is an attempt to clarify for ourselves and other organizers the lessons we have drawn from building a multiracial, low-income people's organization for which lead poisoning has been an important fight.

In a June 1991 article in the *East Bay Express,* journalist Dashka Slater called People United for a Better Oakland (PUEBLO) "the community group that has single-handedly put lead poisoning on the county's agenda." Not apparent in Slater's flattering coverage of PUEBLO's often controversial actions are the real contributions that this small community organization, whose members are 70 percent women of color and 90 percent low-income families of color, has made to the future of multiracial community organizing in California and the United States.

From 1990 to 1992, PUEBLO conducted a citywide campaign to eradicate the problem of lead poisoning in Oakland, California. One of the most pervasive environmental hazards affecting low-income, inner-city children in America, lead poisoning is especially dangerous because its effects are difficult to diagnose without a special blood test.[1] Moreover, its effects are largely irreversible. Using a 1988 study by the state of California as an entry point into the

234

issue, PUEBLO firmly placed the responsibility for public education, screening of children, and removal of lead from homes and public spaces on the shoulders of the Oakland City Council and the Alameda County Board of Supervisors.

The result was not only the most comprehensive lead abatement plan on the West Coast but also growth in the membership and reputation of a two-year-old community organization of color. By organizing directly among the people most affected by lead and most disenfranchised from the health care delivery system, by building a strong base of support among liberal physicians, attorneys, and public workers, and by strategically placing a specific set of demands before decision makers, PUEBLO set a precedent for community organizations fighting lead poisoning.

ORIGINS OF PUEBLO

PUEBLO began in 1989 as the Campaign for Accessible Health Care, a project of the Oakland-based Center for Third World Organizing (CTWO). CTWO had gained a national reputation for training young organizers of color and consulting with a wide range of organizations of color to build issue campaigns. The initiative for the Campaign for Accessible Health Care stemmed from CTWO's interest in a local organizing project that would directly address the concerns of low-income people of color in Oakland and train organizers who would be more able to meet the challenge of building multicultural organizations.

Our own involvement with PUEBLO is rooted in our roles as staff members of CTWO, currently as the center's executive codirectors. Francis Calpotura directed the center's major organizer training program, the Minority Activist Apprenticeship Program, for three years before becoming organizer of the Campaign for Accessible Health Care and is the person directly responsible for the first three years of PUEBLO's development. Rinku Sen is a graduate of the Minority Activist Apprenticeship Program and is coordinator of CTWO's Saturday School for Community Leaders, a key component of PUEBLO's leadership development approach. We write about PUEBLO as a project with which we have been intimately involved, from contributing to strategic decisions to raising necessary moneys for the project's operation.

Three years into its development, PUEBLO is a multi-issue, multiconstituency organization whose mostly Latino American and African American family membership numbers 400. Families pay dues of $24 per year, and the organization's core leadership includes twelve to fifteen individuals who facilitate communication among members and coordinate and inform organizational decision making. PUEBLO's main outreach techniques include doorknocking, house meetings, institutional visits, and public education in a variety of forms. The major languages spoken are English, Spanish, Chinese, Tagalog, and Vietnamese.

The organization has two to three staff people at any time and relies heavily on the ownership and work of its member-leaders and nonmember volunteers. Lead poisoning is only one of the issues PUEBLO has tackled; others include access to immunization and general health care, tenants' rights to decent housing, and racial discrimination in employment.

THE BIG PICTURE

In Oakland, as in small and large cities across the country, quickly changing racial demographics demand political and economic structures that are accountable to communities of color. The 1990 census shows in California a population boom among people of color in relation to non-Hispanic whites or Anglos: Asian Americans have increased by 127 percent; Latino Americans, by 69.2 percent; African Americans, by 21.4 percent; and Native Americans, by 20.3 percent, all contrasted to a 13.8 percent growth in non-Hispanic white populations.[2]

Experts have attributed these changes to high birth rates and significant growth in immigration, leading the California State Department of Finance to predict that people of color will constitute the state's majority by the year 2003. At the same time, childhood poverty rates are climbing, fueled by conservative policies that favor corporate mobility over social responsibility. The end result has been harmful cuts in social services.

The tensions between growing communities of color and the current urban infrastructure are clearly reflected in Oakland. More than twenty-seven different languages are spoken in Oakland, but major institutions responsible for building systems of housing, health care, education, and other basic needs have been slow to adjust to the city's demographic changes. Refusing to take leadership in designing programs that would respond to the needs of multilingual constituencies, these agencies have rendered themselves irrelevant and unreachable to a sizable segment of the community.

This tension between poor people and the government institutions that govern and supposedly serve them has been translated into competition among communities of color for seemingly scarce resources. Historically, community organizations have tended to remain monoracial, and competition rather than cooperation has dominated the relations between African American, Asian American, Latino American, and Native American organizations. Besides splits among racial communities, there is also tension between new immigrants, whose entry into Oakland we can trace largely to U.S. intervention in Third World countries, and their American-born counterparts.

Oakland stands at an important break in poor people's organizing, a break that awaits a widespread multiracial strategy. Into this mix came PUEBLO, founded on the notions that low-income people of color can be organized around issues that cross racial interests and that such organizing must include a reflective process that illuminates oppressive political, economic, and cultural structures. More important, organizers seek to build members' commitment to changing those oppressive structures at their root.

FILLING A NICHE

The Campaign for Accessible Health Care, the organizing project that gave birth to PUEBLO, initially focused on preventing a measles outbreak from claiming Oakland as it had other large cities.

Dallas, Chicago, Milwaukee, and Los Angeles were among the first to be recorded. CTWO had researched and reported on the foreseeable crisis in the November 1988 issue of its *Minority Trendsletter*. Author Madeleine Adamson predicted that a monopolization of vaccine production and marketing, combined with Reagan's health care cuts, would reduce low-income people's access to the vaccines, culminating in a full-blown epidemic. Moving quickly from a door-to-door health survey of 1,000 Oakland families to demonstrations at the Alameda County Department of Health, the Campaign for Accessible Health Care was successful in winning free immunizations for 30,000 children in Oakland and other parts of the county.

Despite its early record of forcing officials to take positive action, the Campaign did not meet with overarching status as a legitimate organization. Externally, it was criticized for its militant actions. Community-based clinics questioned its tactics, which went beyond accepted norms of haggling for more services in settings sanctioned and controlled by the state, frequently seen in the form of public hearings and forums in which community members individually voice their complaints with little or no hope of a response.

The Campaign's targeting of the Child Health and Disability Prevention Program (CHDPP) for access to federally funded children's services and its demand that the County Department of Health set up Saturday immunization clinics made adversaries of the directors of both bodies. Those relationships did not change until well into the lead poisoning campaign.

The Campaign's open support of undocumented immigrants' rights to services also drew criticism from more traditional organizations of color; many of these established organizations had fallen on the conservative side of the immigration debate, favoring punishment and deportation of undocumented immigrants.

Planners also encountered barriers in the internal development of the organization. The notion of building a multiracial organization had been widely discussed but rarely acted on, leaving a vacuum of tested models from which we could learn. On a short-term level, communities of color were mobilized around a well-developed and dramatic issue, but the roots of political solidarity had only just begun to sprout.

The Campaign's relationships with each community, with all its variations, required constant nurturing, and some differences never were breached. For example, Southeast Asian participation in the campaign dropped dramatically as tactics increased in militancy; those communities had to be newly recruited for each action. The challenges of differing language and cultural-political experiences made consensus building painstaking, most obviously at logistic levels. Organizers had to be prepared to provide transportation, child care, and fairly sophisticated translation for meetings. Even a small meeting of ten to twelve people with translation in only one language could easily require five hours, not including preparation or follow-up time before and after the meeting. Our acquisition of 150 simultaneous translation machines in 1991 helped tremendously, but earlier in the organization's development we could borrow or rent machines only for large events.

Although the Campaign did not escape setbacks like these, the immunization fight did form the base from which PUEBLO would develop. This phase of the organizing project built the organization's base membership, as well as legitimacy among communities of color, the public health structures, the media, and a diverse set of allies.

First, the door-to-door organizing style recruited individual members who took increasing leadership as the tactics of the campaigns escalated in militancy. Gwen Hardy, a frequent PUEBLO spokeswoman fond of describing herself as "a mother, grandmother, and wife," noted the importance of the organization's commitment to new members. In an interview with the *Race, Poverty and the Environment Newsletter*, Hardy describes her first interaction with an organizer at her doorstep and her subsequent activism in the organization. "I told her 'I don't drive and I don't have transportation.' They said 'We'll come pick you up!' I went to the meeting and heard what was being discussed. At that point in my life I needed something to get involved in. . . . By becoming involved with this community organization eventually I found out that there were a lot of things that weren't being taken care of. I found that we have to pressure and pressure, push and push in order for them to do the things."[3]

By reaching out to community members on their own turf, and by creating an organizational structure that provided opportunities for members to understand and confront the hidden power structure of their communities and build a social network, PUEBLO began to be as important a locus in members' lives as the places where we first found them—home, work, school, and the hospital.

Second to membership, the question of alliances is the most important to a new organization. Organizer Calpotura's careful interviewing of leaders in Oakland's communities of color created a set of institutional relationships that could be mobilized as needed, particularly in communities of new African, Asian, and Latino immigrants. The recruitment of college students to conduct the initial health survey each Saturday in the spring of 1989 helped solidify the Campaign's university contacts and provided a constant and important source of volunteers. College students bring a high level of energy and enthusiasm to grass-roots organizing.

Finally, the Campaign focused on building relationships with public workers at important places for children's health care, so public school nurses, school administrators, and public health workers played essential roles. All three groups were especially important to the intelligence-gathering activities of the campaign, allowing organizers and members access to information that often changed the direction of the Campaign's strategy.

By the end of 1989, the Campaign for Accessible Health Care could count several victories. The most immediate was the vaccination of 30,000 children at Saturday clinics in the county hospitals. The best structural victory was Oakland's establishment of the Measles Prevention Program, which continues to provide free immunizations on demand. And the most important internal victory was a leadership base that visibly crossed racial lines in working on the issue of children's health care.

But organizations setting out to change communities and their relationship to power in any meaningful way must also struggle with the scarcity of resources and the histories of racial animosity at their most practical, as well as ideological, levels. The Get the Lead Out campaign represents PUEBLO's second effort to tackle the questions of power and cultural diversity.

DEVELOPING THE LEAD ISSUE

When leaders of CTWO first heard of the 1988 California state study documenting the problem of lead poisoning, they knew instinctively that it would point to the prevalence of poisoning in poor communities of color. Although local organizers felt that lead was a potentially important issue, initial exploration revealed several problems with the current discussions about lead poisoning, placing it firmly outside the generally accepted criteria. Research played a key role in helping organizers pinpoint the root causes of lead poisoning and identify workable solutions that would both make significant changes in people's lives and change the way the power structure dealt with affected communities.

First, many residents simply did not see lead poisoning as a critical problem. Lead poisoning is popularly attributed to children's eating leaded paint chips, and many people felt that the 1978 federal government ban on lead-based paint had eradicated the problem. But because there were no mass government efforts to remove lead-based paint from homes built before 1978, and because lead seals paint to make it last longer, the paint remains in older homes, where many poor people live.

Furthermore, while children do ingest lead from paint chips, more subtle sources of lead include fumes and airborne dust particles from automobile exhaust and manufacturing. These findings have been known for decades by the Centers for Disease Control (CDC) and the occupational health movements, but they were not known to the general public. They were not common knowledge among poor people living in leaded homes.

Another reason why people did not consider lead a serious problem is that low-grade lead poisoning is an insidious, cumulative disorder whose effects—ranging from slowness in developing motor skills and loss of hearing or memory to brain damage, kidney failure, and cancer—are often attributed to other causes. Lead poisoning is a "silent" disease. Because the effects build up proportionately to the slow accumulation of lead in the bloodstream, symptoms sometimes do not appear until years later.[4]

Parents like PUEBLO member Ramon Zamora, who noticed his youngest daughter's loss of coordination, excessive nosebleeds, and hair loss, are told that the problems are caused by poor nutrition, birth defects, or behavioral disability, placing the blame on the parent or on the child's heredity. There are no easy solutions to lead poisoning. The most effective measure is to remove the child from the leaded environment, obviously not a viable option for most poor people. It is virtually impossible to reverse poisoning once lead has accumulated in the blood, and it is also difficult to abate lead in homes in a complete and safe way. There is a process called chelation that removes a child's poisoned blood, but it is expensive, lengthy, and painful. And to be completely safe, lead paint in homes has to be covered by a hard, lasting surface, such as wood paneling.

Home owners make the frequent and deadly mistake of stripping the leaded paint, which spreads lead dust everywhere, or covering it with new paint or wallpaper, which only postpones the inevitable leaking of lead. Since PUEBLO's campaign focused on poor people who could not afford to move, the demands clearly had to focus on abatement: providing financial resources to help people make the required changes and training abatement workers to observe careful and high standards in the removal process.

There were not a lot of other fights around the country from which PUEBLO could take example. Most lead poisoning fights had taken place in the courtroom, involving individual plaintiffs filing civil suits against paint companies for damages. While some of these suits had been successful, they had their drawbacks: they took years to win, they did not change general conditions for communities, and they carried with them all the inconvenience and expense of a long court battle. Low-income families who could not afford to retain an attorney or spend workdays in court had little recourse.

LOOKING FOR HANDLES

Sandra Davis, who worked with PUEBLO from its inception, first as an intern, then as an organizer, and now as lead organizer, refers to the products of effective action research as "handles." Handles are facts, events, or laws that solidify an organization's position both ideologically, to gain members' interest and supporters' sympathy, and practically, to give the group leverage with which to deal with decision makers.

The following handles were the turning points for organizers in designing methods to educate parents, service providers, and community leaders about the dangers of lead poisoning as well as in formulating demands that would make a significant dent in the problem and raise the organization's ability to mobilize resources and hold public officials accountable.

The first handle came from the California State Department of Health itself. In 1988, the state conducted a statewide study, testing children in California for excessive blood lead levels.[5] In a media blitz, the state revealed that a shocking 67 percent of children living in Oakland's Nimitz Corridor had elevated levels of lead in their blood; 20 percent of them had blood lead levels considered poisonous under the old CDC guidelines. That was the last heard about the problem of lead poisoning until PUEBLO raised the issue again almost three years later.

Door-knocking in the neighborhoods identified by the state study led PUEBLO to Ramon Zamora and Karleen Lloyd, parents of children who had participated in the study. Karleen Lloyd is a firm, though unassuming, single mother of two girls. After her children were tested, she was told that her younger daughter's lead level was too low for her to worry about, which she believed until two things happened almost simultaneously. A volunteer from PUEBLO knocked on her door, raising questions about the very study she and her children had participated in, at the same time that she had to put her daughter in a special education class. Lloyd is unafraid to assert: "We were just used as laboratory rats. They did this study with no intention to follow up." Lloyd has not heard from the state since.

After discovering that his daughter and several of his grandchildren suffered from lead poisoning, Ramon Zamora abated the lead in his home and paid for the children's medical treatment from his own salary as a worker in a metals factory. Remembering the lack of guidance and financial support he had received in reversing his family's tragedy, Zamora urged the Oakland City Council during testimony by PUEBLO in 1991 to "do something about this problem before it's too late."

In speaking about their experiences of having been recruited, tested, and then dropped, these families were instrumental in raising community awareness and sympathy about this issue. And they exemplified the importance of those most affected by the problem taking the lead in fighting it. Both families remain members of PUEBLO; Karleen Lloyd and her older daughter serve on the organization's leadership council. Both families led PUEBLO into schools, parks, and service organizations, sharing both personal and community resources.

PUEBLO's second set of handles came from researching the national activity on lead poisoning. In the words of Sandra Davis, the "biggest find was a 1989 federal mandate requiring CHDPP to provide free lead tests as part of a complete physical exam for all children aged six months to six years." Organizer Susan Goetz then researched lead abatement plans from Massachusetts, Rhode Island, and New York in search of approaches to blood screening and abatement that would work in Oakland. Taking the best from each plan, and taking advantage of the federal mandate to the CHDPP, PUEBLO formulated its demands to include the following:

1. Environmental screening: immediate testing of homes built before 1950 and all public spaces, including parks, schools, and

adult workplaces, with priority given to those areas where cases of lead poisoning had already been identified.

2. Access to health care: (1) self-certification for CHDPP services for all families meeting the eligibility requirements and (2) immediate blood tests for low-income children, paid for by the CHDPP under the federal mandate.

3. Abatement: a countywide Lead Abatement Plan, including public education, referral for blood lead screening and medical treatment, subsidies to fund the abatement of lead in residential properties, and professional education for contractors and medical workers. Funding would come from the federal government and from a $10-per-year tax levied on all houses built before 1950.

EDUCATION FOR RECRUITMENT

Remembering that an organization without people is just a logo on paper, PUEBLO members and staff set out to build a constituency of low-income people of color, using the issue of lead poisoning as an entry point. The primary vehicle for bringing in community people was Community Lead Action and Information Meetings (CLAIM), interactive one-hour sessions that oriented people to the dangers of lead, the demands of the campaign, and the officials responsible for dealing with the problem.

CLAIM met several organizational objectives: (1) to provide opportunities for emerging leaders, who set up and conducted the sessions, to interact with other community members and develop expertise on the issue; (2) to recruit individual members into the organization; and (3) to provide a role for community institutions in the campaign. These institutions included churches, parent-teacher associations, and service organizations.

PUEBLO conducted twenty-one CLAIM sessions at organizations and ten at members' houses in a house meeting format. Volunteers added to the organization's linguistic capacity, allowing us to conduct the sessions in eight languages. Each session ended with a campaign to recruit new members. In addition to having an active membership, PUEBLO needed to be able to show a broad base of support for the issue among health professionals, elected and appointed officials, students, and other community organizations. The process of developing support included clarifying the self-interest of these people in supporting our campaign, developing clear and important roles for supporters, and recognizing supporters' contributions to the organization.

If the Get the Lead Out campaign were to succeed in winning its demands from the CHDPP, health professionals, as well as low-income people, would have easier access to public health resources. Public officials from our districts wanted to be on the right side of an issue backed by a powerful set of organizations, and progressive students often used our campaign to connect themselves with "the community" as well as to gain class credit for their work. Other organizations, recognizing the effects of lead on their own constituencies, looked forward to offering those benefits once they were set up.

Professionals were asked to host house parties for fund-raising, testify at public events, and write letters to officials. Public officials were asked to lobby other officials and introduce local legislation; students went door to door in wealthier sections of Oakland and other parts of the county to collect postcards supporting the Lead Abatement Plan, and organizations were asked to sponsor CLAIMs and sign onto the plan. While all of these people could attend demonstrations and accountability meetings, they rarely did; those actions were largely the terrain of PUEBLO members.

ORGANIZING STRATEGY

PUEBLO's strategy stresses the use of direct action to build members' understanding of the issue and the power structure surrounding it and to persuade people who control public resources to meet the organization's demands. Important lessons can be drawn from the activities of the campaign. First, we see the campaign identifying clear targets—people who can and should implement the changes that need to be made—and referring consistently to that target's instincts for self-preservation. Targets are always noted as individuals with the power to allocate resources and make decisions.

Second, we see the campaign drawing out those targets through a series of confrontations systematically escalating in tone, in number, and in the importance of the targets chosen. Third, as in any kind of social change, we see a clear use of allies, both internal and external to the mainstream power structure. Finally, we see that the militancy of the tactic is directly related to the political understanding and leadership of the people involved in its implementation.

Drawing clear lines of accountability between the membership and the target does not necessarily require turning out large numbers of people to demonstrate. Some of PUEBLO's most successful activities involved as few as three members, and most activities had no more than thirty, including young people. Using a variety of tactics is more important, both to keep the membership involved at a range of militancy levels and to keep the targets guessing about what we might do next.

Actions of PUEBLO were designed to be confrontational. Sometimes the confrontation took place with quiet tones in a church; sometimes it involved loud chanting on the street. The effectiveness of confrontation is measured not by volume but by how clearly members are able to assert their rights and suggest their capacity to move to the next step.

Members did nothing that they were uncomfortable with, and as we were stonewalled by the system many times over, members gained self-confidence, got mad, and became "comfortable" with different tactics and roles. Leader Teresa Barajas, a recent immigrant from Mexico and a monolingual Spanish speaker, says of her own newly developed ability to question the most powerful people in her city: "Before, I used to be very nervous; we were very timid. But I learned that we don't have to be afraid of anything because we are all equal. Now we don't drop our head before anybody or say we can't do it." Experience proved key to encouraging PUEBLO members to take on new roles and more militant tones.

THE PEOPLE DEMAND ACTION

The earliest targets and actions of the campaign coincided with the least threatening of the demands, those that did not require allocation of new resources, and targets with whom we already had the most experience. The following demands were presented.

DEMAND 1: *Environmental Screening*

Screening involved immediate testing of homes built before 1950 and all public spaces, including parks, schools, and adult workplaces, with priority given to those areas where cases of lead poisoning had already been identified. Targets were David Kears of the Alameda County Department of Health and Rafat Shahid of the county's Hazardous Waste Division.

PUEBLO had contact with David Kears, from whom we had won major concessions during the immunization campaign. In this struggle, the goal was to get these two appointed officials, whose jobs rode on their ability to serve the public and keep the public from bothering their higher-ups, to conduct research that would support our case for free blood lead screening and lead abatement. To shame the Hazardous Waste Division, PUEBLO volunteers gathered soil samples from high-risk sites and had them tested independently and for free by the National Toxics Campaign Laboratory in Boston. Members then marched into David Kears's office, carrying buckets of contaminated soil, and challenged him to test the other sites.

DEMAND 2: *Access to Health Care*

Demands included (1) self-certification for CHDPP services for all families meeting the eligibility requirements and (2) immediate blood tests for low-income children, paid for by the CHDPP under the federal mandate. The target was Martha Bureau, Director of the CHDPP.

This was another target that PUEBLO had dealt with in the immunization campaign, and an especially important one for organizations all over the United States. The CHDPP is the California equivalent of a federally funded child health program called the Early and Periodic Screening, Detection, and Treatment Program (EPSDT), administered at both the state and county levels. This program provides free health care, including mandatory blood lead tests, to children whose families were 200 percent above the federal poverty level, making it an obviously better source of care for kids than MediCal. Public outrage against the CHDPP arose when PUEBLO revealed that the program's outreach was so inadequate that unused funds were routinely handed back to the state at the end of each fiscal year.

Inadequacies of the program include a general unwillingness to post eligibility requirements (potential users had to call the CHDPP and answer a series of questions about their income level before they could know whether they were eligible); a lack of bilingual staff to serve a multiracial constituency; an outreach plan that consisted of waiting in an office for the telephone to ring; and a flat refusal to pay for children's blood lead tests, despite a federal legislative mandate to do so.

PUEBLO's actions here included meetings between Martha Bureau and members at sites chosen by PUEBLO; daytime demonstrations at the CHDPP office in downtown Oakland, chanting "CHDPP, you're no good, test our children like you should"; cultivation of a relationship with a CHDPP junior staff member, who sneaked the eligibility requirements out to a PUEBLO staff member; design and distribution of a self-certification form, which published the eligibility requirements; and the peak action, in which five PUEBLO families piled out of a van at Children's Hospital and demanded free blood lead tests, with a follow-up action presenting poster-sized blowups of the $54 bill that each family received, with a trilingual demand that the CHDPP pay the bills. The very first meeting between Bureau and PUEBLO took place in a church on

East 14th Street and was conducted in Spanish. Bureau brought her own translator.

Simultaneously, PUEBLO pursued a legal strategy to give communities all across California the institutional backup to make the CHDPP do its job. Joining with the Natural Resources Defense Council, the NAACP Legal Defense and Education Fund, the American Civil Liberties Union, and the Alameda County Legal Aid Society, PUEBLO filed a class action lawsuit (*Matthews v. Coye*) to force the CHDPP to comply with the 1989 federal Medicaid provision requiring free blood tests for all low-income children under the age of six. The lawsuit was settled out of court for a $10 million to $15 million program that requires screening more than 500,000 low-income California children for lead.[6]

DEMAND 3: *Abatement*

The goal was to put the Lead Abatement Plan before the Oakland City Council with a positive recommendation from city staff. The target was Henry Gardner, Oakland city manager.

Eventually, PUEBLO was confronted with the realities of public bureaucracy. Before the plan could go before the city council for a vote, it had to go through one of the city departments for a staff evaluation and recommendation. The city stonewalled the plan. Initially, the proposal was placed in the conservative Public Works Committee, where it stayed for several months, until Public Works Director Terry Roberts gave it a negative recommendation. Refusing to meet with PUEBLO to discuss his concerns, Roberts moved the plan to the Office of Community Development, another committee controlled by conservative business and real estate development interests.

Three factors influenced the way in which PUEBLO moved the proposal through the bureaucracy. First was Roberts's refusal to meet with PUEBLO, which infuriated members. Second, an examination of the city's committee structure revealed that PUEBLO allies had the most control in the Health and Human Services Committee, headed by a newly elected city council member from a

PUEBLO district, Nate Miley. Third, research into the city's administrative structure pointed to Henry Gardner, city manager, as simply the most powerful figure in Oakland. Gardner, who had been appointed by former mayor Lionel Wilson, controlled the city budget, and his recommendation could propel a proposal to victory or failure.

Fortified by a clearer understanding of the city's political structure, PUEBLO took the fight directly to the city manager in an action in which thirty members and their children presented Gardner with a three-foot "apple of temptation." Members urged Gardner to resist the temptation to side with large property owners and the realty boards who opposed the Lead Abatement Plan and to make a positive recommendation on Oakland's participation in the plan.

Surrounded by city hall security staff, with city hall itself shut down as a protective measure against the protesters, Gardner finally came out of his meeting, spoke with PUEBLO, and agreed to review the plan. He became a pivotal ally and presented a positive recommendation to the city council.

DEMAND 4: *Comprehensive Abatement*

The goal of this demand was to approve Oakland's participation in the county Lead Abatement Plan, which included public education, referral for blood lead screening and medical treatment, subsidies to fund the abatement of lead in residential properties, and professional education for contractors and medical workers. Funding would come from the federal government and from a $10-per-year tax levied on all houses in Oakland built before 1950.

Allies were city council members Wilson Riles and Nate Miley. Targets were council members Marge Gibson-Haskell, Leo Bazile, Aleta Cannon, Dick Spees, Mary Moore, and Frank Ogawa, and Mayor Elihu Harris.

Since Oakland is the largest city in Alameda County, an agreement from Oakland to join the Lead Abatement Plan would practically guarantee passage of the policy and would clearly influence other cities in the county to follow. Nate Miley and Wilson Riles, two politically progressive African Americans on the city council, represented the two primary districts in which PUEBLO worked. They supported the plan from its inception, during the 1990 elections in which Riles opposed Elihu Harris for the mayoral seat. Miley introduced the motion to join the plan, and its passage gave him his first major victory on the city council. The other council members were not nearly so amenable.

Under pressure from Oakland's homeowners' associations and the real estate lobby, who opposed the $10-per-year tax assessment on older homes, the city council, led by Mayor Harris, delayed the vote twice, each delay weakening the agreements of council members who said that they were for the measure. Actions included conducting lobby meetings with each member who agreed to meet with PUEBLO and buying a full-page ad (designed by the progressive Public Media Center) in the Oakland Tribune, which identified the three council members who had not agreed to support the measure and asked, "How Long Will Oakland Let Children Be Poisoned?"

Public support was overwhelming. Testimony was even taken from physicians and parents at city council meetings. "That ad was the turning point for us," Davis asserts. "It called out individual people from their hiding places and let them know we were watching."

Member Alma Garcia, who was in PUEBLO's office the day the newspaper ad appeared, recalls the wrath of the council members named in the ad. She remembers one in particular: "When we finally met with Leo Bazile, he raved at us for half an hour about how he didn't like our tactics. Whether he liked them or not, though, he did vote yes on the motion." The final city council vote counted five yeses and three abstentions. PUEBLO claimed a victory even in the fact that no one voted no—doing so would have pitted council members against the forces of parents, health professionals, and other public officials PUEBLO had put together in a coalition.

DEMAND 5: *Pass the Countywide Lead Abatement Plan*

Allies were David Kears of the Department of Public Health and Rafat Shahid of the county's Hazardous Waste Division. County targets were the Alameda County Board of Supervisors: Don Perata, Mary King, Bill Aragon, Warren Widener, and Ed Campbell.

The same considerations plaguing the city council—whether to align itself with low-income parents or with middle-class and wealthy real estate owners—also plagued the Board of Supervisors. This set of actions involved forcing the county to include PUEBLO in the discussions for designing the Lead Abatement Plan, gathering postcards from home owners in each district and mailing them to the supervisors, and meeting with each supervisor to elicit his or her support. We note here that the very first targets of the campaign had become allies by this point, having already given PUEBLO enough legitimacy that they could work with us to design the actual plan.

The victory at the level of the Alameda Board of Supervisors was less complete than our victory in Oakland. In December 1991, the board voted to pass the plan, but it put off deciding on the $10-per-house tax. PUEBLO is monitoring the federally funded implementation phase of the plan and is pushing for a complete funding mechanism.

LESSONS LEARNED

We would like to point to a few lessons that we have learned through the Get the Lead Out campaign and other campaigns that we have been involved with. These are not rules but are insights gained from years of trying new tactics, making mistakes, evaluating everything, crying with frustration over things we could not win, and enjoying victories.

1. *Multiracial organizing requires political education and an action plan that contributes experience to that education.* By political education, we mean simply an organizational system of reflection that helps members make connections between their struggles and larger questions of how society is structured to produce and allocate resources. That political education has to be rooted in the experience and issues of the organization, but it also has to broaden the staff's and members' understanding of the connections by asking new questions.

2. *Multiracial organizing is more expensive than monoracial organizing.* If we have any hope of keeping our organizations alive, everybody in the organization has to be trained and willing to raise resources, whether cash or in-kind. Some of our biggest expenses went into supporting an organizational structure in which different sorts of people could be active. They include paying licensed professionals to create a child care program, buying translation machines, training and paying translators, purchasing vans for transportation, and buying food.

3. *Let instinct, not fear, guide your style of direct action.* Sometimes fear of retaliation or simply discomfort with being "impolite" limits the scope and tone of our actions. While repercussions are certainly real, and discomfort is certainly, well, uncomfortable, your instincts will tell you what is the most effective thing to do. Your instincts will also tell you when you are being lied to, when officials will keep their promises and when they will not, and when they are taking you seriously and when they are not. If your instincts do not tell you at the front end, your experience will tell you later. Allow disappointments to make you mad and ready to raise the stakes with more militant action. The very next step might be all your target needs to see the light.

4. *Look under the surface for the real power.* The person who you think has all the resources and the ability to move them around may be controlled by someone entirely different whose name appears nowhere in the public eye. A good research tip is to follow the money—that will often lead you to the real influence in any given city. Do not be afraid to expose relationships—the structure is built on our ignorance of the way things really work.

5. *Actively make links with other organizations, whether they are on the next block or across the country.* Ideas are as important to any organization as skills, and you can get access to both by talking with and listening to others working on similar issues. PUEB-LO's campaigns would not have been possible without the resources of several national organizations that anyone can con-

tact: the Center for Third World Organizing (Oakland), the Public Media Center (San Francisco), the Alliance to End Childhood Lead Poisoning (Washington, DC), and the National Toxics Campaign Laboratory (Boston). Build relationships with these and other groups and use them.

6. *Do not forget to celebrate.* Celebrate your victories—as PUEBLO did after the crucial city council meeting, with confetti, flowers, champagne, and root beer.

7. *There are no shortcuts, and there is no substitute for face-to-face organizing.* Reaching out to people wherever they may happen to be, at school, at work, at home, on their front porch, or at the supermarket, can never be replaced by flyers, ads, a good article in the local paper, or a nice spot on the evening news. We have to be able to build long-lasting political organizations that are modeled on egalitarian values and behavior.

Through the Get the Lead Out campaign, PUEBLO enjoyed the largest amount of press coverage we had ever seen. Our group was able to garner wide coverage from small minority and alternative newspapers. This coverage legitimated PUEBLO's role in the community; reinforced leaders in the organization; escalated pressure on the targets by dramatizing our issues; and helped us to raise money from private foundations and individuals.

14

Women of Color
on the Front Line

CELENE KRAUSS

Toxic waste disposal is a central focus of women's grass-roots environmental activism.[1] Toxic waste facilities are predominantly sited in working-class and low-income communities and communities of color, reflecting the disproportionate burden placed on these communities by a political economy of growth that distributes the costs of economic growth unequally.[2] Spurred by the threat that toxic wastes pose to family health and community survival, female grass-roots activists have assumed the leadership of community environmental struggles. As part of a larger movement for environmental justice, they constitute a diverse constituency, including working-class housewives and secretaries, rural African American farmers, urban residents, Mexican American farm workers and Native Americans.

These activists attempt to differentiate themselves from what they see as the white, male, middle-class leadership of many national environmental organizations. Unlike the more abstract, issue-oriented focus of national groups, women's focus is on environmental issues that grow out of their concrete, immediate experiences.[3] Female blue-collar activists often share a loosely defined ideology of environmental justice and a critique of dominant social institutions and mainstream environmental organizations, which they believe do not address the broader issues of inequality underlying environmental hazards. At the same time, these activists exhibit significant diversity in their conceptualization of toxic waste issues, reflecting different experiences of class, race, and ethnicity.

This chapter looks at the ways in which different working-class women formulate ideologies of resistance around toxic waste issues and the process by which they arrive at a concept of environmental justice. Through an analysis of interviews, newsletters, and conference presentations, I show the voices of white, African American, and Native American female activists and the resources that inform and support their protests. What emerges is an environmental discourse that is mediated by subjective experiences and interpretations and rooted in the political truths women construct out of their identities as housewives, mothers, and members of communities and racial and ethnic groups.

THE SUBJECTIVE DIMENSION OF GRASS-ROOTS ACTIVISM

Grass-roots protest activities have often been trivialized, ignored, and viewed as self-interested actions that are particularistic and parochial, failing to go beyond a single-issue focus. This view of community grass-roots protests is held by most policymakers as well as by many analysts of movements for progressive social change.[4]

In contrast, the voices of blue-collar women engaged in protests regarding toxic waste issues tell us that single-issue protests are about more than the single issue. They reveal a larger world of power and resistance, which in some measure ends up challenging the social relations of power. This challenge becomes visible when we shift the analysis of environmental activism to the experiences of working-class women and the subjective meanings they create around toxic waste issues.

In traditional sociological analysis, this subjective dimension of protest has often been ignored or viewed as private and individualistic. Feminist theory, however, helps us to see its importance. For feminists, the critical reflection on the everyday world of experience is an important subjective dimension of social change.[5] Feminists show us that experience is not merely a personal, individualistic concept. It is social. People's experiences reflect where they fit in the social hierarchy. Thus, blue-collar women of differing backgrounds interpret their experiences of toxic waste problems within the context of their particular cultural histories, starting from different assumptions and arriving at concepts of environmental justice that reflect broader experiences of class and race.

Feminist theorists also challenge a dominant ideology that separates the "public" world of policy and power from the "private" and personal world of everyday experience. By definition, this ideology relegates the lives and concerns of women relating to home and family to the private, nonpolitical arena, leading to invisibility of their grass-roots protests about issues such as toxic wastes.[6] As Ann Bookman has noted in her important study of working-class women's community struggles, women's political activism in general, and working-class political life at the community level in particular, remain "peripheral to the historical record . . . where there is a tendency to privilege male political activity and labor activism."[7] The women's movement took as its central task the reconceptualization of the political itself, critiquing this dominant ideology and constructing a new definition of the political, located in the everyday world of ordinary women rather than in the world of public policy. Feminists provide a perspective for making visible the importance of particular, single-issue protests regarding toxic wastes by showing how ordinary women subjectively link the particulars of their private lives with a broader analysis of power in the public sphere.

Social historians such as George Rudé have pointed out that it is often difficult to understand the experience and ideologies of resistance because ordinary working people appropriate and reshape traditional beliefs embedded within working-class culture, such as family and community.[8] This point is also relevant for understanding the environmental protests of working-class women. Their protests are framed in terms of the traditions of motherhood and family; as a result, they often appear parochial or even conservative. As we shall see, however, for working-class women, these traditions become the levers that set in motion a political process, shaping the language and oppositional meanings that emerge and providing resources for social change.

Shifting the analysis of toxic waste issues to the subjective experience of ordinary women makes visible a complex relationship between everyday life and the larger structures of public power. It reveals the potential for human agency that is hidden in a more traditional sociological approach and provides us with a means of seeing "the sources of power which subordinated groups have created."[9]

The analysis presented in this chapter is based on the oral and written voices of women involved in toxic waste protests. Interviews were conducted at environmental conferences such as the First National People of Color Environmental Leadership Summit, Washington, DC, 1991, and the World Women's Congress for a Healthy Planet, Miami, Florida, 1991, and by telephone. Additional sources include conference presentations, pamphlets, books, and other written materials that have emerged from this movement. This research is part of an ongoing comparative study that will examine the ways in which experiences of race, class, and ethnicity mediate women's environmental activism. Future research includes an analysis of the environmental activism of Mexican American women in addition to that of the women discussed here.

TOXIC WASTE PROTESTS
AND THE RESOURCE OF MOTHERHOOD

Blue-collar women do not use the language of the bureaucrat to talk about environmental issues. They do not spout data or marshal statistics in support of their positions. In fact, interviews with these women rarely generate a lot of discussion about the environmental problem per se. But in telling their stories about their protest against a landfill or incinerator, they ultimately tell larger stories about their discovery or analysis of oppression. Theirs is a political, not a technical, analysis.

Working-class women of diverse racial and ethnic backgrounds identify the toxic waste movement as a women's movement, composed primarily of mothers. Says one woman who fought against an incinerator in Arizona and subsequently worked on other anti-incinerator campaigns throughout the state, "Women are the backbone of the grass-roots groups; they are the ones who stick with it, the ones who won't back off." By and large, it is women, in their traditional role as mothers, who make the link between toxic wastes and their children's ill health. They discover the hazards of toxic contamination: multiple miscarriages, birth defects, cancer deaths, and so on. This is not surprising, as the gender-based division of labor in a capitalist society gives working-class women the responsibility for the health of their children.

These women define their environmental protests as part of the work that mothers do. Cora Tucker, an African American activist who fought against uranium mining in Virginia and who now organizes nationally, says:

> It's not that I don't think that women are smarter, [she laughs] but I think that we are with the kids all day long. . . . If Johnny gets a cough and Mary gets a cough, we try to discover the problem.

Another activist from California sums up this view: "If we don't oppose an incinerator, we're not doing our work as mothers."

For these women, family serves as a spur to action, contradicting popular notions of family as conservative and parochial. Family has a very different meaning for these women than it does for the middle-class nuclear family. Theirs is a less privatized, extended family that is open, permeable, and attached to community. This more extended family creates the networks and resources that enable working-class communities to survive materially given few economic resources.[10] The destruction of working-class neighborhoods by economic growth deprives blue-collar communities of the basic resources of survival; hence the resistance engendered by toxic waste issues. Working-class women's struggles over toxic waste issues are, at root, issues about survival. Ideologies of motherhood, traditionally relegated to the private sphere, become political resources that working-class women use to initiate and justify their resistance. In the process of protest, working-class women come to reject the dominant ideology, which separates the public and private arenas.

Working-class women's extended network of family and community serves as the vehicle for spreading information and concern about toxic waste issues. Extended networks of kinship and friendship become political resources of opposition. For example, in one community in Detroit, women discovered patterns of health problems while attending Tupperware parties. Frequently, a mother may read about a hazard in a newspaper, make a tentative connection between her own child's ill health and the pollutant, and start telephoning friends and family, developing an informal health survey. Such a discovery process is rooted in what Sarah Ruddick has called the everyday practice of mothering.[11] Through their informal networks, they compare notes and experiences and develop an oppositional knowledge used to resist the dominant knowledge of experts and the decisions of government and corporate officials.

These women separate themselves from "mainstream" environmental organizations, which are seen as dominated by white, middle-class men and concerned with remote issues. Says one woman from Rahway, New Jersey: "The mainstream groups deal with safe issues. They want to stop incinerators to save the eagle, or they protect trees for the owl. But we say, what about the people?"

Another activist implicitly criticizes the mainstream environmental groups when she says of the grass-roots Citizens' Clearinghouse for Hazardous Wastes:

> Rather than oceans and lakes, they're concerned about kids dying. Once you've had someone in your family who has been attacked by the environment—I mean who has had cancer or some other disease—you get a keen sense of what's going on.

It is the traditional, "private" women's concerns about home, children, and family that provide the initial impetus for blue-collar women's involvement in issues of toxic waste. The political analyses they develop break down the public-private distinction of dominant ideology and frame a particular toxic waste issue within broader contexts of power relationships.

THE ROLE OF RACE, ETHNICITY, AND CLASS

Interviews with white, African American, and Native American women show that the starting places for and subsequent development of their analyses of toxic waste protests are mediated by issues of class, race, and ethnicity.

White working-class women come from a culture in which traditional women's roles center on the private arena of family. They often marry young; although they may work out of financial necessity, the primary roles from which they derive meaning and satisfaction are those of mothering and taking care of family. They are revered and supported for fulfilling the ideology of a patriarchal family.[12] And these families often reflect a strong belief in the existing political system. The narratives of white working-class women involved in toxic waste issues are filled with the process by which they discover the injustice of their government, their own insecurity about entering the public sphere of politics, and the constraints of the patriarchal family, which, ironically prevent them from becoming fully active in the defense of their family, especially in their protest. Their narratives are marked by a strong initial faith in "their" government, as well as a remarkable transformation as they become disillusioned with the system. They discover "that they never knew what they were capable of doing in defense of their children."

For white working-class women, whose views on public issues are generally expressed only within family or among friends, entering a more public arena to confront toxic waste issues is often extremely stressful. "Even when I went to the PTA," says one activist, "I rarely spoke. I was so nervous." Says another: "My views have always been strong, but I expressed them only in the family. They were not for the public." A strong belief in the existing political system is characteristic of these women's initial response to toxic waste issues. Lois Gibbs, whose involvement in toxic waste issues started at Love Canal, tells us, "I believed if I had a problem I just had to go to the right person in government and he would take care of it."

Initially, white working-class women believe that all they have to do is give the government the facts and their problem will be taken care of. They become progressively disenchanted with what they view as the violation of their rights and the injustice of a system that allows their children and family to die. In the process, they develop a perspective of environmental justice rooted in issues of class, the attempt to make democracy real, and a critique of the corporate state. Says one activist who fought the siting of an incinerator in Sumter County, Alabama: "We need to stop letting economic development be the true God and religion of this country. We have to prevent big money from influencing our government."

A recurring theme in the narratives of these women is the transformation of their beliefs about government and power. Their politicization is rooted in the deep sense of violation, betrayal, and hurt they feel when they find that their government will not protect their families. Lois Gibbs sums up this feeling well:

> I grew up in a blue-collar community. We were very into democracy. There is something about discovering that democracy isn't democracy as we know it. When you lose faith in your government, it's like finding out your mother was fooling around on your father. I was very upset. It almost broke my heart because I really believed in the system. I still believe in the system, only now I believe that democracy is of the people and by the people, that people have to move it, it ain't gonna move by itself.

Echoes of this disillusionment are heard from white blue-collar women throughout the country. One activist relates:

> We decided to tell our elected officials about the problems of incineration because we didn't think they knew. Surely if they knew that there was a toxic waste dump in our county they would stop it. I was politically naive. I was real surprised be-

cause I live in an area that's like the Bible Belt of the South.
Now I think the God of the United States is really economic development, and that has got to change.

Ultimately, these women become aware of the inequities of power
as it is shaped by issues of class and gender. Highly traditional values of democracy and motherhood remain central to their lives. But
in the process of politicization through their work on toxic waste
issues, these values become transformed into resources of opposition that enable women to enter the public arena and challenge its
legitimacy. They justify their resistance as a way to make democracy real and to protect their children.

White blue-collar women's stories are stories of transformations:
transformations into more self-confident and assertive women; into
political activists who challenge the existing system and feel powerful in that challenge; into wives and mothers who establish new relationships with their spouses (or get divorced) and new,
empowering relationships with their children as they provide role
models of women capable of fighting for what they believe in.

African American working-class women begin their involvement
in toxic waste protests from a different place. They bring to their
protests a political awareness that is grounded in race and that
shares none of the white blue-collar women's initial trust in democratic institutions. These women view government with mistrust,
having been victims of racist policies throughout their lives. Individual toxic waste issues are immediately framed within a broader
political context and viewed as environmental racism. Says an African American activist from Rahway, New Jersey:

> When they sited the incinerator for Rahway, I wasn't surprised.
> All you have to do is look around my community to know that
> we are a dumping ground for all kinds of urban industrial proj-
> ects that no one else wants. I knew this was about environ-
> mental racism the moment that they proposed the incinerator.

An African American woman who fought the siting of a landfill on
the South Side of Chicago reiterates this view: "My community is

an all-black community isolated from everyone. They don't care what happens to us." She describes her community as a "toxic doughnut":

> We have seven landfills. We have a sewer treatment plant. We have the Ford Motor Company. We have a paint factory. We have numerous chemical companies and steel mills. The river is just a few blocks away from us and is carrying water so highly contaminated that they say it would take seventy-five years or more before they can clean it up.

This activist sees her involvement in toxic waste issues as a challenge to traditional stereotypes of African American women. She says, "I'm here to tell the story that all people in the projects are not lazy and dumb!"

Some of these women share experiences of personal empowerment through their involvement in toxic waste issues. Says one African American activist:

> Twenty years ago I couldn't do this because I was so shy. . . . I had to really know you to talk with you. Now I talk. Sometimes I think I talk too much. I waited until my fifties to go to jail. But it was well worth it. I never went to no university or college, but I'm going in there and making speeches.

However, this is not a major theme in the narratives of female African American activists, as it is in those of white blue-collar women. African American women's private work as mothers has traditionally extended to a more public role in the local community as protectors of the race. As a decade of African American feminist history has shown, African American women have historically played a central role in community activism and in dealing with issues of race and economic injustice.[13] They receive tremendous status and recognition from their community. Many women participating in toxic waste protests have come out of a history of civil rights activism, and their environmental protests, especially in the South, develop through community organizations born during the civil rights movement.[14] And while the visible leaders are often male, the base of the organizing has been led by African American women, who, as Cheryl Townsend Gilkes has written, have often been called "race women," responsible for the "racial uplift" of their communities.[15]

African American women perceive that traditional environmental groups only peripherally relate to their concerns. As Cora Tucker relates:

> This white woman from an environmental group asked me to come down to save a park. She said that they had been trying to get black folks involved and that they won't come. I said, "Honey, it's not that they aren't concerned, but when their babies are dying in their arms they don't give a damn about a park." I said, "They want to save their babies. If you can help them save their babies, then in turn they can help you save your park." And she said, "But this is a real immediate problem." And I said, "Well, these people's kids dying is immediate."

Tucker says that white environmental groups often call her or the head of the NAACP at the last minute to participate in an environmental rally because they want to "include" African Americans. But they exclude African Americans from the process of defining the issues in the first place. What African American communities are doing is changing the agenda.

Because the concrete experience of African Americans' lives is the experience and analysis of racism, social issues are interpreted and struggled with within this context. Cora Tucker's story of attending a town board meeting shows that the issue she deals with is not merely the environment but also the disempowerment she experiences as an African American woman. At the meeting, white women were addressed as Mrs. So-and-So by the all-white, male board. When Ms. Tucker stood up, however, she was addressed as "Cora":

One morning I got up and I got pissed off and I said, "What did you call me?" He said, "Cora," and I said, "The name is Mrs. Tucker." And I had the floor until he said "Mrs. Tucker." He waited five minutes before he said "Mrs. Tucker." And I held the floor. I said, "I'm not gonna let you call me Cora!" And when he said, "Yes, Mrs. Tucker," I said, "Mr. Chairman, I don't call you by your first name and I don't want you to call me by mine. My name is Mrs. Tucker. And when you want me, you call me Mrs. Tucker." It's not that—I mean it's not like you gotta call me Mrs. Tucker, but it was the respect.

In discussing this small act of resistance as an African American woman, Cora Tucker is showing how environmental issues may be about corporate and state power, but they are also about race. For female African American activists, environmental issues are seen as reflecting environmental racism and linked to other social justice issues, such as jobs, housing, and crime. They are viewed as part of a broader picture of social inequity based on race. Hence, the solution articulated in a vision of environmental justice is a civil rights vision—rooted in the everyday experience of racism. Environmental justice comes to mean the need to resolve the broad social inequities of race.

The narratives of Native American women are also filled with the theme of environmental racism. However, their analysis is laced with different images. It is a genocidal analysis rooted in the Native American cultural identification, the experience of colonialism, and the imminent endangerment of their culture. A Native American woman from North Dakota, who opposed a landfill, says:

Ever since the white man came here, they keep pushing us back, taking our lands, pushing us onto reservations. We are down to 3 percent now, and I see this as just another way for them to take our lands, to completely annihilate our races. We see that as racism.

Like that of the African American women, these women's involvement in toxic waste protests is grounded from the start in race and shares none of the white blue-collar women's initial belief in the state. A Native American woman from southern California who opposed a landfill on the Rosebud Reservation in South Dakota tells us:

> Government did pretty much what we expected them to do. They supported the dump. People here fear the government. They control so many aspects of our life. When I became in-volved in opposing the garbage landfill, my people told me to be careful. They said they annihilate people like me.

Another woman involved in the protest in South Dakota describes a government official's derision of the tribe's resistance to the siting of a landfill:

> If we wanted to live the life of Mother Earth, we should get a tepee and live on the Great Plains and hunt buffalo.

Native American women come from a culture in which women have had more empowered and public roles than is the case in white working-class culture. Within the Native American community, women are revered as nurturers. From childhood, boys and girls learn that men depend on women for their survival. Women also play a central role in the decision-making process within the tribe. Tribal council membership is often equally divided between men and women; many women are tribal leaders and medicine women. Native American religions embody a respect for women as well as an ecological ethic based on values such as reciprocity and sustain-able development: Native Americans pray to Mother Earth, as op-posed to the dominant culture's belief in a white, male, Anglicized representation of divinity.[16]

In describing the ways in which their culture integrates notions of environmentalism and womanhood, one woman from New Mexico says:

> We deal with the whole of life and community; we're not sep-
> arated, we're born into it—you are it. Our connection as
> women is to the Mother Earth, from the time of our conscious-
> ness. We're not environmentalists. We're born into the struggle
> of protecting and preserving our communities. We don't sepa-
> rate ourselves. Our lifeblood automatically makes us respon-
> sible; we are born with it. Our teaching comes from a spiritual
> base. This is foreign to our culture. There isn't even a word for
> dioxin in Navajo.

In recent years, Native American lands have become common
sites for commercial garbage dumping. Garbage and waste companies have exploited the poverty and lack of jobs in Native American communities and the fact that Native American lands, as
sovereign nation territories, are often exempt from local environmental regulations. In discussing their opposition to dumping, Native American women ground their narratives in values about land
that are inherent in the Native American community. They see these
projects as violating tribal sovereignty and the deep meaning of
land, the last resource they have. The issue, says a Native American
woman from California, is

> protection of the land for future generations, not really as a
> mother, but for the health of the people, for survival. Our tribe
> bases its sovereignty on our land base, and if we lose our land
> base, then we will be a lost people. We can't afford to take this
> trash and jeopardize our tribe.
>
> If you don't take care of the land, then the land isn't going to
> take care of you. Because everything we have around us in-
> volves Mother Earth. If we don't take care of the land, what's
> going to happen to us?

In the process of protest, these women tell us, they are forced to
articulate more clearly their cultural values, which become resources of resistance in helping the tribe organize against a landfill.
While many tribal members may not articulate an "environmental"

critique, they well understand the meaning of land and their religion of Mother Earth, on which their society is built.

CONCLUSION

The narratives of white, African American, and Native American women involved in toxic waste protests reveal the ways in which their subjective, particular experiences lead them to analyses of toxic waste issues that extend beyond the particularistic issue to wider worlds of power. Traditional beliefs about home, family, and community provide the impetus for women's involvement in these issues and become a rich source of empowerment as women re-shape traditional language and meanings into an ideology of resistance. These stories challenge traditional views of toxic waste protests as parochial, self-interested, and failing to go beyond a single-issue focus. They show that single-issue protests are ultimately about far more and reveal the experiences of daily life and resources that different groups use to resist. Through environmental protests, these women challenge, in some measure, the social relations of race, class, and gender.

These women's protests have different beginning places, and their analyses of environmental justice are mediated by issues of class and race. For white blue-collar women, the critique of the corporate state and the realization of a more genuine democracy are central to a vision of environmental justice. The definition of environmental justice that they develop becomes rooted in the issue of class. For women of color, it is the link between race and environment, rather than between class and environment, that characterizes definitions of environmental justice. African American women's narratives strongly link environmental justice to other social justice concerns, such as jobs, housing, and crime. Environmental justice comes to mean the need to resolve the broad social inequities of race. For Native American women, environmental justice is bound up with the sovereignty of the indigenous peoples.

In these women's stories, their responses to particular toxic waste issues are inextricably tied to the injustice they feel as mothers, as working-class women, as African Americans, and as Native Americans. They do not talk about their protests in terms of single issues. Thus, their political activism has implications far beyond the visible, particularistic concern of a toxic waste dump site or the siting of a hazardous waste incinerator.

15

The People of Color Environmental Summit

KARL GROSSMAN

It was a seminal event in the environmental justice struggle: the First National People of Color Environmental Leadership Summit, held in Washington, DC, in October 1991. More than 600 African Americans, Latino Americans, Asian Americans, and Native Americans from every state in the United States, and people from other nations, too, struck out at environmental racism and committed themselves to a new movement—a movement for environmental justice.[1]

From the conference came a "Call to Action" declaring that people of color face a disproportionately greater level of environmental pollution—called "environmental genocide"—and setting forth a platform for this "new movement which raises the life and death struggles of indigenous and grass-roots communities of color to an unprecedented multinational integrated level."[2]

"We, the people of color, gathered together," stated a seventeen-point statement titled "Principles of Environmental Justice" adopted at the five-day gathering,

> to begin to build a national and international movement of all peoples of color to fight the destruction and taking of our lands and communities, do hereby re-establish our spiritual interdependence on the sacredness of our Mother Earth; to respect

and celebrate each of our cultures, languages and beliefs about
the natural world and our roles in healing ourselves; to insure
environmental justice; to promote economic alternatives
which would contribute to the development of environmentally safe livelihoods; and, to secure our political, economic
and cultural liberation that has been denied for over 500 years
of colonization and oppression, resulting in the poisoning of
our communities and land and the genocide of our peoples, do
affirm and adopt these principles.[3]

A myth has long existed that environmental issues are mainly a
middle-class white concern. In fact, they affect all classes and
people of all colors—but as found in a landmark study conducted
by the organization that sponsored the conference, the United
Church of Christ Commission for Racial Justice, they affect dark-
skinned people, people of color, the most.[4]

When this is realized and people of all classes and colors come
together to fight pollution, to battle together against the destruction
of the planet and life on it, the struggle for the environment will be
far more winnable. And that is what the First National People of
Color Environmental Leadership Summit and the new energies it
produced could be pivotal in bringing about.

"History was certainly made at the Summit," said Reverend Benjamin Chavis, Jr., executive director of the Commission for Racial
Justice and a conference cochair. A "summary theme that surfaced," he commented, "was that the impact of environmental racism on people-of-color communities is increasingly leading to a
state of environmental genocide." At the Summit, the notion was
"shattered that a multiracial movement is impossible in the United
States because of the prevalence of racism which attempts to pit
some people-of-color communities against other people-of-color
communities." He spoke of a "spiritual bond" he felt "through the
summit that helped to engender mutual respect and unity.

"This country needs a multi-racial movement for change," said
Chavis; a "new movement" came out of the gathering "and is gain-
ing strength and momentum," and that "is good news."[5]

The Summit set forth what must be done in its "Principles of Environmental Justice." The gathering declared that "Environmental Justice . . .

> affirms the sacredness of Mother Earth, ecological unity and the interdependence of all species, and the right to be free from ecological destruction.

> demands that public policy be based on mutual respect and justice for all people, free from any form of discrimination or bias.

> mandates the right to ethical, balanced and responsible uses of land and renewable resources in the interest of a sustainable planet for humans and other living things.

> calls for universal protection from nuclear testing, extraction, production and disposal of toxic/hazardous wastes and poisons and nuclear testing that threatens the fundamental right to clean air, land, water and food.

> affirms the fundamental right to political, economic, cultural and environmental self-determination of all peoples.

> demands the cessation of the production of all toxins, hazardous wastes, and radioactive materials, and that all past and current producers be held strictly accountable to the people for detoxification and the containment at the point of production.

> demands the right to participate as equal partners at every level of decision-making including needs assessment, planning, implementation, enforcement and evaluation.

> affirms the right of all workers to a safe and healthy work environment, without being forced to choose between an unsafe livelihood and unemployment. It also affirms the right of those who work at home to be free from environmental hazards.

> protects the rights of victims of environmental injustice to receive full compensation and reparations for damages as well as quality health care.

considers governmental acts of environmental injustice a violation of international law, the Universal Declaration On Human Rights, and the United Nations Convention in Genocide.

must recognize a special legal and natural relationship of Native Peoples to the U.S. government through treaties, agreements, compacts, and covenants affirming sovereignty and self-determination.

affirms the need for urban and rural ecological policies to clean up and rebuild our cities and rural areas in balance with nature, honoring the cultural integrity of our communities, and providing fair access for all to the full range of resources.

calls for the strict enforcement of principles of informed consent, and a halt to the testing of experimental reproductive and medical procedures and vaccinations on people of color.

opposes the destructive operations of multi-national corporations.

opposes military occupations, repression and exploitation of lands, peoples and cultures, and other life forms.

calls for the education of present and future generations which emphasizes social and environmental issues, based on our experience and an appreciation of our diverse cultural perspectives.

requires that we, as individuals, make personal and consumer choices to consume as little of Mother Earth's resources and to produce as little waste as possible; and make the conscious decision to challenge and reprioritize our lifestyles to insure the health of the natural world for present and future generations.

CIVIL RIGHTS AND ENVIRONMENTAL JUSTICE

Reverend Chavis was the first person to use the term "environmental racism," with the issuance by his commission of a report titled

Toxic Wastes and Race in the United States in 1987. The United Church of Christ Commission for Racial Justice was founded in 1963 in response to the assassination of Medgar Evers; the Birmingham, Alabama, church bombings; and other tensions that gripped the United States as the modern civil rights movement began. As a church-based civil rights arm of a major U.S. Protestant denomination, the commission has focused on many issues: voter registration, access of students of color to education, problems of persons with disabilities, child abuse, and racial violence, among others.

The commission got involved in environmental matters and in connecting environmental degradation and race in 1982, after it was asked by residents of predominantly African American Warren County, North Carolina, for help in their fight against the siting by the state of a dump for PCBs. A campaign of civil disobedience followed, with more than 500 arrested, including Chavis, Dr. Joseph Lowery of the Southern Christian Leadership Conference, and Congressman Walter Fauntroy of Washington, DC.[6]

"We began to ask why the government in North Carolina chose a predominantly black community to dump PCBs," recounted Chavis. He began considering the connection between the Warren County dumping and the U.S. government's Savannah River nuclear facility (long a source of radioactive leaks) being sited in a largely African American area of South Carolina, and what was—and still is—the "largest [hazardous waste] landfill in the nation" being located in Emelle, Alabama, a community that is 80 percent African American.

There seemed to be "evidence of a systematic pattern," said Chavis, and that "led us to do a national study."

The commission correlated the locations of thousands of what the U.S. Environmental Protection Agency deemed "commercial hazardous waste facilities" (defined by the EPA as places licensed for "treating, storing or disposing of hazardous wastes") and "uncontrolled toxic waste sites" (EPA terminology for "closed and abandoned sites") and determined what was suspected: these places of poison were in communities where people of color are concentrated.[7]

"We found it had to do with race," said Chavis. Warren County's African American population was largely poor, but Emelle, Alabama, he noted as an example, is the home of many middle-class African Americans. Race, not income, it was found, is the prime determinant as to where polluting facilities go. The report came to the following conclusions. For "commercial hazardous waste facilities":

> Race proved to be the most significant among variables tested. . . . This represented a consistent national pattern.

> Communities with the greatest number of commercial hazardous waste facilities had the highest composition of ethnic residents.

> Although socio-economic status appeared to play an important role in the location of commercial hazardous waste facilities, race still proved to be more significant.

> Three out of the five largest commercial hazardous waste landfills in the United States were located in predominantly black or Hispanic communities. These three landfills accounted for 40 percent of the total estimated commercial landfill capacity in the nation.

For "uncontrolled toxic waste sites":

> Three out of every five black and Hispanic Americans lived in communities with one or more uncontrolled toxic waste sites.

> Blacks were heavily over-represented in the populations of metropolitan areas with the largest number of uncontrolled toxic waste sites. [These included Memphis, St. Louis, Houston, Cleveland, Chicago, and Atlanta.]

Los Angeles, California had more Hispanics living in communities with uncontrolled toxic waste sites than any other metropolitan area in the United States.

Approximately half of all Asian/Pacific Islanders and American Indians lived in communities with uncontrolled toxic waste sites.

Chavis recalls that as he was preparing to present the report to the National Press Club, he "was trying to figure out how [he] could adequately describe what was going on." "It came to me—*environmental racism*. That's when I coined the term. To me, that's what it is."

As to how he defines it: "Environmental racism is racial discrimination in environmental policymaking, the enforcement of regulations and laws, the deliberate targeting of communities of color for toxic waste facilities, the official sanctioning of the life-threatening presence of poisons and pollutants in our communities, and the history of excluding people of color from leadership of the environmental movement."

On the latter point, former New Mexico governor Toney Anaya, a Latino American and a cochair of the Summit, says, "Environmental groups are typically male-Anglo-dominated." And at the gathering, minorities made it clear, he added, that "we're going to be part of this process, too." The aim was "to empower ourselves."

Getting that message at the meeting were Michael Fischer, executive director of the Sierra Club, and John Adams, director of the Natural Resources Defense Council, both "Big Ten" environmental groups—most of which have had a sharply disproportionate number of minorities in staff and leadership positions compared with their numbers in the U.S. population and have paid inadequate attention to the relationship between racism and the environment. "We know we've been conspicuously missing from battles of environmental justice," said Fischer. "We're here to reach across the table and build a bridge of partnership to you all . . . or we risk becoming irrelevant."

Adams stated that the conference marked "a major turning point in the environmental movement . . . I can tell you, it'll change NRDC."

The tales are horrific of the cost to life because of environmental racism as told by people of color all across America. Increasingly, they are now fighting back. Indeed, as a background paper issued by the Commission for Racial Justice at the Summit stated:

> There exists a prevalent perception among the general public that people of color have not expressed concern for the environment and have not been active in addressing environmental issues. This is a gross misconception which, we believe, is rooted in the narrow definition of environmental issues that has been advanced by traditional environmentalists and media. People of color have taken on environmental issues as community, labor, economic, self-determination and civil and political rights issues.[8]

TALES FROM THE GRASS ROOTS

The tales of environmental racism are many.[9] For example, there are no gardens in Altgeld Gardens. Residents of the housing project where 10,000 people live on Chicago's Southeast Side say that they would not dare to eat anything grown there. Altgeld Gardens is surrounded on all four sides with the most toxic facilities in all of Chicago, and, no surprise, has one of the highest cancer rates in the United States.

Hazel Johnson, mother of seven, tells of "lots of cancer, respiratory problems, and birth deformities," of "babies born with brain tumors. One baby was born with her brain protruding from her head," and now "she's blind and she can't walk. My daughter was five months pregnant. She took ultrasound and the doctors found the baby had no behind, no head. The baby had to be aborted."

Hazel Johnson is sure that the health problems are the result of the community being surrounded by a hazardous waste incinerator that gives off PCBs; seven landfills; several chemical plants; a paint factory; two steel mills; "lagoons" filled with contaminants; and a sludge-drying facility, which smells like "bodies decomposing." Such facilities are concentrated on Chicago's Southeast Side because it is largely inhabited by African Americans and Latino Americans, says Johnson, who has been fighting back as head of People for Community Recovery. Working closely with Greenpeace, the organization's tactics have included civil disobedience.

The African American community of West Harlem in New York City has a sewage plant, which regularly malfunctions as it processes 180 million gallons of raw sewage per day; two huge bus depots; a marine transfer station, where garbage is collected for placement on barges; a six-lane highway; a commuter rail line, on which a four-year-old boy was recently killed; a highway that serves as a major route for hazardous waste through New York City; and a crematorium. "The stereotype of what environmentalism means is wildlife and preservation of open space," says Peggy Shepard, a leader of West Harlem Environmental Action. "But urban environmental problems have been going on for years."

West Harlem has gotten these "exploitive" facilities because of the color of its residents, she charges. Her group fights back through litigation and political organizing and has linked with other community groups in New York and sought assistance from "larger environmental groups. But when you don't have an integrated staff, the priorities of an organization aren't necessarily priorities of communities of color," she says. "We organized around a series of issues in our community that turned out to be all environmental in nature." In the environmental movement nationally, there "has not been sufficient movement on urban environmental problems: incinerators, sewage treatment plants, factories polluting the air, devastating occupational exposure."

Oil refineries and petrochemical plants—more than 100 of them—line an 80-mile strip along the lower reaches of the Mississippi River between New Orleans and Baton Rouge, Louisiana. They have so poisoned the land, air, and water that the African Americans who predominate in the area now call it Cancer Alley, noted Pat Bryant, executive director of the Gulf Coast Tenants Association, at the Summit. A quarter of America's petrochemicals are produced in the corridor, which essentially is a "national sacrifice area," he said. Cancer Alley is also, said Bryant, a product of environmental racism. The placement of toxic facilities in African American areas of the South goes back "hundreds of years," says Darryl Malek-Wiley, the group's director of research. The industrial age has given such sitings new and more terrible forms. The Gulf Coast Tenants Association provides courses in environmental education and assists people in fighting environmental hazards in their communities and in trying to block the siting of new ones. In 1989, it organized the "Great Louisiana Toxics March," and it has been active in organizing drives to block the siting of additional noxious facilities.[10]

In his largely Latino American neighborhood of Albuquerque, New Mexico, notes Richard Moore, codirector of the Southwest Organizing Project and a member of the Summit's national planning committee, there is a landfill, a large pig farm, a dog food plant, a sewage treatment plant, and industrial facilities of Texaco, Chevron, and General Electric. "We have many very sick people with cancers, with leukemia, in this neighborhood. We have sick children, many with blue baby syndrome." Moore says: "We perceive environmental justice issues as issues of racial and social justice, and survival issues. We should not have to survive in these kinds of conditions, to live day by day amidst these poisonous chemicals."

It is not unintentional that these facilities are sited particularly in African American or Latino American communities. Says Moore, "We don't have the complexion for protection." His organization is multiethnic and now covers all of New Mexico. It has stressed door-to-door activity to build "strong organizations" and assists people in exercising political muscle by doing "nonpartisan voter registration—and not only do we register people, but we turn them out. We also have candidate-accountability sessions." Further, "we've done demonstrations and marches, circulated petitions, had small and large community meetings," and pushed meetings with public officials. "You name it, we've done it; and it's borne fruit."

The group was a founder of the Southwest Network for Environmental and Economic Justice (SNEEJ), which takes in seven states.

Native American reservations are more and more being seen—and used—as dump sites for toxic chemical and nuclear waste by corporations and the federal government because the companies and the government think they can use the "carrots" of jobs or payments to place their facilities on Native American lands. "They are targeting reservations because of our low economic status," Christine Valdra of the Good Road Coalition, which is fighting plans for dumps and incinerators on the Rosebud Sioux Reservation in South Dakota, told the Summit. Also, reservations are not subject to local and state environmental restrictions. Outside of reservations, Native Americans get dumped on, too.

Native Americans concentrated in northeastern Oklahoma are heavily affected by a nuclear facility that produces fuel for nuclear plants. Operated by the Sequoyah Fuel Corporation, the facility has a long and extensive record of accidentally releasing radioactive waste into the environment; it also, with approval of the U.S. Nuclear Regulatory Commission, channels 7.8 million gallons per year of its radioactive waste stream out of the plant—as a liquid fertilizer that it calls "raffinate." The company sells the fertilizer in and out of the state and uses it on 10,000 acres surrounding the plant, where cattle destined for market graze and where hay and corn are grown and sold as feed.

Lance Hughes, director of Native Americans for a Clean Environment (NACE) in Tahlequah, Oklahoma, tells of the "unusual cancers" and a high rate of birth defects from "genetic mutation" among Native Americans in the area. "It gets pretty sad, with babies born without eyes, babies born with brain cancers." Wildlife is also born deformed. "We found a nine-legged frog and a two-headed fish. And there was a four-legged chicken," says Hughes, providing photographs of such monstrosities. The white man in America long ago moved to decimate the Native American population, and that "is still going on," says Hughes. "The name of the game has been changed, but I would call it the same—genocide."

NACE has been fighting back with litigation, education, and political action.

Tens of thousands of Asian American women work in the electronic assembly plants of California's Silicon Valley. Asian American women—particularly immigrants—are sought out for this work because of a stereotypical view by plant owners that they will be submissive, that they "won't rock the boat," Young Shin, director of Asian Immigrant Women Advocates, based in Oakland, told the Summit. Meanwhile, the women—mainly from Hong Kong, China, Korea, and Vietnam—are desperate for work. The conditions they labor in are commonly poisonous. "The women work in an environment in which they use highly toxic chemicals," said Shin. She tells of one woman who, after years of work in such a plant, came home one night "and collapsed and was paralyzed. She has been bedridden ever since."

Asian Immigrant Women Advocates also assists the many Asian American women who work as garment workers. They labor in 1990s versions of the turn-of-the-century sweatshop, said Shin. "The lighting is poor; eyesight suffers; many women have backaches and carpal tunnel syndrome." Here, too, employers seeking a vulnerable segment of the population now target Asian American women to labor in bad conditions. "It is environmental racism," Shin said. She told the Summit that racist policies of industry prevent her constituents from achieving environmental justice. "We need the support of a progressive, all-inclusive environmental movement," she added. Since 1983, her group has been educating Asian American women about the poisons in their workplaces and helping them to "exercise their rights."

RACE, CLASS, OR BOTH?

Some people still are not convinced that environmental racism is real. Even some policymakers would have us believe that residents of West Dallas, East Los Angeles, Chicago's South Side, and South Tucson are poisoned because they happen to be poor. These communities also happen to be black and brown. Socioeconomic status is part of the equation, but it does *not* explain the entire story. "It's not a poverty thing. It's not a class thing," said Dr. Robert D. Bullard, professor of sociology at the University of California, Riverside, at the Summit. "It is racism, pure and simple."

Bullard's analyses predate the recent flurry of studies documenting environmental racism.[11] He began his research into environmental racism in 1979 while assisting his wife, an attorney, in a class action lawsuit she was preparing to challenge the planned siting of a municipal landfill in Northwood Manor, an African American "solid middle-class"—Bullard stresses—neighborhood of Houston, Texas. He quickly discovered that since the 1920s, all five of Houston's city-owned landfills and six of its eight incinerators have been sited in African American neighborhoods. That led to wider studies on how "African American communities, because of their economic and political vulnerability, have been routinely targeted for the siting of noxious facilities."

Bullard began working with a colleague, Dr. Beverly Hendrix Wright, who is also a sociology professor (then at the University of New Orleans and now at Xavier University in New Orleans) and a pioneering African American academic involved in investigating environmental racism. In a 1987 article in the *Mid-American Review of Sociology,* they wrote: "Many industrial firms, especially waste disposal companies and companies which have a long history of pollution violations, have come to view the black community as a 'push-over lacking community organization, environmental consciousness.'" Further, "black and lower-income neighborhoods often occupy the 'wrong side of the tracks,' and subsequently receive different treatment when it comes to enforcement of environmental regulations." They added: "Black communities, especially in the South, are just beginning to integrate environmental issues into traditional civil rights agendas. The job vs. environmental argument is now being challenged as black organizations broaden their definitions of civil rights to include air and water quality, hazardous wastes, and other environmental issues."[12]

In a 1990 article in the *Journal of Intergroup Relations* titled

"Mobilizing the Black Community for Environmental Justice,"
Bullard and Wright wrote about how African Americans

> have become increasingly aware of their physical environment
> and the potential threat that pollution may pose to their com-
> munities. Contrary to popular belief, environmental concern is
> not a white middle- and upper-class phenomenon. Blacks,
> however, remain underrepresented in the mainstream environ-
> mental movement. Black communities are beginning to inte-
> grate environmental issues into traditional civil rights agendas
> and to develop viable action strategies to combat environmen-
> tal discrimination and disparate facility siting practices. More-
> over, black community activists are beginning to challenge
> public policies and environmental decisions that have regres-
> sive distributional impact on their communities.[13]

Bullard's 1990 book, *Dumping in Dixie: Race, Class, and En-*
vironmental Quality, detailed how African Americans in Houston
and Dallas; in Alsen, Louisiana; in Institute, West Virginia; and in
Emelle, Alabama, "have taken on corporate giants who would turn
their areas into toxic wastelands." He concluded:

> Limited housing and residential options combined with dis-
> criminatory facility practices have contributed to the imposi-
> tion of all types of toxins on black communities through the
> siting of garbage dumps, hazardous waste landfills, incinera-
> tors, smelter operations, paper mills, chemical plants and a
> host of other polluting industries. These industries have gen-
> erally followed the path of least resistance, which has been in
> economically poor and politically powerless black communi-
> ties. Poor black communities are by no means the only victims
> of siting disparities, however. Middle-income black commu-
> nities are confronted with many of the same land-use disputes
> and environmental threats as their low-income counterparts.
> [And because of housing bias,] increased income has not en-
> abled many blacks to escape the threat of unwanted land use.[14]

Environmental racism has been going on for a long time, notes Charles Lee, an Asian American and research director of the Commission for Racial Justice. He tells the story of the "worst recorded occupational disaster in U.S. history," at Gauley Bridge, West Virginia.

> During the 1930s, hundreds of African-American workers from the Deep South were brought in by the New Kanawha Power Company, a subsidiary of the Union Carbide Corporation, to dig the Hawks Nest tunnel. Over a two-year period, approximately 500 workers died and 1,500 were disabled from silicosis, a lung disease similar to Black Lung. Men literally dropped dead on their feet breathing air so thick with microscopic silica that they could not see more than a yard in front of them. Those who came out for air were beaten back into the tunnel with ax handles. At subsequent congressional hearings, New Kanawha's contractor revealed, "I knew I was going to kill those niggers, but I didn't know it was going to be this soon." An undertaker was hired to bury dead workers in unmarked graves; he agreed to perform the service for an extremely low rate because the company assured him there would be a large number of deaths.[15]

Lee says environmental racism is best seen in historical context. One current is

> the long history of oppression and exploitation of African-Americans, Hispanic-Americans, Asian-Americans and Pacific Islanders, and Native Americans. This has taken the form of genocide, chattel slavery, indentured servitude, and racial discrimination in employment, housing and practically all aspects of life in the United States. We suffer today from the remnant of this sordid history, as well as from new and institutionalized forms of racism.

The problem is exacerbated by "the massive expansion of the petrochemical industry since World War II."

In 1987, the Commission for Racial Justice demanded change. "This report," it declared in *Toxic Wastes and Race in the United States*, "firmly concludes that hazardous wastes in black, Hispanic and other racial and ethnic communities should be made a priority issue at all levels of government. This issue is not currently at the forefront of the nation's attention. Therefore, concerned citizens and policy-makers, who are cognizant of this growing national problem, must make this a priority concern." It called for the U.S. president "to issue an executive order mandating federal agencies to consider the impact of current policies and regulations on racial and ethnic communities"; state governments "to evaluate and make appropriate revisions in their criteria for the siting of new hazardous waste facilities to adequately take into account the racial and socio-economic characteristics of potential host communities"; the U.S. Conference of Mayors, the National Conference of Black Mayors, and the National League of Cities "to convene a national conference to address these issues from a municipal perspective"; and "civil rights and political organizations to gear up voter registration campaigns as a means to further empower racial and ethnic communities to effectively respond to hazardous waste issues and to place hazardous wastes in racial and ethnic communities at the top of state and national legislative agendas."

Government movement on environmental racism in the Reagan and Bush years was at a snail's pace. EPA director William Reilly did not even appear at the Summit—a spokesman said that his schedule was "prohibitive." This showed that the EPA had "utter disrespect for what is happening in our communities," declared Chavis, after sending Reilly a "blistering letter."

After some prodding from academics of color and environmental and social justice activists (the so-called Michigan Coalition), Reilly did establish an internal Work Group on Environmental Equity in 1990. In January 1992, after eighteen months of study, the EPA released its long-awaited draft *Equity Report*.[16] The report came with press disclosure of an EPA committee draft report that said, "Although there are clear differences between ethnic groups for disease and death rates, there are virtually no data to document the environmental contributions to these diseases." George Colling of the Sierra Club said, "There is no new data needed, just a political will and commitment in the face of intensive lobbying by the companies that are making money."

Indeed, Robert Wolcott, the EPA official who headed the committee, acknowledged, "How many times does a tree have to fall before you admit that you heard it?" When the final *Equity Report,* which was part of what the EPA said was a new consideration by the agency of "environmental equity," was issued in June 1992, it had been revised to admit that there is evidence that minorities suffer disproportionately from environmental contaminants.

With the election victory of Bill Clinton and his taking office in 1993 with an administration that is diverse in its leadership and that claims it will bring government attention to all the people of the United States, there is some hope that the specter of environmental racism might begin to be truly addressed by the national government. It is certain that the new administration cannot plead ignorance to the issue. Reverend Benjamin Chavis and Professor Robert Bullard, two of the planners of the Summit, served on Clinton's Transition Team in the Natural Resources and Environment Cluster (i.e., the EPA and the Departments of Energy, the Interior, and Agriculture). How well environmental justice themes are integrated throughout the federal agencies remains to be seen.

Leading up to the Summit was a series of other important events tackling environmental racism. "Focus on Environmental Contamination" was the theme of a 1990 National Minority Health Conference held in Atlanta. The conference was sponsored by the federal Agency for Toxic Substances and Disease Registry (ATSDR) and was attended by 300 community leaders, physicians, and government officials.

Dr. Aubrey F. Manley, deputy assistant secretary of the Department of Health and Human Services (who substituted for Health and Human Services secretary Louis Sullivan), said, "Poor and minority people should not have to bear the responsibility for a mess they haven't made." The Panos Institute, a group based in Washington, DC, went a step further and issued a report, *We Speak for Ourselves: Social Justice, Race, and Environment,* at the conference. The publication included commentary by, among others, Bullard, Lee, and Dana A. Alston, director of the Environment, Community Development and Race Project of Panos and a member of the national planning committee for the Summit. Alston stated in the report:

> Organizing for environmental justice among people of color has grown from a small group of activists in the 1970s to a movement involving thousands of people in neighborhoods throughout the U.S. Although these groups might not be identified as "environmental" organizations, they have nevertheless made environmental issues a priority in their work. Communities of color have often taken a more holistic approach than the mainstream environmental movement, integrating "environmental" concerns into a broader agenda that emphasizes social, racial and economic justice.[17]

In 1990, too, the Commission for Racial Justice organized a workshop on race and environment for the Congressional Black Caucus, whose members—unbeknownst to most people—are rated by the League of Conservation Voters as having among the most proenvironmental voting records in Congress.

Also in 1990, Reverend Jesse Jackson, along with John O'Connor, founder and executive director of the National Toxics Campaign (NTC), and Denis Hayes, a main organizer of both the original Earth Day in 1970 and Earth Day 1990, made a week-long tour of "hot spots" of environmental racism. The tour ended in Cancer Alley, Louisiana. "There is a relationship between environment and empowerment," stated Jackson on that tour.

> When a community is not registered to vote, and therefore lacks the political power, it is easier for multinational corporations to site poisonous facilities in those communities. This

trip, that brings together the largest grassroots community based environmental organization, the National Toxics Campaign, along with Earth Day 1990, is saying it's a new day and a new way. No longer will corporations be allowed to use job blackmail to poison poor people be they black, brown, yellow, red or white. We are demanding that all corporate poisoners sign agreements to stop the poisoning of our communities. We can have safe jobs without pollution if we organize for it.

Since the Summit, other events in the struggle against environmental racism have included the 1992 Conference on Environmental Justice: A Learning Experience, at Xavier University of Louisiana, which is among the historically black colleges and universities (HBCUs). "We are in a period of time that we'll see mass action on environmental racism because the existence of the planet, our existence as people of color, depend on it," Dr. Bunyan Bryant of the School of Natural Resources at the University of Michigan, yet another African American professor who is a pioneer in investigating environmental racism, said at the conference. The conference included faculty members and students from other schools in the grouping of HBCUs and activists, including John Zippert of the Federation of Southern Cooperatives, who told of assaults against him in the battle against the Emelle, Alabama, toxic waste dump, and Native American Oannes Pritzker, who told of being attacked in his native Maine because of his environmental advocacy. Pritzker now lives and works in Florida. The conference was addressed by Louisiana congressman William Jefferson, an African American who pledged that he would try to get the U.S. Congress to focus on environmental racism.

Later that year, also at Xavier, the Southern Community/Labor Conference for Environmental Justice was hosted by the Gulf Coast Tenants Association. It drew more than 2,000 activists, academicians, college students of all races, and elected officials.

Meanwhile, some of the major U.S. environmental organizations have been moving to clean up their racial and ethnic acts. An Environmental Consortium for Minority Outreach was set up in

Washington, DC, by environmental groups after coalitions of minority activists—including Richard Moore and Reverend Benjamin Chavis—sent letters to many of them in 1990 protesting the lack of minority representation on their staffs. Not scored were Greenpeace, the National Toxics Campaign, and Earth Island Institute.

Both Greenpeace and the National Toxics Campaign have long stressed both minority involvement and the fight against environmental racism. As O'Connor of the National Toxics Campaign has stressed: "For the environmental movement to be successful in saving the planet, it must include all races and ethnic groups, rich and poor, black and white, and young and old. When our movement to clean up the nation is truly a reflection of all people in the country, it is at that point that we will succeed in stopping the poisoning of America."

In a breakthrough for minorities and the national environmental movement, since 1989 the president of Earth Island Institute has been an African American. Carl Anthony is an architect for whom environmental issues have long been critical—as has the relationship between environment and race. He is a professor of architecture at the University of California, Berkeley, where he teaches a course on race, poverty, and the environment.

Most environmental groups have had an "elitist perspective," says Anthony. He sees change coming because of a "grass-roots constituency that is challenging them." He is also director of Earth Island's Urban Habitat program. "We're very interested in issues at two ends of the spectrum: global warming, the ozone layer, depletion of global resources—and the negative environmental impacts on communities of poor people and people of color. In order to bring these two concerns together," says Anthony, "we have to develop a new kind of thrust and a new kind of leadership in communities of color to address the needs of our communities and also the larger urban community in making a transition to more sustainable urban patterns."

Anthony, active at the Summit, described as "really incredible" its diversity, the "good balance" between men and women and among African Americans, Latino Americans, Asian Americans, and Native Americans. "I think it set the stage for the decade of the 1990s," he said. "It set out the challenges and opportunities for communities of color and the nation as a whole."

George T. Frampton, Jr., president of The Wilderness Society, a major environmental group that has been actively seeking to become more inclusive, says: "One inescapable truth about the degradation of our environment has received very little attention: those least able to get out of harm's way are people of color." The lack of representation of minorities in national environmental organizations "is beginning to change—and it must—because a movement that is overwhelmingly white will be unable to direct sufficient attention to those environmental problems that disproportionately victimize blacks and minorities. Nor will a monochromatic movement ultimately mobilize the broad-based political support required for the radical environmental policies that our society so urgently needs."

OUR FREE PRESS AND THE MEDIA?

What about the press, which in the United States is, ideally, a watchdog, a monitor revealing social injustice and crusading to rectify it? The media have been largely asleep historically when it comes to dealing with the institutional racism long endemic in the United States. And this has been their behavior regarding environmental racism, too.

For some media, it has been a case of outright denial. "Environmental Racism? Crying Wolf Will Hurt *Real* Discrimination Charges" was the headline of a *Houston Post* editorial (November 5, 1991) following the Summit. The newspaper claimed that "if examined closely, it appears that toxic dumps follow cheap land. White people also have been victims of toxic waste dumps because of cheap land. Just look at Brio, Love Canal, and Times Beach." As for those at the conference: "These folks are crying wolf. That's too bad—because pretty soon, legitimate charges of racism may be at risk of going unheeded, simply because so many people claim racism is around every corner. It often *isn't* there, and those who are saying it should examine exactly what their cries are accomplishing."

Typically, media have treated environmental racism by putting it in a conditional context. "Conference Will Claim Racism of the Environment" was a headline in the Maysville, Kentucky, *Ledger-Independent* (October 21, 1991) above a story on the Summit. Yes, *claim.* "Minority Leaders Say EPA Dumps on Them" headlined the *Las Vegas Sun* (October 25, 1991).

"Dumping on the Poor" was a two-page story in *Time* (August 13, 1990) with a subhead: "America's dispossessed here lived for decades with toxic wastes and garbage. Now they're fighting back." The piece dutifully reported on activism by people of color, but it left the impression that economics, not race, was the issue. "Waste managers deny they are picking on the poor. Some say it is simplistic to attribute the environmental problems of minority communities to racism, even though few challenge the evidence that the poor have more environmental dangers to cope with than do the wealthy. Blacks, Hispanics and Asians have often inherited hazards by moving into older sectors of cities, where decrepit factories and other facilities were built long before anyone worried about pollution."

Charles Lee of the Commission for Racial Justice recalls the 1987 press conference at which *Toxic Wastes and Race in the United States* was released and Chavis first spoke about environmental racism. "When Ben first used the term, the few black reporters accepted it openly. Some white reporters cringed, and then gave us a hard time," related Lee. "You could see: their reaction was visceral, overlayed with emotions."

Where has the investigative reporting, the muckraking, been on environmental racism? What about the press going out and finding out on its own what is really happening? Why did it have to take civil rights activists and some African American academics for the realization of environmental racism to surface? Why did the press, if it was doing its job, not expose a shameful pattern that has been so obvious for so long?

In its landmark report, the National Advisory Commission on Civil Disorders, a panel chaired by Illinois governor Otto Kerner that was formed after widespread urban rioting in 1967, came down heavily on U.S. media—both as being derelict in examining racism in the United States and as being part of a racist society. In a chapter in its 1968 report titled *The News Media and the Disorders,* the Kerner Commission stated:

> The news media have failed to analyze and report adequately on racial problems in the United States and, as a related matter, to meet the Negro's legitimate expectations in journalism. By and large, news organizations have failed to communicate to both their black and white audiences a sense of the problems America faces and the sources of potential solutions. The media reports and writes from the standpoint of a white man's world. The ills of the ghetto, the difficulties of life there, the Negro's burning sense of grievance, are seldom conveyed. Slights and indignities are part of the Negro's daily life, and many of them come from what he now calls the "white press"—a press that repeatedly, if unconsciously, reflects the biases, the paternalism, the indifference of white America. This may be understandable, but it is not excusable in an institution that has the mission to inform and educate the whole of our society.[18]

The report hit at the management and staffing of media institutions principally by white men. "The journalistic profession has been shockingly backward in seeking out, hiring, training and promoting Negroes," said the Kerner Commission. "Fewer than 5 percent of the people employed by the news business in editorial jobs in the United States today are Negroes. Fewer than 1 percent of editors and supervisors are Negroes, and most of them work for Negro-owned organizations."

"Along with the country as a whole," said the Kerner Commission report,

> the press has too long basked in a white world, looking out at it, if at all, with white men's eyes and a white perspective. That is no longer good enough. The painful process of readjustment

that is required of the American news media must begin now. They must make a reality of integration—in both their product and personnel. They must insist on the highest standards of accuracy—not only reporting single events with care and skepticism, but placing each event into meaningful perspective. They must report the travail of our cities with compassion and in depth. In all this, the commission asks for fair and courageous journalism. . . .

The report concluded: "The failings of the media must be corrected and the improvement must come from within the media."

But more than two decades later, there is very, very far to go on the promises made by media groups after the Kerner Commission report was released, promises that changes would be made in the composition of managements and staffs: parity reflecting the diversity of the United States.

A 1990 survey by the Association for Education in Journalism and Mass Communication found that the percentage of nonwhite daily newspaper staff members was 8 percent and that 51 percent of dailies in the United States still employed no minority workers in their newsrooms. The percentage of nonwhites in newspaper management has remained at about 1 percent. In electronic media, which were subject to post–Kerner Commission pressure by the federal government through the Federal Communications Commission, 8 percent of radio news people and 16 percent of television news employees—mainly lower level—were members of minority groups as of 1989, Dwayne Wickham, president of the National Association of Black Journalists, said then.

The U.S. media, Max Robinson, the first African American to anchor a network news broadcast, said in 1981, are "a crooked mirror" through which "white America views itself."

The failure of the media to expose environmental racism is not only a consequence of how a narrow segment of the population—white males—continues to run and staff the U.S. media, a group whose everyday lives are not affected by environmental racism. Also, critically, it is a reflection of who owns U.S. media. In some instances, the connection between the owners of media and who is doing the polluting is direct. Some institutions that should be monitored by media own the very media that should be doing the monitoring. For example, General Electric, one of America's more outrageous corporate environmental outlaws, owns one of the three major U.S. television networks, the National Broadcasting Company. In other instances, the connections are not as direct but indirect linkages exist, controlling the media more and more as fewer and fewer corporations own more of U.S. media.

A very few big corporations have gained control of most of the media in the United States—print and electronic—and are "interlocked in common financial interest with other massive industries and with a few dominant international banks," notes Ben H. Bagdikian in his book on the subject, *The Media Monopoly*. He places the number now at just twenty-six. They "own most of the output of daily newspapers and most of the sales and audiences in magazines, broadcasting, books and movies." Those who head these corporations "would fit in a large room. They constitute a new Private Ministry of Information and Culture."[19]

"When their most sensitive economic interests are at stake, the parent corporations seldom refrain from using their power over public information," writes Bagdikian.

Environmental racism was rated as among the top twenty-five most censored stories in the United States in 1991 by Project Censored, a media research project at Sonoma State University in California.

"Media White-Out of Environmental Racism" was the title of an article in the July–August 1992 issue of *Extra!*, the publication of Fairness & Accuracy in Reporting, a national media watch group based in New York. The story begins: "The young Anglo environmental reporter at the *Albuquerque Journal* stared blankly when Southwest Organizing Project co-director Jeanne Gauna spoke about environmental racism." Still, to help him read up on the subject, she offered him a copy of *Toxic Wastes and Race in the United States*. About a week later, he returned the study. Regarding its findings, he said, "This may be true in other places, but it's not the case in Albuquerque."

The authors of the article, Elizabeth Martinez and Louis Head, concluded that there are three major reasons for media cover-ups on environmental racism: "(1) Corporate interests are at stake, and the mass media hesitate to thoroughly scrutinize them; (2) societal racism encourages the media to be uninterested in people of color unless there's a sensational (usually negative) story; and (3) government agencies, especially the U.S. Environmental Protection Agency, have actively pursued strategies to divert public attention from the issue of environmental racism."

Things are getting a bit better since the Summit. On January 7, 1993, the *Christian Science Monitor* published a story, its headline not conditional—"Pollution in US Cities Hits Minorities Hardest."

And lo and behold, the *New York Times* published a front-page story (January 11, 1993) on environmental racism—"Pollution-Weary Minorities Try Civil Rights Tack"—with a nearly full-page continuation. It reported that "under the banner of environmental justice," African American, Latino American, Asian American, and Native American "groups are battling pollution hazards" and "have developed into a powerful new social movement that is applying the language of the civil rights movement to counter health threats as varied as toxic dumping and lead poisoning."

Well, the movement is here, so mainstream media just have to begin reporting it.

And indeed, what a potentially powerful movement it is: combining the civil rights and environmental movements and challenging two things as American as apple pie—racism and environmental pollution—as they coincide.

"I think when we define the freedom movement, it now includes the environmental issues," says Reverend Chavis. "We now understand the insidious nature of racism. Fighting it does not just involve getting civil rights laws on the books. It goes beyond that. Racism has permeated all facets of American society. We see the struggle against environmental racism as being an ongoing part of the civil rights and freedom movement, something we are going to make part of our agenda, not a side issue but a primary issue. We must be as vigilant in attacking environmental racism as [we are with] racism in health care, housing, and schools."

16

A Call for Justice and Equal Environmental Protection

DEEOHN FERRIS

The environmental justice movement is the confluence of three of America's greatest challenges: the struggle against racism and poverty; the effort to preserve and improve the environment; and the compelling need to shift social institutions from class division and environmental depletion to social unity and global sustainability.

The movement for environmental justice in communities of color is alive and well all across the United States. This movement has matured and can no longer be pushed aside or ghettoized. It is mainstream. Environmental justice activists and academics alike are joining forces to form a much stronger, action-oriented movement. The voices on environmental justice and equity have begun to exert some influence in policy making, as in the case of the federal Environmental Protection Agency (EPA), the Agency for Toxic Substances and Disease Registry (ATSDR), and the National Institute for Environmental Health Sciences (NIEHS).[1]

The October 1991 First National People of Color Environmental Leadership Summit energized and galvanized this movement. The December 1992 Southern Organizing Committee (SOC) conference in New Orleans attracted more than 1,500 environmental justice activists. As a major follow-up activity to the summit, the meeting in New Orleans exceeded everyone's expectations. More-

298

over, the planning that took place under a tree at Xavier University of Louisiana proved to have monumental implications. Grass-roots leaders decided to map out a long-term, directed strategy to address the problem of unequal environmental protection, environmental racism, and disproportionate impact of pollution on communities of color.

The new Clinton administration was now being challenged to reinvent a federal EPA that protects the environment and public health. Two environmental justice leaders, Reverend Benjamin F. Chavis, Jr., and Professor Robert D. Bullard, were selected to serve on the Clinton-Gore Transition Team in the National Resources and Environment Cluster. This cluster consisted of the Departments of Energy, Agriculture, and the Interior and the EPA. With these two individuals working inside the "belly of the beast," the EPA, grass-roots groups from all across the country would have a direct pipeline for getting their message heard by the new EPA administration.[2] This was the thinking behind the development of the environmental justice transition paper discussed in this chapter. The Lawyers' Committee for Civil Rights Under Law took the lead in assembling the community perspectives and recommendations.[3]

AFFECTED COMMUNITIES DEMAND JUSTICE

Contributors to concepts in this chapter represent environmental justice groups, civil rights organizations, and scholars active in the First National People of Color Environmental Leadership Summit and other grass-roots conferences and activities around the nation.[4] This movement has established and documented environmental racism and challenges the existing environmental protection paradigm, which results in disparate impact.

Race is the most significant predictor of the location of pollution sources, ranging from environmental contamination caused by landfills and incinerators to radiation, pesticide poisoning, and deleterious air quality. Furthermore, occupational exposures and indoor air pollution exacerbate ambient environmental risks.

Environmental justice is not anchored in a debate about whether or not decision makers should tinker at the edges of risk-based management. The tenets of environmental justice demand implementation of strategies to eliminate unjust and inequitable effects caused by existing environmental policies.

The mission of the U.S. Environmental Protection Agency must be redefined to address environmental laws, regulations, and agency practices that result in discriminatory outcomes. An environmental justice model must be imposed that incorporates a framework of equal justice and equal protection principles to ensure every citizen's right to be free from pollution.

The need for a comprehensive approach to environmental issues is paramount. Protection of the environment must encompass economic development opportunities that incorporate creation of clean industries and safe jobs. The Environmental Justice Transition Group supports the efforts of people of color in this nation to speak for themselves. The group's transition paper on environmental justice issues is not intended to supersede the activism of community-based groups and Native American governments. Instead, it is a conceptual document highlighting crosscutting concerns.[5]

The transition paper outlines recommendations to the presidential Transition Team for the U.S. Environmental Protection Agency (EPA), centering on three key areas: (1) the agency's institutional focus; (2) targeting of regulatory programs, compliance, and enforcement activities; and (3) new policy.

RECOMMENDATION: *A Shift to Protecting Adversely Affected Communities Must Occur in the EPA's Institutional Focus*

With regard to fulfilling its mission to protect human health and the environment, the EPA must incorporate into its decision-making process factors necessary to safeguard communities facing disproportionate pollution exposures. In this regard, four initiatives can immediately be undertaken to address underprotected populations: (1) the new administration should issue an executive order, and the

EPA's Office of General Counsel should issue a formal opinion, establishing the applicability of civil rights laws and regulations to environmental programs; (2) the EPA should reassess government relationships with indigenous peoples, adequately fund and streamline programs, and facilitate self-determination; (3) the EPA should put priority attention on developing countries; and (4) the EPA should be elevated to cabinet status.

(1) The EPA's Office of General Counsel, in Conjunction with the Department of Justice and the Department's Civil Rights Division, Should Issue a Formal Opinion Establishing the Applicability of Civil Rights Laws and Regulations to Environmental Programs, and the New Administration Should Issue an Executive Order Implementing This Policy

Soon after its creation, the EPA issued an Office of General Counsel (OGC) opinion stating that due to the technical nature of environmental statutes (e.g., setting of discharge limits, regulation of chemicals), civil rights laws are inapplicable to the agency's programs.

In testimony presented in 1971 to the United States Commission on Civil Rights, EPA administrator William Ruckelshaus contended that the agency's role in setting environmental standards precluded the application of this nation's civil rights policies to environmental programs.

This testimony and the OGC opinion are inconsistent with the agency's mandate to protect human health and the environment. The EPA's overarching mission is to ensure equal protection from pollution. Instead, to the detriment of communities of color and low-income communities, program implementation and enforcement produce discriminatory results. Based on the evidence, ostensibly neutral technical standards developed by the agency are implemented in a disparate manner.

It must be made clear at the outset by the new administration that the EPA is not exempt from the tenets of equal protection. The EPA should immediately rescind the OGC's opinion and issue a new opinion establishing that civil rights laws apply to environmental programs.

To reinforce that the principles of equal protection pertain to the entire scope of environmental issues, the president should issue an executive order providing for the equitable implementation of environmental programs. The executive order should do the following:

- Establish a Federal Coordinating Council on environmental justice, including agencies and departments such as the EPA, and the Departments of the Interior, Agriculture, Labor, Health and Human Services, Housing and Urban Development, Energy, Defense, and Transportation; the Centers for Disease Control; the Agency for Toxic Substances and Disease Registry; and the National Institute for Environmental Health Sciences. The principal purpose of the council would be to review federal research and research systems, report on gaps and other deficiencies in environmental data, and research priorities and compatibility of federal research systems. The Federal Coordinating Council should institute a framework for technology assessment and examine related issues in the context of social, cultural, and political impact.

- Direct the White House Council on Environmental Quality to include in its annual report information pertaining to communities in this nation that are experiencing disproportionate pollution risks.

- Mandate inclusion of an equity impact statement that incorporates a presumption equally protecting all people from pollution. The statement would be required for all major federal regulations, grants, and projects.

- Create a Federal Advisory Committee Act board to advise the EPA and the Federal Coordinating Council, the membership of which would include indigenous peoples and representatives of community-based groups experiencing disproportionate impact.

- Direct federal agencies to develop and institute environmentally beneficial procurement practices emphasizing pollution prevention and environmentally friendly products.

(2) The EPA Should Reassess Government Relationships with Indigenous Peoples, Adequately Fund and Streamline Programs, and Facilitate Self-determination

The EPA must reevaluate its programmatic relationships with indigenous peoples. With regard to Native Americans, the EPA should confirm the 1984 EPA Indian Policy and ensure its immediate implementation. Further, the EPA should develop formal policies that determine federal government relationships with indigenous Hawaiians and Pacific Islanders.

Currently, the EPA employs several conflicting approaches vis-à-vis indigenous peoples and their lands. To remedy these conflicts, Pacific Islanders, indigenous Hawaiians, and Native American tribes must be included at all levels in the development of federal environmental policy, including regulation, compliance, and enforcement activities.

The concerns of and problems experienced by Native Americans, Pacific Islanders, and indigenous Hawaiians are distinct, and solutions must be specially tailored. However, federal approaches toward indigenous lands must promote self-determination in implementation of regulatory compliance and enforcement programs.

To enhance efficiency and effective use of targeted resources, the EPA should streamline and consolidate national Indian Program activities into a central office. Currently, Indian Program responsibilities are fragmented into three distinct offices: the Office of Federal Activities; the Office of Regional Operations and State and Local Relations; and the Office of the Deputy Administrator. In addition, in conjunction with Native Americans, the EPA should consider creating a Tribal Operations Committee to commence the process of institutionalizing tribal needs into the agency's budget, planning, and implementation processes.

To facilitate sovereign governance and the ability of Native Americans to protect themselves and their sacred sites from pollution exposure, the EPA must ensure availability of adequate funding and training opportunities, as well as tribal access to EPA program managers and upper-level administrators.

The new administration should support adjustments in basic congressional funding formulas so that environmental programs instituted by tribal governments can be equitably funded at levels sufficient to manage and enforce those programs. Furthermore, resources should be directed to both large and small tribal communities.

In targeting resources and increasing funding for Native American programs, particular attention must be given to enhancing the development of tribal infrastructure. Tribal lands encompass 56 million acres and more than 500 tribal jurisdictions. However, out of 18,000 full-time EPA employees, only 100 are dedicated to the Indian Program.

The EPA must reevaluate federal approaches to regulating the environment of indigenous Hawaiians and Pacific Islanders. These indigenous peoples must be integrated into federal decision-making processes concerning their unique lands, and those lands sacred to them must be afforded special protection, including protection from pollution.

The EPA should institute reporting mechanisms related to the environment of indigenous peoples. The EPA should regularly update the 1990 Indian Resources Task Force Report, and annually the EPA should issue separate reports to Congress on the status of the environment on tribal lands, in the Hawaiian Islands, and in the Pacific Islands.

3. The EPA Should Put Priority Attention on Developing Countries

Consistent with the agency's policy of setting risk-based priorities, the EPA should prioritize African, South American, and Asian programs in its Office of International Activities. In constructing international treaties and United States foreign policy, the new administration must recognize and promote self-determination.

The administration must reevaluate policy conflicts illustrated in the approaches pursued by the United States in eastern Europe and developing countries concerning environment and energy. Currently, the United States is attempting to encourage and reinvigorate the (albeit more environmentally friendly) use of energy and natural resources by eastern European countries in order to rebuild the economy and improve living standards.

However, in developing countries, the United States is using economic and financial aid leverage to discourage (albeit more environmentally unfriendly) use of energy and natural resources— energy and resources on which many developing nations depend to elevate their standard of living. This is inequitable foreign policy, and these approaches must be revised.

In view of the relationship between environmental policy and economic policy in developing countries, the new administration should converge international strategies to preserve the environment and foster economic development in developing nations with an omnibus policy to eliminate drug exports into the United States.

Increasingly in developing countries, ecosystems are being destroyed and replanted with crops that are processed into illegal drugs. United States foreign policy must promote quality economic development as an alternative to drug exports, which destroy the lives and minds of our citizenry.

4. The EPA Should Be Elevated to Cabinet Status, and the New Administration Should Support Other Key Legislative Initiatives

During the 102d Congress, Congressman John Conyers, a Democrat from Michigan, and Senator John Glenn, a Democrat from Ohio, spearheaded a bipartisan campaign to elevate the EPA to cabinet status. Subject to issuance of an executive order, an OGC opinion, and an opinion by the Department of Justice establishing the applicability of civil rights laws to environmental programs, the president should work with Congress to accomplish this goal.

A department-level EPA reorganized to promote overall accountability and efficiency in regulatory, compliance, and enforcement programs would facilitate equitable implementation of statutory programs. Environmental justice must be explicit in the legislation's mission statement as one of the principal areas of focus for the new department and a major area of responsibility for the secretary, who should annually report to Congress on the department's progress.

In addition to creating cabinet-status legislation, the new administration should support legislative initiatives to remedy disproportionate pollution risks. The year 1993 is an unprecedented time for congressional consideration of environmental statutes, including the Clean Water Act; the Comprehensive Environmental Response, Compensation, and Liability Act (Superfund); the Resource Conservation and Recovery Act; the federal Insecticide, Fungicide, and Rodenticide Act; and the Safe Drinking Water Act.

Furthermore, the new administration should work with Congress to develop and enact laws creating job training and economic development opportunities, which would be established and implemented as programs by community-based organizations. Environmental jobs, such as those of inspector and cleanup technician, would provide an employment base for workers of color in such areas as revitalized industrial sectors and federal facilities.

In the legislative context, the new administration has a unique opportunity to redress joblessness, lack of access to health care, and other such tragic and unjust circumstances as elevated health risks and high mortality rates caused by disproportionate environmental exposures in this nation.

RECOMMENDATION: *The EPA Should Substantially Reorient Regulatory, Compliance, and Enforcement Program Priorities*

To redress environmental problems in underprotected communities, the EPA should substantially reorient regulatory, compliance, and enforcement program priorities. The EPA has an obligation to remedy disparate environmental effects by immediately targeting and establishing as high priorities development and implementation of solutions to alleviate discriminatory pollution exposures in communities of color and sensitive populations.

In this regard, the EPA should undertake three initiatives to redress disproportionate pollution risks: (1) prioritize eleven program areas affecting people of color and sensitive populations; (2) target research and development efforts, including restructuring the focus to reporting and data collection on affected populations; (3) target compliance inspections and enforcement to protect communities of color exposed to disproportionate environmental risks.

1. The EPA Should Prioritize Environmental Programs to Redress Disparate Pollution Impact

Due to federal and state resource limitations, the EPA, the states, and Congress have initiated a dialogue on planning sequential or prioritized implementation of environmental programs (e.g., safe drinking water, clean water, and clean air). To the greatest possible extent, sequencing and prioritizing must be based on protecting those most severely exposed, considering factors such as synergistic effects, multiple sources, and sensitive populations.

The agency's work on prioritizing environmental program areas to protect human health should first commence in eleven specific areas: indigenous peoples; farm workers; radiation exposure; waste facility siting and cleanup; clean air; clean water; safe drinking water; urban areas; free trade and border issues; EPA strategic planning and budget; and state program implementation.

- *Indigenous Peoples.* Access to and input into the federal process by indigenous peoples is paramount. Major issues include ensuring basic rights and access to natural resources; protecting groundwater and drinking water; expediting cleanup of federal facilities affecting indigenous lands; restoring funds cut by the Office of Management and Budget to the Bureau of Indian Affairs and infrastructure resources; ameliorating the impact of uranium mining and energy production activities on indigenous lands; and ceasing nuclear testing and radioactive waste disposal affecting Native American tribes and Pacific Islanders.

- *Farm Workers*. On August 13, 1992, after delaying for nearly nine years, the EPA issued the Farmworker Protection Standard (40 C.F.R. §§ 156, 170), revising a prior set of regulations that were widely known to be woefully inadequate. The current set of regulations are deficient and need substantial work in interpretation, implementation, and enforcement to improve protection for migrant farm workers and their families (who are 95 percent African American, Asian American, Native American, and Latino) from exposure to agricultural pesticides.

  In conjunction with efforts on the Farmworker Protection Standard, the EPA should vigorously implement and enforce the risk-reporting requirements set forth in section 6(a)(2) of the federal Insecticide, Fungicide, and Rodenticide Act. The EPA should increase the data base on farm workers' exposure to pesticides and target programs in research and development. The new administrator should acknowledge the priority designation accorded farm worker protection by the agency's Science Advisory Board.

- *Radiation Exposure*. Historically, the EPA is weak on regulating radiation exposure experienced by Native Americans, Mexican Americans, and Pacific Islanders. For example, in Arizona a breach in the mill tailings dam of a uranium-mining operation released thousands of gallons of radioactive water, and mill tailings cascaded down the Rio Puerco, contaminating a nearby Navajo reservation and its inhabitants. The EPA has not taken enforcement action in this case or in other, similar cases because of confusion over federal agency jurisdiction among the EPA, the Department of Energy, and the Nuclear Regulatory Commission.

  The new administration should establish the EPA as the primary enforcement authority over radioactive pollution and clarify the EPA's oversight responsibility under the Federal Facilities Compliance Act. EPA authority should encompass integrating environmental justice concerns into remediations conducted at federal facilities, including assessment of resource needs.

  The new administration should reexamine federal preemption

under the Atomic Energy Act and evaluate whether preemption should be eliminated and state and local governments authorized to control radiation exposures.

- *Waste Facility Siting and Cleanup.* Several studies and reports demonstrate that people of color face significantly higher risks due to disproportionate siting of waste facilities. The litany of data is extensive. Three out of five African Americans live in communities with abandoned toxic waste sites. Sixty percent of, or 15 million, African Americans live in communities with one or more abandoned sites.

  Three of the five largest commercial hazardous waste facilities are located in predominantly African American or Latino American communities, accounting for 40 percent of this nation's total estimated landfill capacity. Communities with hazardous waste incinerators generally have large populations of color—87 percent higher than the national average.

Communities where incinerators are proposed have populations of color 60 percent higher than the national average. Property values in communities that host incinerators are 38 percent lower than the national average, and where incinerators are proposed, property values are 35 percent lower than the national average. Based on these data alone, the conclusions are clear. The impact is discriminatory.

The EPA is obligated to correct these inequities. On an expedited basis, the agency should institute a moratorium on siting in communities already experiencing disproportionate impact; reevaluate implementation of the Resource Conservation and Recovery Act based on the tenets of equal protection; and ensure that future siting of treatment, storage, and disposal facilities (see 40 C.F.R. § 358) does not exacerbate extant risks in communities of color.

The EPA should establish regional procedures and guidelines that ensure contact with and input from affected communities at the outset of federal evaluation of facility sites and government investigations regarding remediation of toxic and hazardous waste sites. Furthermore, it is essential that the EPA expedite Superfund cleanups in communities of color and reassess discriminatory agency buyout policies.

- *Clean Air.* Research on the impact of poor air quality on people of color is incontrovertible. Air quality is the most extensively studied issue associated with disproportionate exposure. If aggressively implemented, the Clean Air Act is potentially one of the most environmentally beneficial pieces of legislation for communities of color in this nation.

  If effectively implemented, the act would address the disproportionate impact of degraded air quality. The section 173(a) program is critical because it mandates EPA review of "social costs." Many of the provisions contained in the clean air law provide communities with access to information regarding siting factors and the permit process for facilities that emit airborne toxins.

  In implementing the public participation requirements of this act, the EPA must ensure that all available information is translated into a form that is easily understandable to citizens. Immediately, the new administration must rescind the giant loophole in the Clean Air Act created by the Bush administration allowing 35,000 refineries, chemical and pharmaceutical plants, utilities, and other environmentally burdensome companies, which already pump billions of pounds of pollutants into the air, to emit more pollutants without subjecting the increases to public review.

  The EPA should identify and ameliorate (or report to Congress on) the regressive impacts of environmental and economic policies such as the gas tax, "green taxes," and Clean Air Act permit trading. The EPA must reassess the new clean air permit-trading system and ensure that it precludes a shifting of the burden of air pollution onto communities of color. Trading that results in disproportionate impact, including reduction in property values, should be prohibited.

- *Clean Water.* The EPA should assess whether sewage treatment facilities and combined sewer overflows are more often located in communities of color. The agency should determine what infrastructure improvements are needed to enhance these facilities to the state of the art through construction grants so that residents are not plagued by noxious fumes and other deleterious exposures.

The EPA should set water quality standards that schedule phasedown of and, where appropriate, ban the discharge of contaminants of concern to people of color who fish and consume those fish. In the interim, the EPA should intervene in the state fish consumption advisory process to guarantee that advisories are issued to citizens on a regular basis and that they are uniform and understandable.

- *Safe Drinking Water.* Many communities of color have insufficient resources to construct and/or maintain public drinking water systems and to implement EPA regulations controlling drinking water contaminants. The EPA should evaluate ways to set regulatory priorities for these communities and provide technical assistance and infrastructure improvement, including appropriate resources.

- *Urban Areas.* The EPA should focus on urban areas to develop pollution prevention initiatives and recycling and hazard abatement programs. Asbestos and lead abatement and removal and cleanup of industrial and formerly industrial areas that contain high amounts of waste should further the goals of creating jobs and community-based economic development.

- *Free Trade and Border Issues.* Industrial dumping on the 2,000-mile Mexico–United States border is causing birth defects, illnesses, and deaths. The EPA should immediately enforce provisions in the Toxic Substances Control Act and other statutory administrative subpoena and data-gathering authorities to collect information from multinational corporations operating on the Mexico–United States border.

The new administration should delay implementation of the North American Free Trade Agreement until a federal study is completed on information associated with chemicals and exposures and conclusions of the study can be factored into treaty considerations.

The EPA should expand the Rio Grande initiative to include both the upper and lower Rio Grande, including geographic considerations, watershed implications, and exposed communities.

- *Strategic Planning and Budget.* The EPA must integrate environmental justice policy into its operating year guidance, the agency's strategic plans, regional work plans, annual agency themes, and state-EPA agreements.

- *State Program Implementation.* The EPA should develop and publish in the *Federal Register* requirements mandating that states equitably implement delegated environmental programs, including grant conditions, permits, compliance, and enforcement activities.

2. The EPA Should Target Research and Development Efforts, Including Restructuring the Focus to Reporting and Data Collection on Affected Populations

The EPA should reconcile federal reporting and data reference systems among agencies and departments to emphasize collecting and analyzing data on populations most exposed to environmental contamination, including synergistic effects, multiple sources, and sensitive populations. The EPA should target research and development and data collection and analysis to support development of rules to protect overexposed populations.

3. The EPA Should Target Compliance Inspections and Enforcement to Protect Communities of Color Exposed to Disproportionate Environmental Risks

The EPA should target enforcement initiatives in communities of color inundated with pollution risks. This initiative should be implemented in areas such as Cancer Alley; Richmond, California; Chicago's South Side; and high-tech industries in the Southwest. In addition, targeting of high-risk populations or areas can be combined with other environmental programs; for example, a farm worker protection initiative could be combined with a pesticide and groundwater pollution initiative and a pesticide farm runoff initiative.

EPA monitoring systems must be revised to encompass communities of color. Even well-recognized toxins, such as lead, are not well monitored. Nor are data well correlated with actual exposures.

The EPA must amend its supplemental environmental projects policy to enable agency attorneys to credit penalties against environmentally beneficial projects in high-exposure areas.

RECOMMENDATION: *New Policy Initiatives Must Be Implemented to Redress Disproportionate Impact*

The EPA must develop new policy initiatives in several critical areas in order to redress disproportionate impact of environmental contamination on communities of color. These new initiatives are as follows:

- Consistent with the presidential campaign theme that coupled environmental protection with economic growth, the EPA and related departments need to support investment in sustainable development and infrastructure.

- The new administration should initiate an environmental-industrial policy of investment in sustainable development, that is, sustainable industries and technologies. The policy, with balanced input from citizens and industry, should shift investment and tax incentives toward conservation, pollution prevention, and a long-term commitment to protecting communities.

- Available public funds should be directed toward economic development opportunities in affected areas (e.g., the new Chrysler Jeep plant in Detroit). These programs must encourage geographic stability so that investments revitalize existing infrastructure instead of creating yet more disposable communities, either foreign or domestic.

- As a means to rebuild infrastructure in communities and around federal facilities, in conjunction with other agencies, states, and educational institutions the EPA should support creation of environmental jobs and training and education in environmental remediation.

- The administration and the EPA must revise cost-benefit analysis guidelines to include intangible costs related to quality of life, health, safety, and environmental justice.

- During the Reagan-Bush era, the administration developed twin crosscutting regulatory relief policies, cost-benefit analysis, and a presumption for federalism in health and environmental standards, which can adversely affect highly polluted communities by causing racial inequities. The EPA should be the lead agency in reviewing these cost-benefit policies.

- The EPA should work with civil rights groups to ensure that pollution prevention initiatives are equitably implemented. As presently conceived by the agency, pollution prevention initiatives will achieve mixed results (e.g., exposure to more concentrated toxic and hazardous chemicals) for workers of color and nearby residents.

- The EPA and the Occupational Safety and Health Administration (OSHA) have issued a limited number of environmental health and safety regulations associated with high-tech industry. The EPA should work with OSHA to review and strengthen the EPA-OSHA memorandum of understanding to address the problems of workers of color and their families who experience high exposure.

- The EPA is scheduled to propose in the *Federal Register* an ill-considered Environmental Excellence Program based on OSHA's VPP Program. An innovative environmental excellence program would be more appropriate, including economic incentives such as long-term capital commitment to an area; environmental protection and long-term planning; jobs, job training, and economic development; multimedia and/or one-stop permitting, and long-term permitting. The critical point is to avoid rewarding inequitable past actions.

- The EPA must support and fund community-based delivery of environmental services (e.g., "communiversities," which link academic institutions with communities in need of research, health assessment, and data analysis) by combining the resources of federal, state, and local environmental protection agencies, local colleges, and universities. These entities should combine to focus a significant portion of their service delivery efforts on environmental and health concerns at the community level.

- To establish credibility in EPA programs, the agency must reverse its historical resistance to cultural diversity and integration in its work force. The EPA should put employees of color in substantive decision-making positions and heed their input.

- EPA regulations and programs should generally shift the burden of proof to polluters seeking permits in areas that affect highly exposed or multiple-exposure communities.

- In conjunction with other agencies, the EPA should set conditions for the World Bank, the Agency for International Development, and the International Monetary Fund on exports of pesticides and wastes. Furthermore, the EPA should be granted oversight responsibility to ensure compliance with these conditions. As mentioned earlier, such actions should be coordinated with an international policy to eliminate drug exports into the United States.

- The EPA should expand the Community Right to Know initiative to include opportunities for communities to be involved in inspections and negotiation or public review of government environmental actions involving siting of industrial facilities. In addition, enhancing community access to information and improved data collection and input are key. Without these tools, informed consent is nonexistent and decision making concerning environmental management in this nation will continue to be hamstrung by community distrust and opposition.

CONCLUSION

Environmental justice is crosscutting, affecting every type of medium (i.e., air, land, and water) as well as regulatory programs, compliance programs, and enforcement. What is ultimately at stake in the environmental justice debate is everyone's quality of life. The goal is equal justice and equal protection from pollution. To combat environmental racism, the new administration and the EPA should immediately adopt the recommendations outlined in this chapter.

Strategies pursued by community-based environmental justice organizations have generated new federal and state legislation, a draft Executive Order on environmental justice, federal and state inter-agency assessments of programs and policies that result in discriminatory placement of environmental hazards and increased industry attention to the environmental justice movement. One signal of the successful momentum attained by the movement surfaced within the first few months of the newly-elected Democratic administration. On Earth Day, 1993, President Clinton announced a commitment to pursue a federal action plan to achieve environmental justice for all Americans.

In pursuit of this commitment, by the summer of 1993, the administration convened a federal inter-agency meeting and circulated for its review and comment a draft Executive Order on Environmental Justice. Formulation of the draft Executive Order occurred during ongoing Congressional deliberations to pass comprehensive legislation to eliminate disproportionate exposure to environmental hazards in communities of color and low-income communities. Adopting policies espoused by environmental justice activists, the order would require data collection and correlation on disparate risk and health effects, assessments by federal environmental programs to identify impacts on affected communities, and inter-agency coordination for eliminating discriminatory siting of polluting facilities. Heeding the plan set forth in the Environmental

Justice Group's EPA Presidential Transition Paper, the Executive Order clarifies the applicability of Title VI of the Civil Rights Act of 1964 by prohibiting discrimination against communities of color and the poor in federally funded environmental programs, including state programs and entities subject to federal oversight.

Recognizing that the administration's Executive Order does not supplant the need for a comprehensive permanent statutory mandate to redress disproportionate environmental risk, activists continue to pressure Congress to pass legislation that will remedy past discriminatory practices, policies, and conduct, and will eliminate environmental discrimination in the future. Legislation has either been introduced or drafted to respond to a range of environmental justice concerns that, if enacted, will affect government as well as the private sector. Both houses of the U.S. Congress are considering bills members have introduced that cover issues including lead exposure, siting of dumps and incinerators, and shipments of hazardous waste to developing countries.

In the House of Representatives, leadership on the issues is spearheaded by influential Democrats of color such as John Conyers, Jr. (D-MI), chairman of the Committee on Government Operations, who has drafted legislation to elevate the EPA to cabinet status; the proposed legislation contains provisions that would integrate environmental justice into the mission and functional responsibilities of this new cabinet-level department. Rep. John Lewis (D-GA) reintroduced legislation entitled the "Environmental Justice Act," which he cointroduced in 1990 with then-Senator, now Vice President Albert Gore. They are joined by women of color Reps. Cardiss Collins (D-IL) and Barbara Rose-Collins (D-MI), who have sponsored legislation to prevent discriminatory siting of waste facilities and to require data collection on disproportionate risk. Rep. Ed Towns (D-NY) has introduced a bill to prevent American shipment of hazardous wastes to developing nations and has cosponsored a bill that would institute a four-year moratorium on permitting new municipal solid-waste incinerators and, after the ban expires, would require a community impact assessment.

Similar issues also are being considered in the Senate. Senator Max Baucus, chairman of the Committee on Environment and Public Works, has introduced a companion bill to Rep. Lewis' Environmental Justice Act legislation pending in the House. Signaling her commitment to aiding people of color in the struggle for environmental justice, Senator Carol Mosely-Braun is one of the first cosponsors of the Baucus bill. Senator Paul Wellstone, a progressive Democrat from Minnesota, successfully amended legislation that would elevate the EPA to cabinet status to require the new department to study and address discriminatory environmental hazards. Similar to Rep. Conyers' draft legislation, the Wellstone amendment creates a high-level Office of Environmental Justice. Senator John Glenn (D-OH) has offered a bill that mirrors Rep. Towns's community impact bill. The Glenn bill would require preparation of a community information statement by new hazardous-waste treatment and disposal facilities.

While Congress and the administration have been focusing on environmental justice concerns, federal agencies have begun to respond to plans articulated by the environmental justice movement by examining their programs and how their implementation has affected communities of color and low-income communities. The EPA has created an Office of Environmental Justice. The Department of Justice and the Department of the Interior are conducting internal program assessments. The National Institute for Environmental Health Sciences has announced that it will convene an interagency conference on environmental health issues to define health research needs in communities of color.

The U.S. Commission on Civil Rights is proceeding with an investigation into the extent to which federal and some state environmental policies discriminate against people of color. Breaking new ground in studies on environmental racism, in a first-ever commission review of environmental policies and practices and discrimination, the commission found that the state of Louisiana failed to establish regulations or safeguards to ensure that communities of color are reasonably protected from a high concentration of hazardous waste, industrial facilities, and risks.[6]

States are taking action as well. Arkansas has set a new standard by signing into law a measure banning construction of waste facilities within twelve miles of one another. According to the stated rationale, the law is designed to prevent saturation of communities of color and low-income communities. Other states considering environmental justice legislation include Louisiana, Virginia, Georgia, South Carolina, North Carolina, New York and California.[7] Some states, California and Texas, for example, have assembled commissions to examine whether environmental injustices against communities of color are occurring within their borders.

These developments at the federal and state levels are key accomplishments that demonstrate that the environmental justice movement is alive, well, and thriving. Due to the hard work of community-based grassroots organizations, pollution issues affecting people of color and poor and working-class communities are more frequently the topics of attention nationally, statewide, and locally. Even so, activists in the movement continue to pressure for change, recognizing that reforms to systems that cause environmental problems experienced by affected communities must be permanent and irrevocable.

Notes

CHAPTER I
ENVIRONMENTAL JUSTICE FOR ALL

1. Robert D. Bullard, *Invisible Houston: The Black Experience in Boom and Bust* (College Station: Texas A & M University Press, 1987), pp. 110–111.

2. National Advisory Commission on Civil Disorders, *Report of the National Advisory Commission on Civil Disorders* (New York: Dutton, 1968), pp. 40–41.

3. See Robert D. Bullard, *Dumping in Dixie: Race, Class, and Environmental Quality* (Boulder, CO: Westview Press, 1990), chap. 3.

4. Interview with Charles Streadit, president of the Houston Northeast Community Action Group, May 30, 1988.

5. Ken Geiser and Gerry Waneck, "PCBs and Warren County," *Science for the People* 15 (July–August 1983): 13–17.

6. Ibid.

7. General Accounting Office, *Siting of Hazardous Waste Landfills and Their Correlation with Racial and Economic Status of Surrounding Communities* (Washington, DC: General Accounting Office, 1983), p. 1.

8. William K. Reilly, "Environmental Equity: EPA's Position," *EPA Journal* 18 (March–April 1992): 18.

9. Marianne Lavelle and Marcia Coyle, "Unequal Protection," *National Law Journal,* September 21, 1992, pp. S1–S2.

10. Ibid., p. S2.

11. See Robert D. Bullard and Beverly H. Wright, "The Politics of Pollution: Implications for the Black Community," *Phylon* 47 (March 1986): 71–78; Bullard, *Dumping in Dixie,* pp. 25–43.

12. See R. B. Stewart, "Paradoxes of Liberty, Integrity, and Fraternity: The Collective Nature of Environmental Quality and Judicial Review of Administrative Action," *Environmental Law* 7 (1977): 474–476; Leonard Gianessi, H. M. Peskin, and E. Wolff, "The Distributional Effects of Uniform Air Pollution Policy in the U.S.," *Quarterly Journal of Economics* 56 (May 1977): 281–301.

13. See W. J. Kruvant, "People, Energy, and Pollution," pp. 125–167 in *The American Energy Consumer,* ed. D. K. Newman and Dawn Day (Cambridge, MA: Ballinger, 1975); Robert D. Bullard, "Solid Waste Sites and the Black Houston Community," *Sociological Inquiry* 53 (Spring 1983): 273–288; United Church of Christ Commission for Racial Justice, *Toxic Wastes and Race in the United States: A National Study of the Racial and Socioeconomic Characteristics of Communities with Hazardous Waste Sites* (New York: United Church of Christ Commission for Racial Justice, 1987); Michel Gelobter, "The Distribution of Air Pollution by Income and Race" (paper presented at the Second Symposium on Social Science in Resource Management, Urbana, Illinois, June 1988); Dick Russell, "Environmental Racism," *Amicus Journal* 11 (Spring 1989): 22–32; Bullard, *Dumping in Dixie;* Paul Ong and Evelyn Blumenberg, "Race and Environmentalism" (Los Angeles: University of California, Los Angeles, Graduate School of Architecture and Urban Planning, March 1990); Eric Mann, *L.A.'s Lethal Air: New Strategies for Policy, Organizing, and Action* (Los Angeles: Labor/Community Strategy Center, 1991); Leslie A. Nieves, "Not in Whose Backyard? Minority Population Concentrations and Noxious Facility Sites" (paper presented at the annual meeting of the American Association for the Advancement of Science, Chicago, February 1991); D. R. Wernette and L. A. Nieves,

"Breathing Polluted Air: Minorities Are Disproportionately Exposed," *EPA Journal* 18 (March–April 1992): 16–17; Robert D. Bullard, "In Our Backyards: Minority Communities Get Most of the Dumps," *EPA Journal* 18 (March–April 1992): 11–12; Bunyan Bryant and Paul Mohai, eds., *Race and the Incidence of Environmental Hazards* (Boulder, CO: Westview Press, 1992).

14. See Gelobter, "The Distribution of Air Pollution."

15. Wernette and Nieves, "Breathing Polluted Air," pp. 16–17.

16. See Mann, *L.A.'s Lethal Air.*

17. See H. P. Mak, H. Abbey, and R. C. Talamo, "Prevalence of Asthma and Health Service Utilization of Asthmatic Children in an Inner City," *Journal of Allergy and Clinical Immunology* 70 (1982): 367–372; I. F. Goldstein and A. L. Weinstein, "Air Pollution and Asthma: Effects of Exposure to Short-Term Sulfur Dioxide Peaks," *Environmental Research* 40 (1986): 332–345; J. Schwartz, D. Gold, D. W. Dockey, S. T. Weiss, and F. E. Speizer, "Predictors of Asthma and Persistent Wheeze in a National Sample of Children in the United States," *American Review of Respiratory Disease* 142 (1990): 555–562.

18. Ong and Blumenberg, "Race and Environmentalism"; Mann, *L.A.'s Lethal Air.*

19. Jane Kay, "Fighting Toxic Racism: L.A.'s Minority Neighborhood Is the 'Dirtiest' in the State," *San Francisco Examiner,* April 7, 1991.

20. Conger Beasley, "Of Pollution and Poverty: Keeping Watch in 'Cancer Alley,'" *Buzzworm* 2 (July–August 1990): 39–45.

21. James O'Byrne, "Death of a Town," *Times Picayune,* February 20, 1991.

22. Bullard, *Dumping in Dixie,* pp. 65–69; James O'Byrne and Mark Schleifstein, "Invisible Poisons," *Times Picayune,* February 18, 1991.

23. Greenpeace, "Home Street, USA," *Greenpeace* (October–November 1991): 8–13.

24. Fernando Ferrer, "Testimony by the Office of Bronx Borough President," *Proceedings of the Public Hearing on Minorities and the Environment: An Exploration into the Effects of Environmental Policies, Practices, and Conditions on Minority and Low-Income Communities* (Bronx, NY: Bronx Planning Office, September 20, 1991), p. 27.

25. Robert Tomsho, "Dumping Grounds: Indian Tribes Contend with Some of the Worst of America's Pollution," *Wall Street Journal,* November 29, 1990; Jane Kay, "Indian Lands Targeted for Waste Disposal Sites," *San Francisco Examiner,* April 10, 1991; Bradley Angel, *The Toxic Threat to Indian Lands: A Greenpeace Report* (San Francisco: Greenpeace, 1992).

26. Angel, *Toxic Threat to Indian Lands.*

27. Samuel S. Epstein, Lester O. Brown, and Carl Pope, *Hazardous Waste in America* (San Francisco: Sierra Club Books, 1983), pp. 33–39.

28. Michael R. Greenberg and Richard F. Anderson, *Hazardous Waste Sites: The Credibility Gap* (New Brunswick, NJ: Rutgers University, Center for Urban Policy Research, 1984), pp. 158–159; Bullard, *Dumping in Dixie,* pp. 4–5.

29. United Church of Christ Commission for Racial Justice, *Toxic Wastes and Race.*

30. Ibid., pp. xiii–xiv.

31. Ibid., pp. 18–19.

32. United Church of Christ Commission for Racial Justice, *Toxic Wastes and Race.*

33. Pat Costner and Joe Thornton, *Playing with Fire* (Washington, DC: Greenpeace, 1990).

34. Agency for Toxic Substances and Disease Registry, *The Nature and Extent of Lead Poisoning in Children in the United States: A Report to Congress* (Atlanta: U.S. Department of Health and Human Services, 1988).

35. Peter Reich, *The Hour of Lead* (Washington, DC: Environmental Defense Fund, 1992), p. 42.

36. Agency for Toxic Substances and Disease Registry, *Nature and Extent of Lead Poisoning.*

37. Bill Lann Lee, "Environmental Litigation on Behalf of Poor, Minority Children; *Matthews v. Coye:* A Case Study" (paper presented at the annual meeting of the American Association for the Advancement of Science, Chicago, April 1992).

CHAPTER 2
CRISIS AT INDIAN CREEK

1. This article was first published in the *Atlanta Journal and Constitution,* January 20, 1980.

2. Barbara Reynolds, "Triana, Alabama: The Unhealthiest Town in America," *National Wildlife* 18 (August 1980): 75.

3. See Robert D. Bullard and Beverly H. Wright, "The Politics of Pollution: Implication for the Black Community," *Phylon* 47 (March 1986): 71–78.

4. Robert D. Bullard, *Dumping in Dixie: Race, Class, and Environmental Quality* (Boulder, CO: Westview Press, 1990), pp. 19–21.

CHAPTER 3
PCBS AND WARREN COUNTY

1. This article was first published in *Science for the People* 15 (1983): 13–17.

2. A great controversy surrounds the attempt to define just *how* toxic these chemicals are. Variables such as acute versus chronic effects, synergism with other environmental factors, route of administration, and species tested all contribute to problems in quantitating a "hazardous exposure." However, the Centers for Disease Control (CDC) in Atlanta considers 50 parts per trillion of dioxin, and 1 part per mil-

lion of PCBs, hazardous based on chronic effects in nonhuman primates; DDT falls somewhere in between.

3. Mary-Jane Schneider, *Persistent Poisons: Chemical Pollutants in the Environment* (New York: New York Academy of Sciences, 1979), p. 13. This book was published by the Academy of Sciences for the general public on the basis of the proceedings of a conference in 1978 titled Health Effects of Halogenated Aromatic Hydrocarbons. The full proceedings of the conference have been published as volume 320 of the *Annals of the New York Academy of Sciences*.

4. Ibid., p. 15.

5. Ibid., p. 59.

6. Ward Worthy, "Both Incidence, Control of Dioxin Are Highly Complex," *Chemical and Engineering News* 61, no. 23 (June 6, 1983), pp. 51–56. This entire volume is devoted to the topic of dioxin. Although most of the articles are apologetic for industry, many of the facts are indisputable regardless of how they are interpreted.

7. Joseph H. Highland, *PCBs: An Environmental Catastrophe* (Washington, DC: Environmental Defense Fund, 1979).

8. Schneider, *Persistent Poisons*, pp. 5–6.

9. U.S. Environmental Protection Agency, Office of Water Regulation and Standards, *Ambient Water Quality Criteria for Polychlorinated Biphenyls*, Publication no. 440/5-80-068 (Washington, DC: U.S. Environmental Protection Agency, October 1980).

10. Schneider, *Persistent Poisons*, p. 15.

11. Kimberly French, "A Community Unites Against Toxic Waste," *Whole Life Times* (January–February 1983), p. 25.

12. Deborah Ferruccio, "Experts Testify Against Hazardous Waste Landfill," letter to the editor, *Franklin Times* (North Carolina), February 16, 1982, pp. 4–5.

13. Ken Ferruccio and Dollie Burwell, "Angry Warren County Rejects Landfill: PCB Direct Action Stuns Local, State Authorities," *Mountain Life and Work* 59, no. 5 (May 1983): 26–27.

CHAPTER 4
BLACK, BROWN, RED, AND POISONED

1. Activist Pat Bryant uses the term "poisoning" in lieu of "pollution" to convey the idea that harm is being caused deliberately with the knowledge and aid of government officials. See Pat Bryant, "Toxics and Racial Justice," *Social Policy* 20 (Summer 1989): 48–52; Pat Bryant, "A Lily-White Achilles Heel," *Environmental Action* 21 (January–February 1990): 28–29.

2. See Community Environmental Health Center at Hunter College, *Hazardous Neighbors? Living Next Door to Industry in Greenpoint-Williamsburg* (New York: Hunter College, Community Environmental Health Center, 1989). This study details the nature of the toxic risks posed by industrial concerns in a community composed primarily of Hasidic Jews and Puerto Ricans.

3. Citizens for a Better Environment, *Richmond at Risk: Community Development and Toxic Hazards from Industrial Polluters* (San Francisco: Citizens for a Better Environment, 1989), pp. 21–22.

4. Conner Bailey and Charles Faupel, "Environmentalism and Civil Rights in Sumter County, Alabama," pp. 159, 170–171 in *Proceedings of the Michigan Conference on Race and the Incidence of Environmental Hazards,* ed. Bunyan Bryant and Paul Mohai (Ann Arbor: University of Michigan, School of Natural Resources, 1990).

5. Ibid., p. 171.

6. Miles Corwin, "Unusual Allies Fight Waste Incinerator," *Los Angeles Times,* February 24, 1991, p. A3.

7. Ibid., p. A36.

8. Harvey White, "Hazardous Waste Incineration and Minority Communities: The Case of Alsen, Louisiana," in Bryant and Mohai, *Race and the Incidence of Environmental Hazards,* pp. 142, 148–149.

9. See Conger Beasley, "Of Pollution and Poverty: Keeping Watch in 'Cancer Alley,'" *Buzzworm* 2 (July–August 1990): 38, 41–42 (describing the Louisiana politics that produced the string of petrochemical plants lining what is known as Cancer Alley).

10. Robert D. Bullard, "Environmental Blackmail in Minority Communities," in Bryant and Mohai, *Race and the Incidence of Environmental Hazards,* pp. 60, 64–65.

11. See Robert D. Bullard, *Dumping in Dixie: Race, Class, and Environmental Quality* (Boulder, CO: Westview Press, 1990), pp. 69–73; Bailey and Faupel, "Environmentalism and Civil Rights in Sumter County," pp. 169–170, 172–173.

12. Bailey and Faupel, "Environmentalism and Civil Rights in Sumter County," p. 163.

13. Sheryl McCarthy, "West Harlem Smells Rat, and More Down Road," *New York Newsday,* August 22, 1990, p. 6.

14. Ibid.; Jeff Bliss, "Not Just Birds and Trees: West Harlem Environmental Action," *City Limits,* May 1990, pp. 7, 8.

15. Dana Alston, *Taking Back Our Lives: A Report to the Panos Institute on Environment, Community Development and Race in the United States* (Washington, DC: The Panos Institute, 1990), p. 11.

16. Robert D. Bullard and Beverly H. Wright, "Blacks and the Environment," *Humboldt Journal of Social Relations* 14 (Summer 1987): 165, 180.

17. Robert D. Bullard, *People of Color Environmental Groups Directory 1992* (Riverside, CA: University of California, 1992), pp. i–v.

18. See generally Dorceta Taylor, "Blacks and the Environment: Toward an Explanation of the Concern and Action Gap Between Blacks and Whites," *Environment and Behavior* 22 (March 1989): 175.

19. Susan Cutter, "Community Concern for Pollution: Social and Environmental Influences," *Environment and Behavior* 13 (1981): 105–124.

20. Dorceta Taylor, "Can the Environmental Movement Attract and Maintain the Support of Minorities?" in Bryant and Mohai, *Race and the Incidence of Environmental Hazards,* p. 35.

21. Taylor, "Blacks and the Environment," pp. 187–190.

22. Arnoldo Garcia, "Environmental Inequities," *Crossroads* (June 1990), p. 16 (interview with activist Richard Moore).

23. Southwest Organizing Project, "Major National Environmental Organizations and the Problem of the 'Environmental Movement,'" (February 1990) (unpublished briefing paper).

24. Daniel Zwerdling, "Poverty and Pollution," *The Progressive* 37 (January 1973): 25, 29.

25. Beasley, "Of Pollution and Poverty," p. 42.

26. Bullard, *Dumping in Dixie,* pp. 95–98.

27. See Jim McNeil, "Hazel Johnson: Talkin' Toxics," *In These Times* (May 23–June 5, 1990), p. 4 (interview with the founder of Chicago's Southeast Side's People for Community Recovery); Claude Engle, "Profiles: Environmental Action in Minority Communities," *Environmental Action* (January–February 1990), p. 22 (profiling Jessie DeerInWater, founder of Native Americans for a Clean Environment; Cora Tucker, founder of Citizens for a Better America; and Francesca Cavazos, director of the Maricopa County Organizing Project); Cynthia Hamilton, "Women, Home, and Community: The Struggle in an Urban Environment," *Race, Poverty and the Environment Newsletter* (April 1990), p. 3.

28. See Mary Pardo, "Mexican American Women Grassroots Community Activists: 'Mothers of East Los Angeles,'" *Frontiers: A Journal of Women Studies* 11 (1990): 1; Dick Russell, "Environmental Racism," *Amicus Journal* 11 (Spring 1989): 22–23, 29–31.

29. Richard Regan and M. Legerton, "Economic Slavery or Hazardous Wastes? Robeson County's Economic Menu," in *Communities in Economic Crisis: Appalachia and the South*, John Gaventa and Alex Willingham, eds. (Philadelphia: Temple University Press, 1990), pp. 146, 153–154.

30. Marguerite Holloway, "The Toxic Avengers Take Brooklyn," *City Limits* (December 1989), p. 8.

31. M. Oliviero, *Minorities and the Environment: An Inquiry for Foundations* (report to the Nathan Cummings Foundation) (New York: Nathan Cummings Foundation, 1991), pp. 17–18, 21–24.

32. Beasley, "Of Poverty and Pollution," p. 45.

33. Sanford Lewis, "Your Legal Recourse," in *Fighting Toxics: A Manual for Protecting Your Family, Community, and Workplace,* ed. Gary Cohen and John O'Connor (Washington, DC: Island Press, 1990), pp 210–211.

34. Telephone interview with Richard Moore of the Southwest Organizing Project, January 25, 1991.

35. Telephone interview with Ellie Goodwin of the Natural Resources Defense Council, March 1, 1991.

36. See generally Richard Youngstrom, "The Neighborhood Inspection," in Cohen and O'Conner, *Fighting Toxics,* pp. 101–146.

37. Ibid., p. 127; telephone interview with Greg Schirm of the Delaware Valley Toxics Coalition, February 26, 1991.

38. Youngstrom, "The Neighborhood Inspection," pp. 126–127; telephone interview with Henry Clark of the West County Toxics Coalition, March 28, 1991.

39. Romona Smith, "After a Leak, Neighbors Smell a Rat," *Philadelphia Daily News,* February 10, 1988, p. 30.

40. See Alix Freedman, "Amid Ghetto Hunger, Many More Suffer Eating Wrong Foods," *Wall Street Journal,* December 18, 1990, p. A1 (lack of nutrition education and cultural and social understanding make

for poor nutrition); Alix Freedman, "Fast-Food Chains Play Central Role in Diet of the Inner-City Poor," *Wall Street Journal*, December 19, 1990, p. A1 (multiple meals per day, pleasant surroundings, and advertising appeals make fast food chains successful in inner-city areas); Alix Freedman, "An Inner-City Shopper Seeking Healthy Food Finds Offerings Scant," *Wall Street Journal*, December 20, 1990, p. A1 (healthier processed foods, fresh fruits, and vegetables either are not stocked or cost more than less healthy alternatives in inner-city stores).

41. Beverly H. Wright, "The Effects of Occupational Injury, Illness, and Disease on the Health Status of Black Americans: A Review," in Bryant and Mohai, *Race and the Incidence of Environmental Hazards*, pp. 128, 135–139. In general, African American men face the highest risk of work-related injury of any major group. The risk for African American women has increased to the point that in 1986 they faced roughly the same injury risk as white men.

42. See Kenneth Manton, Clifford H. Patrick, and Katrina W. Johnson, "Health Differentials Between Blacks and Whites: Recent Trends in Mortality and Morbidity," in *Health Policies and Black Americans*, David P. Willis, ed. (New Brunswick, NJ: Transaction, 1989), pp. 129, 158–159, 180–181, 185.

43. Keith Schneider, "Chemical Plants Buy Up Neighbors for Safety Zone," *New York Times*, November 28, 1990, p. A1.

44. Ibid., p. B8.

45. Ronald J. Rychlak, "Common-law Remedies for Environmental Wrongs: The Role of Private Nuisance," *Mississippi Law Journal* 59 (1989): 657, 661–663.

46. Letter from the Southwest Organizing Project and others to the mainstream environmental organizations, March 16, 1990.

47. Ivette Perfecto, "Pesticide Exposure of Farm Workers and the International Connection," in Bryant and Mohai, *Race and the Incidence of Environmental Hazards*, pp. 187, 193–194.

48. Alston, *Taking Back Our Lives,* p. 15.

49. John Elson, "Dumping on the Poor," *Time,* August 13, 1990, pp. 46, 47.

50. Michael Chamberlin, Michael Gruson, and Paul Weltchek, "Sovereign Debt Exchanges," *University of Illinois Law Review* (1988), pp. 415, 440–450.

51. Letter from Southwest Organizing Project, pp. 2–3.

52. Beasley, "Of Poverty and Pollution," p. 45.

53. Conger Beasley, "Of Pollution and Poverty: Deadly Threat on Native Lands," *Buzzworm* 2 (September–October 1990), pp. 39, 44.

54. Southwest Organizing Project Community Environmental Program Bill of Rights (available from Southwest Organizing Project, 1114 7th Street NW, Albuquerque, NM 87102).

55. Robert D. Bullard and Beverly H. Wright, "Environmentalism and the Politics of Equity: Emergent Trends in the Black Community," *Mid-American Review of Sociology* 12 (1987).

56. Bliss, "Not Just Birds and Trees," p. 8 (quoting activist Vernice Miller, cofounder of West Harlem Environmental Action).

CHAPTER 5
LIVING ON A SUPERFUND SITE IN TEXARKANA

1. See Roberto Contreras, "Texarkana Nightmare," *Voces Unidas* 1 (Second Quarter 1991): 5, 18.

2. See U.S. Environmental Protection Agency, "Koppers Site Update: EPA Announces Amended Record of Decision for Site," *EPA Update* (March 5, 1992).

3. Agency for Toxic Substances and Disease Registry, *Health Assessment for Koppers Company, Inc. National Priority List (NPL) Site, Texarkana, Texas* (Atlanta: U.S. Department of Health and Human Services, 1984).

4. Sanford Lewis, Brian Keating, and Dick Russell, *Inconclusive by Design: Waste, Fraud and Abuse in Federal Environmental Health Research* (Harvey, LA: Environmental Health Network and National Toxics Campaign, 1992), pp. 11–12.

CHAPTER 6
WEST DALLAS VERSUS THE LEAD SMELTER

1. See Agency for Toxic Substances and Disease Registry, *The Nature and Extent of Lead Poisoning in Children in the United States: A Report to Congress* (Atlanta: U.S. Department of Health and Human Services, 1988).

2. See Robert D. Bullard, *Dumping in Dixie: Race, Class, and Environmental Quality* (Boulder, CO: Westview Press, 1990).

3. See J. A. Kushner, *Apartheid in America: An Historical and Legal Analysis of Contemporary Racial Segregation in the United States* (Frederick, MD: Associated Faculty Press, 1980); Franklin J. James, B. I. McCummings, and E. A. Tynan, *Minorities in the Sunbelt* (New Brunswick, NJ: Rutgers University, Center for Urban Policy Research, 1984), p. 138; Joe R. Feagin and Clairece B. Feagin, *Discrimination American Style: Institutional Racism and Sexism* (Malabar, FL: Krieger, 1986); Robert D. Bullard and Joe R. Feagin, "Racism and the City," in *Urban Life in Transition*, ed. Mark Gottdiener and C. V. Pickvance, eds. (Newbury Park, CA: Sage, 1991), pp. 55–76.

4. Bullard, *Dumping in Dixie*, p. 54.

5. Ibid., pp. 54–60.

6. Dallas Alliance Environmental Task Force, *Final Report* (Dallas: Dallas Alliance Environmental Task Force, June 29, 1983), p. 6.

7. D. W. Nauss, "The People vs. the Lead Smelter," *Dallas Times Herald,* July 17, 1983, pp. 18–26.

8. U.S. Environmental Protection Agency, "Report of the Dallas Area Lead Assessment Study" (Dallas: U.S. Environmental Protection Agency, Region VI, 1983), p. 8.

9. Jonathan Lash, Katherine Gillman, and David Sheridan, *A Season of Spoils: The Reagan Administration's Attack on the Environment* (New York: Pantheon, 1984), pp. 135–136.

10. Dallas Alliance Environmental Task Force, *Final Report,* p. 3.

11. Samuel Barrett, environmental quality specialist, Texas Water Commission memorandum, August 28, 1991.

12. Alison Young, "West Dallas Advisors Complain Water Commission Ignoring Them," *Dallas Times Herald,* September 25, 1991, p. A11.

13. Randy Lee Loftis, "Rain Forces Delay of Lead Cleanup in West Dallas," *Dallas Morning News,* December 27, 1991.

14. Alison Young, "EPA's Lead a Shocker: Dirt to Be Stored at Closed Smelter," *Dallas Times Herald,* December 3, 1991, pp. A11, A13; Alison Young, "Mayor Seeks Lead Disposal Outside W. Dallas," *Dallas Times Herald,* December 4, 1991, pp. A21, A24.

15. For an in-depth account of recent developments in West Dallas, see Ronald Robinson, "Lead Kills," *Dallas Examiner,* January 30, 1992, pp. 1–2.

16. Ronald Robinson, "Is W. Dallas Lead Our Own 'Tuskegee Experiment'?" *Dallas Examiner,* February 20, 1992, pp. 1, 6, 9.

17. See Tracy Everbach, "Judge Throws Out '87 Housing Accord," *Dallas Morning News,* January 15, 1992, pp. 21A, 24A.

18. Bullard, *Dumping in Dixie,* pp. 56–57.

19. Dan R. Barber, "EPA Starts Removing Tainted Soil," *Dallas Morning News,* January 1, 1992, pp. 33A, 37A; Ronald Robinson, "Monroe, LA Just Says 'No' to Contaminated Soil," *Dallas Examiner,* February 6, 1992, pp. 1, 6.

20. Robinson, "Monroe, LA Just Says 'No,'" p. 1.

21. See Tamara Mohawk, "EPA Will Resume Shipments Thursday," *News-Star,* February 12, 1992, p. A1.

22. Ibid., p. A1.

CHAPTER 7
COPING WITH POISONS IN CANCER ALLEY

1. See Robert D. Bullard, *In Search of the New South: The Black Urban Experience in the 1970s and 1980s* (Tuscaloosa: University of Alabama Press, 1991), chap. 1.

2. Donald Schueler, "Southern Exposure," *Sierra* 77 (November–December 1992): 45.

3. Robert D. Bullard, *Dumping in Dixie: Race, Class, and Environmental Quality* (Boulder, CO: Westview Press, 1990), chap. 1.

4. Schueler, "Southern Exposure," p. 46.

5. Ibid., pp. 46–47.

6. See Conger Beasley, "Of Pollution and Poverty: Keeping Watch in 'Cancer Alley,'" *Buzzworm* 2 (July–August 1990): 39.

7. Bob Anderson, Mike Dunn, and Sonny Alabarado, "Prosperity in Paradise: Lousiana's Chemical Legacy," *Morning Advocate*, April 25, 1985.

8. Schueler, "Southern Exposure," p. 46.

9. James O'Byrne and Mark Schleifstein, "Dumping Ground: State a Final Stop for Nation's Toxic Waste," *Times Picayune*, March 26, 1991.

10. See Institute for Southern Studies, *1991–1992 Green Index: A State-by-State Guide to the Nation's Environmental Health* (Durham, NC: Institute for Southern Studies, 1992).

11. For a discussion of Lousiana's environmental and economic problems, see Paul H. Templet and Stephen Farber, "The Complementarity between Environmental and Economic Risk: An Empirical Analysis" (Baton Rouge: Louisiana State University, Institute for Environmental Studies, 1992).

12. James O'Byrne and Mark Schleifstein, "Drinking Water in Danger," *Times Picayune,* February 19, 1991, p. A5.

13. Quoted in David Maraniss and Michael Weisskopf, "Jobs and Illness in Petrochemical Corridor," *Washington Post,* December 22, 1989.

14. Quoted in Ginny Carol, "When Pollution Hits Home," *National Wildlife* 29 (August–September 1991): 35.

15. United Church of Christ Commission for Racial Justice, *Toxic Wastes and Race in the United States: A National Study of the Racial and Socioeconomic Characteristics of Communities with Hazardous Waste Sites* (New York: United Church of Christ Commission for Racial Justice, 1987), p. 47.

16. Beasley, "Of Pollution and Poverty," p. 41.

17. Ibid., p. 4.

18. Ibid., p. 39.

19. Daniel Mandell, Sanford J. Lewis, and National Toxics Campaign Fund, *The Formosa Plastics Story: A Report to the People of St. John the Baptist Parish* (Boston: National Toxics Campaign, 1990).

20. Kelly Michelle Colquette and Elizabeth A. Henry Robertson, "Environmental Racism: The Causes, Consequences, and Commendations," *Tulane Environmental Law Journal* 5 (December 1991): 176.

21. See Beverly H. Wright and Florence Robinson, "Voluntary Buy-Outs as an Alternative Damage Claims Arrangement: A Comparative Analysis of Three Impacted Communities" (Baton Rouge: Southern University, Institute for Environmental Issues and Policy Assessment, December 15, 1992), pp. 10–11.

22. Ibid., pp. 8–10.

23. Quoted in James O'Byrne, "The Death of a Town: A Chemical Plant Closes In," *Times Picayune,* February 20, 1991, p. A12.

24. Wright and Robinson, "Voluntary Buy-Outs," pp. 11–13.

25. For a discussion of this topic, see Pat Bryant, "Toxics and Racial Justice," *Social Policy* 20 (Summer 1989): 48–52; Pat Bryant, "A Lily-White Achilles Heel," *Environmental Action* 21 (January–February 1990): 28–29.

CHAPTER 8

IMPACTS OF THE ENERGY INDUSTRY
ON THE NAVAJO AND HOPI

1. Gerald Hausman, *Meditations with the Navajo: Prayer-Songs and Stories of Healing and Harmony* (Santa Fe, NM: Bear, 1989), pp. 13–14.

2. Statement drawn up by six Hopi elders, in Richard O. Clemmer, "Black Mesa and the Hopi," *Native Americans and Energy Development* (Cambridge, MA: Anthropology Resource Center, 1978), p. 29.

3. Matthew L. Wald, "A New Geography for the Coal Industry," *New York Times,* November 25, 1990, p. F5.

4. Joseph G. Jorgensen, Shelton H. Davis, and Robert O. Mathews, "Energy, Agriculture and Social Science in the American West," in Clemmer, *Native Americans and Energy Development*, p. 7.

5. U.S. Department of the Interior, Office of Surface Mining Reclamation and Enforcement, "Proposed Permit Application, Black Mesa–Kayenta Mine, Navajo and Hopi Indian Reservation, Arizona, Volume 1," in *Report: Final Environmental Impact Statement,* OSM-EIS-25 (Denver: U.S. Department of the Interior, Office of Surface Mining Reclamation and Enforcement, June 1990), p. IV-63.

6. Henry J. Brolick, "Statement of Henry J. Brolick, Vice President, Williams Technologies, Inc.," *Hearing before the Committee on Energy and Natural Resources on S. 318,* 101st Cong., 1st sess. (Washington, DC: U.S. Government Printing Office, April 20, 1990), p. 64.

7. U.S. Department of the Interior, "Proposed Permit Application," p. IV-65.

8. Ibid., p. IV-69.

9. Ibid., pp. III-48–49.

10. Ibid., p. IV-69.

11. U. S. Department of the Interior, Office of Surface Mining Reclamation and Enforcement, "Proposed Permit Application, Black Mesa–Kayenta Mine, Navajo and Hopi Indian Reservation, Arizona, Volume 2. Comments and Responses," in *Report: Final Environmental Impact Statement*, OSM-EIS-25 (Denver: U.S. Department of the Interior, Office of Surface Mining Reclamation and Enforcement, June 1990), p. R-2.

12. Ibid., pp. IV-72–75.

13. Testimony of Navajo elders at the Spring Gathering, Anna Mae Survival Camp, Big Mountain, Arizona, April 1–4, 1993.

14. See Lawrence David Weiss, *The Development of Capitalism in the Navajo Nation: A Political-Economic History*, Studies in Marxism, Vol. 5 (Minneapolis: MEP, 1984), p. 37.

15. Ibid., p. 69.

16. Ibid., p. 123.

17. David L. Vinje, "Cultural Values and Economic Development on Reservations," in *American Indian Policy in the Twentieth Century* (Norman: University of Oklahoma Press, 1985), p. 169.

18. For a discussion on current poverty levels on reservations in general and the U.S. government solutions, see "Initiatives for the 1990s," *Hearing before the Select Committee on Indian Affairs*, 101st Cong. 2d sess. (Washington, DC: U.S. Government Printing Office, May 11, 1990).

19. Peter Matthiessen, "Battle for Big Mountain," *Geo* 2 (March 1980): 12–30.

20. See Sandy Tolan, "Showdown at Window Rock," *New York Times Magazine*, November 26, 1989, pp. 28–77.

21. U.S. Commission on Civil Rights, "The Navajo Nation: An American Colony," *A Report of the United States Commission on Civil Rights* (Washington, DC: U.S. Commission on Civil Rights, September 1975), pp. 22, 120; Lorraine Turner Ruffing, "The Navajo Nation: A History of Dependence and Underdevelopment," *Review of Radical Political Economics* 11 (Summer 1979): 25, 28; Ward Churchill and Winona LaDuke, "Native America: The Political Economy of Radioactive Colonialism," Ward Churchill, *Critical Issues in Native North America*, Vol. II, Doc. 68 (Copenhagen: International Work Group for Indigenous Affairs, February 1991), pp. 27–33; Michael Garitty, "The U.S. Colonial Empire Is as Close as the Nearest Reservation: The Pending Energy Wars," in *Trilateralism: The Trilateral Commission and Elite Planning for World Management* (Boston: South End Press, 1980), p. 38.

22. Robert E. Looney and Craig R. Knouse, "Profits of Third World Mineral Producer," *Resource Policy* 13 (1987): 56–57.

23. Ibid.

24. Ward Churchill, "Genocide in Arizona? The 'Navajo-Hopi Dispute' in Perspective," *Critical Issues in Native North America*, pp. 110–116.

25. Interview with Thomas Banyacya at Oraibi, Arizona, April 1, 1993.

26. Ibid.

27. "Peabody Coal Expansion Threatens More Dine with Relocation," *Treaty Council News* (International Treaty Council, San Francisco) 11:21.

28. Clemmer, "Black Mesa and the Hopi," pp. 27–31.

29. Thomas Banyacya, "Statement of the True Traditional Religious Hopi Leaders of Hotevilla," letter to Allen D. Klein, Office of Surface Mining Reclamation and Enforcement, Hotevilla, Arizona, April 9, 1986, pp. 1–5.

30. "Grand Canyon's Air Is Being Polluted on Two Fronts," *New York Times*, October 15, 1989, p. 24L.

31. Lawrence Lack, "Indians Fight Coal Mine in Southwest Water-Use Dispute," *Christian Science Monitor,* July 17, 1990, p. 7.

32. Vinje, "Cultural Values and Economic Development," p. 163.

33. Peter Evans, *Dependent Development: The Alliance of Multinational, State, and Local Capital in Brazil* (Princeton, NJ: Princeton University Press, 1979), pp. 5, 9.

34. Ibid., pp. 6–13.

35. Ibid., p. 10.

36. Ibid., p. 11.

37. "The First 100 Years: A Salute to Peabody Coal," *Congressional Record* (Washington, DC: U.S. Government Printing Office, October 28, 1983), p. S14830.

38. Roger Lowenstein, "Newmont Mining's Market Value Compared with Newmont Gold's Seems a Bit Puzzling," *Wall Street Journal,* November 29, 1989.

39. Keith Bradshaw, "Newmont Selling Stake in Coal Unit," *New York Times,* March 30, 1990, p. D5.

40. Constance Soras and John Stodden, "Over Capacity Forces Change on the Coal Industry," *Coal Age* (September 1987).

41. Churchill, *Critical Issues in Native North America,* p. 138.

42. Wald, "A New Geography for the Coal Industry," p. F5.

43. Matthiessen, "Battle for Big Mountain," p. 16.

44. Ruffing, "The Navajo Nation," pp. 26–27.

45. Churchill and LaDuke, "Native America," p. 28.

46. See "Navajo Bribery Case Almost Ready for Trial," *New York Times,* October 15, 1990, p. A14.

47. "The Toxic Threat to Indian Lands," *Treaty Council News,* August 10, 1990, p. 7.

48. Churchill, *Critical Issues in Native North America,* p. 108.

49. Lack, "Indians Fight Coal Mine," p. 7.

50. Jerry Mander, "Kit Carson in a Three-Piece Suit," *Coevolution Quarterly* (Winter 1981): 53.

51. Larry Evers, *Between Sacred Mountains: Navajo Stories and Lessons from the Land* (Tucson: Sun Tracks and University of Arizona Press, 1982), pp. 204–205.

52. Churchill, *Critical Issues in Native North America,* pp. 116, 132.

53. Ibid., p. 134.

54. Leonard Haskie, "Supplemental Testimony of Leonard Haskie, President of the Navajo Nation," *Department of Interior and Related Agencies Appropriations for 1991,* Hearing before the Subcommittee on Appropriations, Part 11, 101st Cong., 2d sess. (Washington, DC: U.S. Government Printing Office, May 8, 1991), pp. 656–668.

55. James H. Eychaner, "Geohydrology and Effects on Water Use in the Black Mesa Area, Navajo and Hopi Indian Reservation, Arizona," Water Supply Paper 2201 (U.S. Government Printing Office, Washington, DC: U.S. Geological Survey, 1983), pp. 1–4.

56. Brolick, "Statement," p. 71.

57. "Changes to the 1989 CHIA," *Cumulative Hydrological Impact Assessment of the Peabody Coal Company Reclamation and Enforcement* (U.S. Dept. of the Interior, Office of Surface Mining Reclamation and Enforcement: Denver), undated, pp. 1–4.

58. George Harden, "86 Sheep Die, Miner to Pay," *Gallup Independent,* June 27, 1989, p. 150.

59. "Proposed Permit Application, Volume 1," *Final Environmental Impact Statement* (U.S. Dept. of the Interior, Office of Surface Mining Reclamation and Enforcement: Denver), p. IV-22.

60. Betty Reid, "Hopi Tribe to Peabody Coal: No More Water," *Gallup Independent,* August 10, 1989, p. 187; Mark Shaffer, "Mining An-

gers Hopis, Navajos," *Arizona Republic*, August 14, 1989, pp. B1–B2.

61. Quoted in Matthiessen, "Battle for Big Mountain," p. 50.

CHAPTER 9
CALIFORNIA'S ENDANGERED COMMUNITIES OF COLOR

1. Dick Russell, "Environmental Racism," *Amicus Journal* 11 (Spring 1989): 22–32.

2. For an in-depth discussion of environmental problems in South Central Los Angeles, see Jane Kay, "Fighting Toxic Racism: L.A.'s Minority Neighborhood Is the 'Dirtiest' in the State," *San Francisco Examiner*, April 7, 1991, p. A1.

3. Ibid.

4. Jane Kay, "Ethnic Enclaves Fight Toxic Waste," *San Francisco Examiner*, April 9, 1991, pp. A1, A8.

5. Citizens for a Better Environment, *Richmond at Risk: Community Demographics and Toxic Hazards from Industrial Polluters* (San Francisco: Citizens for a Better Environment, 1989).

6. Ibid., p. 121.

7. Jane Kay, "Jackson Joins Earth Day Fight," *San Francisco Examiner*, April 2, 1990, p. A2; Dan Reed, "Jackson to Chevron: Clean Up," *West County Times*, May 8, 1990, p. A1.

8. Jane Kay, "Minority Community Taking Stand Against Toxic Sites," *San Francisco Examiner*, April 7, 1991, p. A12.

9. Ibid.; Miles Corwin, "Unusual Allies Fight Waste Incinerator," *Los Angeles Times*, February 24, 1991, pp. A1, A36; Julia Flynn Siler, "Environmental Racism? It Could Be a Messy Fight," *Business Week*, May 20, 1991, p. 116.

10. Ronald B. Taylor, *Sweatshops in the Sun* (Boston: Beacon Press, 1973); Robert van Bosch, *The Pesticide Conspiracy* (Berkeley: University of California Press, 1989).

11. Jane Kay, "Farm Workers Call It Toxic Racism," *San Francisco Examiner,* April 8, 1991, pp. A1, A8. Figures were supplied by the California Department of Pesticide Regulation, 1993.

12. See Jane Kay, "Toxic Harvest: Farmers Pass a Fatal Legacy to Their Children," *San Francisco Examiner,* January 18, 1987, pp. A1, A12; Conger Beasley, "Of Poverty and Pollution: Reaping America's Unseemly Harvest," *Buzzworm* 2 (May–June 1990): 41–47.

13. California Department of Health Services, "McFarland Child Health Screening Project" (Sacramento: California Department of Health Services, January 1991), pp. 32–34.

14. For a thorough discussion of this problem, see Marion Moses, "Pesticide Related Problems in Farm Workers," *American Association of Occupational Health Nurses Journal* 37 (1989): 115–130.

15. California Department of Health Services, "Epidemiology Study of Adverse Health Effects in Children in McFarland, California," Phase II report (Sacramento: California Department of Health Services, January 1988); Jane Kay, "Farm Chemicals Linked to Town's Cancer Blight," *San Francisco Examiner,* January 29, 1988, p. A1.

16. See Jane Kay, "Indian Lands Targeted for Waste Disposal Sites," *San Francisco Examiner,* April 10, 1990, p. A10; Conger Beasley, "Of Pollution and Poverty: Deadly Threat on Native Lands," *Buzzworm* 2 (September–October 1990): 39–45.

17. Kay, "Indian Lands Targeted," p. A10.

18. Ward Churchill and Winona LaDuke, "Native America: The Political Economy of Radioactive Colonialism," *Insurgent Sociologist* 13 (Spring 1986): 51–68.

19. United Church of Christ Commission for Racial Justice, *Toxic Wastes and Race in the United States: A National Study of the Racial and Socioeconomic Characteristics of Communities with Hazardous Waste*

Sites (New York: United Church of Christ Commission for Racial Justice, 1987).

20. U.S. Environmental Protection Agency, *Environmental Equity: Reducing Risks for All Communities* (Washington, DC: U.S. Environmental Protection Agency, 1992).

21. Marianne Lavelle and Marcia Coyle, "Unequal Protection," *National Law Journal,* September 21, 1992, pp. 1–2.

CHAPTER 10
BUILDING A NET THAT WORKS: SWOP

1. "Environmental Groups Told They Are Racist in Hiring," *New York Times,* February 1, 1990.

2. "DOE Fails to Achieve Many '90 Cleanup Goals," *Albuquerque Journal,* January 15, 1991.

3. "Hispanics Get 'Hot' Jobs, Lab Report Says," *Rio Grande Sun,* January 12, 1984.

4. Testimony provided by Virginia Candelaria and Josephine Rohr, Interdenominational Hearings on Toxics in Minority Communities, unpublished transcript (Albuquerque, NM: Southwest Organizing Project, September 30, 1989).

5. United Church of Christ Commission for Racial Justice, *Toxic Wastes and Race in the United States: A National Study of the Racial and Socioeconomic Characteristics of Communities with Hazardous Waste Sites* (New York: United Church of Christ Commission for Racial Justice, 1987).

6. Ibid.

7. Ibid.

8. Center for Third World Organizing, *Toxics in Minority Communities,* Issue Paper no. 2 (Oakland, CA: Policy Institute for the Center for Third World Organizing, 1986).

9. "U.S.–Mexico Border Bulges with Pollution," *Washington Post,* February 17, 1992.

CHAPTER II
CONCERNED CITIZENS OF SOUTH CENTRAL LOS ANGELES

1. Robert D. Bullard and Beverly H. Wright, "Environmentalism and the Politics of Equity: Emergent Trends in the Black Community," *Mid-American Review of Sociology* 12 (1987): 21–37; Robert Gottlieb and Helen Ingram, "The New Environmentalists," *The Progressive* 53 (1988): 14–15; Dana Alston, ed., *We Speak for Ourselves: Social Justice, Race, and Environment* (Washington, DC: The Panos Institute, 1990).

2. Bunyan Bryant and Paul Mohai, eds., *Race and the Incidence of Environmental Hazards* (Boulder, CO: Westview Press, 1992).

3. This essay was first published in *Race, Poverty, and Environmental Newsletter* 1 (April 1990).

4. All quotes by Charlotte Bullock and Robin Cannon are from a workshop titled Ecofeminist Perspectives: Culture, Values, and Theory held at the University of Southern California, March 1987.

5. See United Church of Christ Commission for Racial Justice, *Toxic Wastes and Race in the United States: A National Study of the Racial and Socioeconomic Characteristics of Communities with Hazardous Waste Sites* (New York: United Church of Christ Commission for Racial Justice, 1987).

6. Center for Third World Organizing, *Toxics and Minority Communities* (Oakland, CA: Center for Third World Organizing, 1983).

7. For an in-depth discussion of feminist perspectives, see Kathy Ferguson, *Feminist Case Against Bureaucracy* (Philadelphia: Temple University Press, 1984).

8. See Cynthia Cockburn, "When Women Get Involved in Community Action," in *Women in the Community,* ed. Marjorie Mayo (New York: Routledge & Kegan Paul, 1977).

9. See Alice Cook and Gwyn Kirk, *Greenham Women Everywhere* (Boston: South End Press, 1984).

10. Cockburn, "When Women Get Involved in Community Action."

11. Russell, "Environmental Racism."

CHAPTER 12
MOTHERS OF EAST LOS ANGELES STRIKE BACK

1. Rodolfo Acuña, "A Community Under Siege: A Chronicle of Chicanos East of the Los Angeles River, 1945–1975," Monograph no. 11 (Los Angeles: California State University, Chicano Studies Research Center, 1984).

2. Eric Mann, *L.A.'s Lethal Air: New Strategies for Policy, Organizing, and Action* (Los Angeles: Labor/Community Strategy Center, 1991).

3. Acuña, "Community Under Siege," p. 75.

4. For a detailed account of early actions by the Mothers of East Los Angeles, see Dick Russell, "Environmental Racism: Minority Communities and Their Battle Against Toxics," *Amicus Journal* 11 (Spring 1989): 22–32; and Mary Pardo, "Mexican American Women Grassroots Community Activists: 'Mothers of East Los Angeles,'" *Frontiers: A Journal of Women Studies* 11 (1990): 1–16.

5. Maura Dolan, "Toxic Waste Incinerator Bid Abandoned," *Los Angeles Times,* May 24, 1991.

6. Thomas W. Hayes, "Review of the Department of Correction's Selection of a Prison Site in Los Angeles County" (Sacramento, CA: Auditor General's Office, 1986), p. 36.

7. "Latino Leaders Vow to Block Prison," *Los Angeles Times*, September 23, 1986.

8. Quoted in Russell, "Environmental Racism."

9. Quoted in Pardo, "Mexican American Women," p. 3.

10. "Juana Beatríz Gutiérrez: La Incansable Lucha de una Activista Comunitaria," *La Opinión*, August 6, 1989, p. 6.

11. Pardo, "Mexican American Women," p. 3.

12. "Eastside Residents Oppose Prison," *La Gente de Aztlan*, October 1986, p. 5.

13. Interview with Ricardo Gutiérrez, East Los Angeles, California, November 11, 1989.

14. "Ties to Prison Site Questioned: Downtown Lot's Value Has Doubled Since '84," *Daily News*, September 23, 1986.

15. Ibid., p. 14.

16. Hayes, "Selection of a Prison Site," p. 7.

17. Ibid., p. 15.

18. Pardo, "Mexican American Women," p. 4.

19. Cerrell Associates, "Political Difficulties Facing Waste-to-Energy Conversion Plant Siting" (Sacramento, CA: California Waste Management Board, 1984).

20. Rodolfo Acuña, "The Armageddon in Our Backyard," *Los Angeles Herald Examiner*, July 7, 1989.

21. Pardo, "Mexican American Women," p. 4.

22. United Church of Christ Commission for Racial Justice, *Toxic Wastes and Race in the United States: A National Study of the Racial and Socioeconomic Characteristics of Communities with Hazardous Waste Sites* (New York: United Church of Christ Commission for Racial Justice, 1987).

23. Acuña, "The Armageddon in Our Backyard."

24. James S. Gomez, "Student Protest Proposed Waste Facility in Vernon," *Los Angeles Times,* July 3, 1988.

25. Dolan, "Toxic Waste Incinerator Bid Abandoned."

26. Quoted in Mark Gladstone, "Plan to Build Prison in L.A. Scuttled after 7-Year Fight," *Los Angeles Times,* September 15, 1992.

CHAPTER 13
PUEBLO FIGHTS LEAD POISONING

1. Joel Schwartz and Ronnie Levin, "Lead: An Example of the Job Ahead," *EPA Journal* 18 (March–April 1992): 42–44.

2. See the *New York Times,* February 26, 1991.

3. Interview with Gwen Hardy, reported in *Race, Poverty and the Environment Newsletter* (Winter 1991): 3.

4. For an in-depth discussion of the nation's childhood lead problem, see Agency for Toxic Substances and Disease Registry, *The Nature and Extent of Lead Poisoning in Children in the United States: A Report to Congress* (Atlanta: U.S. Department of Health and Human Services, 1988); Karen Florini et al., *Legacy of Lead: America's Continuing Epidemic of Childhood Lead Poisoning* (Washington, DC: Environmental Defense Fund, 1990); Herbert L. Neeleman, "Childhood Lead Poisoning: An Eradicable Disease," in *Proceedings: National Minority Health Conference: Focus on Environmental Contamination* (Atlanta: Agency for Toxic Substances and Disease Registry, December 1990).

5. See C. Allenby and K. W. Kizer, *Childhood Lead Poisoning in California, Causes and Prevention: Interim Report to the California Legislature* (Sacramento: California Legislature, June 1989).

6. For a detailed account of this case, see Bill Lann Lee, "Environmental Litigation on Behalf of Poor, Minority Children: *Matthews v. Coye:*

A Case Study" (paper presented at the annual meeting of the American Association for the Advancement of Science, Chicago, February 1991).

CHAPTER 14
WOMEN OF COLOR ON THE FRONT LINE

1. This chapter is a revised version of an article written by Celene Krauss, "Women and Toxic Waste Protests," *Qualitative Sociology* 16, no. 3 (1993): 247–262. For additional reading on women and toxic waste protests, see, for example, Lawrence C. Hamilton, "Concern About Toxic Wastes: Three Demographic Predictors," *Sociological Perspectives* 28 (1985): 463–486; Celene Krauss, "Blue-Collar Women and Toxic Waste Protests," in *Toxic Struggles,* ed. Richard Hofrichter (Philadelphia: New Society, 1993); Mary Pardo, "Mexican American Women Grassroots Community Activists: 'Mothers of East Los Angeles,'" *Frontier* 11 (1990): 1–7; Cynthia Hamilton, "Women, Home, and Community," *Woman of Power* 20 (1991): 42–45; Sherry Cable, "Women's Social Movement Involvement: The Role of Structural Availability in Recruitment and Participation Processes," *Sociological Quarterly* 33 (1992).

2. Writings on the relationship of race, class, and inequities in the siting of environmental facilities include Allan Schnaiberg, *The Environment: From Surplus to Scarcity* (New York: Oxford University Press, 1980); Robert D. Bullard, *Dumping in Dixie: Race, Class, and Environmental Quality* (Boulder, CO: Westview Press, 1990); Robert D. Bullard and Beverly H. Wright, "Dumping Grounds in a Sunbelt City," *Urban Resources* 2 (1985): 37–39; United Church of Christ Commission for Racial Justice, *Toxic Wastes and Race in the United States: A National Study of the Racial and Socioeconomic Characteristics of Communities with Hazardous Waste Sites* (New York: United Church of Christ Commission for Racial Justice, 1987); Phil Brown and Edwin J. Mikkelsen, *No Safe Place: Toxic Waste, Leukemia, and Community Action* (Berkeley: University of California Press, 1990);

Bunyan Bryant and Paul Mohai, eds., *Race and Incidence of Environmental Hazards* (Boulder, CO: Westview Press, 1992).

3. The relationship between environmental grass-roots activism and concrete experience is developed in Krauss, "Blue-Collar Women and Toxic Waste Protests"; Celene Krauss, "Community Struggles and the Shaping of Democratic Consciousness," *Sociological Forum* 4 (1989): 227–238; Vandana Shiva, *Staying Alive: Women, Ecology and Development* (London: Zed, 1989); Dorceta Taylor, "Can the Environmental Movement Attract and Maintain the Support of Minorities?," pp. 28–59 in *Proceedings of the Michigan Conference on Race and the Incidence of Environmental Hazards,* ed. Bunyan Bryant and Paul Mohai (Ann Arbor: University of Michigan, School of Natural Resources, 1990).

4. For a complex analysis of single-issue community protests, see Joseph M. Kling and Prudence S. Posner, eds., *Dilemmas of Activism: Class, Community, and the Politics of Local Mobilization* (Philadelphia: Temple University Press, 1990). Also see Robert Bellah, "Populism and Individualism," *Social Policy* (Fall 1985).

5. For illustrations of feminist theories and methodologies that develop this perspective, read Patricia Hill Collins, *Black Feminist Thought: Knowledge, Consciousness, and the Politics of Empowerment* (Boston: Unwin Hyman, 1990); Nancy Hartsock, *Money, Sex and Power* (Boston: Northeastern University Press, 1984); Dorothy Smith, *The Everyday World as Problematic: A Feminist Sociology* (Boston: Northeastern University Press, 1987).

6. For an analysis of the private-public split in feminist political theory, see Susan Okin, *Women in Western Political Thought* (Princeton, NJ: Princeton University Press, 1979); Jean Bethke Elshtain, *Public Man, Private Woman* (Princeton, NJ: Princeton University Press, 1981); Martha A. Ackelsberg, "Communities, Resistance, and Women's Activism: Some Implications for a Democratic Polity," pp. 53–76 in *Women and the Politics of Empowerment,* ed. Ann Bookman and Sandra Morgen (Philadelphia: Temple University Press, 1988).

7. Sandra Morgen, " 'It's the Whole Power of the City Against Us!' : The Development of Political Consciousness in a Women's Health Care Coalition," in *Women and the Politics of Empowerment*, p. 97.

8. See George Rudé, *Ideology and Popular Protest* (New York: Pantheon, 1980). Others include Herbert Gutman, *Work, Culture and Society in Industrializing America* (New York: Vintage, 1977); Sheila Rowbotham, *Women, Resistance and Revolution* (New York: Vintage, 1974); E. P. Thompson, *The Making of the English Working Class* (New York: Vintage, 1966).

9. Sheila Rowbotham, *Women's Consciousness, Man's World* (New York: Penguin, 1973).

10. The relationship of extended families, friendship networks, and the community activism of working-class women is explored by numerous writers. See, for example, Terry Haywoode, "Working Class Feminism: Creating a Politics of Community, Connection, and Concern," Ph.D. diss., The Graduate School and University Center of the City University of New York, 1990. For the importance of this relationship in African American communities, read Nancy Naples, "Activist Mothering: Cross-Generational Continuity in the Community Work of Women from Low-Income Urban Neighborhoods," *Gender and Society* (May 1992); Patricia Hill Collins, *Black Feminist Thought: Knowledge, Consciousness, and the Politics of Empowerment* (Boston: Unwin Hyman, 1990); Karen Sacks, "Generations of Working-Class Families," pp. 15–38 in *My Troubles Are Going to Have Trouble With Me: Everyday Trials and Triumphs of Women Workers,* ed. Karen Sacks (New Brunswick, NJ: Rutgers University Press, 1984); Carol Stack, *All Our Kin: Strategies for Survival in a Black Community* (New York: Harper Colophon, 1974). Family networks also play an important role in Native American communities. See, for example, Rayna Greene, "American Indian Women: Diverse Leadership for Social Change," in *Bridges of Power: Women's Multicultural Alliances,* ed. Lisa Albrect and Rose Brewer (Philadelphia: New Society, 1990).

11. See Sara Ruddick, *Maternal Thinking: Towards a Politics of Peace* (New York: Ballantine, 1989).

12. Terry Haywoode, "Working Class Feminism: Crating a Politics of Community, Connection, and Concern" (paper presented at the annual meeting of the American Sociological Association, Pittsburgh, Pennsylvania, August 1992); Ida Susser, *Norman Street: Poverty and Politics in an Urban Neighborhood* (New York: Oxford University Press, 1982).

13. Paula Giddings, *When and Where I Enter: The Impact of Black Women on Race and Sex in America* (New York: Morrow, 1984). Also, in *Black Feminist Thought,* Patricia Hill Collins develops the history of African American women as "othermothers" in her discussion of community activism.

14. Robert D. Bullard, *Dumping in Dixie: Race, Class, and Environmental Quality* (Boulder, CO: Westview Press, 1990).

15. Cheryl Townsend Gilkes, "Building in Many Places: Multiple Commitments and Ideologies in Black Women's Community Work," in *Women and the Politics of Empowerment.*

16. See Teresa Amott and Julie Mathaei, *Race, Gender & Work: A Multicultural Economic History of Women in the United States* (Boston: South End Press, 1991); Rayna Greene, "American Indian Women: Diverse Leadership for Social Change"; Annette M. Jaimes and Theresa Halsey, "American Indian Women at the Center of Indigenous Resistance in North America," in *The State of Native America,* ed. Annette M. Jaimes (Boston: South End Press, 1992).

CHAPTER 15

THE PEOPLE OF COLOR ENVIRONMENTAL SUMMIT

1. For a detailed account of the speakers and events at the Summit, see the ninety-page publication by the United Church of Christ Commission for Racial Justice, *First National People of Color Environmental Leadership Summit: Program Guide* (New York: United Church of Christ Commission for Racial Justice, 1991).

2. The delegates drafted and adopted "A Call to Action" at the Washington, DC, Summit on October 27, 1991.

3. The "Principles of Environmental Justice" were adopted by the Summit attendees on October 27, 1991. The express purpose of the meeting was to have a working document developed by grass-roots leaders to take back to their respective communities.

4. See United Church of Christ Commission for Racial Justice, *Toxic Wastes and Race in the United States: A National Study of the Racial and Socioeconomic Characteristics of Communities with Hazardous Waste Sites* (New York: United Church of Christ Commission for Racial Justice, 1987).

5. The full text of Reverend Chavis's speech is published in United Church of Christ Commission for Racial Justice, *Proceedings: The First National People of Color Environmental Leadership Summit* (New York: United Church of Christ Commission for Racial Justice, 1993), pp. 7–9.

6. See Ken Geiser and Gerry Waneck, "PCBs and Warren County," *Science for the People* 15 (July–August 1983): 13–17; Robert D. Bullard, *Dumping in Dixie: Race, Class, and Environmental Quality* (Boulder, CO: Westview Press, 1990), pp. 35–40.

7. United Church of Christ Commission for Racial Justice, *Toxic Wastes and Race*, pp. 18–19.

8. For the full text of the paper, see Robert D. Bullard and Dana Alston, "People of Color and the Struggle for Environmental Justice," pp. 211–213 in United Church of Christ Commission for Racial Justice, *Proceedings*.

9. Many of these stories were first published in Karl Grossman, "From Toxic Racism to Environmental Justice," *E: The Environmental Magazine* 3 (October–November 1991): 28–35.

10. Pat Bryant, "Toxics and Racial Justice," *Community Activism Social Policy* (Summer 1989): 48–52; Pat Bryant, "A Lily-White Achilles Heel," *Environmental Action* 21 (January–February 1990): 28–29.

11. See Robert D. Bullard, "Solid Waste Sites and the Black Houston Community," *Sociological Inquiry* 53 (Spring 1983): 273–288; Rob-

ert D. Bullard, "Endangered Environs: The Price of Unplanned Growth in Boomtown Houston," *California Sociologist* 7 (Summer 1984): 84–102; Robert D. Bullard and Beverly H. Wright, "The Politics of Pollution: Implications for the Black Community," *Phylon* 47 (March 1986): 71–78; Robert D. Bullard, *Invisible Houston: The Black Experience in Boom and Bust* (College Station: Texas A & M University Press, 1987), pp. 60–75.

12. Robert D. Bullard and Beverly H. Wright, "Environmentalism and the Politics of Equity: Emergent Trends in the Black Community," *Mid-American Review of Sociology* 12 (Winter 1986): 21–37.

13. Robert D. Bullard and Beverly H. Wright, "Mobilizing the Black Community for Environmental Justice," *Journal of Intergroup Relations* 17 (Spring 1990): 33–43.

14. Bullard, *Dumping in Dixie,* pp. 103–117.

15. See Joseph A. Page and Mary Win-O'Brien, *Bitter Wages: Ralph Nader's Study Group Report on Disease and Injury on the Job* (New York: Grossman, 1973), p. 161; Anil Agarwal, Juliet Merrifield, and Rajesh Tandon, *No Place to Run: Local Realities and Global Issues of the Bhopal Disaster* (New Market, TN: Highlander Center and Society for Participatory Research in India, 1985), pp. 20–21.

16. U.S. Environmental Protection Agency, *Environmental Equity: Reducing Risks for All Communities* (draft) (Washington, DC: U.S. Environmental Protection Agency, January 1992).

17. Dana Alston, ed., *We Speak for Ourselves: Social Justice, Race, and Environment* (Washington, DC: The Panos Institute, 1990), p. 3.

18. National Advisory Commission on Civil Disorders, *Report of the National Advisory Commission on Civil Disorders* (New York: St. Martin's Press, 1968).

19. Ben H. Bagdikian, *The Media Monopoly,* 3d ed. (Boston: Beacon Press, 1990).

CHAPTER 16
A CALL FOR JUSTICE
AND EQUAL ENVIRONMENTAL PROTECTION

1. A workshop sponsored jointly by the EPA, the ATSDR, and the NIEHS titled Environmental Health Needs was held in Research Triangle, North Carolina, in 1992. The impetus behind this scientific conference came from environmental justice academics and activists external to the government agencies.

2. Drs. Benjamin F. Chavis and Robert D. Bullard were part of a twenty-two-person team detailed to the EPA, where they interviewed key agency staff members on operations, met with congressional staff members on pending legislation, reviewed government documents, received public input, and assisted in writing a "briefing book" for the new administrator.

3. The Washington, DC–based Lawyers' Committee for Civil Rights Under Law is a nonpartisan, nonprofit organization formed in 1963 at the request of President John F. Kennedy to involve the private bar in provision of legal services to victims of racial discrimination. The Lawyers' Committee implements its mission through legal representation, public policy advocacy, and public education on civil rights matters. Its Environmental Justice Project focuses on developing interdisciplinary cooperation and strategies to prevent and remedy the disproportionate environmental risks experienced by people of color and the poor.

4. This chapter represents comments submitted by the Environmental Justice Transition Group, which includes the following organizations (in alphabetical order): Earth Island Institute, the Gulf Coast Tenants Organization; the Indigenous Environmental Network; the Lawyers' Committee for Civil Rights Under Law; Native Action; the Southern Organizing Committee for Economic and Social Justice; the Southwest Network for Environmental and Economic Justice; the Southwest Organizing Project; and the United Church of Christ Commission for Racial Justice.

5. Environmental Justice Transition Group, *Recommendations to the Presidential Transition Team for the U.S. Environmental Protection Agency on Environmental Justice Issues* (Washington, DC: Lawyers' Committee for Civil Rights Under Law, Environmental Justice Project, December 21, 1992).

6. Louisiana Advisory Committee to the U.S. Commission on Civil Rights, *The Battle for Environmental Justice in Louisiana: Government, Industry and the Public,* September 1993.

7. David F. Kern, "State Praised for Shielding Poor from Waste," *Arkansas Gazette,* August 26, 1993.

About the Contributors

REGINA AUSTIN is a professor at the University of Pennsylvania Law School. Previously, she practiced law with the firm of Schnader, Harrison, Segal, & Lewis. She has written on a wide range of topics addressing African American culture, the underground and informal economies, African American feminist legal scholarship, and harassment of low-status employees. Professor Austin has been a visiting professor at Harvard and Stanford law schools.

PAT BRYANT is director of the Gulf Coast Tenants Organization (GCTO), a federation of grass-roots groups primarily along the gulf coasts of Mississippi, Alabama, and Louisiana. Much of his work with the GCTO has focused on housing, health care, jobs, and environmental education. Mr. Bryant's leadership has made the GCTO one of the leading organizing forces against toxic dumping in the southern United States.

ROBERT D. BULLARD is a professor of sociology at the University of California, Riverside. His more than fifteen years of work on environmental justice issues have made him a leading expert in the field. He was one of the planners of the First National People of Color Environmental Leadership Summit. Among his books that address environmental racism are *Invisible Houston: The Black Experience in Boom and Bust* (College Station: Texas A & M University Press, 1987), *Dumping in Dixie: Race, Class, and Environmental Quality* (Boulder, CO: Westview Press, 1990), and *Confronting Environmental Racism: Voices from the Grassroots* (Boston: South End Press, 1993).

FRANCIS CALPOTURA is codirector of the Oakland-based Center for Third World Organizing (CTWO). He is an active organizer and leader in the Bay Area's Asian American community.

BENJAMIN F. CHAVIS, JR., is executive director of the National Association for the Advancement of Colored People (NAACP). Before coming to the NAACP, Reverend Chavis directed the United Church of Christ Commission for Racial Justice. He is a twenty-five-year veteran of the civil rights movement and has championed the cause of environmental justice for more than a decade. Under his leadership, the commission issued its landmark study, *Toxic Wastes and Race in the United States,* and coordinated the First National People of Color Environmental Leadership Summit.

DEEOHN FERRIS is an environmental attorney and directs the Lawyers' Committee for Civil Rights Under Law's Environmental Justice Alliance Project. Before joining the Lawyers' Committee, she was director of environmental quality for the National Wildlife Federation. She also worked for eight years with the U.S. Environmental Protection Agency as director of its Special Litigation Division.

KEN GEISER is a professor of environmental studies and director of the Toxics Use Reduction Program at the University of Massachusetts, Lowell. He has written about and worked on environmental policy issues for more than a decade.

KARL GROSSMAN is a professor of journalism at the State University of New York/College at Old Westbury. He is the author of three books on environment and energy: *Cover Up: What You Are Not Supposed to Know about Nuclear Power* (Sag Harbor, NY: Permanent Press, 1982); *The Poison Conspiracy* (Sag Harbor, NY: Permanent Press, 1983); and *Power Crazy* (New York: Grove Press, 1986). He has specialized in environmental journalism for more than twenty-five years. Professor Grossman is program director and vice president of EnviroVideo, a New York–based company that produces environmental television documentary and news programming.

GABRIEL GUTIÉRREZ was born and raised in East Los Angeles. He has participated in various community campaigns, such as the successful battle to prevent the building of a state prison in East Los Angeles and the struggle to keep an unwanted incinerator out of neighboring Vernon. His mother, Juana Gutiérrez, was a founding member of Mothers of East Los Angeles. He is a doctoral candidate in history at the University of California, Santa Barbara.

MICHAEL HAGGERTY is a free-lance environmental writer. His chapter on Triana, Alabama, first appeared as an article in the *Atlanta Journal and Constitution* in 1980.

KATHY HALL was coordinator of the Siskiyou Citizens Against Toxic Sprays in the Salmon River area of California. She is a graduate student in sociology at the University of California, Santa Cruz.

CYNTHIA HAMILTON has been active in grass-roots organizing for almost twenty years. She is currently an associate professor in the Pan African Studies Department at California State University, Los Angeles, and a lecturer in the Graduate School of Architecture and Urban Planning at the University of California, Los Angeles. She has conducted research on urban restructuring and its consequences for African American communities.

LOUIS HEAD is a community organizer and staff member of the New Mexico–based Southwest Organizing Project (SWOP). His responsibilities with that organization have included media relations, fund-raising, and a variety of other tasks. He is presently grants administrator for SWOP and coordinates development work that takes him to urban ghettos, Native American reservations, pueblos in New Mexico, barrios in Texas and California, and the *colonias* and *maquiladoras* along the Mexico–United States border.

JANE KAY is a veteran environmental writer with the *San Francisco Examiner.* She teaches environmental reporting at the University of California, Berkeley, Graduate School of Journalism. She has twice won the prestigious Scripps Howard Foundation's Edward J. Meeman Award for outstanding conservation reporting. Her series uncovering widespread exposure to chemicals in groundwater in Tucson, Arizona, won her the Sigma Delta Chi Public Service Award and resulted in an $84.2 million settlement for Tucsonans from Hughes Aircraft Company. Her April 1991 four-part series on toxic racism is widely used in the environmental justice arena.

CELENE KRAUSS is an assistant professor of sociology and co-coordinator of women's studies at Kean College of New Jersey. She writes and lectures on the process of politicization in community environmental struggles. Her recent work develops a feminist perspective for understanding women's leadership role in the environmental justice movement.

JOHN LEWIS was elected to the U.S. House of Representatives in 1986 from the Fifth Congressional District of Georgia. He was reelected by an overwhelming majority to a fourth term in Congress in November 1992. In 1990, the *National Journal* named him as one of eleven "rising stars in Congress." Congressman Lewis is currently chief deputy majority whip and cochair of the Congressional Urban Caucus. He sits on the influential Steering and Policy Committee, Ways and Means Committee, and Committee on Aging. His work and deeds over the past three decades have set him apart as a giant in the civil rights and social justice movement.

RICHARD MOORE is a founding member of the Southwest Organizing Project (SWOP) and the Southwest Network for Environmental and Economic Justice (SNEEJ). He has been a resident of New Mexico for more than twenty years, working on a variety of issues, such as welfare rights, police brutality, low-cost health care, child nutrition, and environmental racism. He serves on the board of directors of the Eco-Justice Working Group, the National Council of Churches, Interfaith Impact for Justice and Peace, and the Coalition for Justice in the Maquiladoras.

PATSY RUTH OLIVER is a native Texan. She is a former resident of the Carver Terrace neighborhood in Texarkana and a current board member of the National Toxics Campaign. Ms. Oliver's and her neighbors' homes were built on top of a toxic waste dump. She was one of the leaders in getting the community declared a Superfund site and getting the residents moved out of the contaminated neighborhood.

RONALD ROBINSON is a journalist with the *Dallas Examiner,* an African American–owned weekly newspaper. He has written extensively on the West Dallas lead contamination, local citizen concerns, the cleanup actions of the federal EPA, and related issues of the Dallas African American community.

MICHAEL SCHILL is an assistant professor at the University of Pennsylvania Law School. Prior to joining the faculty at Pennsylvania in 1987, he was associated with the law firm of Fried, Frank, Harris & Jacobson in New York City, where he specialized in real estate law. He teaches in the areas of property law, real estate transactions, and urban affairs.

RINKU SEN is codirector of the Oakland-based Center for Third World Organizing (CTWO). She is also editor of *Third Force,* a bimonthly publication of the center.

GERRY WANECK was a graduate student in immunology at Tufts University's Sackler School when his coauthored paper was published in *Science for the People* in 1983. He was also a representative of Federation for Progress, based in New York City.

BEVERLY H. WRIGHT is an associate professor of sociology at Xavier University of Louisiana and directs the Deep South Center for Environmental Justice. Professor Wright is a leading environmental justice scholar and advocate of university-community partnerships in addressing local environmental problems.

Selected Bibliography

Acuna, Rodolfo. *Community under Siege: A Chronicle of Chicanos East of the Los Angeles River, 1945–1975*. Los Angeles: California State University, Chicano Studies Research Center, 1984.

Agency for Toxic Substances and Disease Registry. *The Nature and Extent of Lead Poisoning in Children in the United States: A Report to Congress*. Atlanta: U.S. Department of Health and Human Services, 1988.

———. *Health Assessment, Koppers Superfund Site, Texarkana, Texas*. Atlanta: U.S. Department of Health and Human Services, April 1989.

Albrect, Lisa, and Rose Brewer (eds.). *Bridges of Power: Women's Multicultural Alliances*. Philadelphia: New Society Publishers, 1990.

Alston, Dana. *We Speak for Ourselves: Social Justice, Race, and Environment*. Washington, D.C.: The Panos Institute, 1990.

Amott, Teresa, and Julia Mathaei. *Race, Gender and Work: A Multicultural Economic History of Women in the United States*. Boston: South End Press, 1991.

Anderson, Bob. "Plant Sites: Is Racism an Issue?" *Baton Rouge Morning Advocate* (May 12, 1992).

Anderson, Bob, Mike Dunn, and Sonny Alabarado. "Prosperity in Paradise: Louisiana's Chemical Legacy." *Morning Advocate* (April 25, 1985).

Angel, Bradley. *The Toxic Threat to Indian Lands: A Greenpeace Report*. San Francisco: Greenpeace, 1992.

Austin, Regina, and Michael Schill. "Black, Brown, Poor, and Poisoned: Minority Grassroots Environmentalism and the Quest for Eco-Justice." *Kansas Journal of Law and Public Policy* 1 (1991):69–82.

Bachrach, Kenneth M., and Alex J. Zautra. "Coping with Community Stress: The Threat of a Hazardous Waste Landfill." *Journal of Health and Social Behavior* 26 (June 1985):127–41.

Beasley, Conger. "Of Pollution and Poverty: Keeping Watch in Cancer Alley." *Buzzworm* 2:4 (July–August 1990):39–45.

———. "Of Pollution and Poverty: Deadly Threat on Native Lands." *Buzzworm* 2:5 (September–October 1990):39–45.

Blumberg, Louis, and Robert Gottlieb. *War on Waste: Can America Win Its Battle with Garbage?* Washington, D.C.: Island Press, 1989.

Brown, Michael H. *Laying Waste: The Poisoning of America by Toxic Chemicals.* New York: Pantheon Books, 1980.

———. *The Toxic Cloud: The Poisoning of America's Air.* New York: Harper & Row, 1987.

Brown, Phil, and Edwin J. Mikkelsen. *No Safe Place: Toxic Waste, Leukemia, and Community Action.* Berkeley: University of California Press, 1990.

Bryant, Bunyan, and Paul Mohai. *Race and the Incidence of Environmental Hazards.* Boulder: Westview Press, 1992.

Bryant, Pat. "Toxics and Racial Justice." *Social Policy* 20 (Summer 1989):48–52.

Bullard, Robert D. "Solid Waste Sites and the Black Houston Community." *Sociological Inquiry* 53 (Spring 1983):273–88.

———. *Invisible Houston: The Black Experience in Boom and Bust.* College Station, Tex.: Texas A&M University Press, 1987.

———. "Ecological Inequities and the New South: Black Communities under Siege." *Journal of Ethnic Studies* 17 (Winter 1990):101–15.

———. *Dumping in Dixie: Race, Class, and Environmental Quality.* Boulder: Westview Press, 1990.

———. "Environmental Racism." *Environmental Protection* 2 (June 1991):25–26.

———. "Environmental Justice for All." *EnviroAction* Environmental News Digest for the National Wildlife Federation (November 1991).

———. "In Our Backyards: Minority Communities Get Most of the Dumps." *EPA Journal* 18 (March–April 1992):11–12.

———. "The Environmental Justice Framework: A Strategy for Addressing Unequal Protection." Paper presented at the Resources for the Future Conference on Risk Management, Annapolis, Md. (November 1992).

———. *Directory of People of Color Environmental Groups 1992.* Flint, Mich.: Charles Stewart Mott Foundation, 1992.

———. "Urban Infrastructure: Social, Environmental, and Health Risks to African Americans." In Billy J. Tidwell (ed.), *The State of Black America 1992*, pp. 183–96. New York: National Urban League, 1992.

———. "Environmental Racism and Land Use." *Land Use Forum: A Journal of Law, Policy & Practice* 2 (Spring 1993):6–11.

———. "Waste and Racism: A Stacked Deck?" *Forum for Applied Research and Public Policy* 8 (Spring 1993):29–35.

———. *Confronting Environmental Racism: Voices from the Grassroots.* Boston: South End Press, 1993.

———. "Race and Environmental Justice in the United States." *Yale Journal of International Law* 18 (Winter 1993):319–35.

———. "The Threat of Environmental Racism." *Natural Resources & Environment* 7 (Winter 1993):23–26, 55–56.

Bullard, Robert D., and Joe R. Feagin. "Racism and the City." In M. Gottdiener and C. V. Pickvance (eds.) *Urban life in Transition*, pp. 55–76. Newbury Park, Calif.: Sage, 1991.

Bullard, Robert D., and Beverly H. Wright. "Environmentalism and the Politics of Equity: Emergent Trends in the Black Community." *Mid-American Review of Sociology* 12 (1987):21–37.

———. "The Quest for Environmental Equity: Mobilizing the African Community for Social Change." *Society and Natural Resources* 3 (1990):301–11.

———. "The Quest for Environmental Equity: Mobilizing the African American Community for Social Change." *Society and Natural Resources* 3 (1991):301–11.

Carroll, Ginny. "When Pollution Hits Home." *National Wildlife* 29 (August–September 1991):30–39.

Center for Investigative Reporting and Bill Moyers. *Global Dumping Grounds: The International Trade in Hazardous Waste.* Washington, D.C.: Seven Locks Press, 1990.

Cerrell Associates, Inc. *Political Difficulties Facing Waste-to-Energy Conversion Plant Siting.* Los Angeles: California Waste Management Board, 1984.

Churchill, Ward (ed.). *Critical Issues in Native North America.* Copenhagen: International Work Group for Indigenous Affairs, 1991.

Churchill, Ward, and Winona LaDuke. "Native America: The Political Economy of Radioactive Colonialism." *Insurgent Sociologist* 13 (Spring 1983):51–63.

Citizens for a Better Environment. *Richmond at Risk: Community Demographics and Toxic Hazards from Industrial Polluters.* San Francisco: Citizens for a Better Environment, 1989.

Cohen, Gary, and John O'Connor. *Fighting Toxics: A Manual for Protecting Your Family, Community, and Workplace.* Washington, D.C.: Island Press, 1990.

Collins, Patricia Hill (ed.). *Black Feminist Thought: Knowledge, Consciousness, and the Politics of Empowerment.* Boston: Unwin Hyman, 1990.

Colquette, K. C., and Elizabeth A. Henry Robertson. "Environmental Racism: The Causes, Consequences, and Commendations." *Tulane Environmental Law Journal 5* (1991):153–207.

Corwin, Miles. "Unusual Allies Fight Waste Incinerator." *Los Angeles Times* (February 24, 1991), A1, A36.

Costner, Pat, and Joe Thornton. *Playing with Fire.* Washington, D.C.: Greenpeace USA, 1990.

Daschle, Thomas. "Dances with Garbage." *Christian Science Monitor* (February 14, 1991).

Denton, Nancy A., and Douglas S. Massey. "Residential Segregation of Blacks, Hispanics, and Asians by Socioeconomic and Generation." *Social Science Quarterly* 69 (1988):797–817.

Dolan, Maura. "Toxic Waste Incinerator Bid Abandoned." *Los Angeles Times* (May 24, 1991).

Dunlap, Riley E., and Angela G. Mertig (eds.). *American Environmentalism: The U.S. Environmental Movement, 1970–1990.* New York: Taylor and Francis, 1992.

Edelstein, Michael R. *Contaminated Communities: The Social and Psychological Impacts of Residential Toxic Exposure.* Boulder: Westview Press, 1988.

Evers, Larry. *Between Sacred Mountains: Navajo Stories and Lessons from the Land.* Tucson: Sun Tracks and the University of Arizona Press, 1982.

Feagin, Joe R., and Clairece B. Feagin. *Discrimination American Style: Institutional Racism and Sexism.* Malabar, Fla.: Robert E. Krieger, 1986.

Florini, Karen, et al. *Legacy of Lead: America's Continuing Epidemic of Childhood Lead Poisoning.* Washington, D.C.: Environmental Defense Fund, 1990.

Freeman, Myrick A. "The Distribution of Environmental Quality." In Allen V. Kneese and Blair T. Bower (eds.), *Environmental Quality Analysis,* pp. 243–78. Baltimore: Johns Hopkins University Press for Resources for the Future, 1972.

Gelobter, Michel. "The Distribution of Air Pollution by Income and Race." Paper presented at the Second Symposium on Social Science in Resource Management, Urbana, Illinois (June 1988).

Geschwind, Sandra A., Jan Stolwijk, Michael Bracken, Edward Fitzgerald, Alice Stark, Carolyn Olsen, and James Melius. "Risk of Congenital Malformations Associated with Proximity to Hazardous Waste Sites." *American Journal of Epidemiology* 135 (1992):1197–207.

Gianessi, Leonard, H. M. Peskin, and E. Wolff. "The Distributional Effects of Uniform Air Pollution Policy in the U.S." *Quarterly Journal of Economics* (May 1979):281–301.

Gibbs, Lois M. *Love Canal, My Story.* Albany: State University of New York Press, 1982.

Giddings, Paula. *When and Where I Enter: The Impact of Black Women on Race and Sex in America.* New York: Morrow, 1984.

Godsil, Rachel D. "Remedying Environmental Racism." *Michigan Law Review,* vol. 90, no. 394 (1991):394–427.

Goldman, Benjamin. *The Truth About Where You Live: An Atlas for Action on Toxins and Mortality.* New York: Random House, 1992.

Goldstein, I. F., and A. L. Weinstein. "Air Pollution and Asthma: Effects of Exposure to Short-Term Sulfur Dioxide Peaks." *Environmental Research* 40 (1986):332–45.

Gottlieb, Robert, and Helen Ingram. "The New Environmentalists." *The Progressive* 53 (1988):14–15.

Greenberg, Michael, and Richard Anderson. *Hazardous Wastes Sites: The Credibility Gap.* New Brunswick, N.J.: Rutgers University Center for Urban Policy Research, 1984.

Greenpeace. "The 'Logic' Behind Hazardous Waste Export." *Greenpeace Waste Trade Update* (First Quarter 1992):1–2.

———. "Home Street, USA." *Greenpeace Magazine* (October–November 1991):8–13.

Grossman, Karl. "Environmental Racism." *Crisis* (April 1991): 14–17, 31–32.

———. "From Toxic Racism to Environmental Justice." *E: The Environmental Magazine* 3 (June 1992):28–35.

Hacker, Andrew. *Two Nations: Black and White, Separate, Hostile, Unequal*. New York: Scribner's Sons, 1992.

Haggerty, Michael. "Crisis at Indian Creek." *Atlanta Journal and Constitution Magazine* (January 20, 1980):14–25.

Hamilton, Cynthia. "Home, Family, and Community." *Race, Poverty and Environment Newsletter* 1 (April 1990).

Hamilton, Lawrence C. "Concern About Toxic Waste: Three Demographic Predictors." *Sociological Perspectives* 28 (1985):463–86.

Hofrichter, Richard (ed). *Toxic Struggles: The Theory and Practice of Environmental Justice*. Philadelphia: New Society Publishers, 1993.

Institute for Southern Studies. *1991–1992 Green Index: A State-by-State Guide to the Nation's Environmental Health*. Durham, N.C.: Institute for Southern Studies, 1992.

Jaimes, M. Annette (ed.). *The State of Native America: Genocide, Colonization, and Resistance*. Boston: South End Press, 1992.

Jaynes, G. D., and R. M. Williams, Jr. *A Common Destiny: Blacks and the American Society*. Washington, D.C.: National Academy Press, 1989.

Jones, J. M. *Prejudice and Racism*. Reading, Mass.: Addison-Wesley, 1972.

———. "The Concept of Racism and Its Changing Reality." In Benjamin P. Bower and Raymond G. Hunt (eds.), *Impact of Racism on White Americans*, pp. 27–49. Beverly Hills, Calif.: Sage, 1981.

Kay, Jane. "Fighting Toxic Racism: L.A.'s Minority Neighborhood is the 'Dirtiest' in the State." *San Francisco Examiner* (April 7, 1991).

———. "Indian Lands Targeted for Waste Disposal Sites." *San Francisco Examiner* (April 10, 1991).

Kazis, Richard, and Richard Grossman. *Fear at Work: Job Blackmail, Labor, and the Environment.* New York: The Pilgrim Press, 1983.

Kern, David. "State Praised for Shielding Poor from Waste." *Arkansas Gazette* (August 26, 1993).

Kling, Joseph, and Prudence S. Posner (eds.). *Dilemmas of Activism: Class, Community, and the Politics of Local Mobilization.* Philadelphia: Temple University Press, 1990.

Kneese, Allen V., and Blair T. Bower. *Environmental Quality Analysis.* Baltimore: Johns Hopkins University Press for Resources for the Future, 1972.

Knowles, L. L., and K. Prewitt. *Institutional Racism in America.* Englewood Cliffs, N.J.: Prentice-Hall, 1969.

Kozol, Jonathan. *Savage Inequalities: Children in America's Schools.* New York: Crown, 1991.

Krause, Celene. "Community Struggles and the Shaping of Democratic Consciousness." *Sociological Forum* 4 (1989):227–38.

Kreiss, K., M. M. Zack, R. D. Kimbrough, L. L. Needham, A. L. Smrek, and B. T. Jones. "Cross-sectional Study of a Community with Exceptional Exposure to DDT." *Journal of the American Medical Association* 245 (May 15, 1991):1926–30.

Kruvant, W. J. "People, Energy, and Pollution." In D. K. Newman and Dawn Day, eds., *The American Energy Consumer,* pp. 125–67. Cambridge, Mass.: Ballinger, 1975.

Kushner, J. A. *Apartheid in America: An Historical and Legal Analysis of Contemporary Racial Segregation in the United States.* Frederick, Md.: Associated Faculty Press, 1980.

Lavelle, Marianne, and Marcia Coyle. "Unequal Protection." *The National Law Journal*, September 21, 1992.

Lee, Bill Lann. "Environmental Litigation on Behalf of Poor Minority Children: Matthews *v.* Coye: A Case Study." Paper presented at the Annual Meeting of the American Association for the Advancement of Science, Chicago (March 1992).

Levine, Adeline. *Love Canal: Science, Politics, and People.* Lexington, Mass.: D.C. Heath, 1982.

Lewis, Sanford, Brian Keating, and Dick Russell. *Inconclusive by Design: Waste, Fraud and Abuse in Federal Environmental Health Research.* Boston: National Toxics Campaign, 1992.

Limerick, Patricia Nelson. *The Legacy of Conquest: The Unbroken Past of the American West.* New York: W. W. Norton, 1987.

Loftis, Randy Lee. "Louisiana OKs Dumping of Tainted Soil." *Dallas Morning News* (May 12, 1992).

Logan, John R., and Harvey Molotch. *Urban Futures: The Political Economy of Place.* Berkeley: University of California Press, 1987.

Looney, Robert E., and Craig R. Knouse. "Profits of Third World Mineral Producers." *Resource Policy* 13 (1987):56–57.

Louisiana Advisory Committee to the U.S. Commission on Civil Rights. *The Battle for Environmental Justice in Louisiana: Government, Industry and the Public.* Kansas City, Mo.: Regional Office, U.S. Commission on Civil Rights, 1993.

Mak, H. P., H. Abbey, and R. C. Talamo. "Prevalence of Asthma and Health Service Utilization of Asthmatic Children in an Inner City." *Journal of Allergy and Clinical Immunology* 70 (1982):367–72.

Mann, Eric. *L.A.'s Lethal Air: New Strategies for Policy, Organizing, and Action.* Los Angeles: Labor/Community Strategy Center, 1991.

Maraniss, David, and Michael Weisskopf. "Jobs and Illness in Petrochemical Corridor." *Washington Post* (December 22, 1987).

Mohai, Paul. "Black Environmentalism." *Social Science Quarterly* 71 (1990):744–65.

Morris, Aldon D. *The Origins of the Civil Rights Movement: Black Communities Organizing for Change.* New York: The Free Press, 1984.

Morrison, Denton E. "How and Why Environmental Consciousness Has Trickled Down." In Allan Schnaiberg, Nicholas Watts, and Klaus Zimmermann (eds.), *Distributional Conflict in Environmental Resource Policy,* pp. 187–220. New York: St. Martin's Press, 1986.

Moses, Marion. "Pesticide Related Problems in Farm Workers." *American Association of Occupational Health Nurses Journal* 37 (1989):115–30.

National Advisory Commission on Civil Disorders. *Report of the National Advisory Commission on Civil Disorders.* New York: Dutton, 1968.

Nauss, D. W. "The People *vs.* the Lead Smelter." *Dallas Times Herald* (July 17, 1983).

Newman, Dorothy K., and Dawn Day. *The American Energy Consumer.* Cambridge, Mass.: Ballinger, 1975.

Nieves, Leslie A. "Not in Whose Backyard? Minority Population Concentrations and Noxious Facility Sites." Paper presented at the Annual Meeting of the American Association for the Advancement of Science, Chicago, February 9, 1992.

O'Byrne, James. "The Death of a Town." *Times Picayune* (February 20, 1991).

O'Byrne, James, and Mark Schleifstein. "Invisible Poisons." *Times Picayune* (February 18, 1991).

Omi, Michael, and Howard Winant. *Racial Formation in the United States: From the 1960's to the 1980's.* New York: Routledge and Kegan Paul, 1986.

Pardo, Mary. "Mexican American Women Grassroots Community Activists: Mothers of East Los Angeles." *Frontiers: A Journal of Women's Studies* 11 (1990):1–6.

Pollack, Sue, and JoAnn Grozuczak. *Reagan, Toxics, and Minorities.* Washington, D.C.: Urban Environment Conference, Inc., 1984.

Reed, Dan. "Jackson to Chevron: Clean Up." *West County Times* (May 8, 1990).

Reich, Peter. *The Hour of Lead.* Washington, D.C.: Environmental Defense Fund, 1992.

Reilly, William K. "Environmental Equity: EPA's Position." *EPA Journal* 18 (1992):18–22.

Reynolds, Barbara. "Triana, Alabama: The Unhealthiest Town in America." *National Wildlife* 18 (August 1980):75.

Russell, Dick. "Environmental Racism." *The Amicus Journal* (Spring 1989):22–32.

Sanchez, Jesus. "The Environment: Whose Movement?" *California Tomorrow* 3 (1988):10–17.

Sanchez, Roberto. "Health and Environmental Risks of the Maquiladora in Mexicali." *Natural Resources Journal* 30 (Winter 1990):163–86.

Savage, David G. "High Court Rejects Curbs on Waste Dumps." *Los Angeles Times* (June 2, 1992).

Schnaiberg, Allan. "Redistributive Goals Versus Distributive Politics: Social Equity Limits in Environmentalism and Appropriate Technology Movements." *Sociological Inquiry* 53 (Spring 1983):200–19.

Schueler, Donald. "Southern Exposure." *Sierra* 77 (November–December 1992):42–49.

Schwartz, J., D. Gold, D. W. Dockey, S. T. Weiss, and F. E. Speizer. "Predictors of Asthma and Persistent Wheeze in a National Sample of Children in the United States." *American Review of Respiratory Disease* 142 (1990):555–62.

Scott, Steve, and Randy Lee Loftis. "Slag Sites' Health Risks Still Unclear." *Dallas Morning News* (July 23, 1991).

Shrader-Frechette, K. S. *Risk and Rationality: Philosophical Foundations for Populist Reforms.* Berkeley: University of California Press, 1992.

Shiva, Vandana. *Staying Alive: Women, Ecology and Development.* London: Zed, 1988.

Siler, Julia Flynn. "Environmental Racism? It Could Be a Messy Fight." *Business Week* (May 20, 1991):116.

Stewart, R. B. "Paradoxes of Liberty, Integrity, and Fraternity: The Collective Nature of Environmental Quality and Judicial Review of Administrative Action." *Environmental Action* vol. 7, no. 3 (1977):474–76.

Summerhays, John. *Estimation and Evaluation of Cancer Risks Attributable to Air Pollution in Southeast Chicago.* Chicago: U.S. Environmental Protection Agency, 1989.

Taylor, Dorceta A. "Blacks and the Environment: Toward an Explanation of the Concern and Action Gap Between Blacks and Whites." *Environment and Behavior* 21 (1989):175–205.

Templet, Paul, and Stephen Farber. *The Complementarity Between Environmental and Economic Risk: An Empirical Analysis.* Baton Rouge, La.: Louisiana State University Institute for Environmental Studies, 1992.

Tomsho, Robert. "Dumping Grounds: Indian Tribes Contend with Some of the Worst of America's Pollution." *Wall Street Journal* (November 29, 1990).

Truax, Hawley. "Beyond White Environmentalism: Minorities and the Environment." *Environmental Action* 21 (1990):19–30.

Unger, Donald G., Abraham Wandersman, and William Hallman. "Living Near a Hazardous Waste Facility: Coping with Individual and Family Stress." *Journal of Orthopsychiatry* 62 (1992):55–70.

United Church of Christ Commission for Racial Justice. *Toxic Wastes and Race in the United States: A National Study of the Racial and Socioeco-*

nomic Characteristics of Communities with Hazardous Waste Sites. New York: United Church of Christ, 1987.

———. *Proceedings: The First National People of Color Environmental Leadership Summit*. New York: United Church of Christ Commission for Racial Justice, 1992.

U.S. Environmental Protection Agency. *Environmental Equity: Reducing Risk for All Communities*. Washington, D.C.: U.S. EPA, 1992.

———. *EPA Headquarters Cultural Diversity Survey: Draft Final Report*. Washington, D.C.: U.S. EPA Cultural Diversity Task Force, 1992.

———. "Geographic Initiatives: Protecting What We Love." *Securing Our Legacy: An EPA Progress Report 1989–1991*. Washington, D.C.: U.S. EPA, 1992.

———. *Strategies and Framework for the Future. Final Report*. Washington, D.C.: U.S. EPA, 1992.

———. *Toxic Release Inventory & Emission Reductions 1987–1990 in the Lower Mississippi River Industrial Corridor*. Washington, D.C.: U.S. EPA, Office of Pollution Prevention and Toxics, 1993.

———. *Women, Minorities and People with Disabilities*. Washington, D.C.: U.S. EPA, 1992.

Weisskopf, Michael. "EPA's 2 Voices on Pollution Risks to Minorities." *Washington Post* (March 9, 1992).

Wellman, D. T. *Portraits of White Racism*. New York: Cambridge University Press, 1977.

Wernette, D. R., and L. A. Nieves. "Breathing Polluted Air." *EPA Journal* 18 (March–April 1992):16–17.

West, Pat C., F. Fly, and R. Marans. "Minority Anglers and Toxic Fish Consumption: Evidence from a State-Wide Survey of Michigan." In B.

Bryant and P. Mohai (eds.), *Race and the Incidence of Environmental Hazards,* pp. 108–22. Boulder: Westview Press, 1992.

Willis, David P. (ed.). *Health Policies and Black Americans.* New Brunswick, N.J.: Transaction Publishers, 1989.

Wright, Beverly H., and Robert D. Bullard. "Hazards in the Workplace and Black Health." *National Journal of Sociology* 4 (1990):45–62.

Index